# THE COMPLETE
# INTERNET
# COMPANION
## FOR LIBRARIANS

Allen C. Benson

**Neal-Schuman Publishers, Inc.**
New York       London

Published by Neal-Schuman Publishers, Inc.
100 Varick Street
New York, NY 10013

Printed and bound in the United States of America

**Library of Congress Cataloging-in-Publication Data**

Benson , Allen C .
    The complete Internet companion for librarians  /  by Allen C.
Benson .
        p .    cm .
    Includes   bibliographical references and index .
    ISBN  1-55570-178-7
    1.  Internet ( Computer  network ) --Handbooks , manuals , etc. .
I. Title .
TK5105 . 875 . I57B46     1995
004 . 6 ' 7--dc20                                              94-3560
                                                                    CIP

# Contents

# Foreword

## ≡ Connecting Your Library to the Internet

The Internet is the latest technology that librarians have embraced in an ongoing attempt to deliver better library and information services. Communication technologies have long had a marked influence on the practice of librarianship. Librarians have usually been quick to adopt the best developed communication technologies of their time in order to expand and extend the scope of library service. They have used couriers, the postal service, telegraph, telephone, and most recently electronic mail, and facsimile transmission to obtain materials from other collections for their users. There is evidence, as early as the 13th century, of a union catalog of the holdings of monastic libraries compiled to facilitate the location and borrowing of manuscripts to be read or copied. More contemporary interlibrary loan networks have relied on teletype machines as an inexpensive, rapid means of communication with potential lending libraries. In the mid-1960s librarians first attempted to use facsimile transmission to support interlibrary lending. However, the fax technology of the time was neither technically nor economically adequate to the challenge. When fax technology improved markedly in the 1980s, librarians were quick to reconsider it. In the early 1970s, there were few commercial applications of interactive, data communication technologies. Nonetheless, in 1971 librarians *invented* OCLC, an interactive, teleprocessing system, and refashioned library technical services and resource sharing among libraries. Thus, it should be no surprise that librarians have been among the first to incorporate the Internet into their activities, and have been among the most avid students of its capabilities and potential.

The Internet is a special purpose electronic network that enables computers to communicate with each other. More precisely, it is more than 10,000 computer networks all of which adhere to common data transmission standards, hence, permitting ready communication among the millions of computers on those networks. On a more metaphorical level the Internet is a first step in the evolution of a *global computer*. The Internet enables anyone using a terminal connected to a computer on any of the interconnected networks to have access to the computer facilities on any other network. Admittedly, at the present time not all communication paths are open to all users and some of the communication paths are better developed than others; nonetheless, users of any network computer can request services from any other computer. They may be denied access because they are not recognized users, but they have a reliable communication path to all computers.

If we consider the rapid growth of information sources in electronic form, we cannot fail to comprehend the significance of the Internet for a profession dedicated to helping people to satisfy their information needs. Previous communication technologies, and resource sharing programs, required librarians to think beyond the limited resources of their local collections. They enhanced the services librarians could provide, but they also made their jobs more challenging. The Internet with its enormous number of potential resources, most of which are undocumented substantially extends both the challenge and the potential of communication technology for libraries and librarians.

Anyone who has heard or read about the Internet is eminently aware of its potential. Anyone who has had experience with it is equally aware of its challenges *and its present limitations*. The Internet and its myriad resources will not replace libraries, but they will change libraries. The Internet and its gadgets will not replace librarians, but they will change how librarians do their jobs. The computing facilities distributed throughout the Internet will not diminish the value of the traditional skills that librarians have, but they will require that librarians add to their repertoire of working skills.

The new electronic technologies are no threat to libraries or librarians. They magnify the role and value of skilled librarians. Current technological trends, in fact, threaten those who have *only* specialized, technical skills to offer. Increasing amounts of intelligence are being incorporated into software and electronic devices making them ever easier to implement and use. Consider for a moment how much easier it is to install and use a modern, highly sophisticated word processing program than it was to set up and use a much more modest program a decade ago; consider how much easier it is to install and use a modem to communicate with a remote system than it was a decade ago; consider how many librarians, working in very small libraries without technical assistance, have installed microcomputer-based systems that rival the capabilities of systems that only the largest libraries could afford two decades ago. One hardly has to know much about a computer system any longer. The hardware identifies itself to the software in most cases and the software configures itself appropriately to use it. On the other hand, the skills that librarians possess knowledge of the existence, characteristics, strengths and weaknesses, etc. of information sources; the ability to analyze information needs and to match them with the properties of available information sources; a service orientation in which *users'* information needs are more important than the intricacies of their problems have enduring value regardless of technical advances.

The challenge then for librarians is not to compete with fifteen year old computer hackers, but to be aware of the new tools and sources available to them and how to use them *when appropriate*. Electronic sources, whether available on CD-ROM, mounted on local systems or accessible from remote corners of the earth via the Internet, will not precipitately replace traditional sources, but they will complement them. The challenge for librarians is to learn the characteristics of this expanded palette of information sources and to learn how to use it most effectively. Librarians have in the long history of their profession absorbed many new tools and technologies. The Internet and its resources is simply the latest.

Eventually, the Internet will do many things, but what librarians need to know is *what can it offer now*, and how does one find his or her way through the electronic maze to its widely distributed caches of gems. The Internet has tediously been likened to an *information superhighway*. If it is a *superhighway*, it is, for the moment, at least, one with few discernible directional signs, few maps, and entrances and exits that are neither readily found, nor uniform in appearance. To continue this tired highway analogy, it may be an ever exhilarating experience for aimless, restless pleasure drivers, but an enormous frustration for goal oriented motorists.

The present book helps to guide anyone interested in exploring how the Internet can be used to satisfy complex and simple information needs. It provides him or her with the necessary technical information to begin to use this fecund resource and in so doing further increase one's ability to use it. Allen Benson gently leads the reader through the welter of acronyms and jargon that besot such an undertaking. He explains the various ways a user can connect to the network. and step through the looking glass into a dazzling albeit sometimes bewildering new world. He describes in language comprehensible to lay persons the technical components of the Internet, the facilities needed to effect a connection, the potential pitfalls, and how to avoid them. For example, the present text provides simple, though complete tutorials on modems, communication software, and the special software needed to effect a connection to the Internet. It also discusses the numerous services and facilities that are available on the Internet for communication (e-mail), access to remote computers (Telnet), file transfer (FTP), searching for files and data resources on the network (Archie, Veronica, Wais, etc.), navigation (Gopher, Mosaic, etc.). With this as background, he describes the numerous, different services available on the network.

Unlike most writers on this subject, Benson does not end after performing a dazzling array of electronic parlor tricks and introducing colorful acronyms. He thoughtfully describes the areas in which the Internet is likely to be an excellent source of information that should be considered early in a search, and the many areas in which it might only be worth a try. The text describes 12 subject areas for which the Internet may be a particularly good source: agriculture, astronomy, biology, computers, education, electronic texts, government and politics, health, history, the Internet, law, and libraries. It provides a detailed treatment of the major sources in these fields accessible through the Internet, and it gives step-by-step instructions for accessing them; as well as detailed information for accessing many other important resources available on the network.

Equally important, Allen Benson provides sufficiently detailed information for people who want to explore this fascinating, new electronic world and to become more at home in it.

This book is an excellent resource for the novice and experienced user of the Internet. The novice will find in it all that he or she needs to unravel the Internet's arcane, cryptic secrets, including step-by-step instructions to access most of the resources discussed in the book. The experienced user will discover in a convenient place a wealth of information about resources available on this global computer known as the Internet.

The present book will serve as a user's manual that one can use to access many of the Internet's best known and most useful resources. Upon completing this book, the reader will have a clear understanding of what the Internet is today, how it may evolve to satisfy future needs, and he or she will have experienced in vivid detail how this potent electronic technology is reshaping librarianship.

S.Michael Malinconico
University of Alabama

# Acknowledgments

I was introduced to the Internet as part of my curriculum at the University of Alabama's School of Library and Information Studies. I would like to thank everyone there, especially Dr. J. Gordon Coleman, Jr., who offered me my graduate assistantship working in the Information Processing Lab. Special thanks to Greg Goldstein, the administrator for the School's local area network, who answered countless questions about network technology and Internet services. I owe a special debt of gratitude to Professor S. Michael Malinconico for it was he who gave me the inspiration to begin this project and offered continuous support until its completion.

Thanks to Linda M. Fodemski at the University of Arkansas, Fayetteville, for being a wonderful sounding board and for reading the final manuscript and offering editorial suggestions.

# Introduction

## ≡ What This Book Is About

The Internet offers libraries an extraordinary opportunity to take advantage of the value of resource sharing. Using the Internet, libraries can connect with computers on the other side of the globe just as easily as they could connect to computers in the next room. Once the computers are connected, users can search full-text databases or download essays, research papers, books, software, pictures, and sound files. Although a growing number of companies charge a fee for accessing these resources, there's also an increasing amount of information that is available at no cost.

You can see the power of resource sharing by considering this scenario: You have one copy of *O Pioneers* by Willa Cather in your library and one day it is checked out. A patron comes in and requests a copy of *O Pioneers*. You are faced with an issue that is common in the current paper- based library. You can either (1) Place the copy you have on reserve, (2) Request another copy through inter-library loan, or (3) Purchase another copy, catalog it, and add it to the collection. All three solutions take time—days or weeks—and the request may still go unfilled.

The Internet offers a fourth and the most promising solution to date. An Internet service called FTP enables you to access a remote computer and copy a file to your local computer. These files might consist of anything from a single page of text to an entire book. Anyone connected to the Internet who needs a copy of *O Pioneers* can get it. The easiest way to retrieve a book on the Internet (*etext*, or electronic text, as it is commonly called) is to locate it on another computer and copy it.

For this scenario I chose a book that already has been translated into electronic format and made available on the Internet by an organization called Project Gutenberg. If your library doesn't own a copy of *O Pioneers*, the value of resource sharing in the context of an electronic network like the Internet becomes even more evident. One etext version of *O Pioneers* is accessible by many. No matter how many times it's "checked out," there still remains one copy sitting on the Internet's "virtual" library shelf. When a library patron requests a copy, you download a digitized version of the book and copy it to a floppy disk for the patron (and maybe keep an extra copy on the library computer's hard drive for future use). Whether you have only one request for *O Pioneers* or three requests in the same week, you can serve all of the patrons at point of need.

You can connect to the Internet several different ways. Depending on which method you use, it could be a daunting task, or, it might be relatively simple . The chapters in this book that discuss hardware, software, and connection procedures were written for do-it-yourself individuals who are not yet connected to the Internet (and are quite detached physically from any local computer network that is connected.)

Whether you're an information broker working out of your home or small storefront office or the director of a small rural library, a medium sized metropolitan public library, a corporate library, or a Junior College library, if you are the person responsible for setting up an Internet connection, this book will walk you through the steps necessary for establishing that connection.

Your challenge is twofold: Not only do you have to connect with the Internet physically, but you must also connect with it in a cognitive sense. Here the focus of the book shifts to help you become familiar with the interface you use to operate in a global network environment.

What does the word *interface* mean? Consider this analogy: When you go from your home to the grocery store, you get into your car, start the engine, and begin driving down the road. Your interface is the steering wheel, the dashboard filled with various gauges, pedals on the floor, and a view of the world as seen through the windshield. The automobile's underlying architecture—the engine and transmission, etc.—is hidden from you and for the most part irrelevant.

When you search a database at Penn State University via the Internet, you sit down behind a computer, press the On switch and begin pushing keys. Your interface with the Internet is the keyboard and what appears on the video display terminal in front of you. Like the engine and transmission in an automobile, the technology used to interconnect the multiple physical networks that make up the Internet and allow your personal computer to communicate with Penn State's mainframe is also hidden. You know that you are connected and can communicate, and that is all that's relevant.

This level of communication, however, does require that you understand the Internet on a software application level. This book explains the basic software tools upon which most of the Internet services are built.

All along I have been keenly aware of the debate about the value of providing libraries with access to the information superhighway. It is clear, however, that the Internet is having an impact on libraries that have already linked up with it. The Internet has created new possibilities for libraries, from the smallest to the largest, enabling them to participate in global resource sharing. The Internet has successfully provided greater access to more information resources and services without adding mass to already overflowing collections.

Although great care was exercised in writing this book, there will undoubtedly be some areas that you'd like to know more about. In these instances, don't hesitate to ask for assistance from a library patron who is a computer hobbyist, the dealer who sold you your equipment, or a computer-literate friend in another department or organization.

You might also find assistance at a local technical college or university. Consider hiring an undergraduate student in the computer engineering department to work a few hours each week during the summer months. The hourly wages a student demands are far less than a professional consultant's fees. The student could help you with anything from purchasing your first computer and setting up a simple dial-up connection to setting up more complex hardware configurations and connection methods.

## ≡ Organization

This book is organized in six parts.

**Part I "Overview of the Internet,"** explains what the Internet is, the hardware and software requirements for establishing a link with the Internet, and lists various vendors with whom these links can be made.

**Part II "Tools and Protocols,"** introduces the "big three" Internet applications: FTP, TELNET, and Email. These are the three basic services that enable users to communicate with others, share information, and find information.

**Part III "Search Utilities and the Client/Server Model,"** introduces popular resource discovery tools and special front-end applications that access multiple services while using a single interface.

**Part IV "General Resources,"** gives a broad overview of information services available on the Internet.

**Part V "Integrating the Internet into Traditional Library Services,"** discusses what the librarian's role is in a global network environment and how and why Internet affects the kind of services libraries can deliver.

**Part VI "Internet Resources Arranged by Subject A–Z,"** is a selective list of Internet resources and services.

## ≡ Audience

The primary audience for this book is comprised of librarians responsible for planning and setting up their organization's computer system and/or for providing online reference services. Librarians who want to integrate Internet services into their reference practice will find this book useful for locating specific resources listed by subject or for learning more about resource discovery tools.

This book appeals more broadly to other individuals that deal in the exchange of information such as information brokers, lawyers, teachers, and business managers and will be useful to anyone already connected to the Internet, but who would like to learn more about accessing the many services to their fullest potential.

## ≡ Scope

Even though you can use a variety of methods to access the Internet, this book is for the individual who wants to connect one machine to the Internet. The computer might be at someone's house, at a library, or in a classroom. This book is not a how-to manual for connecting a network to the Internet.

Although this book starts with the basics in terms of accessing and using the Internet, it does assume that you have a basic knowledge of computer applications. For example, step-by-step instructions are provided on how to retrieve a text file from a remote computer on the Internet and bring it back to your own personal computer. What you do with the file after you retrieve it will be a function of your own computing skills.

## ≡ Conventions

This book applies the following conventions relating to typography, special word meanings, and formats for displaying certain types of data:

- Characters that you type—commands or statements—are shown in boldface and the computer response is plain text. The following example shows that when you type "type recent-files.txt", the computer responds with "This is a list of all the files..."

```
$ type recent-files.txt
;This is a list of all the files which have been created or modified in the
;past three weeks. It is created every night at 2AM Pacific time.
;
;Flags Size    Modified        File Name
;
-r       187 May 12 02:00 ./help/recent-files.txt
-r       154 May 12 02:00 ./help/all-files.txt
-r    559872 May 11 20:59 ./util/DW_3.1.sea.bin
-r    116447 May 11 20:07 ./help/popular-files.txt
```

  Unless stated otherwise, pay careful attention to upper- and lowercase letters when entering data.

- Special keys such as SHIFT, CTRL, ENTER, and ESC are shown in uppercase letters.

- When you read the phrase "enter the command..." you should type whatever expression follows and then press the ENTER or RETURN key.

- In specifying the form of a command, words enclosed in angle brackets (<>) indicate variables. In other words, you are to insert your own input in place of the bracketed information. For example, if you are asked to enter the command get <filename>, you supply the name of the file. If the filename were *net.bib.txt*, you would enter get net.bib.txt. If you are asked to type subscribe <your name>, you would type subscribe John Doe(assuming your name is John Doe).

- For ease of reading, computer addresses and user names are printed in lowercase *italic* type. For example, *abenson3@ua1vm.ua.edu* and *cse.ogc.edu*. When an Internet address comes at the end of a sentence, please note that the last dot is a period, not part of the address.

- Filenames and directory names are printed in *italic* type. For example, you may be told to go to the */pub/history/doc* directory and retrieve a file called *constitution.txt*.

- New terms also are presented in *italic* type. These are terms being introduced and defined for the first time.

- By convention, the computer system you connect to is referred to as the *host* system. If it is your dial-up host—the computer you dial-up to as your link to the Internet—it is referred to as a *local host*. If it is a host you springboard to from the local host (that is, reach by means of the local host), it is referred to as a *remote host*.

The terms *local* and *remote* have no significant meaning in geographic terms. The local host may be in the same room as you and the remote host may be on the other side of the globe, or your local host may be in another city and the remote host you use may be in the building adjoining your library.

- Depending on which host you connect with, prompts will vary. A *prompt* is a symbol, word, or phrase that appears on the screen for the purpose of informing the user that the computer is ready to accept input. Common prompts are $ and %, but they may also consist of names or parts of Internet addresses. The terms *system prompt* or *host prompt* refer to the prompt used on a local or remote computer, a computer other than your own personal computer.

- *Command prompts* are prompts that appear when you run a particular program on a host computer. Examples of typical command prompts that you'll see include *FTP> MAIL> TELNET>* and *archie>*, etc. When these and other prompts such as *help>* prompts are included in the text, they are printed in *italic* type. For example, you will see the phrase, "enter the command **help** at the *archie>* prompt."

- Three address formats are used in this book and each will be explained in more detail as they are introduced in the text. Briefly, they are

    1. Electronic mail (email) addresses, whether they be email addresses for individuals or pieces of software running on a computer. Email addresses consist of two parts separated by an at sign (@).

        ```
        username@domain.com
        listserv@domain.edu
        info-server@domain.gov
        ```

    2. Domain name addresses , which are computer addresses.

        ```
        dra.com
        sklib.usask.ca
        ```

3. Internet Protocol addresses, which are also computer addresses, consist of four numbers separated by dots, such as

```
128.174.252.1
35.8.2.1
```

- Many terms used in this book are synonymous with the word *computer*. These include *remote host*, *local host*, *machine*, *personal computer*, *server*, and *system*.

- The word *site* refers to a computer's location or address. For example, to say that a file is available at site *netcom.com* means that the file resides on a computer whose address is *netcom.com*.

- When the term *argument* is used, it refers to the word(s) or number(s) that are entered on the same line as the command and modify or expand the command. For example, in the Archie expression **find mpeg, find** is the command and **mpeg** is the argument. When running another special Internet application called FTP, you might type the phrase **get echo.zip.** The word **get** is the command and the filename **echo.zip** is the argument.

- When the term *string* is used, it refers to any series of alphanumeric characters (any character you can type, for example A to Z, a to z, 0 to 9 and punctuation marks). The term *substring* refers to a series of alphanumeric characters that occur anywhere within the filename or directory name. For example, the substring *to* matches any of the following: *to, stop, toe, stove.*

Note: Throughout the book a number of Internet addresses, FTP paths, Gopher menus, and other directories are given. Be aware that many of these will change over time, especially Gopher menus and the location of files in FTP archives.

# PART I

# OVERVIEW OF THE INTERNET

This first part explains what the Internet is, provides you with a brief outline of its evolution, and explains how it is organized. My perspective as a librarian helps me explain the communication systems and information resources that are coming forth from this emerging global village, not the technical concepts behind the networks connecting its citizens.

First, I discuss how the Internet began and provide a brief outline of its evolution. Then I describe the global addressing system that enables Internet users to connect with other objects and people on the Internet. I discuss where to go online for information that relates to the Internet itself and also where to go for general assistance in using the Internet. Finally, I describe the various organizations that are concerned with issues like Internet services, standards, security, and operations.

If you are not yet familiar with the Internet and its various protocols, the information in Chapter 1's "Sources of Network Related Information" and "Where To Get Assistance" will be meaningless until you have read Parts 2 and 3 of this book. For veteran Internauts who already know how to use the Web, WAIS, Gopher, FTP, TELNET, and the Internet email services, these resources can serve a more immediate purpose.

# What Is the Internet?

The Internet is a worldwide network of computers and people. Built upon state-of-the-art technology, the Internet makes it possible for thousands of dissimilar physical networks—networks that are not connected to one another and that use diverse hardware technologies—to connect and operate as a single communication system.

The Internet began as an effort by the Advanced Research Projects Agency (ARPA) to create a large scale network so the computer systems of government agencies and universities could be interconnected. In 1969, the first four connection points were linked together forming what was called the Advanced Research Projects Agency Network (ARPANET). The four sites that were selected included the University of Utah, the University of California at Los Angeles, the University of California at Santa Barbara, and Stanford Research Institute (now SRI International).

The Department of Defense (DoD) was interested in the early development of the Internet as a framework for building an indestructible command and control network. ARPA was to invent a system for transferring data across its network in such a way that if parts of the network were destroyed as the result of a nuclear attack, alternate paths would be available.

This goal led to the development of a technology called *packet switching*. In packet switching, one large piece of data, such as a book, is divided into smaller chunks before being routed to its destination. Each one of these chunks, called *datagrams*, "knows" its final destination, but in getting there the datagrams will take different paths and go in different directions at different times. Eventually they all end up at the same place and all of the different chunks will be put back together in the correct order to form the original book.

Another development that came out of the ARPANET project was called *dynamic rerouting*. In the above example, if this book were being transmitted during an enemy attack and one of the network links was destroyed, the datagram traveling on that particular link could be recovered and automatically rerouted to other links.

During its early years, ARPANET experienced continued growth as it recognized the need to communicate with other developing networks. In 1983 it became known as the ARPA Internet and the DoD divided it into two connected networks: MILNET, a network of military computers, and ARPANET, the network of research computers.

The National Science Foundation (NSF) came along next and created a network of supercomputers called NSFNET and in 1986 connected to ARPANET. NSFNET's sophisticated communications technology surpassed ARPANET's and as a result, ARPANET was phased out in the latter part of that decade. Those computer systems that had been a part of ARPANET joined NSFNET.

In the early days of the Internet, ARPANET was considered a backbone network. Backbone networks are designated as such because of their ability to transfer data at very high speeds and with great reliability. Today, various backbone networks combine to form a framework for the worldwide Internet.

Today, the NSFNET provides a major service with its 45- megabits-per-second (45,000,000 bps)-backbone carrying data between the regional mid-level networks that in turn connect up the research and educational institutions. NSFNET is currently being funded under the High Performance Computing Act (1991). Other national backbones like NASA's NSI and the U.S. Department of Energy's ESNET provide additional backbone services. In Europe, there are international backbone services provided by networks such as EBONE. Various smaller networks have formed alliances with each other and support the Internet on a regional level. Local support comes from private industry and from state and federally funded research and educational organizations in the form of membership dues and service fees. In other parts of the world, support comes from national research organizations and international cooperatives.

Since its creation, the Internet has grown exponentially in terms of the number of networks that are connecting to it and the amount of information being transferred. Network traffic measured in bytes totaled 1.88 trillion during October 1991. By September 1992, that figure had increased to a total of 3.32 trillion bytes per month. Mark K. Lottor of SRI International provided statistics on Internet growth during a 10-year period in *RFC 1296* (January 1992). This data showed that Internet growth between 1981 and 1991 went from 213 hosts in August 1981 to 617,000 hosts in October 1991. According to the January 1994 "Internet Domain Survey" from SRI International, this number has now grown to 2,217,000 hosts.

Today, the Internet is a collection of high-speed networks composed of major backbones with the capacity to transfer data at rates up to 45 megabits per second. The amount of traffic traveling across a single U.S. backbone can exceed a terabyte (one trillion bytes) per month. In February of 1994, over 11 trillion bytes were sent to the NSFNET backbone services alone. Attached to these backbones are more than 5,000 federal, regional, state, campus and corporate networks. The Internet includes network links to every continent on the globe.

Corporations are discovering the value of Internet connectivity in their day-to-day operations. In fact, now more than half of all Internet traffic is commercial.

Business managers use the Internet's global communications capabilities for maintaining contact with customers and employees, for staying on top of international developments that relate to their business, and for collaborative projects in the areas of research and development. Businesses advertise their products and services in electronic marketplaces like CommerceNet—an online shopping mall with virtual storefronts. (CommerceNet is discussed further in Chapter 9.)

## ≡ The Internet Addressing System

Every computer (referred to as a *host* on the Internet) has its own unique address, and every person that uses the Internet has his or her own address. Two addressing systems are used on the Internet: One uses a hierarchical naming system called the Domain Name System.

A domain name looks like this: *opac.sfsu.edu*

As you can see, domain names consist of a series of subnames separated by periods. When you read the address from left to right the subnames go from most specific to most general. Subnames make references to values such as country, type of organization, organization name, and computer name. The above address tells you that there is a computer named "opac" located at San Francisco State University which is an educational institution.

Here is another example of a domain name: *uafsysb.uark.edu*

In this example, the top level domain is *edu*, which refers to an educational institution. The second level domain is *uark.edu*, which is the domain name for the University of Arkansas. The lowest level domain, *uafsysb.uark.edu*, is the domain name for the System B computer at the University of Arkansas, Fayetteville.

If you wanted to send email to an individual at the preceding address, you would attach his or her username in front of the domain name and it would appear like this:

*gitshaw@uafsysb.uark.edu*

In this example, the at sign (@) separates the username from the domain name. Your username will be assigned to you and it may include all or part of your first name, last name, or anything else for that matter. Other top-level domain names look like these:

| | |
|---|---|
| *edu:* | educational institutions |
| *com:* | commercial businesses and for-profit organizations |
| *gov:* | U.S. government organizations |
| *int:* | international organizations |
| *mil:* | U.S. military organizations |
| *net:* | Networking organizations |
| *org:* | non-profit organizations |

When machines in foreign countries are assigned addresses, geographical top-level domains are used. This is the country's two-letter international standard abbreviation. Thus, the domain name **hydra.uwo.ca** has as its top-level domain *ca,* which stands for Canada. Examples of other geographical top-level domains include these:

**ar**   Argentina (Argentine Republic)
**aq**   Antarctica
**au**   Australia
**be**   Belgium
**cl**   Chile (Republic of)
**fi**   Finland (Republic of)
**de**   Germany (Federal Republic of)

Larry Landweber at the Computer Sciences Department of the University of Wisconsin—Madison, maintains a complete list of country codes and levels of connectivity. You can find the latest version of this list in the *connectivity_table* directory at FTP site *ftp.cs.wisc.edu.* The phrase *FTP site* refers to both a protocol and a computer. FTP stands for File Transfer Protocol which is a method used for transferring files from one computer to another. A computer that makes files available on the Internet via FTP is referred to as an FTP site. FTP sites have Internet addresses—in this case *ftp.cs.wisc.edu.*

As you can see by this reference to Landweber's file, understanding how to use an Internet address is essential if you want to retrieve any information from the Internet. The procedures for using FTP and connecting with FTP sites" will become more apparent after reading Chapter 4, Basic Internet Tools.

Every host on the Internet is also assigned a unique identifier called an *Internet address* or *IP address* (Internet Protocol address). The IP address is a numerical address consisting of four numbers separated by periods. An IP address looks like this: 128.86.8.7

In actuality, your computer system uses only numbers, turning all domain name addresses into numbers. This translation process is taken care of behind the scenes by software, so it isn't necessary to discuss the details of how it's done. The reason domain names exist in the first place is because names are more convenient for people to use and easier to remember than numbers. For this reason, you are more apt to use domain names for addressing hosts than IP addresses.

Each domain name address has a corresponding IP address and you can use either one when contacting other hosts. For example, the Carl System can be reached with either the domain name **pac.carl.org** or with its IP address **192.54.81.128.** The details of how you can contact another person or computer on the Internet by using domain name addresses and IP addresses will become clearer when the various Internet services are discussed in subsequent chapters.

## ≡ Network Etiquette

Much has been written about Internet etiquette and customs. Once you're connected to the Internet, a Veronica search on the word *etiquette* will yield several resources. *Veronica* is a resource discovery tool that was built specifically for searching Gopher servers. *Gopher servers* are Internet programs mounted on computers around that world that provide menu-driven interfaces to large quantities of information on the Internet. Veronica is a program that enabled you to type in keywords to initiate a search of titles in the Gopher menus.(Veronica searches are discussed in Chapter 7.) You can retrieve additional information on Internet etiquette by sending the command **sendme mail manners** in the body of an email message to *listserv@bitnic.educom.edu*. Here also are a few basic principles with which you should become familiar:

- Networks and Internet hosts have developed what are called *Acceptable Use Policies*. These are policy statements that outline an organization's core principles and explain what they consider to be acceptable and unacceptable use of their services. When you obtain your Internet account, you will be asked to sign an Acceptable Use Policies or some form of membership agreement where you agree to adhere to rules.

- When using another system besides your own, either through FTP or TELNET, remember that you are a guest on that system and you should conduct yourself appropriately, complying with any stated restrictions.

- When you're logged onto a remote computer, do your work and then logoff when you're finished. Don't leave the connection open unnecessarily.

- When logging into a public FTP site, login as "anonymous" and enter your email address when prompted for a password. (Some FTP sites can only be accessed if you have proper authorization. To copy files to or from these sites you will need a userid and password. FTP sites that require no special registration are referred to as *anonymous FTP sites*. These are sites where the system administrator has set the FTP server up with a special userid named "anonymous" that anyone is permitted to use.)

- When possible, avoid logging onto remote machines during periods of heavy usage such as peak business hours. The best time to login without running into a lot of traffic (which results in slow response times) is on weekends or very early in the morning and late at night on weekdays.

Email is a medium of communication that mixes two older forms of communication. In one sense it's like writing a letter, but in another sense it's like making a phone call—somewhat spontaneous and informal. If you apply common courtesy and the Golden Rule, which is "do unto others as you would have them do unto you," you should have no problems. Keep in mind that although it may seem like you are talking to a computer, you are indeed talking to other people when using communication services like email.

After your first few days of email discussion, you'll no doubt learn something about *flaming* and *smileys*, expressions you can send in your email messages. Those of you who were raised during the time of flowing ink and writing paper may find it a little odd at first, but over time you'll get used to it. :-) (Tilt your head 90 degrees to the left to see the two eyes, nose, and smile.)

There are hundreds of smileys representing different emotions and facial expressions such as winking ;-) and surprise. :-0 If you'd like more information on smileys, run a Veronica search on the word *smiley* once you're connected to the Internet.

Flaming occurs when someone sends an angry email response. A *flame* might just be a strong statement or opinion. It might also include !SHOUTING!, which is text typed in uppercase letters, or it may include profane language.

Some aspects of the Internet are going through constant change. New ideas are continually being introduced that relate to how the Internet is accessed and used. Existing applications for locating information or transferring different types of data are being revised and new ones are under development. Methods of connecting to the Internet are expanding and being improved upon with the creation of new protocols and friendlier user interfaces.

The remainder of this chapter discusses information resources and services that deal closely with these issues. As you become an active participant in the Internet community, it's important to become aware of the existence of these network related resources early on. They will help you gain a broader understanding of what the Internet is all about and can serve as a source of "help" when you're faced with network related questions.

## ≡ Sources of Network-Related Information

Internet documentation called *Request For Comments* (RFC) and *For Your Information* (FYI) provide background information on various technical details relating to the Internet. RFC documents can be retrieved from numerous sites and by various means. To get a complete list of RFC's, send email to *refc-info@isi.edu*. In the subject field of your electronic mail message enter **accessing RFCs** and in the body of the message enter the following text:

```
Help:ways_to_get_rfcs.
```

RFC documents can also be obtained via FTP from *nic.ddn.mil* in the directory */rfc* as filenames *rfc\*.txt* (the asterisk is a variable which should be replaced with one of the RFC numbers listed in that directory).

If you have access to a PostScript printer, you may want to retrieve and print a collection of PostScript-format maps of the Internet available in the */maps* directory at FTP site *ftp.merit.edu*.

### Monthly Reports

Monthly reports from the Internet Research Group are available in the */internet/newsletters/internet.monthly.report* directory at FTP site *nis.nsf.net*. These reports contain articles from regional networks, the Internet Architecture Board, some Internet Engineering reports, and a calendar of events. The reports also list newly published RFCs and publishes usage reports from organizations such as InterNIC.

## National Research and Education Network (NREN)

Information on the National Research and Education Network (NREN) can be found in the */nren* directory at FTP site *nis.nsf.net*. This directory contains a wide variety of information about government activity pertaining to NREN. For example, one of the documents it includes is the *NREN Program—Report to Congress*, issued by the Director of the Office of Science and Technology. These are subdirectories leading to information about The High Performance Computing Act and The Information and Infrastructure and Technology Act.

## National Information Infrastructure Documents (NII)

During President Clinton's first year in office, he created the United Stated Advisory Council on the National Information Infrastructure. President Clinton's executive order creating the advisory council defined the purpose of NII to be this:

> "The National Information Infrastructure shall be the integration of hardware, software, and skills that will make it easy and affordable to connect people with each other, with computers, and with a vast array of services and information resources."

Some of the more important issues concerning the future of the NII are issues libraries will have to face if they intend to remain viable resources to their clientele. These issues not only relate to the librarian's role in creating a bridge between the library user and networked information resources, but it also relates to insuring network accessibility by all members of the public, the importance of creating interfaces that are easily understood by the masses, and making the information resources available at affordable prices.

Information on the NII is available from various sources on the Internet. To access via FTP, connect with the FTP server at *isdres.er.usgs.gov* and change directories to */pub/npr*. The NII file may be available both as a self extracting compressed file called *niiagend.exe* and as a text file with a *.txt* extension.

FedWorld National Technical Information Service is a Bulletin Board System that makes NII files available. You can access FedWorld by calling direct or by TELNETing via Internet. The TELNET address is *fedworld.doc.gov*. To call direct, dial 703-321-8020. After you have registered your name, address, and password, the FedWorld main menu appears. Enter "F Library of Files, and then "F Find Files," and lastly "F By filename, alphabetically." You will then be required to enter a search string. Here type "nii" (without quotes) and press ENTER. This will bring up a list of files with NII in their names. Instructions are provided on the screen for downloading the files.

To access NII documents via Gopher, connect with the Gopher server at *ace.esusda.gov*. From the main menu, choose */5. Americans Communicating Electronically/11. National Policy Issues/4. National Information Infrastructure (NII)*. Pictured below are the choices that are available in the NII directory.

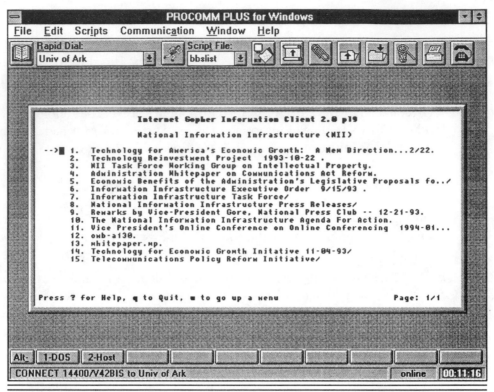

**Figure 1-1:** View of the National Information Infrastructure Gopher menu maintained by the USDA Extension Service.

## LISTSERV

A LISTSERV mailing list called Network News will update you automatically on new Internet resources. To join this list, use email to send a one-line message that reads **subscribe nnews <your_name>** where **<your_name>** is your full name (not your email username and address). Send your message to *listserv@vm1.no-dak.edu*.

## Gopher

The Gopher server at the Internet Society offers access to a tremendous amount of information relating to the Internet. Gopher is a program that enables you to access information on the Internet by browsing through a system of menus. It also provides a search mechanism for finding documents stored on the Internet that contain certain keywords or phrases. (Gopher is described in detail in Chapter 7.) Using Gopher, connect to site *ietf.cnri. reston. va.us.*

To receive a copy of the *Internet Glossary*, type the command **send rfc1392** in the body of an email message and send it to *mail-server@nisc.sri.com.*

## ≡ Where To Get Assistance

Whether you access the Internet through a dial-up host or you are directly connected through a campus or corporate computer, every node usually has an on-line help system. To learn more about the operating system and services offered by the host you dial, enter the command **help**, **?**, **/?**, or **/h** at the system prompt. On UNIX systems, the **man** (short for *manual*) command followed by a topic will pull up any available online manuals for topics you specify. Contact the system administrator if you have difficulty finding where help files are located.

### Frequently Asked Questions

Popular Internet help sheets called FAQs (Frequently Asked Questions)answer commonly asked questions about the Internet and are cited often throughout this book. FAQs are available via FTP to site *rtfm.mit.edu* in directory */pub/usenet-by-group*. In this directory, FAQs are organized by news group headings. Check under the news group *alt.internet.services* for one relating specifically to Internet services.

### InterNIC

InterNIC is an Internet information system run by three separate organizations. Network Solutions, Inc. provides registration services, AT&T provides directory and database services, and General Atomic/CERFnet provides information services. Probably the most valuable services to you will be the information services provided by General Atomic/CERFnet. This component of InterNIC offers the following service areas:

1. A service called the Reference Desk assists with questions about how to connect to the Internet and how to find information. The Reference Desk can be reached any of the following ways:

   > Toll-free hotline: 1-800-444-4345
   > Email: *info@internic.net*
   > Fax: 1-619-455-4640
   > Mail: InterNIC Information Services
   > General Atomics
   > P.O. Box 85608
   > San Diego, CA 92186-9784

2. Two discussion lists are available: One is called Announce and it introduces new InterNIC services. To join, send the email message *subscribe announce <your name>* to *listserv@is.internic.net*. Another discussion list covers general developments. To join this list, send the email message *subscribe net-resources <your name>* to *listserv@is.internic.net*.

   The *discussion list* itself is an email address. When someone sends email to the discussion list address, it is sent out to everyone subscribing to the list. A running conversation takes place as the people who receive mail respond to the messages. See Chapter 13 for further details on discussion lists.

3. InfoSource is a service that provides information about the Internet—how it's used and organized. You can access it in these different ways:

   - FTP to site *is.internic.net* and go to the directory *infosource*.
   - Email to *mailserv@is.internic.net*. Send the word **help** in the body of the message for details on what services are offered.
   - Logon to WAIS. Once connected, look for a source called *internic-infosource*.
   - Use your own Gopher client by entering *gopher is.internic.net* at your system prompt, or by using InterNIC's client by TELNETing to *is.internic.net*. Login: *gopher*. Choose the menu item */2.InterNIC Information Services* in the root menu. This will bring you to the this submenu:

```
       InterNIC Information Services (General Atomics)

     1.  Welcome to the InfoSource/
     2.  Infosource Update <As of 11/9/93>.
     3.  InfoSource Table of Contents.
     4.  Getting Connected to the Internet/
     5.  InterNIC Store/
     6.  About InterNIC Information Services/
     7.  Getting Started on the Internet/
     8.  Internet Information for Everybody/
     9.  Just for NICs/
     10. NSF, NREN, National Information Infrastructure Information/
     11. Beyond InterNIC: Virtual Treasures of the Internet/
     12. Top Documents Requested at InterNIC IS/
     13. Searching the InfoSource by Keyword/
```

   Choosing item */8. Internet Information for Everybody/* takes you to the next menu:

```
          Internet Information for Everybody

     1.  Internet Statistics, Size, and Connectivity/
     2.  Things to Do on the Internet/
     3.  Learning to Use the Network/
     4.  Government Agencies on the Internet.
     5.  Internet Monthly Reports/
     6.  Introduction to Internet Protocols.
     7.  Organizations/
     8.  Other Networks/
     9.  All About Request for Comments (RFCs) Documents & Retrieval/
     10. Historical Internet Documents and Archives/
```

4. InterNIC Information Services also produces a quarterly CD-ROM-based periodical that is called NICLink. For more information, call the InterNIC Reference Desk at 1-800-444-4345 or send email to *info@internic.net*.

## Online Help Services

Once you are running a particular Internet application like TELNET, Archie, or FTP, enter the command **help** or **?** at the corresponding *TELNET>*, *archie>*, or *FTP>* command prompts for online assistance.

## Assistance with Computer Terminology

Source of information on terminology is *Babel: A Listing of Computer Oriented Abbreviations and Acronyms* by Irving Kind. To retrieve a copy of this paper, send the command **GET BABEL93A TXT F=MAIL** in the body of an email message to *listserv@vm.temple.edu.*

## The Internet Encyclopedia or Interpedia

In late October 1993, a mailing list was established for discussing a suggestion made by Rick Gates that an Internet Encyclopedia, or Interpedia, be established on the Internet. If you're interested in its development as a potential resource tool, contact the Interpedia mailing list at *interpedia-request@telerama.lm.com.* Include the word **subscribe** in your message.

## HELP-NET

A good place to ask questions about how to navigate the Internet is HELP-NET. For additional information, send an email message to *listserv@vm.temple.edu* and in the body of the message type *GET HELP-NET PURPOSE F=MAIL* and *GET HELP-NET FILELIST F=MAIL.* Type each command on a separate line.

## The Global Network Navigator

The *Global Network Navigator* (GNN) is dedicated to helping online users explore information resources on the Internet. To read more about GNN, use a Web browser to connect to URL: *http://nearnet.gnn.com/wel/welcome.html.* A *Web Browser* is a special application that you use to access information that is stored on the WorldWide Web or "The Web." One of the most popular Web browsers on the Internet today is called Mosaic. You access Web files either "browsing" through hypertext documents or by directing your search. When you direct your search, you "point" your browser at a particular file by entering its URL (Uniform Resource Locator). (See Chapter 9 for details on using Web clients.)

GNN contains publications include *GNN NetNews, GNN Magazine, The Whole Internet Catalog, GNN Arcade, The Travelers' Center* and *The Internet Center.* You must be a registered subscriber to have access to this information. Subscription is free, but you must fill out a GNN registration form and agree to its terms and conditions. To receive a copy of this form, send an email request to *info@gnn.com.* Fill the form out online and return it via email.

## Magazines about the Internet

To help stay up-to-date on new developments on the Internet, the following publications are recommended:

*Internet World*
Internet World
Meckler Corp.
11 Ferry Lane West
Westport, CT 06880
Phone: 203-226-6967
email: *meckler@jvnc.net* or *70373.616@compuserve.com*

*Internet/NREN Business Journal*
Michael Strangelove, Publisher
1-60 Springfield Road
Ottawa, Ontario, CANADA, KIM 1C7
Phone: 613-747-0642
FAX: 613-564-6641
email: *441495@acadvm1.uottawa.ca*

*Matrix News*
Matrix Information and Directory Services
1106 Clayton Lane, Suite 550W
Austin, TX 78723
Phone: 512-451-7602
email: *mids@tic.com*

*MultiMedia Schools*
Online Inc.
462 Danbury Road
Wilton, CT 06897
Phone: 800-248-8466
FAX: 203-761-1444

*Internet Business Advantage*
P.O. Box 10488
Lancaster, PA 17605-0488
Phone: 717-393-1000
FAX: 717-393-5752
email: success@wentworth.com

*Inside the Internet*
9420 Bunsen Parkway, Suite 300
Louisville, KY 40220
Phone: 800-223-8720
email: ineteditor@merlin.cobb.ziff.com

## Organizations Involved in Network Activity

Although the Internet is not a centralized establishment and on the whole is self-governing, there are certain organizations that do exert influence over the Internet and coordinate many of the Internet's activities. The following list introduces organizations and explains their basic functions.

- **The Internet Architecture Board.** Back in the early 1980's when this organization was first formed, it was known as the Internet Activities Board, or IAB. Its goals were to "coordinate research and development of the TCP/IP protocols and to give other research advice to the Internet community." Today, the IAB is responsible for the "oversight of the architecture of the worldwide multiprotocol Internet." IAB receives reports from the Internet Engineering Task force and the Internet Research Task Force.

- **Internet Engineering Task Force (IETF).** This group specializes in the development and approval of specifications that become Internet Standards. Email: *ietf-info@isoc.org*

- **The Internet Research Task Force (IRTF).** This is a research wing of the Internet Architecture Board. The IRTF concentrates on developing technologies that may be needed in the future. Topics currently under consideration are resource discovery, privacy, security, and library use of the Internet. In June 1992, the IAB, the IETF, and the IRTF joined with the Internet Society.

- **The Internet Society (ISOC).** The Internet Society is a nonprofit organization whose purpose is to facilitate and support the technical evolution of the Internet as a research and education tool. The Internet Society publishes the *Internet Society News*, a valuable source that provides news about Internet developments. For more information, write to the following:

  Internet Society
  1895 Preston White Drive, Suite 100
  Reston, VA 22091
  Voice: 703-648-9888
  FAX: 703-620-0913
  Email: *isoc@isoc.orgisoc@nri.reston.va.us*

  The Internet Society archives its files at FTP site *nnsc.nsf.net* in the */internet-society* directory.

- **Internet Assigned Numbers Authority (IANA).** This group provides a standardized way for systems to refer to network resources. Operated by the University of Southern California Information Sciences Institute, IANA maintains a registry of identifiers associated with Internet protocols. This enables systems to apply some standards when referring to network resources.

- **The Federation of American Research Networks (FARNET).** Established in 1987 as a non-profit corporation, FARNET's mission is to promote research and education in a computer network environment. Among other things, they offer members educational programs and assistance in improving information services. FARNET publishes a monthly online newsletter for its members. For further information, contact:

  FARNET
  100 Fifth Ave., 4th Floor
  Waltham, MA 02154
  Voice: 800-72-FARNET
  FAX: 617-890-5117

- **Clearinghouse for Networked Information Discovery and Retrieval (CNIDR).** CNIDR was established in 1992 as a support center for the development of wide-area information retrieval tools such as World Wide Web, Wide Area Information Servers, and Gopher. With so many information resources available on the Internet, resource discovery or information discovery has become a critical issue. CNIDR provides a repository for such systems. It is also active in the development of standards and provides continuing education for Internet users. For further information, contact:

  CNIDR
  MCNC Center for communications
  P.O. Box 12889
  Research Triangle Park, NC 27709-2889
  Voice: 919-248-1499
  Email: *info@cnidr.org*
  FTP: *ftp.cnidr.org*

- **The Electronic Frontier Foundation, Inc. (EFF).** The Electronic Frontier Foundation was established to make the new telecommunications technology useful and available not just to the technically elite, but to everyone. In keeping with the belief that the individual's constitutional rights should be preserved, the society places a high priority on maintaining the free and open flow of information and communications. For further information contact:

  The Electronic Frontier Foundation, Inc.
  155 Second Street
  Cambridge, MA 02142
  Voice: 617-864-0665
  FAX: 617-864-0866
  Email: *eff@eff.org*
  Electronic Frontier Foundation Gopher address: *gopher.eff.org.*
  FTP address: *ftp.eff.org.* Look in the */pub/EFF* directory.

- **The Internet Anonymous FTP Archive Working Group (IAFA-WG).** This organization was formed under the auspices of the Internet Engineering Task Force. It's chartered to define a set of procedures for accessing and administrating anonymous FTP archive sites. For additional information connect to FTP site *ftp.unt.edu* and download the file called *iafa-charter* found in the */pub/resource-discussion* directory. You can also subscribe to a mailing list discussion group by sending your request to *iafa-request@cc.mcgill.ca.*

## ≡ For Further Study

The mailing list *namedroppers@nic.ddn.mil* discusses various issues relating to the Domain Name System. Send a message to *namedroppers-request@nic.ddn.mil* if you'd like to subscribe. (For details on subscribing to discussion lists, see Chapter 13.)

Some of the RFCs that relate to the Domain Name System include these:

- RFC 1034—Mockapetris, P.V. *Domain Names-Concepts and Facilities*
- RFC 974—Partridge, C. *Mail Routing and the Domain system*

# Chapter 2

# Hardware and Software Requirements

The hardware and software requirements for connecting to the Internet will vary from person to person and organization to organization. This chapter concentrates on one configuration that will be useful to the majority of librarians who are working towards establishing their first link with the Internet. Connecting to the Internet involves four basic components: Personal computer, modem, telephone line, and communications software.

If you are working in an academic or corporate library where Internet access is already provided through a terminal or personal computer that's connected to your organization's mainframe or minicomputer, your link with the Internet has already been established for you. If you would also like to access the Internet services from your home, then the information in this chapter may prove helpful.

## ≡ How Computers Communicate

The symbols you and I use to communicate, such as the 26 characters of the English alphabet, have to be translated into a form that computers can understand. Computers understand only two electrical states: on and off—a pulse of electricity or no pulse. This on/off system based on 0s (zeros) and 1s (ones) is called the *binary number system*. A single 0 or 1 is called a *bit* (short for binary digit), the smallest unit of information that can be represented in binary notation.

Each one of the characters you and I use are represented by a decimal number and these in turn are given a binary equivalent. For example, the character B is represented in the decimal number system by 66. The number 66 is represented in binary code by a set of on/off switches, 01000010, which are the binary equivalent of 66. These eight bits(01000010) are considered a basic unit of measurement called a *byte* (pronounced "bite"). A byte is the equivalent of one character.

A kilobyte is another basic unit of measurement, equal to about 1,000 bytes (1,024 bytes). The abbreviation 16Kb is read as 16 kilobytes, which is roughly equivalent to about 16,000 bytes.

A megabyte, abbreviated as M, is equivalent to about 1,000,000 bytes (1,048,576 bytes). This is the common unit of measurement for personal computer memory. For example, you might own a personal computer with 4Mb (4 million bytes) of RAM expandable to 32Mb (32 million bytes).

With the large amount of information being transferred on the Internet, it isn't uncommon to see measuring units such as gigabytes (about 1 billion bytes) and terabytes (units equaling about 1 trillion bytes).

## ≡ Standard Codes for Representing Numbers

*ASCII* (pronounced "ass-kee") stands for American Standard Code for Information Interchange. The ASCII character set consists of 128 seven-bit codes (the binary equivalents of the numbers 0 or "null" through 127) that represent the upper- and lowercase alphabet, numbers, standard keyboard characters such as ?, ;, !, $, etc. and certain control characters like the carriage return and line feed.

In theory, any system that supports the ASCII standard can communicate with any other ASCII system, and it is a standard that has been accepted widely in the computer industry with the notable exception of IBM. In its tradition of doing things differently, IBM developed its own code called *EBCDIC* which stands for Extended Binary-Coded Decimal Interchange Code.

IBM's code uses 8 bits of data to represent a character. EBCDIC is widely used in IBM mainframes, but it isn't used in non-IBM machines nor is it used in the IBM PC and PS/2 computers. The IBM PC uses what IBM calls Extended ASCII. Extended ASCII uses an 8-bit code allowing for a total of 256 characters. The standard ASCII characters are represented by values 0 through 127. Then there are 128 higher characters that define such things as diacritical marks and international punctuation.

When your PC, which supports the ASCII standard, connects through a modem to an IBM mainframe, which supports EBCDIC, there's usually a converter on the mainframe that automatically changes EBCDIC to ASCII. This is a process that takes place behind the scenes and one that you don't have to be concerned with.

## ≡ Introduction to Modems

The telephone system was designed to transmit audio tones like those generated in human conversations, not digital computer data. The on/off pulses of digital data must be converted into audio signals before they can be carried by a telephone line. Converting digital 1s ("on" switches) and 0s ("off" switches) into audio tones is called *modulation*. Converting audio tones back into digital on/off pulses that a computer can understand is called *demodulation*.

A *modem* (MOdulator/DEModulator) is a hardware device that enables one computer to communicate with another computers via telephone lines. Modems convert computer data, which consists of on/off digital pulses, into audio signals. These audio signals travel along telephone lines until they reach a receiving modem on a remote computer. The modem on the remote computer converts the audio tones it receives back into on/off pulses and sends them on to the host computer with which you are connecting.

Modems are connected to telephone lines by way of an RJ-ll plug. That's the little clear plastic telephone plug with which you are probably already familiar. Modems have two phone jacks. One phone cable runs from a modular phone jack in the wall to the modem jack labeled "line" or "telco." The second jack on the modem is reserved for your telephone's phone line connection. This allows the phone to be used, but only when the modem is not in use.

Be aware that when your computer is using the modem, it ties up your phone line. If you are working in a library with only one phone line, patrons will hear a busy signal when they call in. If anyone working with you picks up an extension phone, it will ruin your online connection. Call waiting is another service that can't be used if a computer is sharing the line. You should consider installing a dedicated line for your computer because tying up the line will most definitely cause problems, at least during open hours.

## External and Internal Modems

You can use either an external modem or an internal modem to communicate with the Internet. An external modem is a separate device that sits on your desktop next to your computer. A power adapter cord provides the external modem with electricity.

An internal modem is a circuit board (also called a *card*) that fits into an expansion slot inside your computer. Internal modems connect to telephone lines in the same manner that exterior modems do, but in the case of internal modems, the two telephone jacks are part of the circuit board and are accessed from the back of your computer.

When choosing between an internal or external modem, consider the following seven points:

1. If you compare an internal modem to an external modem with the same features, you will find that the internal modem is always less expensive.

2. An internal modem will occupy one of the expansion slots inside your computer. Check to see whether you have an extra expansion slot available.

3. External modems need to plug into a serial port. A *port* is a communication channel where data flows into and out of the computer. A *serial port*, as one of its functions, transmits and receives asynchronous data which is data that flows in a stream on bit after another. If you don't have a spare port, you'll need to install an expansion card with a serial port for the exterior modem. If you have an expansion slot available, you may want to install a Multi I/O (multiple input/output) card. Then again, if you have an extra expansion slot, why not use it to install an internal modem and save on desk space?

4. Having an external modem allows you the freedom to move it from one computer to another by simply unplugging it. As long as you have the right connecting cable, you can plug it into any other personal computer, including a Mac. (Modem cables for Macs have a round cable connector on the Mac end.)

5. Getting an internal modem for portable computers like laptops and note-books could present special problems. They may not have expansion slots, or if they do, they may not be standard ISA (industry standard architecture) expansion slots. You might have to get a proprietary internal modem (a modem developed by a company to be used only in the machine they create) to fit the brand of portable computer you have, or if your portable computer supports the new standard expansion slot called PCMCIA, you can use a PCMCIA-compatible modem.

6. There are external modems for portable computers called *pocket* modems which are ideal for portable communications. Some plug directly into the serial port. Others are packaged with acoustic couplers, allowing users to link from pay phones, hotels, and other phones where jacks aren't removable.

7. Although internal modems don't usually include a diagnostic display, external modems do. These displays, called LEDs, are located on external modem front panels. There may be an LED that lights indicating that the power is on and this is all you will ever need to check, but LEDs can also be helpful when troubleshooting. For example, you can look at the DC LED to see whether the modem is able to compress data or look at the EC LED to see if the modem is able to detect errors.

If you're using an internal modem, you can run a TSR program (terminate-and-stay-resident program) on your computer that creates the equivalent of LEDs on your screen. *TSR programs* are programs that are designed to stay in the computer's RAM (random-access memory) at all times, and can be activated by the user with a keystroke. Once you have your modem and communications software running, you may want to explore local Bulletin Board Systems for this kind of program or it may be included with the modem you purchase. Be aware, however, that TSR programs may interfere with the successful running of your other applications. Unless you're experiencing modem problems, there shouldn't be any real need to run a program like this at all times.

When you add a new device to your computer it could conflict with another device for the computer's attention. If you have problems installing your modem, either have a knowledgable friend help you or pay a little extra to have your dealer install and configure your modem so that it works properly with your software.

## Modem Standards

Modems share certain things in common. Most are compatible with a standard set of commands called Hayes Standard AT Command Set for controlling modem features. Modems offer different options that affect their ability to detect data error and compress and uncompress data. Modems also transfer data at a variety of speeds. These details are all dictated by modem communication standards and the modem you use will have to conform to these standards.

Hayes Microcomputer Products developed a set of commands called the *Hayes AT Command Set*. Most modems sold today are compatible with this standardized set of commands that enable you to talk to a modem through the computer keyboard and thus control the modem's operations. The letters AT tell the modem that you are going to send it a command. For example, if you want to dial a modem, you type ATDT followed by the phone number you are calling. (Enter no space between the command and the numbers that you are dialing.) The D tells the modem to dial the numbers, and the T is a subcommand that tells the modem to dial in touch-tone mode. With newer versions of communications programs, you don't have to know this command to dial your modem because your program does it for you.

Another detail which is governed by standards is the speed at which your modem transfers data. CCITT (Consultative Committee on International Telephony and Telegraphy), a European-based standards-setting organization, set the technical standards for the 2400bps modem in 1985 and designated them V.22bis. In subsequent years standards were developed for the 9600bps modem which were designated V.32, and the 14,400bps modem which were designated V.32bis.

The ITU (International Telecommunications Union) is the successor to the CCITT standards committee. The latest standard currently being developed by the ITU is v.Fast 28,800bps. As of the writing of this book, the 14,400bps modems are the fastest official ITU standard. Some companies, however, are speculating on what the final ITU v.Fast standard will be and are manufacturing something called a v.Fast Class or v.FC 28,800bps modem.

The abbreviation *bps* stands for bits per second. The speed at which modems can transfer information is measured in bits per second. A 2400bps modem can transfer information at a rate of 2,400 bits per second. The faster the transfer rate, the more quickly you can send and receive information.

*Baud* is a unit of measurement that is used less frequently than bits per second and its meaning is slightly different. Technically speaking, the *baud rate* is the rate at which the state of the line changes every second. (*State* can refer to frequency, amplitude, phase, or voltage.) Back when modem speeds were 300 baud, the terms baud and bits per second could be taken to mean the same thing. At today's higher modem speeds, however, the baud rate is much slower than the number of bits per second.

When a modem uses a compression standard, it compresses data that the computer sends to it and then transmits it in that compressed state to another modem. *Data compression* is a process which reduces the size of a file by minimizing the amount of space it requires. The data compression standard V.42bis, which is now standard with 14,400bps modems, compresses up to four characters into one character before sending it over the telephone lines. When the compressed character is received, it's decompressed back into its original four-character state. Theoretically, a 14,400bps modem could transmit 4 X 14,400bps, or 57,600 bits of data in one second.

In reality, the potential benefits of data compression are not always fully realized. The transfer speed of textual data increases greatly after compression because all of the blank spaces it contains in its uncompressed form are removed. Executable files are packed tight to begin with so these files can't be compressed as much as text files. Files that are already stored in a compressed state, such as ZIP files (discussed in Chapter 4) aren't going to transfer noticeably faster than the normal connect speed of your 14,400bps modem.

Another standard that is important to the operation of your modem is the error correction protocol V.42.

Telephone lines are prone to distortion and noise, and this can garble the data being transmitted between two modems. When you're downloading information from an online database that charges for its services, it would be beneficial to have a high speed modem that removes garbage characters resulting from line noise. To make sure your communications with a remote modem remain error free, your modem should support the V.42 error correction protocol.

Another protocol you will come across is called the *MNP Protocol*, or Microcom Networking Protocol. MNP is a protocol developed by Microcom, Inc., which has the capability of performing error correction and data compression when your modem is communicating with another modem that supports MNP.

Your modem will not operate at a speed any faster than the top speed of the modem to which you connect. In order for these various standards to work, the modems at both ends of the telephone link have to have the same standards. If your modem is 14,400bps with error correction and data compression, but the modem that your dial-up host uses is 2400bps without data compression, then 2400bps will be the top speed at which you can transfer data.

## Serial Cables and Plugs

The communication process between you and the Internet begins when the computer sends data (binary code) through a cable that runs from the computer's *serial port* to a modem. The serial port is a connection point, a place where data enters and leaves the computer, one bit after the other in a single file, by way of a cable leading to the modem. This cable, called an *RS-232C cable*, usually doesn't come with the modem and has to be purchased separately.

The RS-232C cable is named after an electronic communications standard developed by the Electronic Industries Association. The RS-232C standard defines the serial port connections for terminals and communications hardware and also how data is transported over communications links.

For example, an RS-232C cable connection specifies a 25-pin D-Shell connector (the pins form the shape of an elongated D) with a male plug at the terminal end and a female plug at the modem end. A few years later, IBM broke the 25-pin rule and created a 9-pin connector and these are also commonly seen today.

The RS-232C standard also specifies that pin 2 sends data from the terminal to the modem and pin 3 receives data from the modem, while pin 7 serves as the ground for both circuits. (In 1987, the official name for the RS-232 standard was changed to EIA-232D, but it is still commonly referred to as RS-232C.)

## Serial Port Settings: Talking the Talk

Each byte of information, such as the character A, is sent along the phone lines as a separate data item. In order for one byte to be discernible from the next, it is packaged with a *start bit* in front and a *stop bit* in back. The start bit is just an extra bit that lets the system know that what follows is a byte of information—a set of data bits. If the data you're sending is ASCII characters, seven bits is all that is needed. In this instance you would say that your modem is "set to seven data bits." If you were sending a file that contained something other than text, you would use a setting of eight data bits. The last bit in the line is the stop bit and it just tells the computer receiving the information that the transmission of a byte of data is complete. In communicating this idea you would say you have "a setting of one stop bit."

There is a special bit that comes right after the data bit and just before the stop bit called a *parity bit*. The purpose of this bit is to make sure that all of the data bits are correct—that no garbage was inadvertently added during transmission. If *even parity* is used, the sum of all the 1s between the start bit and stop bit must be even. For example, if there were four 1s in the data bits, the parity bit would be set to 0 to keep the total number of 1s even. If you were using even parity and a byte of information arrived with an odd number of 1s between the start bit and stop bit, this would be a signal that the byte contained an error.

The above principle can be applied in reverse by using *odd parity*. The sum of all the 1s must be an odd number and so the parity bit is adjusted accordingly. *No parity* means that a parity bit isn't used to check the accuracy of the data bits. This is the most common setting for communication systems using personal computers.

Most hosts that you dial-up to will use a setting of 8-N-1, which means you will have to use those same settings before your computer will communicate properly with theirs. The 8 stands for eight data bits, the N means no parity bit, and the 1 refers to one stop bit.

Because each byte of information ends up being 10 bits long (8 data bits plus 1 start bit and 1 stop bit), and a byte of information equals one character, then a transfer rate of 9600 bits per second equals a transfer rate of about 960 characters per second. Another common setting is 7-E-1, which means that you use 7 data bits, even parity, and one stop bit. A byte of information at the setting 7-E-1 also contains 10 bits: 1 start bit, 7 data bits, a parity bit, and a stop bit.

As a real-life example of what you might encounter while navigating online resources, the following is an extract from the instructions given to users who would like to use a modem for accessing the Eccles Library Online Catalog owned by the Spencer S. Eccles Health Sciences Library, Utah Health Sciences Library Consortium (UHSLC).

```
HARDWARE and SOFTWARE REQUIREMENTS:  1200 baud modem
connected to the phone port (i.e., the serial or RS232 port) on your computer
and communications software (MAC examples: Kermit, MacTerminal; PC
examples: Kermit, Procomm). Follow the instructions in your
communications software manual for setting up the parameters for accessing
another computer. Follow the instructions in your communications software
manual for dialing the online catalog.
```

```
MODEM   SET-UP   PARAMETERS
Phone Number:    (801) 581-5410

8 Data Bits        1200 Baud
1 Stop Bit         Xon Xoff Data Flow Control
Full duplex        Caps Lock On
No Parity          VT100 Emulation
```

One concept that isn't represented in the 8-N-1 notation discussed earlier is *full duplex* and *half duplex* connections. When data is moving in both directions at the same time you have a full duplex connection. When you press a key on your keyboard in a full duplex connection, your computer sends the character to the remote computer which then sends—or "echoes"—it back to your computer , where it is displayed on your screen.

When data is moving in only one direction you have a half duplex connection. When you press a key on your keyboard in a half duplex connection, it is displayed on your screen and sent to the remote computer at the same time.

It's important that you use the same communications connections that the remote host is using. If you communicate in full duplex with a remote computer that's using half duplex, you won't see any characters appearing on your screen as you type. If this happens, change your settings to half duplex. If you see double letters (lliikkee tthhiiss) on your screen, change your setting to full duplex. If you're not sure how to do this, refer to your communications software user's manual or online help menus.

*Flow control* keeps the various components of a telecommunications system from delivering more data than the receiving end can handle. The flow control takes place between your computer and the modem, your modem and the other modem, and between the other modem and the remote host to which it is connected. One modem, for example, asks the other modem how fast it can exchange information. The highest transfer rate that is common to both of them is the transfer rate upon which they agree.

Communications software enables you to set the flow control between your computer and your modem. The software usually arrives with certain default (preset) settings, but you may have to change these for your particular applications. The most common techniques used are hardware flow control and software flow control. XON/XOFF data flow control (sometimes called *XON/XOFF handshaking*) was listed earlier in the instructions for connecting to the Eccles Library Online Catalog. This refers to a type of software-based method of adjusting the flow of information between a computer and modem. It is important that your communications software is using the same method of flow control as your modem.

## ≡ Buying a Modem

The following graph shows that the time it takes to download a file varies depending on the speed at which the data is transferred. For purposes of this illustration, I used a file called elec.rights1-4, which is housed in the electronic document archive maintained by the Electronic Frontier Foundation. This file is a

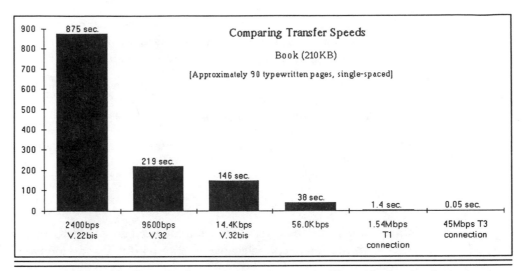

**Figure 2-1:** Graph illustrates how connection speeds affect the time it takes to transfer a book from one point on the Internet to another.

210,000 byte text file called *Citizen's Rights and Access to Electronic Information*—a booklet distributed at the 1991 ALA conference and now made available on the Internet. The calculations for transfer speed assume 100 percent efficiency.

This graph illustrates a wide spectrum of performance. On the low end, the graph shows that it takes a 2400bps modem operating on a standard telephone line 14.5 minutes to download this 90 page booklet. On the high end, the download time is 5/100ths of a second on a 45Mbps high speed dedicated line connection.

Simple math will illustrate the financial advantages of owning a modem that's capable of high connect speeds. A 9600bps modem transfers data four times as fast as a 2400bps modem. A 14,400bps modem transfers data six times faster than 2400bps. This means that a file that might take an hour to transfer at 2400bps would only take 10 minutes at 14,400bps. If you're paying for an online connect charge, you can reduce your costs by roughly 80 percent.

When you query online databases, write email, browse through menus, and so on, you will use about the same amount of connect time no matter how fast your modem is. During these operations the biggest factor that effects the amount of time you spend online is not how fast your modem runs, but rather how fast you type and read. When you're transferring files across telephone lines, you should definitely have a high speed modem because the transfer speed will effectively reduce your online time and in turn your connection costs. A 14,400bps modem with error correction and data compression (CCITT v.42/v.42bis Protocol) is highly recommended.

You must be able to give your modem instructions by issuing commands, telling it what to do. A good standard to follow for issuing these commands is the Hayes Command Set (also called the AT Command Set). Hayes and Hayes-compatible modems respond to these commands and are therefore the recommended models to buy.

Many modems now include FAX (document facsimile) communication features that allow you to send and receive FAX messages from your word processor or other Windows applications. This is a feature you may be interested in exploring.

### Summary of Hardware Requirements

To summarize, the basic hardware items necessary for establishing your dial-up Internet connection include the following:

1. A personal computer.
2. A telephone line.
3. If you're using an external modem, you need an RS-232C serial cable, the modem itself, a telephone cable with an RJ-ll plug, and a power adapter cord.
4. If you're using an internal modem, you need an RJ-ll telephone cable that runs from your internal modem to the modular phone jack mounted in the wall.

## ≡ Understanding Terminals and Multiterminal Systems

Mainframe computers are very large scale, expensive computers that require full-time staffs to keep them running. Thousands of these systems have been installed at universities and businesses worldwide. Being connected to the Internet will at some point bring you face-to-face (not literally) with one of these machines.

You may, for example, discover that a particular document you want resides on a mainframe located at the University of Alabama. The only way you can get a copy of this document is by connecting to their IBM 3090 mainframe via the Internet, sending the remote computer commands through your keyboard to locate the file you want, and then bringing a copy of the file back to your local machine.

While you are doing this, there will be several others using the same mainframe system. This illustrates a technology called *time sharing*—a system where many people, sometimes several hundred, share the same computer simultaneously. Typically, if you are a university or corporate librarian, your Internet access will be through a multiterminal system like a mainframe or minicomputer. You will either be using a terminal or a personal computer that is connected to your local host via a cable (*hardwired*, as it is often called), or you will have a personal computer that is equipped with a modem and this is how you'll access the local host. *Minicomputers* are multi-user computers that are typically more powerful than a personal computer but not as powerful as a mainframe.

If you are directing a small- or medium-sized public library with a modest budget, as I am, it is most likely that you will also make your connection to the Internet through a multiterminal system because it is the most convenient and inexpensive means of connecting. You won't have the choice of using a terminal and hardwire connection, however, because your organization won't have a million dollar mainframe setting in the director's office with which to connect. You will instead find someone else who *does* have a multi-user computer which you can access via telephone lines.

## Terminals vs. Personal Computers

Exactly what is the difference between a terminal and a personal computer? Terminals, which look something like personal computers, consist of three basic elements, as follows:

- The monitor—also called a video display unit (VDU) or cathode-ray tube (CRT) is the screen that displays everything you see.
- The keyboard is the device on which you input data.
- The serial interface, consisting of the cables and plugs that connect the terminal to the host. (Terminals can't do much unless they are connected to a host computer.)

The major element that terminals don't have, the one thing that makes them quite different from a personal computer, is the box that holds the central processing unit (CPU) and the disk drives. Because a terminal does not have a CPU, which is often referred to as the "brain" of the computer—terminals are sometimes called "dumb" terminals. In actuality, not all terminals are dumb because some do contain some processing circuitry.

## Communications Software

*Communications software* (sometimes referred to as *terminal emulation software*) enables your computer to communicate with modems, phone lines, and remote hosts. Software packages offer different features, and although some are DOS based, others are designed for Windows environments.

One feature that every communications program should offer is the capability of emulating different terminals. *Terminal emulation* is the feature that enables your personal computer to link with minicomputers and mainframes around the world.

Another common feature is called *file transfer protocols*. These are programs that help you send and receive data between your personal computer and a host computer. More sophisticated programs may offer other features like automatic dialing, cut and paste editing, scripting, and bulletin board functions .

### Terminal Emulation

When personal computers first came on the market in the late 1970's, they were used as stand-alone systems. Terminals were used to communicate with mainframes or minicomputers, and personal computers were used to run one or more specialized applications like Microsoft Word for Windows, WordPerfect, or Lotus 1-2-3.

In many libraries today, personal computers are used for more than running word processing, spreadsheet, and database programs. They also perform as terminals in online communications. With the aid of communications software, a personal computer can now be used as a terminal in addition to all of the other functions it serves. In fact, with the new communications programs available today, personal computers are able to offer users much more than the terminals they replace.

"Why would anyone want to make a powerful microcomputer act as though it were just a terminal?" you may wonder. The answer is simple. When you dial a host computer, the host is expecting to communicate with a terminal, not a full-fledged computer like your PC or Mac. The only way your personal computer can interact with a host is if you make the host believe your computer really is a terminal.

### Terminal Types

All the various hosts you'll be connecting to on the Internet recognize a limited set of terminal types. The most common one is VT100, which stands for VAX Terminal, Model 100. When you purchase your communications software, make sure that VT100 is included among the list of terminals it emulates. You should also be able to emulate an ANSI terminal, that will aid you in communicating with bulletin board systems (described in Chapter 20).

The basic goal is to make sure that your terminal emulation is set to the same terminal type as the host's. VT100 is the default setting on most hosts and it is a good one to choose if you are in doubt.

### File Transfer Protocols

File transfer protocols are sets of rules that regulate how your personal computer communicates with a remote host when sending or receiving data. The communications program you choose should support the most common protocols (Kermit, ZModem, YModem, and XModem). File transfer protocols are explained in more detail in Chapter 4.

### Other Communications Software Features

Some communications programs offer ways to store one or more telephone numbers in a dialing directory. When you want to contact a particular host, the program retrieves the desired number and dials it automatically, making the connection for you.

Most communication programs allow you to capture information so that you can save it to a disk or send it to the printer. When the capture feature is turned on, the characters you type and receive during a session are saved to a disk. When you're being charged by the minute for online time, this is an economical way to retrieve data quickly and then disconnect. Once you're offline, you can pull your file into a word processor for reading, editing, and printing at your convenience.

Some communications programs support *scripting*. A *script* is a list of instructions that are written in such a way that a program can understand them. Scripting is typically used to write programs that automate routine tasks. For example, if you login to FirstSearch or CompuServe on a regular basis, a login script could be written to take care of the connecting and logging in process automatically. Instructions for writing and compiling scripts usually is explained in the user manual that accompanies your communications software.

Lastly, your communications program may have a review feature, sometimes called *scroll back* or *replay*, that enables you to go back and view data that has already scrolled off the screen. This feature is very convenient when part of a directory has scrolled off your screen and you'd like to go back and confirm a filename.

## Summary of Software Requirements

The software you need depends on the kind of connection you will make with the Internet. For a dial-up Internet connection, you need communications software on your end of the connection. The rest of the connection, which involves a multitude of applications, communication links, and host computers, is all outside your realm of responsibility. These items are put into place by other individuals.

A few of the more popular commercial communications packages that are available include, Crosstalk, Crosstalk for Windows, Procomm Plus, Procomm Plus for Windows, and Smartcom for Macs. If you're using Microsoft Windows and looking for a recommendation, I would suggest trying Procomm Plus for Windows. Produced by Datastorm Technologies, it provides an excellent Windows interface with several useful features.

There are also shareware and freeware packages that can provide you with the basic requirements necessary for connecting to both the Internet and bulletin boards systems. Some names to look for are Procomm (shareware version for DOS), Qmodem, MicroLink (a simple Microsoft Windows shareware program), and White Knight and ZTerm for Macs.

## ≡ For Further Study

One source of communications software you should check out before you get online is the *Libris Britannia* CD-ROM. This CD-ROM contains over 600Mb of shareware and freeware for the IBM PC and compatible. It's available from Walnut Creek CDROM, 4041 Pike Lane, Suite E, Concord CA 94520. Once you are online with the Internet, you can conduct your business with Walnut Creek CDROM via the Internet email system. For additional information on products, send a message to *info@cdrom.com*, or for orders, write to *orders@cdrom.com*.

For additional information on modems, explore FTP site *oak.oakland.edu* in the directory */pub/misc/modems*.

For an interesting history of the International Telecommunications Union, Gopher to site *info.itu.ch* and follow the path */2.About ITU/13.ITU's History/1.ITU General History/1.[ASCII Lanag: E Bytes: 12667*.

# Chapter 3

# Connecting to the Internet

In Chapter 2, you learned about the basic hardware and software requirements for establishing a connection to the Internet. This chapter helps you put that theory into practice by showing you the various methods of connecting to the Internet. Emphasis is placed on the one mode of connection that matches the hardware and software configuration detailed in Chapter 2.

Basically, you can connect to the Internet by using either a direct connection or a remote connection. With a *direct connection,* you either link your computer to the Internet through high-speed dedicated lines or use a modem and special purpose software (SLIP or PPP combined with TCP/IP) on standard telephone lines. With a *remote connection,* your computer is linked via modem and telephone lines to a host machine that is directly connected to the Internet. This method of connecting is often called a *shell account* or a *dial-up* connection.

If your library is a small- to medium-sized organization and you plan to utilize the Internet as a supplementary information resource accessible only by the reference department, you might settle for a simple dial-up service, which is the lowest priced option and the easiest to install. If your library is an integral part of a larger organization that uses the Internet on a large scale, then by virtue of this association you may have the ability to easily connect to an existing LAN (Local Area Network) that is directly connected to the Internet.

## ≡ Direct Connections

Most universities already are connected to the Internet, as are many large government agencies and corporations. In these organizations, computing resources are often a department in themselves. Larger institutions may have multiple LANs, each with its own network administrator. Typically, these organizations use expensive, high-speed, dedicated, leased lines for connecting to the Internet.

This type of connection is appropriate for organizations that transfer large amounts of data and have many users and workstations that must be connected to the Internet. This option requires that dedicated lines be leased through a network provider and special network hardware be installed onsite—making this a complicated operation.

If you are part of an organization that has a dedicated Internet connection, but for security or other reasons your library hasn't been allowed access, your best option for gaining access to the Internet is to first try linking to the existing system. You probably will need to present your proposal to a network administrator or someone in computing services.

Before approaching them, however, read through the rest of this manual and develop a clear understanding of the advantages of connecting to the Internet. When you present your request, be ready with the answers to the following questions:

1. Who will be using the Internet? Do you plan to allow access only to professional staff in the reference department or do you want to provide public access, too?

2. What services do you want to make accessible? (Here you should cover all the available services, email, FTP, TELNET, Gopher, and so on.)

3. How will these services benefit you and your patrons? You may see email as a valuable tool for keeping abreast of the most current developments in the library profession or as a convenient method of sending purchase orders to vendors. You may feel that TELNET is a more cost-effective service for connecting to commercial databases such as Dialog or FirstSearch than is TYMNET or SPRINTNET. Or, you might see the value in allowing patrons direct, unmediated access to other library's online catalogs anywhere in the world.

## SLIP and PPP Connections

A scaled-down version of a direct connection through dedicated leased lines is a dedicated dial-up connection made with a high speed modem using software called SLIP (Serial Line Internet Protocol) or PPP (Point to Point Protocol). With SLIP and PPP connections, a 14,400 bps connection is highly recommended.

With this type of connection, you still have a full Internet connection with the capability of sending and receiving data directly with any other machine on the Internet. Unlike a dedicated connection, which remains up and running at all times, SLIP and PPP connections are only up and running when you call in and make a connection, and then they are down and non-operational when you disconnect.

With either of these two connection methods, your own personal computer has a full Internet connection and you work directly with other hosts on the Internet, sending and receiving data straight from your personal computer. This offers the benefit of being able to run your own applications for finding and retrieving data on the Internet.

If you are accessing a university system, you may find that it not only offers direct, dedicated access to students and faculty through an Ethernet connection, but also through a SLIP or PPP connection to users with modems located on or off campus.

SLIP and PPP dial-up connections are probably within financial reach of most libraries, but they can be difficult to set up and run properly. If you have minimal computer skills, you no doubt will have to enlist the services of a computer hobbyist or professional to configure this kind of system.

Another option, CSLIP (compressed SLIP), makes the file transfer process work faster than SLIP or PPP. No matter what application you choose, you and the service provider you connect to must support the same software. Check with the system administrator to see what options are available.

The equipment requirements for this type of connection are a computer, a modem, and a telephone line. For optimal performance, you should acquire the highest speed modem available. If you are working on a LAN, you might consider exploring specially designed routers that include the SLIP or PPP software and the modem. A *router* is a machine that serves as a gateway between a LAN and the Internet. Rockwell International produces a router called the NetHopper.

## UUCP Connections

UUCP is an acronym for Unix to Unix CoPy, a protocol that started on UNIX but is now implemented on other platforms including MS-DOS and Macintosh OS. UUCP is a program that enables the transfer of files between remote dial-up sites. If there is a college or university computer within local calling distance of your library, and it supports UUCP, there is a possibility that you could establish a low cost email link with the Internet through that host. Although UUCP limits you primarily to a mail-only connection with the Internet, it will become evident in subsequent chapters that a lot of resource discovery and file transfer operations can be executed with email service only. Other services that involve interactive communication like TELNET, Gopher, and WWW (all explained in later chapters) are not available via a UUCP connection.

To connect to a UUCP mail network you have to have UUCP software installed on your own personal computer. Even though a UUCP connection is fairly inexpensive and easy to set up, it doesn't provide the range of services a full Internet connection provides. An excellent book for MS-DOS users that includes UUCP software is: *A DOS User's Guide to the Internet: E-mail, Netnews, and File Transfer with UUCP*, by James Gardner (Prentice Hall, ISBN: 0-13-106-873-3).

## WinNET

Computer Witchcraft, Inc. has designed a shareware software program called WinNET that sends and receives electronic mail and USENET News articles through a UUCP Internet connection. You can make the Internet connection through a UUCP service provider of your choice or through Computer Witchcraft's WinNET system. If you use a provider other than Computer Witchcraft, there is a shareware registration fee of $99.00 for the software. Your other option is setting up a UUCP account with Computer Witchcraft, Inc., via a 1-800 telephone number. In this instance, WinNET software is provided to you free of charge. The WinNET computer system is your connection with the Internet and USENET and usage is billed to you on a connect-time basis.

To run WinNET, you need at least an 80386 with 2Mb RAM, a Hayes compatible modem, and one of the following applications: Microsoft Windows version 3.1 or higher, Microsoft NT, or OS/2. By installing WinNET and dialing up to the WinNET computer system, you can establish a UUCP Internet connection in just a matter of minutes.

The rate for online usage of the WinNET system if you connect with the WinNET system is $8.00 per hour. There is a monthly minimum charge of $9.95 per hour and payments are made by credit card. Rates for 1-800 number service are as follows:

Monday through Friday, 8am–5pm(ET): 18 cents/minute
All other times: 12 cents/minute

Unlike other connection methods described in this chapter, with a UUCP connection you are online just long enough to send or receive any pending email. This transaction takes place as fast as your modem will transfer data. With other connection methods, you must go online to create and send your email messages.

Setting up the WinNET software is quite easy. Included with the software is a file called *READ_1ST.TXT*, which completely explains the setup process. At each stage of the setup process, you can access online help information by simply clicking on the More Information button. A sample setup screen is shown in Figure 3-1.

You can download a copy of WinNET via FTP from *oak.oakland.edu* in the */pub/msdos/windows3* directory. The filename is *wnmai211.zip*. If you are unfamiliar with FTP, refer to Chapter 4. If you are not yet connected to the Internet, ask a friend who is to download a copy of this file for you. For additional information, contact:

Computer Witchcraft, Inc.
P.O. Box 4189
Louisville, KY 40204
Tel: 502-589-6800
FAX: 502-589-7300
Internet email: *winnet@win.net*

## Bulletin Board Connections

*Bulletin board systems* (sometimes called *Conferencing Systems*), like Prodigy and GEnie, provide partial, indirect connections to the Internet by giving you access only to email and maybe USENET news. Bulletin board systems such as Delphi

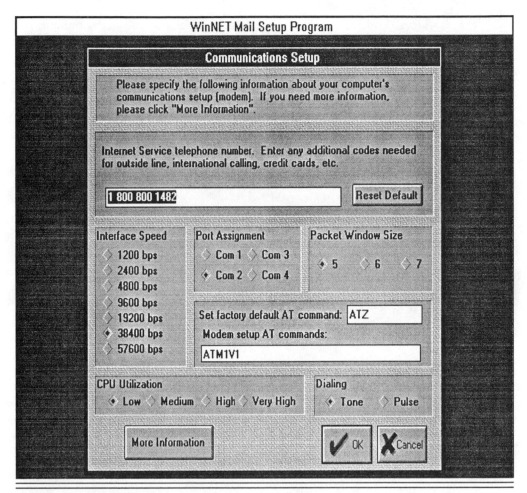

**Figure 3-1:** WinNET Mail Setup Program Screen

offer their subscribers a full range of Internet services and are included in the section covering dial-up Internet hosts.

Connecting to a bulletin board that provides mail access and maybe news is much like connecting to any dial-up Internet host—you use a modem and standard telephone line. Although the amount of information these systems offer as a whole is less voluminous than what is accessible on the Internet, they do provide some services that aren't available on the Internet, such as up-to-date news, weather, sports, entertainment, traveler's information, and many other specialized databases.

Commercial bulletin board systems have very wide coverage in terms of *PoPs* (points of presence—a point where a person can attach to a service provider locally), so connections are available to more people who aren't living within local calling distance of large metropolitan areas. To subscribe to one of these services, you will pay a monthly fee for basic access and additional charges for specialized services. For additional information, contact any one of the bulletin board service providers listed below:

GEnie
GE Information Services
P.O. Box 6403
Rockville, MD 20850-1785
1-800-638-9636

CompuServe
P.O. Box 20212
5000 Arlington Centre Blvd.
Columbus, OH 43220
1-800-848-8990

Prodigy
Prodigy Services Company
P.O. Box 791
White Plains, NY 10601
1-800-284-5933

## ≡ Dial-up Connections

Connecting via a modem and telephone line to a local host computer that is directly connected to the Internet is the quickest system to set up and the simplest, least expensive option of all. Many information brokers, public librarians, school librarians, and small college and corporate librarians will find a modem connection such as this to be an affordable and adequate means of linking to the Internet.

The primary disadvantage of a dial-up connection is that you are required to go through an intermediary computer—the local host—before gaining access to the Internet. This limits you to the Internet applications running on the service provider's computer which may not be as friendly as those applications designed for personal computers. You also have to learn to use the operating commands on the host computer, which will be quite different from those on your personal computer.

When you transfer information to or from the Internet using a dial-up connection, you have to go through a two- step process. When you transfer a file from a remote machine on the Internet to your own personal computer, you first have to download it to your service provider's machine and then download it one more time from there to your own personal computer.

In some situations, this two-step process can be advantageous. If you download a large text file to your local host and are not sure whether it's relevant to your needs, you can first view it on the local host, and then decide whether you want to download it to your personal computer. Viewing the file on your local host first gives you the option of editing the file before downloading, downloading the file as-is, or discarding it.

Transferring files from your local host to your personal computer takes much longer than transferring files from the remote host to your local host. This is because you are linked to your local host with a standard telephone wire and, at tops, a 28.8Kbps modem. Your local host, however, is linked to the Internet via high speed dedicated lines transferring data at rates of 56Kbps to 1.544Mbps.

Table 3-1 gives you information on ten commercial providers that offer nation-wide dial-up services plus other services as noted. Contact any potential provider for current rates and other details that aren't included here. Depending on which service provider you choose, variations will exist in price, quality of service, and how many features a service provider offers. It's best to consider all of the options available and compare them to the needs of your individual library.

If you access the Internet through a dial-up connection to a commercial service provider, you connect to this local host one of the following three ways:

1. By making a free telephone call, if the host happens to be within local calling distance,

2. By using a nation-wide toll-free number, if one is offered, or

3. By accessing a public data network.

The first two choices will be simple to set up. If you are within local calling distance of your host, you have it made—you won't have to pay long-distance charges on top of online fees. If the nearest host is long distance and toll-free access is offered, compare the price of that with the hourly connect rate charged by a public data network. If you can't make a local call and there isn't a toll-free number available, you will have to connect with your Internet host by going through a public data network. Here are four of the better known public data network services:

SPRINTNET, 12490 Sunrise Valley Drive, Reston, VA 22096. To find your local SprintNet number, call SprintNet at 800-736-1130. Internationally, call (404)859-7700.

BT TYMNET, Inc., 2560 North First, San Jose, CA 95131. To find a local Tymnet number, call Tymnet at 800-937-2862. Internationally, call 215-666-1770.

CompuServe Packet Network (CPN): To get the nearest CPN number, call 800-848-8980 from within the 48 contiguous United States.

PSI's Global Dial-up Service, Performance Systems International, Inc., 510 Huntmar Park drive, Herndon, VA 22070. For information on local access numbers, send the word **help** in the body of an email message to *numbers-info@psi.com* or call 800-827-7482.

## ≡ Miscellaneous Other Connection Options

Integrated Service Digital Network, or ISDN, is an access method that uses a telephone line to transfer both data and voice transmissions simultaneously at transfer rates as high as 128Kbps. A call to the local phone company in your area will

**Table 3-1:**   Commercial Providers Nationwide Services

| Name | Mail Address | Telepone | Email Address |
|---|---|---|---|
| Delphi | Delphi<br>1030 Massachusetts Ave.<br>Cambridge, MA 02138 | 800-695-4005<br>800-544-4005 | walthowe@delphi.com |
| Amigos | AMIGOS Bibliographic Council, Inc.<br>12200 Park Central Drive, Suite 500,<br>Dallas, Texas 75251 | 214-851-8000<br>Nat'l 800-843-8482 | amigos@amigos.org |
| HoloNet | Information Access Technologies<br>46 Shattuck Square, Suite 11<br>Berkeley, CA 94704-1152 | 510-704-0160<br>FAX 510-704-8019 | info@holonet.net |
| BIX | General Videotex Corp.<br>1030 Massachusetts Ave.<br>Cambridge, MA 01238 | 800-695-4775<br>617-354-4137 | tjl@mhis.bix.com<br>bix@genvid.com |
| PSI | Performance Systems International<br>510 Huntmar Park Drive<br>Herndon, VA 22070 | 800-827-7482<br>703-620-6651 | info@psi.com<br>psilink-info@psi.com |
| DIAL n' CERF USA | CERFnet<br>California Education & Research<br>Federation Network<br>P.O. Box 85608<br>San Diego, CA 92186 | 800-876-2373<br>619-455-3900 | help@cerf.net |
| PANIX | PANIX<br>Alexis Rosen<br>110 Riverside Drive<br>New York, NY 10024 | 212-787-6160<br>212-877-4854 | info@panix.com |
| WELL | Whole Earth 'Lectronic Link<br>27 Gate Five Road<br>Sausalito, CA 94965-1401 | 415-332-4335<br>8–6 M–F<br>Pacific time | info@well.sf.ca.us |
| CLASS | Cooperative Library Agency for<br>Systems and Services<br>1415 Koll Circle, Suite 101<br>San Jose, CA 95112-4698 | 800-488-4559<br>FAX 408-453-5379 | class@class.org |
| ANS | Advance Networks and Services<br>2901 Hubbard Road<br>Ann Arbor, MI 48150 | 703-758-7701 | info@ans.net |

| Services | 800 Number Access | Public Data Network Access | Fees and Requirements |
|---|---|---|---|
| Basic Internet services along with BBS services such as entertainment and games, travel services, news, weather and sports, conferences, etc. | No | Tyment and SprintNet 6pm–6am wkdys no charge, 6am–6pm $9/hr. | 10/4 Plan: $10/mo, after 4 hrs of use add $4 ea. add'l hour. 20/20 Advantage Plan: $20/mo, after 20 hours of use add $1.80 ea. add'l hour. One-time enrollment $19. |
| Basic Internet Services including FTP, TELNET, Elm & Pine mailer, Archie, SLIP & PPP. | Yes | No | Access Fee (per Institution) $150/yr member, $300/yr non-member; account fee (per user) first account $200/yr, each addt'l $100/yr. Connect chrg $9.75/hr. |
| Basic Internet services including TELNET, FTP, email and USENET. | No | yes | Membership fee of $6/mo or $60/yr; $4/hr peak, $2/hr non-peak. |
| Basic Internet services including FTP, email, Archie, Gopher, WHOIS, finger, and USENET. | No | SprintNet and Tymnet: $3/hr evenings/wknds $9/hr wkdys. (Weekday is M–F, 6am–6pm your local time.) | $13/mo membership; 20/20 Advantage Plan for high volume users: Add $20/mo first 20 hrs, additional use $1.80/hr. |
| Basic Internet services including TELNET, FTP, email, and USENET. | Yes | yes | $39 registration; $39/mo TELNET only; $19/mo additional for email; FTP $10/mo; $29/mo for 9600bps. |
| Basic Internet services including TELNET, RLOGIN, USENET, email, and SLIP. | yes | No | For 800 service, $50.00 installation fee, $20/month per user ID; weekday connect charge$10/hr, weekend rate $8.00/hr. |
| Full Internet services including TELNET, FTP, Gopher, USENET, etc. Individual SLIP or PPP $35/month, UUCP $35/mo + $1/hr. | No | SprintNet provides up to 30 hrs of long distance modem time per month for $30.00. | $40 start up fee; $57/quarter. |
| Basic Internet Services including TELNET, FTP, RLOGIN, Gopher and USENET. | No | CompuServe Packet Network. | $15/mo, $2/hr; add $4/hr for CPN. |
| Provides TELNET, FTP, email, and USENET. | yes | No | Initial membership fee $135/yr then $150/yr thereafter. $10.50/hr for toll-free access in 48 states. |
| ANSRemote Service: Basic Internet services including Email, USENET, FTP, TELNET, and Archie. | Yes | No | ANSRemote (TELNET only service): $25/month + $8.50/hour. ANSRemote/IP (SLIP and PPP service): $35/month +$8.50/hour. $25 one-time subscription fee. |

help you determine whether ISDN is available in your area. A modem isn't needed with ISDN connections, but your system does need a special ISDN interface card.

ISDN has been offered as a near term alternative to a fully fiber-optic network. ISDN is a technology that enables the copper telephone lines that already exist to carry digital signals instead of analog signals. Unlike fiber-optic lines, copper lines already run to almost every American home. ISDN is available to over a third of these households. Estimates are that in the next four years, ISDN will be available to anyone living in the United States with a copper phone line connection. ISDN can move data 27 times faster than a 2400bps modem, thus permitting quick transfers of large data files like those required for graphics and photographs. The faster data transfer rates of ISDN makes online searching less expensive and easier to use.

If you are within local calling distance of an educational institution, you should investigate the possibility of dialing-up to one of their computers. This link might be a simple dial-up connection to a university terminal server, a UUCP connection, or a SLIP connection. Try contacting Academic Computing Services, or a similar department, at the institution closest to you and find out what criteria has to be met to get an account for your library. Be prepared for the question "Why do you want access?" (see "Direct Connections," earlier in this chapter). Also, inquire about any networks that might already be involved with helping public libraries and schools in your state connect to the Internet.

A free community computing service, such as a FreeNet, may be available in your area. Although these services usually don't offer full Internet access, they do offer a free email link with the Internet and also carry USENET news. See Chapter 18 for additional information on FreeNets.

## ≡ For Further Study

For a directory of public access Internet providers, consult the *Public Dialup Internet Access List (PDIAL)* compiled by Peter Kaminski. Some of these service providers offer access to a shell account or BBS program running on a host connected directly to the Internet, while others can connect you directly to the Internet via SLIP or PPP. A copy of this list can be obtained by sending email to *info-deli-server@netcom.com*. In the subject field of the message, enter **send pdial**. This file called *pdial* can also be found at FTP site *ftp.netcom.com* in the */pub/info-deli/public-access/pdial* directory and at FTP site *nic.merit.edu* in the */internet/pdial* directory.

A USENET newsgroup called *alt.internet.access.wanted* specializes in helping individuals and organizations find access links to the Internet.

For an annotated list of public, open access UNIX sites FTP to site *gvl.unisys.com* and go to the */pub/pubnet* directory for a file called *nixpub.long*.

A comprehensive document including many of these files is *Individual Access to Internet* compiled by James Milles. This file includes the Public Dialup Internet Access List, the list of open-access UNIX sites, and more. To retrieve a copy, FTP to site *liberty.uc.wlu.edu* and go to the */pub/lawlib* directory, filename *internet.access*.

Susan Estrada has written a book on how to establish SLIP/PPP and dedicated line Internet connections. The title is *Connecting to the Internet* (O'Reilly and Associates, 1993).

# PART II

# TOOLS AND PROTOCOLS

This section discusses three basic Internet services: FTP, TELNET, and Email—plus the underlying communication protocols that form the basis of the Internet.

This part doesn't deal with the technical concepts behind the protocols, but rather with the services they provide to those who use them. From this standpoint, you may view the Internet and its underlying technology as a set of application programs that are made available to you as an Internet user.

Having access to the Internet means having access to special Internet applications and services provided by a suite of protocols called *TCP/IP*. TCP/IP stands for Transmission Control Protocol/Internet Protocol and it is the underlying principle that ties together all of the thousands of networks forming the Internet. *Protocols* are rules defining how something will be done. TCP and IP are the key protocols in a whole family of protocols, thus the entire suite is named after them. This suite of more than 100 communication protocols specify the details of how computers communicate with one another, how networks interconnect, and how information is routed from one machine to another. Together they define the operations that take place within the Internet.

IP is the set of rules and regulations that determine how packets of information make their way from a source host to a destination host. TCP allows an application on one computer to connect to an application on another computer, and then to transmit data across this connection as though there were a direct hardwired link. When you transfer a file from a remote machine to your local machine, TCP ensures that pieces of the file won't be duplicated or misplaced. When you send an electronic mail message, TCP keeps track of what is sent. It will retransmit anything that doesn't make it through. If a message is too large, TCP will divide it into smaller pieces and make sure they all arrive correctly. When computer applications need to communicate with other computer applications on the Internet, they use TCP.

# Chapter 4

# Transferring Files on the Internet

## ≡ Introduction to File Transfer Protocol (FTP)

File transfer is one of the most frequently used Internet applications, enabling you to copy files from over a thousand different archives around the world. You can think of these archives as libraries—electronic libraries housing digitized information. Although information in traditional paper-based libraries is stored in books and magazines, the file is the unit of storage in electronic libraries.

These files hold such things as text, images, sound, and executable programs. Tools like Archie assist you in exploring the staggering number of files that reside in these archives. (Archie is discussed in detail in Chapter 10).

The set of conventions that govern how this file transfer process takes place on the Internet is called *File Transfer Protocol* or FTP. The FTP protocol enables you to list directories on remote machines and to transfer files in either direction. When a file is transferred, it is not actually moved; rather, the file is copied from one machine to another. The computer from which the file is copied is sometimes referred to as the *source host* and the computer to which the file is copied is called the *destination host*.

Like most of the Internet applications discussed in this book, FTP is based on a client/server model (see the introduction to Part III for further details). You run a program on your local machine called an FTP client, which in turn connects to another program running on a remote machine called a *server*. As with other Internet protocol names, FTP is sometimes used as a verb. For example, you may see a sentence like "You can obtain a copy of *The Library Bill of Rights* by FTPing to the Electronic Frontier Foundation's Library Policy Archive."

Some sites enforce a strict FTP authorization that prohibits you from accessing files until you obtain a login name and password for their computer. Many other sites, the ones you will most often be connecting to, allow *anonymous FTP* which provides unrestricted access to public files. Anonymous FTP access means that you don't have to be a registered user to connect to the remote host.

In order to provide a reasonable level of performance and to avoid overloading their system, FTP sites install user limits for anonymous FTP during working hours. Working hours are usually defined as 8 a.m. to 5 p.m. local time Monday through Friday. When one site is busy, there are usually one or more archives around the world that can provide the same files. These archives are referred to as *mirror* sites.

Throughout this book, you will find numerous references to files located on FTP servers around the world. Directions for accessing these files always include three elements:

1. The remote computer's Internet address (either the Domain Name System address or the Internet Protocol address);

2. The pathname that tells you the path of directories you must follow to get from the root directory to the directory where the file resides; and

3. The filename itself. This information is usually presented in a format similar to this: FTP to site *ftp.eff.org* and download the file called *README* located in the */pub/academic/civics* directory.

## Downloading ASCII Text Files

In this section, examples of anonymous FTP sessions are presented, demonstrating basic principles in downloading ASCII text files. ASCII text files contain plain text and are usually given the extension *.txt*, *.doc*, or in some cases, no extension at all. You are *downloading* a text file when you transfer it from a remote computer to a local computer. When you transfer a text file from your local computer to a remote computer, you are *uploading*. The details of transferring other file types are discussed later in this chapter.

The text files you create with a text editing program such as DOS Editor are plain text files. Usually, these files don't create any problems when being sent over a network. A file saved in a word processing program such as Microsoft Word for Windows usually includes ASCII text, but it also includes formatting codes for such things as bold, italic, and underlining. These formatted files are actually binary files, not ASCII text files, and cannot be easily moved from computer to computer without some difficulties. If you were to view a file with formatting in another application that couldn't read and interpret these codes, you would see unrecognizable characters mixed in with the text.

Most word processing programs offer you the option of saving text as a plain ASCII file or text only. If you plan to send your word processing files over a network, make sure that you save them using this option. Some word processing programs enable you to save your file with all the formatting so that it can be transferred from one application to another. Microsoft Word for Windows Version 2.0, for example, uses a process called Rich Text Formatting (RTF) to convert the formatting into instructions that other applications can read and interpret. This allows you to transfer files between a DOS system and a Macintosh, for example, while keeping the formatting intact.

## Exercise 1

### *Connecting to an FTP Site and Downloading a File*

In the first exercise, you FTP to an archive containing historical texts maintained by the Electronic Frontier Foundation. Once there, you download a copy of *The Declaration of Independence,* which is a text file called *dec_of_ind* residing in the */pub/academic/civics* directory. The Domain Name System address for the computer on which all of this is located is *ftp.eff.org*.

### A. Making the Connection

To make a connection to the FTP server, begin by typing **FTP** at your system prompt and then pressing ENTER. Depending on whether you connect to the Internet by using a university account or a commercial service provider such as Delphi, there may be slight variations in how you issue the FTP command. If an *FTP>* prompt is displayed, type the **open** command, followed by the destination host's address. Some systems will allow you to type **ftp ftp.eff.org** all on one line.

Once connected, you must first enter your username, which is **anonymous.** (Some systems require that you type **user anonymous**). Then you are prompted to provide a password, at which point you enter your email address (which is not echoed). You then see an *FTP>* prompt, or some other prompt like *FTP.EFF.ORG>,* which indicates that you have connected and can begin communicating commands to the server. So far, the session looks something like this:

```
$ ftp ftp.eff.org
athena.ualr.edu MultiNet FTP user process 3.2(106)
Connection opened (Assuming 8-bit connections)
ftp.eff.org FTP server (Version 2.1WU(1) Thu May 20 15:21:04 EDT 1993) ready.
Username: anonymous
Password:
If your ftp client chokes on this message, log in with a '-' as the
first character of your password to disable it.

If you have problems with or questions about this service, send mail to
ftphelp@eff.org; we'll try to fix the problem or answer the question.

Electronic Frontier Foundation newsletters and other information are in
pub/EFF and subdirectories thereof. If you're interested in official
EFF positions and philosophies, look here.

For general information on the EFF, get pub/EFF/about-eff.

**** NOTICE ****
The files ending in ".z" are gzip'ed files. Either get gzip from a
GNU archive site (ftp.uu.net:/packages/gnu, say) or use "get filename"
(without the .z) to have it ungzip'ed on the fly. (If you have UNIX
compress compatible software, "get filename.Z" will convert gzip files
to compress files on the fly.)

Remember to use binary mode with compressed or gzip'ed files.
****************
```

```
Please read the file README
   it was last modified on Thu Nov 18 10:38:40 1993 - 17 days ago
Please read the file README.bigdummy
   it was last modified on Mon Nov 22 22:23:05 1993 - 13 days ago
Guest login ok, access restrictions apply.
FTP.EFF.ORG>
```

## B.  Issuing the dir (directory) Command

To better understand how directories and files are organized, type **dir** at the prompt and press ENTER. This display the following directory, called the *root directory*—the directory that you land in when you first connect.

```
FTP.EFF.ORG>dir
<Opening ASCII mode data connection for /bin/ls.
total 556
-rw-r--r--  1 root     daemon        0 Oct 17  1991 .notar
lrwxrwxrwx  1 mech     mech          7 Nov  9 16:18 Eff -> pub/EFF
-rw-rw-r--  1 pmiller  brown       358 Nov 18 15:38 README
-rw-r--r--  1 mech     mech        307 Nov 23 03:23 README.bigdummy
dr-xr-xr-x  2 root     daemon      512 May 29 00:34 bin
dr-xr-xr-x  3 root     daemon      512 Nov 24 00:04 etc
-rw-r--r--  1 root     daemon    56163 Dec  5 07:08 ls-lR.Z
-rw-r--r--  1 root     daemon   211034 Dec  4 07:08 ls-lR.old
drwxrwsr-x 17 pmiller  doc         512 Nov 23 23:58 pub
drwxr-xr-x  4 root     daemon      512 Oct 18  1991 users
<Transfer complete.
```

## C.  Working in UNIX Directories

The directory shown here is one displayed on a computer running the UNIX operating system, the most prevalent operating system on the Internet. UNIX organizes files into directories, which are in themselves a special kind of file. In the directory illustrated above, the system has stored information about other files and directories.

Each line, read left to right, displays information about a particular file or directory. The type of file is listed in the left column. A **d** in this first column indicates a directory and a – indicates a file of some kind. Next is information relating to access modes for different users (**-rw-rw-r--**). The letters r, w, and x stand for read, write and execute. Depending on their position in line, they are rights given to individuals, groups, or everyone.

The next column lists the number of files or directories linked to the particular file. For example, on the third line the *README* file has one file linked to it. The column after this lists **pmiller** as the creator or owner of the file. The next word **brown** refers to the group that owns the file. Next is the file's size given in bytes, and just past this is the date the file was made or last modified. Current year entries are expressed in month, day, and time. The file and directory names are listed in the last column.

UNIX file and directory names are case sensitive. This means that in order to successfully change directories or transfer files, you must type the name of the directory or file just as it is shown. You cannot download a file called *INDEX.rfc* if you ask for **index.rfc,** nor can you change to a directory called *XFree86* if you type **xfree86.**

UNIX organizes files into a hierarchical structure which has been compared to a family tree. When you first connect to an FTP server, you are in the parent directory, which is the top of this imaginary tree. This directory is known as the root directory and is designated with a forward slash (/).

## D.  Pathnames and Subdirectories

As you can see, in the root directory of *ftp.eff.org* illustrated in the example, there are directories under the root called *bin* and *pub,* etc. These are called *subdirectories* of the root. Each directory, except for the root, has one parent directory and one or more subdirectories.

The file you are looking for resides in the */pub/academic/civics* directory. This series of directory names separated by slashes (/) is called a *pathname.* Note that UNIX directory path separators are forward slashes, not backslashes (\), as they are in DOS. The pathname tells you the path you must follow through the hierarchical file structure to find the file you want. For example, the root directory is the first /. The directory *pub* is a subdirectory of *root.* The directory *academic* is a subdirectory of *pub,* and so on.

## E.  Changing to a Different Directory

You can change your working directory (the directory you are currently working in)by using the **cd** (change directory) command. The **cd** command uses the form

```
cd <pathname>
```

where the argument **<pathname>** is the pathname for the directory to which you want to change. The command **cd ..** or **cdup** will move you up one directory.

Moving ahead with the first exercise, type the following command and pathname, and then press ENTER.

```
FTP.EFF.ORG>cd pub/academic/civics
CWD command successful.
```

You can use the command **cd** to change only directories, not files. That is why the filename *dec_of_ind* was not included in the above pathname.

In the preceding example, you moved through all the directories at one time by issuing the cd command once, followed by a pathname that included all the necessary subdirectory names. You could have moved one directory at a time by typing **cd pub** and pressing ENTER, **cd academic** and pressing ENTER, and **cd civics** and pressing ENTER once again. Either way, you will arrive at the desired destination.

Now you can enter the **dir** command and to confirm that you are indeed in the directory that contains the file *dec_of_ind* along with several other interesting files.

```
FTP.EFF.ORG>dir
<Opening ASCII mode data connection for /bin/ls.
```

```
total 1064
lrwxrwxrwx  1 ftp      caf            6 May 28 19:32 Index -> README
-rw-r--r--  1 kadie    caf         8690 Oct 18 17:38 README
-rw-rw-r--  1 ftp      caf         1076 Sep  2  1992 administration.address
-rw-rw-r--  1 ftp      caf        16488 Jan 12  1993 affirmative-action.info
-rw-rw-r--  1 ftp      caf         9918 Aug  5 03:32 alawon-2-31
-rw-rw-r--  1 ftp      caf          192 Mar 14 19:36 bill.status.pointer
-rw-rw-r--  1 ftp      caf         2517 Mar 20 03:00 cabinet.contact-info
-rw-rw-r--  1 ftp      caf          125 Apr  4 22:16 cabinet.resumes.pointer
-rw-rw-r--  1 ftp      caf         1071 Feb  8  1993 campus-news.pointer
-rw-rw-r--  1 ftp      caf        82640 Nov 16  1992 canada.constitution
-rw-rw-r--  1 ftp      caf        20354 Nov 16  1992 canada.meech-accord
lrwxrwxrwx  1 ftp      caf           18 May 28 19:32 charter.can -> ../law/char
ter.can
lrwxrwxrwx  1 ftp      caf           34 May 28 19:32 civil-disob -> ../../EFF/n
ewsletters/effector4.04
-rw-rw-r--  1 ftp      caf         5879 Aug  5 03:32 clinton-appointees
-rw-rw-r--  1 ftp      caf         1387 Mar 14 19:37 clinton.press.pointer
-rw-rw-r--  1 ftp      caf         1304 Dec 11  1992 columnist.contact-info
-rw-rw-r--  1 ftp      caf          307 Mar 20 03:09 congress.info.pointer
-rw-rw-r--  1 ftp      caf        34709 Aug 24 14:59 congress.phones
-rw-rw-r--  1 ftp      caf          879 Aug 14  1992 constitution.az.us
-rw-rw-r--  1 ftp      caf        45483 Jun 10  1992 constitution.us
-rw-rw-r--  1 ftp      caf         8496 Oct  4  1991 dec_of_ind
-rw-rw-r--  1 ftp      caf         1428 May 24 01:52 executive.phone-numbers
-rw-rw-r--  1 ftp      caf         1653 Oct 31  1991 fcc
-rw-rw-r--  1 ftp      caf        11442 Jul 24 19:35 fed-register.internet
-rw-rw-r--  1 ftp      caf        18114 Nov 16  1992 federalist-paper-10
-rw-rw-r--  1 ftp      caf        11812 Nov 16  1992 federalist-paper-51
-rw-rw-r--  1 ftp      caf         1875 Nov 14  1992 federalist-papers.pointer
-rw-rw-r--  1 ftp      caf         8874 Dec  4  1992 foia.insight
-rw-rw-r--  1 ftp      caf        37138 Feb 27  1992 foia.nlg
-rw-rw-r--  1 ftp      caf         2830 Mar 21  1992 gov.contact
-rw-rw-r--  1 ftp      caf          866 Jan 12  1993 historical-documents.point
er
-rw-rw-r--  1 ftp      caf         3122 May 24 01:52 judiciary-comm.phone-numbe
rs
-rw-rw-r--  1 ftp      caf          865 May 24 01:52 library-of-congress.pointe
r
-rw-rw-r--  1 ftp      caf         5703 Mar  1  1992 media.fax
-rw-rw-r--  1 ftp      caf          181 Aug 14  1992 umd.edu
-rw-rw-r--  1 ftp      caf         5725 Nov 16  1992 virginia.decl-of-rights
-rw-rw-r--  1 ftp      caf         1225 Feb  8  1993 white-house.email-address
-rw-rw-r--  1 ftp      caf        10785 Apr  4 22:16 white-house.pr.pointer
-rw-rw-r--  1 ftp      caf       139671 May  5 22:18 wtp.zip
drwxrwsr-x  2 ftp      caf         1536 Aug  5 03:34 zzz
<Transfer complete.
```

## F.  The pwd (Print Working Directory) Command

While you are in the *civics* directory, you can practice another useful FTP command. At the FTP prompt type **pwd**. The server responds by telling you the name of the working directory.

```
FTP.EFF.ORG>pwd
"/pub/academic/civics" is current directory.
```

## G. Transferring a File Using the get Command

Now you are ready to transfer a copy of the *dec_of_ind* file from the remote computer to your local computer. This is done by issuing the command get <filename>. This means that to download a copy of *The Declaration of Independence*, you would enter the command **get dec_of_ind**. Some systems will prompt you for a "local" filename after you have entered the remote host's filename. You may need to rename the file when you transfer it in order to follow the DOS conventions that limit filenames to eight or fewer characters plus a three-character extension. Enter **get dec_of_ind declar.txt** (notice that there is only one space separating the original filename and the shortened name that you have assigned it). When the transfer is complete, the *FTP>* prompt will reappear.

## H. Using the Statistics Command

Just how long does this file transfer take? One way to find out is by using the **statistics** command. The **statistics** command turns the print timing statistics for file transfers OFF and ON. When this feature is turned OFF and you **get** a file, the following information is displayed on your screen:

```
FTP.EFF.ORG>get dec_of_ind
  To local file: declar.txt
Opening ASCII mode data connection for dec_of_ind (8496 bytes).
Transfer complete.
FTP.EFF.ORG>
```

If you type **statistics** at the *FTP>* prompt and press enter, you then switch the print timing statistics feature ON. Now when you **get** a file, the screen will also display information describing the file transfer rate in bits per second (bps) and the elapsed time in milliseconds (ms).

```
FTP.EFF.ORG>statistics
[Transfer statistics printing is ON]
FTP.EFF.ORG>get dec_of_ind
  To local file: declar.txt
<Opening ASCII mode data connection for dec_of_ind (8496 bytes).
<Transfer complete.
8659 bytes transferred at 1135 bps.
Run time = 0. ms, Elapsed time = 61006. ms.
```

To turn this feature OFF, enter the **statistics** command once again.

## I. Checking Your Local Directory with the ldir Command

You can confirm that the file arrived on your local machine without closing your FTP session by entering the **ldir** command at the *FTP>* prompt. This command displays the working directory on your local computer without breaking the FTP connection. In the following example, you can view the working directory on my local computer and see that I did indeed download *The Declaration of Independence* as file DECLAR.TXT (see line three).

```
FTP.EFF.ORG>ldir
DISK$USER:[ACBENSON]

00-ABSTRACT.TXT;1        70   5-DEC-1993 09:52 [ARKNET,ACBENSON] (RWED,RWED,,)
00-INDEX.TXT;1           75   5-DEC-1993 09:52 [ARKNET,ACBENSON] (RWED,RWED,,)
DECLAR.TXT;1             18   5-DEC-1993 09:59 [ARKNET,ACBENSON] (RWED,RWED,,)
GOPHERRC.;5              4   22-JUN-1993 20:56 [ARKNET,ACBENSON] (RWD,RWD,R,)
MAIL.MAI;1              36    3-DEC-1993 16:13 [ARKNET,ACBENSON] (RW,RW,,)
NEWS-EXTRACTS.DIR;1      1   31-OCT-1993 09:22 [ARKNET,ACBENSON] (RWE,RWE,,E)
PROC.;1                  6    4-DEC-1993 09:25 [ARKNET,ACBENSON] (RWED,RWED,,)
SEND.EXE;2               8    8-SEP-1993 11:31 [ARKNET,ACBENSON] (RWED,RWED,RE,)
SEND.EXE;1               8    8-SEP-1993 11:30 [ARKNET,ACBENSON] (RWED,RWED,RE,)
TT.;2                    1    5-DEC-1993 09:56 [ARKNET,ACBENSON] (RWED,RWED,,)
TT.;1                    8    5-DEC-1993 09:51 [ARKNET,ACBENSON] (RWED,RWED,,)
```

## J. *README* Files

Before leaving The Electronic Frontier Foundation, you should go back to the root directory and download two potentially important files. This will also give you an opportunity to practice two new commands. Entering the **cd/** command will take you all the way back to the root directory. Once there, you can enter the **pwd** command just to confirm that your working directory is now the root ("/").

```
FTP.EFF.ORG>cd/
FTP.EFF.ORG>pwd
<"/" is current directory.
```

If you enter the **dir** command you will display the holdings of the root directory as illustrated earlier.

Notice the two files listed in the right column called *README* and *README.bigdummy*. There are special purpose files located in FTP archives that will assist you in understanding what things are stored at that particular site. The most common file is a README file (also named Readme, read.me, AAA_README.1ST, Index, 00README, 00-index.txt, and other similar variations). If you recall, when you first connected to the Electronic Frontier Foundation, the message on the opening screen requested that users read the file README and README.bigdummy. *Readme* files are usually text files describing the contents of a directory, special instructions, or a brief explanation of the archive's contents and/or purpose.

## K. Using the mget (multiple get) Command and Wildcards

To transfer both of these files with one command, use the command *mget* (multiple get). Along with this command, you can use the wildcard characters ? and *. The question mark represents a single character and the asterisk represents one or more characters.

Because there are no other filenames beginning with the letter R, simply enter *mget R\** at the *FTP>* prompt and you will successfully transfer both of the readme files.

### L.  Using the bell Command

Type the pathname necessary to move back to the *civics* directory (FTP.EFF.ORG>cd pub/academic/civics):then type the command **bell**. This causes a tone to sound when you complete your operations—a handy device if you are transferring a large file and want to work on something else during the downloading process. The beep will let you know when the transfer is complete. To turn the bell off, simply type **bell off** at the prompt. Practice this procedure by downloading the file called README after issuing the bell command and then turn the bell off when you are finished. Type **quit** at the prompt to end your session and close the connection. Your session should look something like this:

```
FTP.EFF.ORG>bell
[Bell will now ring when operations complete]
FTP.EFF.ORG>get README
   To local file: readciv.txt
Opening ASCII mode data connection for README (8690 bytes).
Transfer complete.
FTP.EFF.ORG>bell off
[Operations will complete silently]
FTP.EFF.ORG>quit
Goodbye.
$
```

This particular readme file contains brief descriptions of every file residing in the *civics* directory. Because the filenames are somewhat cryptic when viewed on-line, readme files like this one are most helpful when you are trying to attach some meaning to an archive's holdings. These files are also called *index.txt, abstract.txt, 00-INDEX.TXT,* or something similar.

## Exercise 2

### *Downloading Text Files and Saving Directory Information*

In the next search exercise, you download a file called *proclamation-of-neutrality* in the subdirectory */pub/docs/history/USA/early_republic* on machine *ra.msstate.edu.* To retrieve a copy of this file, first log in to your own site and then execute the following commands:

```
$ ftp ra.msstate.edu
athena.ualr.edu MultiNet FTP user process 3.2(106)
Connection opened (Assuming 8-bit connections)
<Ra.MsState.Edu FTP server (Version wu-2.1c(4) Wed Sep 1 09:00:41 CDT 1993) ready.
Username: anonymous
Password:
RA.MSSTATE.EDU>get pub/docs/history/USA/early_republic proclamation-of-neutrality
proc.txt
Opening ASCII mode data connection for proclamation-of-neutrality (2586 bytes).
Transfer complete.
RA.MSSTATE.EDU>quit
Goodbye.
$
```

## A.  Using One Command Line for Finding and Transferring a File

In this example, you connected to an archive containing historical texts and images maintained by Mississippi State University. Once there, you downloaded a copy of *The Proclamation of Neutrality (1793)*. Rather than going to the subdirectory *early_republic* one directory at a time, issuing the **dir** command to view the contents of that directory, and then issuing the **get** command to download the desired file, you typed the **get** command followed by the pathname and filename all on one line in the root directory.

If you know where you are going and what file you want to download, the above example demonstrates a quick way to execute the transfer. Note also that the 26-character filename was renamed *proc.txt* before transferring. Once you complete the transfer, you should have a file on your local machine that begins as follows:

```
THE PROCLAMATION OF NEUTRALITY (1793):


BY THE PRESIDENT OF THE UNITED STATES

A PROCLAMATION

     Whereas it appears that a state of war exists between
Austria, Prussia, Sardinia, Great Britain, and the United
Netherlands, of the one part, and France on the other; and
the duty and interest of the United States require, that they
should with sincerity and good faith adopt and pursue a
conduct friendly and impartial toward the belligerent Powers;
     I have therefore thought fit by these presents to declare
the disposition of the United States to observe the conduct
aforesaid towards those Powers respectfully; and to exhort and
warn the citizens of the United States carefully to avoid all
acts and proceedings whatsoever, which may in any manner tend
to contravene such disposition.
     And I do hereby also make known, that whatsoever of the
citizens of the United States shall render himself liable to
punishment or forfeiture under the law of nations, by
committing, aiding, or abetting hostilities against any of the
said Powers, or by carrying to any of them those articles which
are deemed contraband by the modern usage of nations, will not
receive the protection of the United States, against such
punishment or forfeiture; and further, that I have given
instructions to those officers, to whom it belongs, to cause
prosecutions to be instituted against all persons, who shall,
within the cognizance of the courts of the United States,
violate the law of nations, with respect to the Powers at war,
or any of them.
     In testimony whereof, I have caused the seal of the United
States of America to be affixed to these presents, and signed
the same with my hand.  Done at the city of Philadelphia, the
twenty-second day of April, one thousand seven hundred and
ninety-three, and of the Independence of the United States of
America the seventeenth.

GEORGE WASHINGTON
April 22, 1793
```

```
-----------------------------------

   France declared war against Great Britain and Holland
early in April, 1793.  President Washington called a special
cabinet meeting, which resulted in this declaration of
neutrality.


-----------------------------------

Prepared by Gerald Murphy (The Cleveland Free-Net - aa300)
Distributed by the Cybercasting Services Division of the
   National Public Telecomputing Network (NPTN).

Permission is hereby granted to download, reprint, and/or otherwise
   redistribute this file, provided appropriate point of origin
   credit is given to the preparer(s) and the National Public
   Telecomputing Network.
```

## B. Saving Remote Filenames to a Local Machine

Another FTP command that is quite useful enables you to take the output of the **dir** command and put the output in a file on your local machine. You can then read the file's contents after you break the FTP connection. This is useful when the directories are very long and you would like to review their contents offline, especially when you are paying by the minute for connect time.

The command for accomplishing this is **dir * <local filename>**, where * represents all the subdirectories and the files they contain in your current working directory and **<local filename>** specifies the name you would like to assign this file on your local machine. The following session demonstrates how this command works. After FTPing to site *ftp.eff.org*, I changed directories to *pub* and there issued the **dir** command. After viewing the output from this command, I entered the command **dir * pub.txt**, which took all of the directories shown below and the files contained in those directories and placed them in a local file named *pub.txt*.

```
$ ftp ftp.eff.org
athena.ualr.edu MultiNet FTP user process 3.2(106)
Connection opened (Assuming 8-bit connections)
<ftp.eff.org FTP server (Version 2.1WU(1) Thu May 20 15:21:04 EDT 1993) ready.
Username: anonymous
Password:
FTP.EFF.ORG>cd pub.txt
<CWD command successful.
FTP.EFF.ORG>dir
<Opening ASCII mode data connection for /bin/ls.
total 40
-rw-r--r--   1 mech      mech       804 Jun  1 19:08 .message
-rw-r--r--   1 mech      doc       2544 Aug  4 23:11 00-INDEX.pub
-rw-r--r--   1 mech      mech       456 Aug  2 21:30 00-links.html
lrwxrwxrwx   1 mech      mech        23 Aug  4 22:44 00-master_filelist.Z -> ..
/00-master_filelist.Z
drwxr-xr-x   4 mech      mech       512 Jul 22 23:31 Alerts
drwxrwsr-x  16 kadie     caf       1024 Jun 25 17:48 CAF
drwxrwxr-x   7 mech      doc       1024 Jul 30 01:48 EFF
drwxr-xr-x  26 mech      mech      1024 Aug  3 20:03 Groups
```

```
drwxr-xr-x 12 mech      mech         2048 Jul 11 20:33 Net_info
drwxr-xr-x 14 mech      mech          512 Aug  4 15:35 Publications
lrwxrwxrwx  1 mech      mech            9 Jan 27 16:46 README -> ../README
-rw-r--r--  1 mech      mech         3984 Aug  1 20:17 README.changes
lrwxrwxrwx  1 mech      mech           13 Dec 21 19:08 about.eff -> EFF/about.eff
lrwxrwxrwx  1 mech      doc             3 Aug 24  1993 eff -> EFF
<Transfer complete.
FTP.EFF.ORG>dir * pub
<Opening ASCII mode data connection for /bin/ls.
<Transfer complete.
FTP.EFF.ORG>exit
<Goodbye.
```

## C. Saving a List of Filenames Contained in a Single Directory

Change to the directory */pub/EFF/papers* and enter the dir command.

```
FTP.EFF.ORG>cd pub/EFF/papers
<CWD command successful.
FTP.EFF.ORG>dir
<Opening ASCII mode data connection for /bin/ls.
total 3274
-rw-rw-r--  1 ftp       ftp         11054 Nov  8 22:19 Index
-rw-rw-r--  1 ftp       ftp          8974 Jun 19  1991 across-electronic-frontier
-rw-r--r--  1 mech      ftp          8440 Nov  4 00:04 announce.op2
-rw-r--r--  1 ftp       ftp        361840 Sep  2 21:23 bdummy.txt
drwxrwsr-x  3 ftp       ftp           512 Dec  1 16:06 big-dummys-guide-texi
-rw-r--r--  1 ftp       ftp        285659 Aug 20 13:51 big-dummys-guide.sit.hqx
lrwxrwxrwx  1 mech      ftp            10 Nov 23 03:49 big-dummys-guide.txt ->
bdummy.txt
-rw-r--r--  1 ftp       ftp         24122 Aug 11  1992 civil-liberties-in-cyberspace
-rw-rw-r--  1 ftp       ftp         63838 Feb 23  1991 crime-and-puzzlement
-rw-rw-r--  1 ftp       ftp          7850 Jun 19  1991 crime-and-puzzlement-2
drwxrwxr-x  2 ftp       ftp          1024 Nov  9 17:57 cyber
-rw-r--r--  1 ftp       ftp         32934 Aug 11  1992 decrypting-puzzle-palace
-rw-r--r--  1 mech      mech         32560 Nov  9 22:48 denning.ppr
-rw-rw-r--  1 ftp       ftp          8972 May 23  1991 eff-and-virtual-communities
-rw-r--r--  1 ftp       ftp         14825 Aug 11  1992 eff-comments-dialtone
-rw-r--r--  1 ftp       ftp         22165 Aug 11  1992 eff-comments-intel-nets
-rw-r--r--  1 ftp       ftp         59825 Mar  9 00:18 eff-on-isdn-applications
-rw-rw-r--  1 ftp       ftp          7812 Jul 22  1991 fcc-network-testimony
-rw-r--r--  1 ftp       ftp         13244 Aug 11  1992 first-year-law-school
-rw-r--r--  1 ftp       ftp         17245 Aug 11  1992 great-work
-rw-rw-r--  1 ftp       ftp          6476 Jun 19  1991 isdn-testimony
-rw-r--r--  1 mech      ftp          5779 Nov 30 16:32 kapornyt.op
-rw-rw-r--  1 ftp       ftp         28006 Mar 16  1992 nsfnet-testimony
-rw-rw-r--  1 ftp       ftp          6300 Sep 27  1992 nsfnet-testimony-notes
-rw-r--r--  1 mech      ftp         25054 Nov  3 17:44 op2.0
-rw-r--r--  1 mech      ftp        345658 Nov  3 23:58 op2.0.ps.z
lrwxrwxrwx  1 mech      ftp            12 Nov  4 00:02 op2.0.readme -> announce.op2
lrwxrwxrwx  1 root      ftp            29 Oct 22 20:19 open-platform-discussion ->
open-platform-discussion-1993
-rw-r--r--  1 ftp       ftp         20202 Jul 21 20:14 open-platform-discussion-1993
-rw-rw-r--  1 ftp       ftp         16616 Nov 12  1991 open-platform-overview
-rw-rw-r--  1 ftp       ftp         35502 Jul 16  1992 open-platform-proposal
-rw-rw-r--  1 ftp       ftp         36478 Nov 12  1991 open-platform-testimony
-rw-rw-r--  1 ftp       ftp         61654 Sep 19  1991 open-road-nren
```

```
-rw-rw-r--   1 ftp        ftp          4182 Oct 16  1991 open-road-overheads
-rw-rw-r--   1 ftp        ftp          4946 Sep 27  1992 prodigy-stumbles
-rw-rw-r--   1 ftp        ftp         34014 Aug  7  1991 search-and-seizure
-rw-rw-r--   1 ftp        ftp          5386 Nov 15 18:08 why-joined-eff
<Transfer complete.
```

Notice that in the displayed directory there is a subdirectory called *cyber*. If you would like to create a file that displays the files contained in that directory, enter the following command:

```
FTP.EFF.ORG>dir cyber cyber.dir
<Opening ASCII mode data connection for /bin/ls.
<Transfer complete.
```

In this example, you begin by typing the command **dir** followed by the subdirectory name *cyber*; then follow that with the output filename *cyber.dir*. When you view this file, which is named *cyber.dir* on your local machine, you will see a listing of the contents of the directory called *cyber*, which should resemble this:

```
total 1894
-rw-rw-r--   1 ftp        ftp          6337 Nov  8 22:21 Index
-rw-r--r--   1 ftp        ftp         44305 Aug 28  1992 cfp1-summary
-rw-rw-r--   1 ftp        ftp         40674 Jul 16  1992 cfp2-summary
-rw-rw-r--   1 ftp        ftp         19465 Aug  2  1991 computer-conferencing-intro
-rw-rw-r--   1 ftp        ftp         58773 Aug 20  1991 concerning-hackers
-rw-r--r--   1 ftp        ftp         45988 Jan 25  1993 cpsr-berkeley-platform
-rw-r--r--   1 ftp        ftp         20230 Aug 28  1992 cpsr-privacy-for-nren
-rw-rw-r--   1 ftp        ftp         44153 Oct  1  1992 cud3.09-hollywood-hacker
-rw-r--r--   1 mech       mech       184284 Nov  9 17:57 cybrpoet.gvc
-rw-r--r--   1 ftp        ftp          5386 Aug 28  1992 educom-comment-nsfnet
-rw-rw-r--   1 ftp        ftp          4422 Jul 16  1992 getting-internet-info
-rw-rw-r--   1 ftp        ftp         34462 Mar 27  1992 global-civil-society
-rw-rw-r--   1 ftp        ftp         32650 Jul 16  1992 gurps-labor-lost
-rw-r--r--   1 ftp        ftp         58985 Jul 28 17:09 innkeeping
-rw-r--r--   1 ftp        ftp        154297 May 25 17:08 internet-individual-access
-rw-rw-r--   1 ftp        ftp         11798 Jul 16  1992 isdn-technology
-rw-rw-r--   1 ftp        ftp         59067 Jul 16  1992 life-in-virtual-community
-rw-r--r--   1 ftp        ftp         12887 Apr  5 21:12 net-during-russian-coup
-rw-rw-r--   1 ftp        ftp         13701 Jul 16  1992 prodigy-where-is-it-going
-rw-r--r--   1 ftp        ftp         10558 Aug 21  1992 select-bbs
-rw-r--r--   1 ftp        ftp         28030 Jul 29 00:16 telluride.ideas
-rw-r--r--   1 ftp        ftp         28023 Sep 21 16:09 town-on-internet-highway
-rw-rw-r--   1 ftp        ftp         18319 Jul 16  1992 what-is-cyberspace
```

## Exercise 3

### *Moving Files from Your Dial-up Host to Your Personal Computer*

If you executed the preceding text file transfers, you now have the following files copied to your workspace on the local host (their local filenames will vary depending on what names you have assigned them):

| *Remote host filename* | *Local filename* |
|---|---|
| dec_of_ind | delar.txt |
| README | readeff.txt |

| *Remote host filename* | *Local filename* |
|---|---|
| README.bigdummy | bigdum.txt |
| README | readciv.txt |
| proclamation-of-neutrality | proc.txt |

If your personal computer is connected directly to the Internet, the files you download using FTP will come right to your personal computer. If you are using a modem and telephone line to connect to the Internet through an intermediary such as Amigos or Delphi, you will have to transfer the files one more time before they actually arrive on your own personal computer. You began by transferring the files from the remote computer to your workspace on the intermediary computer using FTP. It was not your responsibility to install the FTP application, which consists of both the client and server programs. If the remote and intermediary computers support the TCP/IP protocol suite, this installation had already taken place.

Now you have to transfer the files from the intermediary computer to your own personal computer using one of a group of other standard file transfer protocols, such as Kermit, Xmodem, Ymodem, or Zmodem. When you choose a communication program, it more than likely will support one or more of these common protocols.

These protocols are simply agreed-upon standards that govern how your personal computer communicates with another computer when exchanging files. For example, if the communication software on your personal computer supports Zmodem and the local host that you dial-up to supports Zmodem, you tell the local host to *send* using Zmodem and you tell your communication software to *receive* using Zmodem. The local host's Zmodem is not your responsibility, but you do have to confirm that it is installed.

## A. Downloading a File Using Zmodem

To demonstrate this process, let's download the file *declar.txt*. You must first determine which of the mentioned protocols is supported by both your communication software and the local host to which you are connecting. Because most communication programs support Zmodem, that is the protocol used in the following demonstration.

On most systems, the Zmodem program is called *sz*, which stands for *send using Zmodem*. Its companion program is named *rz*, which stands for *receive using Zmodem*.

To download a text file from your personal workspace on the dial-up host to your personal computer, type sz -a <filename>, in this case sz -a declar.txt. You use the -a parameter when downloading ASCII text files. If you are downloading a binary file, use -b.

Depending on the communication software you use, as soon as you enter the sz command, your communication program may detect that you have initiated a Zmodem transfer and automatically start transferring the file without any further action on your part.

With other communication programs, you will have to tell them to start downloading using Zmodem. The exact procedure you follow will vary from program to program, so consult the documentation that came with the particular communication program you use.

Again, depending on the communication software you are using, you will see different things on the screen while the file is being downloaded. Procomm Plus for Windows displays a status window that tracks the downloading process, showing the number of bytes being transferred per second, the estimated time until completion, and the percentage of the total file that has transferred at any given time. When the download is complete, the program beeps three times and the window disappears.

Most communication programs allow you to switch over to a DOS prompt without quitting the communication program or breaking your connection with the dial-up host. You can use this feature to confirm that the transfer took place successfully; you can make sure that the file you downloaded is residing on your disk. With this established, you can exit back to the communication program and continue your communications with the dial-up host. A good file management habit is to delete the *declar.txt* file from your personal workspace on the dial-up host while it is still clear in your mind what that file's purpose is and that you no longer need it.

Zmodem also permits downloading multiple files with one command. If you wanted to download all of the files with the .txt extension, you could enter **sz -a *.txt**.

## Exercise 4

### *Connecting to a Machine Running VMS*

In the next search exercise, you connect to a computer running a VMS operating system. The most noticeable difference from UNIX is how the directory information is displayed. Directory and filenames are listed in the left column and directories are designated with a .DIR extension. In the second column, the file size is given in kilobytes. (To translate this number into bytes, simply multiply times 1,000.)

### A.  Making the Connection

Begin this session by entering the **ftp hydra.uwo.ca** command. This connects you with the FTP archive at the University of Western Ontario where there is a directory of files that will be of particular interest to librarians. After logging in, enter a **cd** command to change to the *LIBSOFT* directory, and then enter a **dir** command. Limited space allows only a sampling of the *LIBSOFT* directory to be printed out here. If time allows, explore this directory to its fullest—it is one of the more important software and text depositories for librarians on the Internet. So far, the session should look something like the following:

```
$ ftp hydra.uwo.ca
Connection opened (Assuming 8-bit connections)
<HYDRA.UWO.CA MultiNet FTP Server Process 3.1(14) at Sun 5-Dec-93 10:45AM-EST
Username: anonymous
Password:
<Guest User GUEST logged into PUB:[000000] at Sun  5-Dec-93 10:46, job 25d13.
<Directory and access restrictions apply
HYDRA.UWO.CA>cd libsoft
<Connected to PUB:[000000.LIBSOFT].
HYDRA.UWO.CA>dir
<List started.

PUB:[000000.LIBSOFT]

00-ABSTRACT.TXT;1          70    6-JUN-1993 09:59 [35007_321] (RWE,RWED,RE,RE)
00-INDEX.TXT;61           75   28-NOV-1993 14:46 [35007_321] (RWE,RWED,RE,RE)
AAA_README.1ST;13          8    6-JUN-1993 09:58 [35007_321] (RWE,RWED,RE,RE)
ACADLIST.TXT;1            14    8-NOV-1992 14:39 [35007_321] (RWE,RWED,RE,RE)
AGGUIDE.DOS;1           178   30-JUN-1992 10:33 [35007_321] (RWE,RWED,RE,RE)
AGGUIDE.WP;1            230   30-JUN-1992 10:33 [35007_321] (RWE,RWED,RE,RE)
APRA_EC.DIR;1             1   28-SEP-1993 10:37 [35007_321] (RWE,RWE,RE,RE)
ARCHIE.COM;1             35   11-SEP-1991 14:16 [35007_321] (RWE,RWED,RE,RE)
ARCHIE_GUIDE.TXT;1        7    3-NOV-1991 13:05 [35007_321] (RWE,RWED,RE,RE)
ARTBASE.TXT;1            31   14-NOV-1991 18:45 [35007_321] (RWE,RWED,RE,RE)
AUT103-4.TXT;1          200   26-APR-1992 20:26 [35007_321] (RWE,RWED,RE,RE)
AUT1101.TXT;1           246   26-APR-1992 20:26 [35007_321] (RWE,RWED,RE,RE)
BAR_CODE.ZIP;1          106   22-NOV-1992 21:54 [35007_321] (RWE,RWED,RE,RE)
BGI12.ZIP;1             179   28-NOV-1993 14:45 [35007_321] (RWE,RWED,RE,RE)
BIBL771.ZIP;1           492    8-NOV-1992 20:34 [35007_321] (RWE,RWED,RE,RE)
BIBNET27.ZIP;1          527    8-NOV-1992 20:34 [35007_321] (RWE,RWED,RE,RE)
BIG-DUMMYS-GUIDE.TXT;1   731   26-SEP-1993 20:21 [35007_321] (RWE,RWED,RE,RE)
BINARIES.TXT;2           23   11-MAY-1993 18:14 [35007_321] (RWE,RWED,RE,RE)
BINARIES_FTP.TXT;1       14    3-DEC-1991 19:01 [35007_321] (RWE,RWED,RE,RE)
BIOGREF.DOC;1             8   18-JAN-1993 22:11 [35007_321] (RWE,RWED,RE,RE)
BIOGREF.ZIP;1           548   18-JAN-1993 22:12 [35007_321] (RWE,RWED,RE,RE)
BIOLOGY.TXT;1           214    9-JUN-1993 13:40 [35007_321] (RWE,RWED,RE,RE)
BITNET_FTP.TXT;1         18    9-FEB-1992 14:20 [35007_321] (RWE,RWED,RE,RE)
BITWORK_FAC.WP5;1       246    8-MAR-1993 16:44 [35007_321] (RWE,RWED,RE,RE)
BSD.ZIP;2                38    3-JUL-1992 09:57 [35007_321] (RWE,RWED,RE,RE)
CARL.TXT;1               60    3-MAR-1992 19:23 [35007_321] (RWE,RWED,RE,RE)
CASSY.EXE;1             308   19-SEP-1991 11:05 [35007_321] (RWE,RWED,RE,RE)
CASSY.TXT;2               3   29-MAY-1992 12:54 [35007_321] (RWE,RWED,RE,RE)
CATALIST.TXT;1           11    8-AUG-1991 15:29 [35007_321] (RWE,RWED,RE,RE)
CATALIST10.EXE;1        323   22-NOV-1992 21:47 [35007_321] (RWE,RWED,RE,RE)
```

This directory contains many interesting text files such as Lee Hancock's comprehensive list of health science resources that are available on the Internet; John Sadler's list of Canadian Library OPAC's you can TELNET to on the Internet; Michael Strangelove's *The Electric Mystic's Guide to the Internet: A Complete Bibliography of Networked Electronic Documents Relevant to Religious Studies*; and executable programs such as Tim Craven's thesaurus construction program; cataloging and indexing programs; and Clyde W. Grotophorst's government documents check-in system for IBM PC's.

## B. Downloading a File

The best file to download for a complete description of this directory's contents is *00-abstract.txt*. When you **get** this file, be aware that VMS file and directory names are not case-sensitive as they are in UNIX. You can type **get 00-abstract.txt** or **get 00-ABSTRACT.TXT**. The first few lines of this file look like this:

```
  __    __      __   __   __                  _____    _____    _____     __    _____
 /_ /|      /_/| /_ /|       /_____/|  /____/ \ /_____ /|   /_____ /|
 | | |      | || | | |       |  ____|/ / /-\ \/| | ____|/   |___   ___|/
 | | |      | || | | |___    | | |__    | |   | || | |____        | | |
 | | |      | || | |/___/| | | |/___/| | |   | || | |/___/ |      | | |
 | | |      | || |  ___ || |_____ || | |   | || | ___|/       | | |
 | | |___   | || | |  | ||      | || | |   | || | | |         | | |
 | |/___/| | || | |__| ||  ___| || |  \ __/ |/ | | |         | | |
 |_____|/ |_|/ |_____|/ |_____|/   \_____/   |_|/         |_|/
```

```
                        FTP ARCHIVE
                UNIVERSITY OF WESTERN ONTARIO


----------------------------------------------------------------
     Directory CCSDISK:[PUB.LIBSOFT]    Last Update: May 12, 1993 EDT
----------------------------------------------------------------


ACADLIST.TXT   The 5th Revision of the Directory of Scholarly Electronic
               Conferences. (How to obtain it - not the actual list!)

AGGUIDE.WP     NOT JUST COWS. A Guide to Internet/Bitnet Resources in
               Agriculture and Related Sciences. Written and compiled by
               Wilfred Drew. This is in WordPerfect 5.1 format.
>>>AAGUIDE.DOS    NOT JUST COWS in ASCII format.

ARCHIE.COM     Documentation on the Archie archive listing and indexing
               database at McGill. Contains a user's guide in WordPerfect
               5.1 format (uses info from archive) and a text file from
               Robert Maas (Maasinfo). Self-extracting archive file.

ARCHIE_GUIDE.TXT
               Richard Hintz's  What is an Archie?  text file.

ARTBASE.TXT    Bob Gale's Bibliography of Arts Online - not all on Internet.

AUT103-4.TXT   Automatome V10 nos 3/4. REVIEWS OF 10 AUTOMATED LIBRARY SYSTEMS
               The Assistant                Jacqueline S. Wright and Timothy
N. Holthoff
               BiblioTech Software          Betty Howell
               Carlyle Systems              Steve Hunt
               Data Trek Library Software   Linda Register
               INMAGIC                      Robert E. Riger
               INNOPAC                      Jane Walsh
               Information Navigator        Sandy Gold
               NOTIS:  An Overview          Diane I. Hillman
               PALS Integrated Library System   Christopher Noe
               Sydney Library System        Jane Reynolds
```

For additional practice in downloading text files, explore any one of the following sites:

1.  Host: *ifcss.org*

    Subject: Chinese Community Information Center

2.  Host: *borg.lib.vt.edu*

    Subject: The Scholarly Communications Project of Virginia Tech

3.  Host: *vm1.nodak.edu*

    Subject: Several discussion list archives covering subjects such as genealogy, new list announcements, and disability information

4.  Host: *ftp.funet.fi*

    Subject: Finnish University and Research Network (FUNET) archive

5.  Host: *ftp.cs.cmu.edu*

    Subject: Artificial Intelligence (Look in the */user/ai* directory)

6.  Host: *info.umd.edu*

    Subject: U.S. Supreme Court decisions (Look in the */info/Government/US/SupremeCt* directory)

Use the same commands relating to connecting, moving through directories, and downloading files that were explained in earlier exercises. At most FTP sites, you'll find the interesting files and directories located under */pub*.

If you find a text file you'd like to refer to later, record the following information for future reference: document title, host address, pathname, and filename. Remember, always insert the *ftp* command before the host's Internet address when trying to connect.

## ≡ Downloading Binary Files

Any data that is not plain text is binary data and a file that contains binary data is referred to as a *binary* file. Some examples of binary files are sound recordings, pictures, and executable programs.

Because binary files contain binary data, they must be transferred in binary mode. ASCII text is the default mode of file transfer in FTP, so unless you tell the program something different, the FTP application will assume you are working with text files. Switching to a binary setting is a simple process. Simply enter the **binary** command before you enter the **get** or **mget** command. When you have changed the transfer mode to binary, that mode remains in effect until you **quit** your session or until you enter the **ascii** command again.

If you find that after transferring your files, they are corrupted, you may have failed to set the transfer type to binary before you transferred the file from the remote host to your local machine. If you are using a dial-up service, make sure that you also set the file transfer type to binary when you transfer the file from your service provider's computer to your own personal computer.

Software resources on the Internet can be divided into three classifications: public domain, freeware, and shareware. *Public domain* software carries no copyright and is made available by the programmer without any restrictions . No limitations are imposed on its distribution and it can be transformed or modified by anyone without first obtaining permission from the author or paying the author a fee.

*Freeware* is copyrighted software made available for public use without charge. By retaining the copyright, the author can restrict the redistribution and modification of the software.

*Shareware* programs are also copyrighted but are made available on a trial basis; if, after you try it out, you decide to keep it and use it, you are required to pay the author a small fee. In return, you become a registered user and receive certain benefits such as a printed manual and technical support. If you decide not to keep the program, you must destroy the copies you have in your possession.

In an effort to conserve storage space and keep related files grouped together, system managers running anonymous FTP archives use two special file formats. You must become familiar with these if you want to take full advantage of the binary holdings in FTP archives.

The first of these formatting procedures takes large files and compresses them into smaller files that require less storage space and downloading time. These are called *compressed* files and they must be transformed back into their original, or *decompressed*, state before they can be used.

The second format takes a set of related files and packs them together into a single file called an *archive*. For example, the separate documentation files and programs that constitute a piece of software are usually packed together into a single archive for easier storage and downloading. After you download an archived file to your own machine, you then have to unpack it to convert it back into its original state.

Many utilities like *tar*, *StuffIt*, and *pkzip* transform files into different formats. Most of the text and data compression programs used for performing these operations use standard public domain software that can be found at one of two sights:

- in the United States, *wuarchive.wustl.edu* [128.252.135.4], at Washington University in St. Louis, and

- in Europe, *garbo.uwasa.fi* [128.214.87.1]

Many other sites that have the same programs, in particular *oak.oakland.edu* [141.210.80.117], the primary mirror site of SIMTEL20 (US Army Information Systems Command at White Sands Missile Range in New Mexico) which closed down in September 1993.

The Oak Software Repository is an FTP archive maintained by Oakland University, Rochester, Michigan. If you are looking for MS-DOS files, **cd** to **/pub/msdos**. For a complete list of MS-DOS files, **cd** to **/pub/msdos/filedocs** and download the file called *simlist.zip*. If you have access to a gopher client, this software repository can also be accessed through *gopher.oakland.edu*. (Gopher is explained in Chapter 7.)

For Macintosh programs, you can refer to the official home of the Info-Mac archives at FTP site *sumex-aim.stanford.edu* [36.44.0.6]. A CD ROM of this archive is available from Pacific HiTech. The cost is approximately $45.00 and you can order the CD ROM by contacting the company by phone at 800-765-8369, FAX at 801-278-2666, or email at *71175.3152@compuserve.com*.

There is a 35-user limit for anonymous FTP into *sumex-aim.stanford.edu* from 8a.m. to 5 p.m. Pacific time, Monday through Friday. When you find they are busy, use one of the mirror archives such as the University of Michigan's Macintosh Public Domain and Shareware Archive *mac.archive.umich.edu* [141.211.32.2]. The Washington University archive mentioned earlier maintains mirror archives of *summex-aim.stanford.edu* and *mac.archive.umich.edu*. Look in */mirrors/infomac* and */mirrors/archive.umich.edu* respectively.

## Downloading ZIP files

A *zip* file is a single file in which one or more compressed files are stored. In the next exercise, you download a zip file and the special software needed for transforming the zip file into a normal file (also called *unzipping* the file).

## Exercise 5

### *How To Download a Zip File*

To retrieve a zip file, begin by FTPing to site *oak.oakland.edu* and download the file called *bkache56.zip* in the */pub/msdos/*info directory. This file is a zip-formatted version of Backache Relief Now!, a shareware package from Jim Hood & Seattle Scientific Photography. The session will look something like this:

```
$ ftp oak.oakland.edu
athena.ualr.edu MultiNet FTP user process 3.2(106)
Connection opened (Assuming 8-bit connections)
<gatekeeper FTP server (Version 4.19 Wed Jul 1 18:27:52 EDT 1992) ready.
Username: anonymous
Password:
OAK.OAKLAND.EDU>cd pub/msdos/info
<CWD command successful.
OAK.OAKLAND.EDU>binary
Type: Image, Structure: File, Mode: Stream
OAK.OAKLAND.EDU>get bkache56.zip
  To local file:
<Opening BINARY mode data connection for bkache56.zip (191371 bytes).
<Transfer complete.
OAK.OAKLAND.EDU>quit
<Goodbye.
```

Notice that after logging in and moving to the desired directory, I entered the **binary** command before entering the **get** command.

You may want to enter the **ldir** command to confirm that the file arrived before quitting the FTP session. If you have a dial-up connection to a local host, the next step is to download the file from your local host to your personal computer using Zmodem or one of the other file transfer protocols mentioned earlier.

When the transfer is complete, store the **bkache56.zip** file in its own directory on your personal machine and proceed to the next step by downloading the necessary software for transforming it into a usable file.

## Exercise 6

### *Getting a Copy of PKUNZIP*

The most commonly used DOS programs for transforming zip files are PKZIP and PKUNZIP. These are shareware programs produced by PKWARE Inc., 9025 N. Deerwood Drive, Brown Deer, WI 53223. The latest official version of these applications is version 2.04g. You need to have the latest version of PKUNZIP; if you have an older version, such as version 1.1, you can decompress only those files made with PKZIP version 1.1 or earlier. If you have the latest version, you can decompress any zip file made with PKZIP 2.04g or earlier.

The file that contains these and other related programs can be downloaded from any of the following FTP archives:

1.  Host: *ctron.com* (134.141.197.25)

    Pathname: */pub/General.Info*
    Filename: *pk204g.exe*

2.  Host: *csd4.csd.uwm.edu* (129.89.7.4)

    Pathname: */pub/msdos*
    Filename: *pk204g.exe*

3.  Host: *oak.oakland.edu*

    Pathname: *lpc/arcers*
    Filename: *pkz204g.exe*

Remember to set the transfer mode to binary before downloading the file. The session should look something like this:

```
$ ftp ctron.com
athena.ualr.edu MultiNet FTP user process 3.2(106)
Connection opened (Assuming 8-bit connections)
<gatekeeper FTP server (Version 4.19 Wed Jul 1 18:27:52 EDT 1992) ready.
Username: anonymous
Password:
<Usual restrictions apply, priority modified.
<umask modified such that uploaded files cannot be downloaded.
CTRON.COM>cd pub/General.Info
<CWD command successful.
CTRON.COM>binary
Type: Image, Structure: File, Mode: Stream
CTRON.COM>get pk204g.exe
   To local file:
<Opening data connection for pk204g.exe (binary mode) (202574 bytes).
<Transfer complete.
CTRON.COM>quit
<Goodbye.
```

## Exercise 7

### Transferring a Binary File with Kermit

Now transfer the *pk204g.exe* file from your dial-up host to your personal computer, using one of the standard protocols described earlier. For demonstration purposes, this section illustrates how the session looks if you are using Kermit. (If Kermit isn't available to you, use one of the protocols that is.)

After quitting the FTP session and retiring to your local host, type **kermit** and press ENTER. Next, type **set file type binary** and press ENTER. Now, type **send pk204g.exe** and press ENTER. Using Kermit to download the file to your personal computer will look something like this:

```
$ kermit
VMS Kermit-32 version 3.3.128
Default terminal for transfers is: _LTA5756:
Kermit-32>set file type binary
Current block size for file transfer is 512
Kermit-32>send pk204g.exe
```

## Exercise 8

### Decompressing the pk204g.exe File

When the *pk204g.exe* file is on your own computer, create a separate directory and copy it to that directory. Because the file has an .exe extension, it may look as though it is an executable file. Actually it is a self-extracting MS-DOS executable file. *Self-extracting files* decompress themselves on disk when you run them.

To run the program, type **pk204g** and press ENTER. After a few moments, the directory displays over a dozen normal files, one of which will be *PKUNZIP.EXE*. If you are working on an IBM-compatible computer, this is the program you will use to decompress any files you download with the .zip extension. These files have been compressed and archived with PKZIP, a companion program which is also included in the pk204g.zip file.

## Exercise 9

### Unzipping and Installing bkache56.zip

Now that you have PKUNZIP available for your use, you can convert the file you downloaded earlier called *bkache56.zip*. You can use two different procedures to decompress the file. The preferred method is to list the directory that contains *PKUNZIP.EXE* in the DOS PATH. This would allow you to run PKUNZIP from any directory. A less favorable alternative is to move the file you want to unzip into the same directory where PKUNZIP resides.

Finally, enter this command to decompress the file:

```
C:\pkunzip bkache56
```

It isn't necessary to include the .zip extension.

Now use the **dir** command to display the files that are extracted from the archive. Once *bkache56* is unzipped, you see eleven new files as well as the original file *bkache56.zip*. The original zip-formatted file was not changed and can be deleted if you see that everything is in order.

Notice that one of the files is called README. View this file in a word processing program, or simply print it to the screen with the DOS **type** command. The README file provides a description of the program, installation instructions, and registration information in case you decide to keep the program.

You will need to install the software before you can use it. To install the program, type **install** and press ENTER. A notice will appear asking you whether you want to proceed with the installation. If so, installation will create a target subdirectory on your hard drive. After installation is complete, the program can be started by entering the command **go**.

## Exercise 10

### *Zipping a File*

PKUNZIP's companion program, PKZIP, takes one or more normal files and compresses them into a single zip-formatted file. If, for example, you have written an article that you'd like to upload to a remote computer's FTP archive, first save the document as a plain ASCII text file, compress the file using PKZIP, and then upload it to your local host computer. From there, you again upload it to a remote computer of your choosing by using the **put** command.

For example, the following command creates a zip-formatted file called *BKLIST.ZIP* from the normal file called *BKLIST.TXT*:

```
c:\ pkzip bklist.txt
```

As when using PKUNZIP, this operation must also take place in the directory where both the file and PKZIP reside, or make sure PKZIP can be located by the DOS PATH statement.

## ≡ Downloading Pictures

Two of the most common formats for storing pictures are GIF and JPEG. GIF (Graphics Interchange Format) files were originally developed by CompuServe. These files are usually given the extension .gif. JPEG pictures are stored in files with .jpg extensions. The name JPEG stands for the Joint Photographic Experts Group, the organization that developed this particular image format.

GIF and JPEG images are stored as binary files, so the same procedure used for downloading compressed or executable files is also used for downloading picture files. The difference comes in how these pictures are displayed. In order to view a GIF or JPEG file, you must run a program called a *viewer* which transforms the file into an actual image. The following exercise takes you through the necessary steps for downloading and viewing a GIF file.

## Exercise 11

### *Downloading a Viewer Program*

In this exercise, you download a shareware viewer program called VPIC, which was developed by Bob Montgomery. VPIC version 6.0 is a DOS viewer for GIF images and it can be found at various FTP archive sites on the Internet. Two of these locations are the following:

1. Host: *ftp.cis.ksu.edu* [129.130.10.80]
   Pathname: */pub/PC/useful-msdos/section-C/area-4/graphics*
   Filename: *vpic60.zip*

2. Host: *seq1.loc.gov* [140.147.3.12]
   Pathname: */pub/1492.exhibit/viewers*
   Filename: *vpic60.zip*

FTP to the second source listed above, **cd** to */pub/1492.exhibit/viewers*, and download the ZIP file called *vpic60.zip*. Notice that there is another viewer program in this directory called DVPEG, a DOS program for viewing both JPEG and GIF files. If time allows, you might try transferring and unzipping this program, too. Both programs include documentation on how to set up your system and run the programs.

Remember that ZIP files are binary files, which means you need to set the FTP transfer mode to binary before transferring *vpic60.zip* to your local computer. If you must download the file a second time from a dial-up machine to your own personal computer, continue to take the necessary steps for properly downloading binary files.

## Exercise 12

### *Unzipping vpic60.zip*

Place *vpic60.zip* in its own directory and use PKUNZIP to extract all of the compressed files. If the directory that contains *PKUNZIP.EXE* is in the DOS PATH, go to the directory containing *vpic60.zip*, type **pkunzip vpic60**, and press ENTER. If everything goes as it should and all of the files are properly extracted from the archive, you may want to delete the original zip-formatted file or save it to a disk.

Enter a **dir/p** command so you can page through all of the filenames. Note the files called *readme.1st*, *config.doc*, and *vpic.doc*. These are text documents that provide information on how to configure VPIC and VPIC's general features.

For additional information on picture files, consult the frequently asked questions (FAQ) list on viewing pictures. This list consists of three files called *part1*, *part2*, and *part3*. These files reside in the */pub/usenet/news.answers/pictures-faq* directory at FTP site *rtfm.mit.edu*.

In the last part of this exercise, download one or more GIF files and save them to the same directory where the VPIC viewer program resides. If all goes well, the viewer program should run when you type **vpic** and press ENTER. The names of the GIF files you downloaded and saved to that same directory will be displayed on the screen. Select the file you want to view by moving the highlight bar to the appropriate line; then press ENTER. If everything is in proper working order, the image will appear on the screen.

Several sources are available for GIF files and information relating to GIF files. One FTP source you might like to explore is site *ames.arc.nasa.gov*. Once connected, change to the */pub/GIF* directory. Here you'll find the following list of files (the one called *best0.gif* is an image of the planet Venus taken from Voyager 2):

```
-rw-r--r--  1 108   wheel     1209 Aug 30  1989  README
-rw-r--r--  1 108   10      149414 Feb  6  1991  best0.gif
-rw-r--r--  1 108   10      199159 Feb  6  1991  best1.gif
-rw-r--r--  1 108   10      202638 Feb  6  1991  best2.gif
-rw-r--r--  1 108   10       65049 Feb  6  1991  best3.gif
-rw-r--r--  1 108   10      222458 Feb  6  1991  best4.gif
-rw-r--r--  1 108   10      172101 Feb  6  1991  best5.gif
-rw-r--r--  1 108   10      170108 Feb  6  1991  best6.gif
-rw-r--r--  1 108   10      199159 Feb  6  1991  clouds.gif
-rw-r--r--  1 108   10      164219 Feb  8  1991  shuttle.gif
-rw-r--r--  1 108   10       52158 Feb  6  1991  triton.gif
-rw-r--r--  1 108   10       28691 Feb  6  1991  whole.gif
```

A site maintained by the University of Central Florida's College of Engineering, *apocalypse.engr.ucf.edu*, maintains GIF image files in the */pub/images/gif* directory and JPEG image files in the */pub/images/jpeg* directory.

The GIF files include:

```
-rw-r--r--  1 ssd   ipg      455 Sep  1  1991  README
-rw-r--r--  1 ssd   ipg   162440 Feb  3  1992  bridge.gif
-rw-r--r--  1 root  ipg   149223 Aug  5 17:49  earth.gif
-rw-r--r--  1 root  ipg   237431 Jul 16 02:20  flower.gif
-rw-r--r--  1 root  ipg   165134 Jun 30  1990  hub_dep3.gif
-rw-r--r--  1 root  ipg   189180 Jun 30  1990  hub_dep7.gif
-rw-r--r--  1 root  ipg   131381 Jun 30  1990  hub_dep8.gif
-rw-r--r--  1 root  ipg   145595 Jun 30  1990  hub_grf5.gif
-rw-r--r--  1 root  ipg   230970 Jun 30  1990  hub_grf5.scr
-rw-r--r--  1 root  ipg   217029 Jun 30  1990  hub_plb0.gif
-rw-r--r--  1 root  ipg   199154 Jun 30  1990  hub_plb1.gif
-rw-r--r--  1 root  ipg   195707 Jun 30  1990  hub_plb2.gif
-rw-r--r--  1 ssd   ipg   176358 Nov 20  1990  mandrl.gif
-rw-r--r--  1 root  ipg   743845 Oct 29  1990  oldmill.gif
-rw-r--r--  1 ssd   ipg   262189 May 13  1992  oldmill.pgm
-rw-r--r--  1 ssd   ipg   308930 Sep 18  1992  oldmill2.gif
-rw-r--r--  1 root  ipg    54272 Oct 29  1990  orangutan.gif
-rw-r--r--  1 ssd   ipg   159329 Aug  4  1992  rose-640x512.gif
-rw-r--r--  1 root  ipg   191308 Jul 16 02:20  spaceman.gif
```

A colorful image of a parrot can be found at site *oak.oakland.edu* [141.210.10.117] in the directory */pub/msdos/gif* as filename *parrot.gif*. This directory is worth exploring—there are several other GIF images and GIF utilities stored in this directory. A few sample descriptions of GIF files extracted from the *00_index.txt* file (which is also located in that directory) are shown here:

```
blastoff.gif  B   27776  880510  Space Shuttle roars skyward, use CSHOW
clown.gif     B   51200  890115  GIF picture of a clown
mouse.gif     B   31049  890608  320x200 256-color GIF picture of a mouse
mthood.gif    B   11904  880505  Color GIF picture of Mt. Hood
parrot.gif    B   58368  880829  Tropical bird - great for VGA
pepsi.gif     B    5120  900201  320x200x32 GIF of a Pepsi can
seashore.gif  B  252928  900113  640x480x256 GIF picture of seashore scene
```

You might also try exploring FTP site *nic.stolaf.edu* [130.71.128.8]. Once logged on, **cd** to */pub/travel-advisories/gifs/flags/world-almanac-1992.* Here you will find GIF files containing images of flags from countries ranging from Afghanistan to Zimbabwe.

Now go back to one of the first sites introduced in this chapter, *ra.msstate.edu*, and **cd** to */pub/docs/history/gifs.* Here you'll find an interesting image file called *egypt.gif.* Before leaving this site, change directories to */pub/docs/history/USA/Vietnam/gifs* and there you will find a storehouse of color images depicting scenes from the Vietnam War.

## ≡ FTP Commands Reviewed

The following list outlines the major FTP commands that were introduced in this chapter. For a more complete listing online, enter **help** or **?** at the *FTP>* prompt.

**ascii**—This command puts FTP in the mode to transfer ASCII text files. It is the default mode for FTP.

**binary**—This command puts FTP in the mode to transfer binary files.

**cd <directory>**—The **cd** command changes directories on the remote host, where **<directory>** is the name of the directory to which you want to move. When you enter a path, separate directory names with the slash character. For example, **cd pub/docs/history.**

**cd ..**—This command makes the directory above the one you're working in the current directory on the remote host.

**cdup**—This command also changes the directory to the directory one level up on the remote host.

**dir**—This is the "directory" command, and it lists the contents of the current directory on the remote machine.

**dir <remote filename or directory> <local filename>**—When you use the **dir** command with these two arguments, the remote filename or directory that you specify is moved to your local machine with a "local" filename that you have assigned it.

**get <filename>**—The **get** command transfers or downloads the specified file from the remote host to the local host.

**get <remote filename> <local filename>**—Attaching these two arguments to the **get** command enables you to transfer the file and also rename it with a local filename.

**help**—The **help** command prints online user help.

**mget <filenames>**—The **mget** command transfers multiple files from the remote host to the local host.

**pwd**—This command displays the current directory on the remote host.

**quit**—This command, or the **exit** command, causes the FTP program to terminate.

**statistics**—The **statistics** command acts as a toggle switch, turning on or off the feature that prints file transfer timing statistics.

## ≡ For Further Study

For a printout of FTP sites, FTP to site *piolot.njin.net* and download the file *ftp.list* in directory */pub/ftp-list*.

For further studies relating to TCP/IP, consult RFC739 and RFC791. To retrieve a document called "Network Reading List: TCP/IP, UNIX, and Ethernet," send an email message to *archive-server@ftp.utexas.edu* with the message **send docs net-read.txt**.

A very good introduction to audio formats and information relating to sound files on various platforms is provided by Guido van Rossum in the FAQ "Audio file Formats." To obtain a copy, FTP to site *ftp.cwi.nl* and go to directory */pub* to get a file called *AudioFormats2.10*.

San Diego State University has one of the most extensive collections of sound files on the Internet. To browse their archive, FTP to site *athena.sdsu.edu* and change to the */sounds* directory. Most of the available files are in the .AU format used by Sun workstations. The sound player program that came with your sound board may not support this file type. If this is the case, you can also download a sound conversion program from FTP site *athena.sdsu.edu* in the */pub/SoundConversion* directory. One sound conversion program that's available for most platforms is SOX (SOund eXchange) and it supports several sound file types including Sun SPARC .AU.

If you need an FTP client to run on your Macintosh computer, one possible source is FETCH. This is an FTP client for Macintosh designed by Jim Matthews. You can get the FTP client by FTPing to site *sumex-aim.stanford.edu* in the directory */info-mac/comm* or by contacting Software Sales, Dartmouth College, 6028 Kiewit Computation Center, Hanover, NH 03755-3523. (This implementation requires MacTCP.)

One USENET newsgroup that discusses issues relating to new FTP archives is *comp.archives*.

A wealth of GIF files are stored at FTP site *wuarchive.wustl.edu* in the */graphics/gif* directory. When you are in this directory, download the file called *00Index.930210* for an index of available files. An interesting source of space-related GIFs can be found at site *ames.arc.nasa.gov* in the directory *filelist/NASA/GIF*.

Terry Rover has compiled a list of anonymous FTP sites which he updates once each month. Rover's list is approximately 100K compressed and 400K uncompressed. To obtain a copy, look for a file named *ftp-list.zip* in the */pub/msdos/info* directory at FTP site *oak.oakland.edu*.

*Chapter* **5**

# TELNET: Remote Login

TELNET is a powerful Internet application in the TCP/IP protocol suite that enables you to login to remote systems.

The resources that are accessible via TELNET are quite diverse. Although much of the emphasis in TELNET is placed on scientific and research topics, some sites are relevant to the humanities as well.

Some TELNET sites serve very specific purposes, like the one at the University of Michigan called the Geographic Name Server. This server is a menu-driven database that provides information about cities, including population, elevation, latitude, and longitude. This server can be reached by TELNETing to *martini.eecs.umich.edu 3000*. You also will find systems like PENpages that offer full menus of services relating to one topic and including online keyword searching of their full-text databases. PENpages, a database of agricultural information provided by the College of Agricultural Sciences at Pennsylvania State University, is explained in more detail in Part VI.

Other gateway systems, like *library.wustl.edu* at Washington University, provide access to several other systems. You are in effect TELNETing to reach machine A, and then invoking TELNET on machine A to reach machine B.

The TELNET service also enables you to access libraries worldwide and interact with the online catalogs at their sites. Accessing other library catalogs may assist you in verifying information for acquisitions, inter-library loan, and copy cataloging. One of the largest library catalogs accessible via TELNET is the Library of Congress. Details for accessing this library and others are given in Chapter 15.

The TELNET service also enables librarians to access commercial online bibliographic utilities and services. Accessing commercial database utilities via Internet can save the cost of going through public data networks like TYMNET and SprintNet. Some of the more common commercial databases and their corresponding Internet addresses are listed below.

| | | |
|---|---|---|
| BRS | *brs.com* | |
| CARL UnCover | *database.carl.org* | [192.54.81.76] |
| DIALOG | *dialog.com* | [192.132.3.234] |
| Dow Jones News/retrieval | *djnr.dowjones.com* | |
| EPIC | *epic.prod.oclc.org* | [132.174.100.2] |
| FirstSearch | *fscat.oclc.org* | |
| LEXIS/NEXIS | *lexis.meaddata.com* | [192.73.216.20 or 192.73.216.21] |
| Medlars | *medlars.nlm.nih.gov* | |
| ORBIT | *orbit.com* | [192.188.13.234] |
| STN | *stnc.cas.org* | [142,243.5.32] |

Accessing commercial vendors may lower the cost of online searching if you have free access to a local university computer. (See Part V for more information.)

TELNET, like FTP, is based on the client/server model. The client program, running on your machine, initiates the connection with a server program, running on a remote machine. Keystrokes are passed from your terminal directly to the remote computer just as though they were being typed at a terminal on the remote computer. Output from the remote computer is sent back and displayed on your terminal.

## ≡ Running TELNET

To run the TELNET software and open the connection, you must issue the appropriate command. The command to invoke your TELNET client will be similar to this one:

```
telnet <domain_address>
```

In this case, **telnet** is the command you enter to run the TELNET software, and <domain_address> is the domain name or IP address of the remote machine you want to use (which may be a commercial database service like those listed in the previous section). You log into the remote host using an account number, password, or special username. For example, to connect to the machine NASA Spacelink, you would enter the following:

```
$ telnet spacelink.msfc.nasa.gov
```

A few moments later, the message shown in Figure 5-1 and a Welcome screen appears. Because I have already registered, I was asked to enter my username and password, which then brought me to the main menu. The process of entering your name and password is called *logging in* or *logging on*. First-time callers must type NEWUSER as their username and password.

```
Trying... Connected to SPACELINK.MSFC.NASA.GOV, a DG MV1000 running AOS.


                              W E L C O M E

                                   to

                            NASA SPACELINK

                   A Space-Related Informational Database
                  Provided by the NASA Educational Affairs Division
                   Operated by the Marshall Space Flight Center
                   On a Data General ECLIPSE MV7800 Minicomputer

                          ******IMPORTANT!******
            Do not press RETURN until you have read the following information.
            You are about to be asked to provide a Username and a Password.
                    If this is your first call to NASA Spacelink,
            Enter NEWUSER as your Username and enter NEWUSER as your Password.
            If you have called before, enter your assigned Username and Password.
                  You may send Carriage Returns or Line Feeds but NOT BOTH.


                            You may now press RETURN, or
                      To redisplay this message press CONTROL-D.



AOS/VS II 2.20.00.66 / EXEC-32 2.20.00.07          1-Jan-94 15:57:18       @TCON3
Username: acbenson
Password:
--------
Last message change       22-Dec-93        8:55:26


]**** IMPORTANT MESSAGES *****

Internet callers may try our FTP site under development.  Username is anonymous
and Password is guest.  Address is 192.149.89.61   READ README!

Network callers: For downloads please use Kermit instead of XMODEM or YMODEM.

Accounts unused for 90 days are automatically deleted.

Our modem line is 205-895-0028.

For info on the recent Shuttle mission (Hubble Servicing) enter STS-61 at
the GO TO prompt.  Remember the hyphen!


--------
Most recent logon       10-Nov-93        10:04:56
====PRESS RETURN TO CONTINUE====
```

**Figure 5-1:**   Login screen and opening menu for NASA Spacelink database

```
NASA/SPACELINK      MENU SYSTEM       Revision:1.68.00.00   [@TCON3 NETWORK]


NASA Spacelink Main Menu


1.    Log Off NASA Spacelink
2.    NASA Spacelink Overview
3.    Current NASA News
4.    Aeronautics
5.    Space Exploration: Before the Shuttle
6.    Space Exploration: The Shuttle and Beyond
7.    NASA and its Centers
8.    NASA Educational Services
9.    Instructional Materials
10.   Space Program Spinoffs/Technology Transfer


11.   LIVE FROM...OTHER WORLDS (Interactive Program for Teachers and Students)


Enter an option number, 'G' for GO TO, ? for HELP, or
  press RETURN to redisplay menu...1
```

**Figure 5-1:**   *(continued)*

## The TELNET Command Mode

If you enter the **telnet** command by itself without a target host's address, a *telnet>* client prompt appears and you are be placed in what is called *TELNET command mode*. You will use TELNET command mode for only a few instances. You can type a question mark (?) at the *telnet>* prompt to display a list of valid TELNET client commands. Among the various TELNET commands, you'll probably use **open, quit, close, set, carriage return,** and **display** most often.

The **open** command allows you to initiate a session from the *telnet>* prompt by typing **open <domain_name>**. For example, if the *telnet>* prompt is displayed on your screen, which means you are in command mode, you initiate a TELNET connection by entering **open hpcwire.ans.net** to TELNET to HPCwire, the High-Performance Computing Daily News & Information Service. If command mode is not active and the only thing displayed on your screen is the system prompt, you initiate this session by entering **telnet hpcwire.ans.net.**

The **set** command allows you to set various operating parameters. Entering **set?** at the *telnet>* prompt provides you with a complete listing of these parameters. The **display** command displays the operating parameters in use for the current TELNET session.

## Exiting a TELNET Session

Exiting a TELNET session is fairly simple. If you are using the menu, just choose Quit. If you are in command mode, use the **quit** command to exit TELNET. If you are currently connected to a remote machine, use the **close** command to disconnect from the remote machine without stopping the TELNET program.

If you get stuck in the session, however, and it appears that things are locked up, try using the *TELNET escape character* to quit. On UNIX systems, the TEL-NET escape character is CTRL ]. Press the CTRL key and hold it down while pressing the right square bracket (]): this moves you into command mode. Press RETURN without entering a command to get out of command mode and get back into the TELNET session with the remote computer. (Note: In some documentation, you will see the CTRL key indicated with the caret (^) . In these cases, CTRL Z is written as ^Z.)

Sometimes it may appear that the escape character doesn't work. Although the remote host acts immediately on the input it receives from your keyboard, the information it sends back to you is buffered. A little time may pass before the information appears on your screen. As a result, if you use the escape character, it may seem as though it's not working because the data that has already left the remote host and found its way into the buffer will still arrive and be displayed on your screen.

## Port Numbers

Occasionally, you will be asked to specify a port number when you make a TEL-NET connection. *Port numbers* are positive integers that represent different destinations within a given host computer. Each destination provides a different service and these services are kept separate by giving each one a different port assignment.

Some ports are always reserved for certain standard services such as electronic mail. Other numbers are used for special services. A host computer called *downwind.sprl.umich.edu* at the University of Michigan provides weather reports for the United States and Canada. In order to connect to this special service, you must specify a port number of 3000. The command **telnet downwind.sprl.umich.edu 3000** tells the host that you want to use the weather service.

If the above format for specifying the port number doesn't work at your site, check your local documentation on using TELNET. On some systems, such as the VAX/VMS system that I connect to, it's necessary to specify the port number in the following manner:

```
telnet downwind.sprl.umich.edu /port=3000
```

When you connect to this server, your TELNET session will look something like Figure 5-2.

The TELNET client software on your local machine provides terminal emulation and you should be aware of what kind of terminal it is emulating. The remote host may ask you what type of terminal emulation you are using or give you a number of choices from which to pick. The most common type of terminal emulation is VT100 and most hosts accept VT100 emulation or something similar. An exception to this is IBM mainframes which neither accept nor use VT100 terminal emulation.

```
$ telnet downwind.sprl.umich.edu /port=3000
Trying... Connected to DOWNWIND.SPRL.UMICH.EDU, an IBM-RS/6000-320 running AIX31
.


------------------------------------------------------------------------------
*                        University of Michigan                               *
*                        WEATHER UNDERGROUND                                   *
------------------------------------------------------------------------------
*                                                                             *
*                 College of Engineering, University of Michigan              *
*                 Department of Atmospheric, Oceanic, and Space Sciences      *
*                 Ann Arbor, Michigan  48109-2143                             *
*                 comments: sdm@madlab.sprl.umich.edu                         *
*                                                                             *
*  With Help from:  The UNIDATA Project,                                      *
*                   University Corporation for Atmospheric Research           *
*                   Boulder, Colorado  80307-3000                             *
*                                                                             *
------------------------------------------------------------------------------
*  NOTE:----------> New users, please select option "H" on the main menu:     *
*                   H) Help and information for new users                     *
*                                                                             *
------------------------------------------------------------------------------



Press Return for menu, or enter 3 letter forecast city code:

                 WEATHER UNDERGROUND MAIN MENU
                 *****************************
                 1) U.S. forecasts and climate data
                 2) Canadian forecasts
                 3) Current weather observations
                 4) Ski conditions
                 5) Long-range forecasts
                 6) Latest earthquake reports
                 7) Severe weather
                 8) Hurricane advisories
                 9) National Weather Summary
                 10) International data
                 11) Marine forecasts and observations
                 X) Exit program
                 C) Change scrolling to screen
                 H) Help and information for new users
                 ?) Answers to all your questions
                  Selection:x
------------------------------------------------------------------------------
*                                                                             *
*                        Have a good one!                                     *
*                                                                             *
------------------------------------------------------------------------------

Connection closed by Foreign Host
```

**Figure 5-2:**   Welcome screen and main menu for Weather Underground

### TN3270 Application

You may need a special version of the TELNET application called *tn3270* on rare occasions when trying to establish a connection with an IBM mainframe. These machines are accustomed to dealing with 3270 terminals which work differently from others. For example, 3270 terminals use special PF keys (programmed function keys).

Sometimes, the IBM machines to which you are connecting automatically handle the appropriate terminal emulation. Other times, the system may freeze up and you must enter a TELNET escape character to break the connection. In these instances, you can then try using *tn3270* to reach the IBM computer.

The way the 3270 system works with input and output is different from other systems, and you may have to go through some trial and error in order to determine which keys have what functions. The 3270 runs a full-screen application, which means that you are expected to move around the screen by using the TAB key, entering information in different fields. You will notice with 3270 systems that the screens do not scroll upward one line at a time; instead, the screen goes blank and a whole new screen appears.

If you have to clear the screen, try pressing CTRL HOME or CTRL Z. Instead of using the function keys (F1, F2, etc.), try pressing the ESC key and a number. For example, instead of pressing F1, hold the ESC key down and press 1 at the same time. In place of F10, hold the ESC key down and press 0.

Aside from the extra effort involved in TELNETing to an IBM mainframe, using TELNET is a rather simple operation. Once you learn the basic TELNET commands and the procedure for logging on to a remote host, the only challenge you face is in making use of the resources you're accessing on the remote computer.

### Recording Information and Troubleshooting

TELNET is not a service that makes it easy to move information from the remote computer to your own. If you want to record what occurs during a session, it's best to capture a log file of your session. Check with your computer department or the manual accompanying the communication software you use to learn just how this can be done on your system. PROCOMM PLUS for Windows, for example, gives the option of capturing to a file or directly to the printer during a TELNET session. Both methods are initiated by clicking on the appropriate button.

Sometimes, you may experience problems trying to connect to a remote host. If you fail to connect to a host using TELNET, an error message appears on your screen, stating something like ?UnKnown INTERNET host. One reason this may occur is that you mistyped the domain name or IP address.

Another reason you may be unable to connect is because all the connections that the remote host supports are already in use. When this happens, you get a *time out* message saying something like Connection refused or There are too many interactive users at the moment.

Another cause may be that the host you are trying to reach is down. Other times some part of the network may be down or too congested. A program called *ping* can help in testing this kind problem. You may have to find out how to do this on your particular system, but you can begin by simply typing the word **ping** at your system prompt, followed by the host address. Then press ENTER.

When you enter the command **ping ua1vm.ua.edu**, you may see output as simple as *ua1vm.ua.edu is alive*, or it may look something like this:

```
Ping V2R2: Pinging host UA1VM.UA.EDU (130.160.4.100). Enter #CP EXT to
interrupt.
PING: Ping #1 response took 2.568 seconds. Successes so far 1.
```

The ping program sends data packets to the host, which in turn should echo them back if a connection is made. The IP address from which it is echoed back, the time it takes in milliseconds, and sometimes the size of the packet are given in the above report. If you receive a message that says no such host exists, there may be a problem with the domain network software and its attempt to translate the corresponding IP address. If you know the IP address, try using that to contact the host. If this works, the problem was the domain name.

A list on the Internet called a *host table* gives the domain names and corresponding IP addresses. This list is distributed by the Internet Network Information Center, but it is by no means complete. You can retrieve a copy of this list via anonymous FTP from *nic.ddn.mil* in the */hosts* directory.

## ≡ For Further Study

Several RFC documents pertaining to TELNET are available. Two that may be of particular interest are *#854 Telnet Protocol Specification. 5/83* and *#855 Telnet Option Specifications. 5.83*. To obtain copies of these and other documents, FTP to site *nic.ddn.mil* and go to the */rfc/rfc directory*.

# Chapter 6

# Simple Mail Transfer Protocol (SMTP)

Electronic mail, or *email*, is the most widely used service on the Internet. Email enables people to exchange electronic messages much as they would conventional mail, but with certain added conveniences.

The standardized system for delivering Internet mail is called *Simple Mail Transfer Protocol (SMTP)*. SMTP is the part of the TCP/IP protocol suite that makes it possible for an individual with one computer system to exchange email with someone who has an entirely different computer system. This protocol describes how email messages are to be handled during delivery and what their format should be.

## ≡ Email Advantages

One of the more notable conveniences is the speed with which email travels. Email messages travel on high-speed networks and usually arrive at their destination within minutes of being sent. As a result, Internet users have come to refer to the regular postal service as *snail mail* when comparing it to the speed at which email travels.

Unlike a paper letter, email can be stored in file form on a computer, which in turn enables you to pull it into a word processor for editing and printing. Email can be forwarded easily to another person without the inconvenience and cost of making a paper copy, stuffing it in an envelope, affixing a stamp, addressing it, and taking it to the post office. Further, one email message can be directed easily to multiple recipients—no more printing out multiple paper copies and mailing each one separately.

Location and distance are irrelevant factors when you are communicating via email. If you live in a remote area of the Ozark Mountains and have access to the Internet mail system, you'll find that it is just as easy to send a message to a colleague in Switzerland as it is to send one to your closest neighbor just a hollering distance away.

In addition to these conveniences, email also serves as a powerful tool for discovering and transmitting various kinds of information. Later in this chapter, you learn the details for using email to send and receive binary files, such as software programs. Chapter 11 shows you how to use email to retrieve special information from mail servers—programs running on remote computers that are set up to respond to certain commands via email. Chapter 13 introduces a way to exchange information on the Internet through a service called LISTSERV.

## ≡ Transport and User Agents

Two different operations are involved when you are exchanging email. One of these operations involves a program called a *transport agent* that runs in the background without direct contact from the user. This is the program that is actually responsible for sending and receiving email via the SMTP standard. The Internet mail system works because every network that is part of the Internet has at least one computer that runs a transport agent.

The other operation involves a program called a *user agent*. This is a program that serves as your interface with the Internet email system. Many different user agents are available, and each one looks and feels a little different from the next. All the various user agents offer mail management features for handling basic tasks such as reading messages, composing messages, sending messages, deleting messages, and so on.

## ≡ Sending and Receiving Messages

The process of sending and receiving email is fairly simple. The operation begins when you enter a command that starts the user program (user agent). The user program provides an editor you use to compose the message you want to send. The user agent then sends the completed message to a mailer program (transfer agent). The mailer program works behind the scenes and is responsible for transmitting the message to the remote host.

The remote host's mailer program receives the message and stores it in a file system. The last step of the process comes when the person to whom the message was addressed receives it and views the message by running his or her own user program.

The file system where messages are stored is called the user's *mailbox*. If you send a message to a user who doesn't have a mailbox at the Internet address you specify, the transport agent at that address creates an error report and sends it back to you as a message. When this happens, your mail is described as having been *bounced back*.

### Anatomy of an Email Message

Email messages contain lines of text that follow a certain format. As illustrated in the sample message below, the opening section consists of a list of field names (each of which is followed by a colon) and one or more items of information. These field names are referred to as *message headers*, or collectively as a *message header*.

The message header is followed by another section called the *body* of the message. The message body, which is separated from the header by a blank line, is where the actual text is entered by the person composing the message. You do not see the header as part of the message when you compose it. The header is attached automatically when you send your message.

```
From:    IN%"mtracy@arrl.org"
Return-path: <mtracy@arrl.org>
Received: from uu7.psi.com by UALR.EDU (PMDF V4.2-11 #4503) id
  <01H89MVVXD00000XUT@UALR.EDU>; Sat, 29 Jan 1994 20:12:14 CDT
Received: from mgate.arrl.org by uu7.psi.com (5.65b/4.0.071791-PSI/PSINet) via
  SMTP; id AA06608 for acbenson@ualr.edu; Sat, 29 Jan 94 21:12:02 -0500
Received: from jrb by mgate.arrl.org with smtp (Smail3.1.28.1 #6) id
  m0pQRco-000B9DC; Sat, 29 Jan 94 21:10 EST
Received: from mt by jrb with SMTP id AA9360 ; Sat, 29 Jan 94 21:05:00 GMT
Date: Sat, 29 Jan 1994 21:09:47 -0500 (EST)
From: mtracy@arrl.org (Michael Tracy)
Subject:
To: ACBENSON@ualr.edu
Message-id: <57640@mt>

Dear ARRL Information Service user:

The way we have set up our server, incoming messages for information
are sent to info@arrl.org.  The outgoing response comes from
info-serv@arrl.org.  As warned in our HELP file, if you use the reply
function of your mailer to reply to the index list, it does not get sent
to the mail server, but gets sent to info-serv@arrl.org, which gets
redirected to a mailbox on my machine.

The system was set up this way so that failed mail would not loop
endlessly, annoying system administrators. :-).

A few of the more common address errors get directed this way, too
(such as info-server@arrl.org, etc.)

Please re-try your request, sending it to info@arrl.org. That is the
ONLY address that works to access the server. :-)

If you have any questions, contact mtracy@arrl.org.
```

You don't need to understand what every field in the header means before you can use the Internet mail system effectively. The following brief descriptions provide basic definitions of the different header fields.

- The From field describes the person who sent the message. Note that email addresses consist of two parts separated by the at (@) sign . The part that comes before the @ is usually the username—the name that a person uses when logging on. The part after the @ is the domain name.

- The Return-Path field provides information about the address of the person who originated the message.

- The Received field tells when the message was received by a particular computer, the path that the message took, and which mail programs were being used. Depending on how many computers handled your message along the way, your message header may show one or more of these Received fields.

- The Date field shows the time and date the message was sent. After the Date field there is another From field which is different from the first From field in that it gives the real name of the person who sent the message.

- The Subject field is specified by the sender and summarizes what the message is about.

- The To field gives the names of all the people who are to receive copies of the message. If the message is sent only to you, only your address appears here.

- The Message-id field is meaningless to us humans, but it does contain a unique identifier that computers find interesting.

- The CC field shows the address of anyone who has received a copy of the message.

- The Status field tells the status of the message. R means the message is being read for the first time; N means the message is new; O means the message is old; and U means the message is unread.

Email enables you to connect not only with other Internet hosts, but also with non-Internet systems through *mail gateways*, special purpose computers that transfer information to and from the Internet. The non-Internet systems include BITNET, FidoNet, the UUCP Mail Networks, mail services such as MCI Mail, and commercial bulletin boards like Compuserve and Prodigy.

## Popular Mail Programs

Providing complete documentation for every available user agent is impractical and beyond the scope of this book. Instead, you shouldfirst determine which software is on the machine at your service provider's site, and then obtain whatever support documentation is available.

To learn more about a mail program called Elm, for example, you could enter the UNIX **man** (manual) command followed by the name **elm**. UNIX will display a brief description of the program and its command line options. In many cases, the online help screens in the mail program will constitute your main source of documentation.

UNIX systems are the most widely used systems on the Internet and many of the more popular user agents are found on UNIX systems. The following list is a brief description of some of the more popular UNIX-based user agents.

- *Pine* is designed for inexperienced users and offers a simple and straight forward menu from which to pick commands. One of Pine's more notable features is that it has MIME capabilities (Multipurpose Internet Mail Extensions), which allows it to send and receive multimedia email.

- *Elm*, like Pine, is also a full-screen, interactive mail system. Although Elm is easy to use, it does offer advanced mail management features.
- *MH* (Mail Handler) is a set of single-purpose programs. You use a different program for each task you want to perform.

## Mailing Binary Data

As discussed earlier, SMTP describes how messages that contain ASCII characters can be sent and received. Another protocol currently in development is called *Multipurpose Internet Mail Extensions (MIME)*. MIME enables the transfer of binary data through the Internet mail system. The user attaches a binary file, often referred to as *richtext*, to a message containing regular text, and then transports the entire message using SMTP. In order for this system to work, however, both the sender and the receiver must be running user mail programs that support MIME. Although MIME may become widely used in the future, most current mail programs do not yet support it.

Another way to send binary data through the mail system is to encode the binary data as text. This encoded text is then sent as a regular message. The recipient decodes the message and converts it back into its original binary format. One program called *UUENCODE* is used to encode the binary data as text, and another program called *UUDECODE* is used to change it back into a binary format.

If you have a software program (a binary file) that you want to send to a friend on the Internet, for example, and you have to do it via email, you would do it like this: You'd UUENCODE the binary file and upload it to your local host as an ASCII text file. Because the file, as an ASCII file, is comprised of printable characters, you can incorporate it into an email file and send it to your friend. When the mail file arrives at its destination, your friend downloads it to his or her personal computer and uses UUDECODE to translate the coded version of the file back into its binary state. If the file is extremely large, the coded version is automatically sent in more than one mail message. Your friend must save the multiple messages to a single file and keep them in their correct order. (Both UUENCODE and UNDECODE are used in operations that use the mail system as an information retrieval tool in Chapter 11.)

The computer output that follows was extracted from a UUENCODEd document before translation back into its binary state:

```
-------the file starts directly below this line--------
begin 666 WAIS.res
M*#IS;W5R8V4*(#IV97)S:6]N(#,*(#II<"UN86UE(")S;F5K:V%R+F5N<RYF
M<B<(*(#IT8W M<&]R=" R,3 *(#ID871A8F%S92UN86UE(")B:6(M9&UI+65N
M<RUF<B<(*(#IC;W-T(# N,# "B Z8V]S="=UU;FET%(#IF<F5E( H@.FUA:6YT
M86EN97(@(F-H;W5971 <VYE:VMA<BYE:G,,N9G(B"B Z9&5S8W)I<'1I;VX*
M(@Z3397)V97(@(@8W)E871E9"!W:71H(%==!I25,@@4<F5L96%S92 X(&(U(@@,+
M.

end
-------the UUENCODED file ended just above this line------
```

A UUENCODEd file always starts with the word *begin*, followed by some numbers (the file-mode) and then the UUENCODEd filename, in this case

*WAIS.res*. The encoded data ends with a line containing a closing quotation mark, followed by a line containing the word *end*.

If you tried to read this file in its original binary state with a text editor, you wouldn't be able to because binary data consists of nonprintable characters. This example is readable and shows what the binary data looks like after it has been translated into a file consisting of printable characters. This is what a UUEN-CODEd file looks like.

The programs for coding and decoding binary files are available via anonymous FTP. o find out where these files reside on the Internet, use the Archie service or FTP to site *oak.oakland.edu* and look in the directory */pub/msdos/filutl* for a file called *uuexe521.zip*.

### Using UUENCODE

To use UUENCODE, begin by saving a binary file to the same directory where the UUENCODE program resides. Then enter the command in this form:

```
uuencode <filename>
```

In this case, **<filename>** is the name of the binary file you want to encode. For example, to encode a file called *foo.bar*, you enter this command:

```
uuencode foo.bar.
```

UUENCODE then produces a file with the name **foo.uue**.

### Using UNDECODE

If you receive an encoded file and need to decode it, use the UUDECODE program. Do this by entering the command in this form:

```
uudecode <filename>
```

In this case, **<filename>** is the name of the ASCII text file you want to transform back into a binary file. For example, **uudecode foo** will look for a file called *foo.uue* and decode it. If the file has an extension other than *.uue*, specify it in the command. For example, if the filename is *foo.bar* you would enter **uudecode foo.bar**.

## ≡ For Further Study

Details of SMTP are explained in J. Postel *Simple Mail Transfer Protocol, RFC 821*, USC/Information Sciences Institute, August 1982.

The format of email messages is discussed in D. Cocker's *Standard for the Format of ARPA Internet Text Messages, RFC 822*, Department of Electrical Engineering, University of Delaware, August 1982.

For further reading on the subject of multimedia data such as bitmaps, voice and graphics being transported via computer mail, see J.Postel's, *A Structured Format for Transmission of Multi-Media Documents, RFC 767*, USC/Information Sciences Institute, August 1980; J. Reynolds, J. Postel, A. Katz, G. Finn and

A. DeSchon, *The DARPA Experimental Multimedia Mail System*, IEEE Computer, Vol. 18, No.10, October 1985; and *MIME (Multipurpose Internet Mail Extensions) Mechanisms for Specifying and Describing the Format of Internet Message Bodies, RFC 1341*, PS, June 1992.

Details on sending email from one network to another are given in *inter-Network Mail Guide* by John J. Chew. A copy of this document can be accessed via FTP to site ra.msstate.edu. Look in the */docs* directory for a file called *internet-work-mail-guide*.

For an introduction to sending and receiving electronic mail using a UNIX Mail System, FTP to site *ftp.sura.net*, go to the */pub/nic/network.service.guides* directory, and download a copy of the file *how.to.email.guide*.

# PART III

# SEARCH UTILITIES AND THE CLIENT/SERVER MODEL

Most of the services that are used for seeking out information on the Internet are based on the *client-server* model. The terms *client* and *server* refer to types of programs. These programs have a special relationship because client programs send requests to server programs and server programs respond. This is the reason why clients are sometimes referred to as *masters* and server programs as *slaves*. When you are learning how to use the Internet, you are actually learning how to use various client programs.

Services such as Gopher are based on the client-server model. When you are using Gopher, you are actually running a program called a Gopher client and it is communicating with a server program called a Gopher server. A Gopher client formulates a request and then sends it to the server. The Gopher server receives it, performs its service, and then returns the results to the Gopher client. The same is true for Archie and other search utilities.

If you have a direct connection to the Internet, you can choose your own client programs that are designed to run on a variety of platforms ranging from Macintosh and MS-DOS machines to Sun workstations. There are many client programs to choose from with names like HyperWAIS, WAIStation, XMosaic, and TurboGopher. When you have the opportunity to run your own client program, you can choose one that provides a friendly, more intuitive interface that prompts you for what information it needs.

If your connection to the Internet is through a local host, you'll be limited to using the client programs that are running on that service provider's system. If the local service provider doesn't run the client program you need, you must TELNET to a remote computer site that not only has the server you want, but also a public client. For example, if the local computer you connect with doesn't run an Archie client, you'll have to TELNET to a remote computer that runs not only an Archie server but also an Archie client. You'll TELNET to a public Archie site when you want to use the Archie service. The computer I dial into runs a Gopher client, so when I want to use the Gopher service, I simply type the word **Gopher** and the Gopher client starts running.

There is no real disadvantage to either method because when you get connected to Gopher or Archie—no matter how you do it—you can take advantage of most of the services Gopher and Archie offer. The only thing you need to know is where the public sites are in case your local computer doesn't offer a particular service.

As each Internet service is discussed in this part, Internet addresses are given for accessing public sites. Sources are also be given for downloading the client programs to run on your own personal computer should that opportunity be available to you.

# Chapter 7

# Gopher

Gopher was originally developed in April of 1991 by a team at the University of Minnesota Microcomputer and Workstation Networks Center. The team included Bob Alberti, Farhad Anklesaria, Paul Lindner, Mark McCahill, and Daniel Torry. The originators define Gopher as "a software following a simple protocol for burrowing [as a gopher does] through a TCP/IP Internet. The protocol and software follows a client-server model."

Gopher is a distributed system that is used for organizing information in a hierarchical manner. Gopher is considered a front-end application because it provides one interface for accessing different types of services.

Information on Gopher is organized into a hierarchical menu structure (tree structure) with a root menu and submenus. When you place the cursor on a particular menu item and press ENTER, Gopher automatically links you to other files and other services. For example, one menu item may connect you to another computer by implementing a TELNET session.

Gopher clients are available for most computer systems. The one used as a basis for this discussion is the character-based UNIX Gopher client.

## ≡ Accessing Gopher

To use Gopher, just type **gopher** at your system prompt and press ENTER. If this doesn't connect you with a Gopher server, you still can use Gopher by TELNETing to a public Gopher site. One such site is located at the University of Minnesota and can be reached by TELNETing to *consult.micro.umn.edu*. At the login prompt, type **gopher** (locations for other sites are listed later in this chapter).

If a Gopher client is running on your local machine and you enter the **gopher** command, a screen similar to the one shown in Figure 7-1 should appear.

```
                              CMS Gopher 2.2.0
                             gopher.micro.umn.edu

<menu>       Information About Gopher
<menu>       Computer Information
<menu>       Discussion Groups
<menu>       Fun & Games
<menu>       Internet file server (ftp) sites
<menu>       Libraries
<menu>       News
<menu>       Other Gopher and Information Servers
<menu>       Phone Books
<search>     Search lots of places at the U of M
<menu>       University of Minnesota Campus Information
```

**Figure 7-1:**   Connecting to Gopher

The top line tells you which version of the Gopher client software is running and the line below that is the name of your "home" server. This is the Gopher server your client connects to by default. The client you use is pre-configured with the address of a particular home server (in my case, it's the University of Minnesota Gopher server). You can redirect the Gopher client to an alternative server, such as the server at The Whole Earth 'Lectronic Link (The Well), by entering the necessary parameters in the command line like this:

```
$ gopher gopher.well.sf.ca.us
```

Here the command **gopher** is followed by the Gopher server's address. Between the time you enter the command **gopher** and the time the root menu appears on your screen, the following simple client/server interaction takes place:

Client: The client opens connection to *gopher.micro.umn.edu.*

Server: The server accepts connection but says nothing.

Client: The client sends an empty line which is interpreted as meaning "What do you have?"

Server: The server returns a series of lines.

The client interface receives these lines and then displays the root menu—the first visible sign of the interaction that's taking place between client and server.

For each menu selection, there are submenus providing access to a broad range of information. For example, when you select the menu item *Libraries*, a new menu screen appears, giving you another set of menu choices. Selecting one of these leads you to such things as other libraries on the Internet, select full-text electronic journals, 30 full-text books, and other information resources.

In Minnesota's root menu, Item 1 is a directory, which the submenu offers additional choices, including a document titled "About Gopher." To view this document, use the arrow keys to move the cursor to that line and press ENTER. You can also choose a menu item by typing its line number and pressing ENTER. Upon doing so, the client software sends a unique retrieval string to the servers name and port number. The server responds by sending back the document and then closes the connection. This process of closing the connection when the server isn't in use makes Gopher an efficient mechanism for accessing information. Because there is no state existing between the client and server between transactions, the resources of the server aren't being used unnecessarily.

The Gopher client interface enables reference librarians to access information on the Internet without knowing precisely where it is located or the method required for retrieving it. All you need to know is what you want and the best means for finding it (via Veronica, etc.), not the actual command structure for retrieving the data. This is a process which remains transparent to you.

Gopher clients list one menu item per line, and each line has an extension that identifies what it is. Table 7-1 lists these identifiers.

If you access a directory, a submenu appears, but this one is more specific in subject demonstrating a powerful feature of Gopher. The submenu displayed may in fact be on a different computer and in a different geographic location. The process required for making this link is completely transparent to the user.

If you access a text file, a document appears, but only the first screen of the file is presented. To page down, press the space bar.

You can also type a slash (/), followed by a search string in order to locate a particular phrase or section in the document. This search capability is a very important feature of Gopher because it makes every text file you pull up on Gopher a searchable document.

Numbers and percent signs also appear on Gopher screens. These items tell you what percentage of the total file has already been viewed.

Table 7-2 lists some of the commands available when you are running a UNIX Gopher client.

When a text file is displayed, you are given several choices:

1. You can press **q**, and then press ENTER to quit the operation.

2. Press **m** and you are given the option to mail the file to yourself or someone else. When using a public Gopher, are limited to using the mail option. You can't save or print files to a remote computer without having an account on that computer.

**Table 7-1:** Gopher Line Identifiers

| Identifier | Description |
| --- | --- |
| / | indicates a directory (another menu) |
| . | indicates a text file |
| <?> | indicates a searchable index |
| <tel> | indicates a TELNET session |
| <cso> | indicates a searchable campus phone book |
| <) | indicates a sound file |
| <picture> | indicates a picture you can view (Note: Your client software must be able to support this capability in order for it to work. The UNIX character-based client does not.) |
| <bin> | indicates a binary file that can be downloaded |

**Table 7-2:** UNIX Gopher Commands

| Command | Description |
|---|---|
| ? | displays a Help screen |
| / | searches for item |
| O | changes options |
| = | displays source information about current item |
| < | previous page |
| > | next page |
| S | saves item to a file |
| D | downloads a file |
| q | quits Gopher |
| n | next search-item |
| m | mails file |
| u | goes up one level in the menu tree |
| 0–9 | moves to line number |
| ENTER | views the current line item |
| T | go to the top level menu |
| END | move cursor to last item |
| HOME | move cursor to first item |
| ↑ | moves cursor up |
| ↓ | moves cursor down |

3. Press **d** and you are given the option to download the file using one of the available file transfer protocols. (Choose one that your communications software supports.)

4. Press **s** to save the file to your local host. You will be prompted for a file-name.

5. If you happen to be working in close proximity with the local host and you are provided with printing services, you can press **p** to print the file.

## ≡ Public Gopher Sites

If your service provider isn't running a Gopher client and you can't run one on your own machine, you can still utilize the Gopher service by using TELNET and logging onto any one of the following public Gopher sites. Unless otherwise stated, at the login prompt type **gopher**. No password is necessary.

*Sites in North America:*

| | |
|---|---|
| The University of Minnesota: | *consult.micro.umn.edu* |
| The University of Illinois: | *ux1.cso.uiuc.edu* |
| The University of Iowa: | *panda.uiowa.edu* or *gremlin.isca.uiowa.edu* |
| The University of North Texas: | *gopher.unt.edu* |

*Other sites around the world:*

> *gopher.sunet.se*
> *info.anu.edu.au* login: info
> *gopher.chalmers.se*
> *grits.valdosta.peachnet.edu*
> *fatty.law.cornell.edu*
> *cat.ohiolink.edu*
> *gopher.ora.com*
> *tolten.puc.cl*
> *ogpher.denet.dk*
> *gopher.th-darmstadt.de*
> *ecnet.ec*
> *ecosys.drdr.virginia.edu*
> *gopher.isnet.is*
> *siam.mi.cnr.it*
> *sunic.sunet.se*

## ☰ Searching with Veronica

*Veronica* (Very Easy Rodent-Oriented Net-wide Index to Computerized Archives) is a resource discovery tool used for searching Gopher servers on the Internet. Veronica is a server to which you must connect through your Gopher. This service maintains an index of titles of Gopher items and provides keyword searches of those titles. Veronica is not a full-text index.

The Veronica database is updated every two weeks. Locally generated indexes are collated at a central data site and then redistributed to sites running Veronica search engines. This service is maintained by various sites such as *gopher.psi.com* and *veronica.sunet.se.*

The purpose of the following Veronica search was to locate and connect to a Campus Wide Information System (CWIS) called the Princeton News Network (PNN). When I first started writing this book, PNN was offering a searchable full-text document called *Internet - Accessible Library Catalogs & Databases* by Dr. Art St. George and Dr. Ron Larsen. Before I had finished writing this book, I went back to verify that the service was still being offered by PNN and found that it was not. The following search, although it took some odd turns, is still included here because it shows the thought process that you can apply when navigating the Internet via Gopher. My purpose in searching Art St. George's *Catalog of Databases* was to find all of the entries pertaining to agriculture.

My search began at the University of Minnesota using Veronica, which I accessed through the following series of menu choices:

> 8. *Other Gopher and Information Servers/*
> 2. *Search titles in Gopherspace using veronica/*

Upon choosing menu item number 2 shown above, I arrived at the screen shown in Figure 7-2.

```
 1.
 2.  FAQ:  Frequently-Asked Questions about veronica  (1993/08/23).
 3.  How to compose  veronica queries (NEW June 24) READ ME!!.
 4.  Search Gopher Directory Titles at PSINet <?>
 5.  Search Gopher Directory Titles at SUNET <?>
 6.  Search Gopher Directory Titles at U. of Manitoba <?>
 7.  Search Gopher Directory Titles at University of Cologne <?>
--> 8.  Search gopherspace at PSINet <?>
 9.  Search gopherspace at SUNET <?>
10.  Search gopherspace at U. of Manitoba <?>
11.  Search gopherspace at University of Cologne <?>
```

**Figure 7-2:**    Accessing Veronica

In the figure, notice that when you choose menu items 4 through 7, you are searching directory titles only. When choosing menu items 8 through 11 , your search results may also include items that are pointers to TELNET sessions, items that are binary files, images, or sounds, etc. The various names listed (PSINet, SUNET, etc.) are sites where Veronica servers are located.

I chose menu item 8. *Search gopherspace at PSINet* and pressed ENTER. Upon choosing this server, a search window like the one shown in Figure 7-3 popped up on the screen. This is where I entered the search statement **PNN**. A single-word query is the simplest Veronica search you can use.

Veronica enables you to use the Boolean operators AND, OR, and NOT in your search statement. AND retrieves titles of Gopher items that contain all of the search terms you specify. OR retrieves titles of Gopher items that contain at least one of the search terms. NOT eliminates a search term or group of search terms.

The order of execution of a query starts from the right-hand side and interprets operators as they are encountered. Veronica also understands parentheses, which specify a different order of execution. Terms within parentheses are executed first.

You can us either upper- or lowercase letters, which means that the words MOSAIC and mosaic are interpreted to mean the same thing.

When the search is completed, all the relevant document titles found (up to 200) are collected and presented to you in the form of a Gopher menu with direct links to the information requested. If you would like to retrieve more than the default setting of 200, add at the end of your query the option **-m**, followed by a

```
+------------------------Search gopherspace at PSINet----------------------+
|                                                                          |
| Words to search for                                                      |
|                                                                          |
|   PNN                                                                    |
|                                                                          |
|               [Cancel: ^G] [Erase: ^U] [Accept: Enter]                   |
+--------------------------------------------------------------------------+
```

**Figure 7-3:**    Entering the search statement

number to indicate the number you'd like to see. For example, if you want to increase your search results to include the first 300 menu items, add **-m300** to your query.

Truncation is also offered to permit variation in word length or spelling. The * symbol is used at the end of a character string to find items with any number of characters following the stem. For example, **librar\*** matches **library, libraries, librarian,** and **librarians.**

You can restrict your search further by adding the **-t** option, followed by a character that represents a certain Gopher type. Examples of Gopher types are as follows:

| 0 | files |
|---|---|
| 1 | directories |
| s | sound |
| I | image |
| 8 | pointers to TELNET sessions |

If, for example, you want to restrict your search to items that point to TELNET sessions, add **-t8** to your query. The search statement **elementary education -t0 -m400** requests up to 400 items containing the words *elementary* (the AND operator is implied) and *education*. The statement specifies that the only Gopher items wanted are file type items.

For additional information on Veronica title searching and retrieval, see the appropriate menu items listed in Figure 7-2 (such as "Frequently-Asked Questions about veronica" and "How to compose veronica queries").

The search results from the PNN search are shown in Figure 7-4.

```
Press ? for Help, q to Quit, u to go up a menu              Page: 1/1
             Internet Gopher Information Client 2.0 p19


             Search gopherspace at U. of Manitoba: PNN

      1.  Map of PNN gopher.
      2.  About PNN and Gopher/
      3.  Credits for PNN.
      4.  Index to Information in PNN.
      5.  What's New on PNN.
      6.  How to Contribute to PNN.
      7.  Using PNN.
      8.  About PNN: Princeton News Network.
      9.  Gopher vs. PNN .
      10. Re: Gopher vs. PNN .
      11. Re: Gopher vs. PNN.
      12. Gopher vs. PNN.
      13. Re: Gopher vs. PNN.
      14. Re: Gopher vs. PNN.
      15. 7.14 Princeton News Network PNN.
  --> 16. PNN - Princeton News Network/
      17. PNN - Princeton News Network/
      18. Princeton News Network PNN.
```

**Figure 7-4:** The PNN search results

```
+----------------------PNN - Princeton News Network---------------------+
|                                                                       |
| Warning!!!!!, you are about to leave the Internet                     |
| Gopher program and connect to another host. If                       |
| you get stuck press the control key and the                          |
| ^ key, and then type q.                                              |
|                                                                       |
| Connecting to pucc.princeton.edu, port 23 using tn3270.              |
|                                                                       |
| Use the account name "When you see the VM 370 logo, clear it, " to log in |
|                                                                       |
|                                           [Cancel: ^G] [OK: Enter]    |
|                                                                       |
+-----------------------------------------------------------------------+
```

**Figure 7-5:** Making the TELNET connection with Veronica

The items listed may be text files, menu trees, search engines, or items that connect you to remote hosts via TELNET sessions. Because of the redundancy of resources existing on Gopher servers, Veronica searches often list duplicate results. In the above search example, Veronica found four servers that all pointed to an object titled "Re: Gopher vs. PNN" (see lines 10, 11, 13, and 14).

I guessed that selecting menu item number 16 would connect me to PNN via TELNET. This was the right choice, and the screen shown in Figure 7-5 appeared before the TELNET connection was made.

I pressed ENTER and the TELNET connection was made. When I arrived at the VM logo screen, I cleared it by pressing CTRL Z and then typed **pnn** and pressed ENTER. I was then presented with the following message:

```
To provide better, more comprehensive access to information on the Internet,
CIT has moved to Gopher as its on-line information system navigator. PNN
Gopher provides access not only to the resources found in PNN but also to
information from the entire universe of Gopher resources. To use PNN Gopher,
log on to any public machine: PUCC, UNIX, Mac or PC and either type gopher or
select the Gopher icon. Choose Help and Information from the main menu for
further assistance.

PNN as such is no longer available as of Monday, December 6. Public
(anonymous) PNN is no longer available. If you are a University student,
faculty or staff member, you can get an account to use PNN Gopher from Unix or
the IBM mainframe; PNN Gopher is also available on CIT campus cluster Macs
and PCs. Gopher clients are available for network-connected office Macs and
PCs; for more information, see the document "Accessing Information Everywhere
with Gopher," available from the CIT Information Center.

If you have comments or suggestions about this expanded service, please send
e-mail to gopher@Princeton.edu.
```

As the message states, PNN has a new Gopher interface accessible by connecting to the Princeton Gopher (gopher.princeton.edu). I went back to do another Veronica search, this time using the key words **ron larsen**, one of the authors of the book. This search resulted in the menu shown in Figure 7-6.

```
     1.  Art St. George & Ron Larsen list: Verzeichnis der Bibliotheken.
-->  2.  Art St. George & Ron Larsen list of internet-accessible libr./
     3.  Art St. George & Ron Larsen list: Verzeichnis der Bibliotheken.
     4.  Art St. George & Ron Larsen list of internet-accessible libr./
     5.  4 out of 4  (get info here).
```

**Figure 7-6:** Results of the Veronica search for Ron Larsen

I chose menu item number 2 and pressed ENTER, which brought me to another screen with the message

`Art St. George & Ron Larsen list of internet-accessible libr.`

When I pressed ENTER, Gopher connected me to a full-text version of the book in question. To search this online version of *Internet - Accessible Library Catalogs & Databases* using a Gopher interface, I simply press the slash (/) and a search window popped up on the screen, superimposed on top of text already there. I entered the keyword *agriculture* and pressed ENTER.

The search engine immediately took me to the first occurrence of the word *agriculture* and it was a relevant entry. To find the next occurrence, I pressed / and the search window appeared again with the keyword *agriculture* still entered. I pressed ENTER and the search continued to find the next occurrence of the word. When all was said and done, I found the following four references:

1. The MELVYL catalog, an online union catalog with collection strengths in agriculture. The MELVYL system can be accessed via TELNET using the host name *melvyl.ucop.edu* or any four Internet addresses [31.1.0.1, 31.0.0.11, 31.0.0.13, 31.1.0.11].

2. PENpages, a database of agricultural and Extension related information ranging from daily, weekly, and monthly agricultural news and alerts to permanent reference material. PENpages can be accessed via TELNET using the host name *psupen.psu.edu*.

3. Three bulletin boards:

    [301-344-85180] ALF, Agriculture Library, Berwyn, MD. Agricultural information.

    [314-882-8289] AgEBB, Columbus, MO. Agricultural information.

    [402-472-6615] HPRCC, Weather Data, Lincoln, NE. Regional agricultural weather.

4. A published resource directory called *Directory of Computerized Data Files, 1989*. This is a guide to U.S. Government information in machine-readable form, NTIS, U.S. Department of Commerce, National Technical Information Service (PB89-191761). Federal Computer Products Center, NTIS, Springfield, VA 22161, 703-487-4763.

## ≡ What Is Jughead?

*Jughead*, an acronym for Jonzy's Universal Gopher Hierarchy Excavation and Display, is a search engine similar to Veronica except that it searches a smaller, more defined area of Gopherspace. Jughead might index all menu items on just one Gopher server, or it might index all gopher sites but selectively, only including high-level menu items.

Like Veronica, searches may use *and*, *or*, and *not* connectors and words may be truncated with * as the last character. When two words are used in the command line like *virtual reality*, a Boolean *and* is implied. That is, matches will contain both *virtual* and *reality*.

If Jughead isn't on your home server, connect to the server at *gopher.cc.utah.edu* and look at menu Item /4. *Use Jughead to search menus of the University of Utah <?>*. Here you can conduct an experimental search.

## ≡ Reference Services and Gopher

As a reference librarian, you can make use of the Gopher services in several different ways. One approach is to become familiar with information rich servers and learn what resources are available at those sites. Librarians need to know at which site the server is located and also what menu choices to make or what path to follow in order to arrive at a particular piece of information.

### Creating Your Own Bookmarks

If you locate items that you think you might return to on a frequent basis, you can use a feature called *bookmarks* to help you keep track of these items you will use often. *Gopher bookmarks* are references to Gopher menus and files. Typing the letter **a** after you've selected an item will automatically add that item to your bookmark list. Other bookmark commands include these:

A    Makes the current menu a bookmark
d    Deletes items from your bookmark list
v    Allows you to view your bookmark menu

At any point during your gopher session you can press the letter **v** and your custom bookmark menu will appear. If you choose one of the bookmarked entries, you'll be taken instantly to that source, no matter where you are in Gopherspace at the time. If you'd like to view your list of bookmarks as the first screen of your Gopher session, type the command **gopher -b** at your system prompt and press ENTER.

### Finding "Information Rich" Servers

Examples of servers that carry a wealth of resources are the University of California, Santa Cruz InfoSlug System (*gopher.scilibx.ucsc.edu*) and the Gopher server at the North Carolina State University (*dewey.lib.ncsu.edu*). (Other specialized Gopher servers are included under in Part VI.)

Another very comprehensive Gopher server was developed by the graduate students in the English department of Carnegie Mellon University. All the choices available in the root menu of this server are listed below. To connect, type the command **gopher english-server.hss.cmu.edu** and press ENTER. The root menu on this server fills three screens.

```
        Root gopher server: english-server.hss.cmu.edu

-->  1.  -New Stuff/
     2.  About this server (27k).
     3.  Art and Architecture/
     4.  Books/
     5.  Classes/
     6.  CMU Women's Center/
     7.  Conferences/
     8.  Contributions/
     9.  Cultural Theory/
    10.  Cyber/
    11.  Drama/
    12.  Economics/
    13.  English Server Party Line <TEL>
    14.  Environmental Activism/
    15.  Fiction/
    16.  Gender and Sexuality/
    17.  Government, Law and Politics/
    18.  Graduate Students Only/

    19.  Gulf War/
    20.  History/
    21.  Internet/
    22.  Invention/
    23.  Journals/
    24.  Judiciary/
    25.  Languages and Linguistics/
    26.  Libraries/
    27.  Literacy/
    28.  Macintosh/
    29.  Marx/
    30.  MS-DOS and Windows/
    31.  MUDs/
    32.  Other Servers/
    33.  Philosophy/
    34.  Pittsburgh/
    35.  Poetry/
    36.  Pop Culture/

    37.  Progressive/
    38.  Pterodactyl Speedway/
    39.  Queer Resources Directory/
    40.  Race/
    41.  Recipes/
```

```
42. Reference
43. Rhetoric/
44. Search English Server <?>
45. Search Gopherspace/
46. Technical Communications/
47. The Academy/
48. Unix/
49. Usenet/
50. White House/
```

Depending upon where your interests lie and what the needs of your particular patrons are, there may be zero, one, or many resources worth noting that are accessible through the Gopher servers mentioned in this book. Rather than relying on memory to relocate relevant documents at a later date, use bookmarks to create your own personal lists of frequently accessed items.

*Infopop software*, described fully in Part V, provides another alternative. You can use this application for creating a personalized, menu-driven database that has the capability of cutting and pasting Internet addresses from the database's window onto the command line of the underlying screen.

## Listing Gopher Servers

If you aren't accessing a particular resource using the bookmark feature, you must begin your journey by connecting to the target server's root menu. You can do this in one of two ways: Either by making a menu choice on a Gopher server that lists all other Gopher servers in the world, or by connecting directly to the server you want at the beginning.

The disadvantage of the former method is that it takes time to work through several submenus before arriving at a list of Gopher servers. You also must connect to a Gopher server initially before you can begin the process of searching through a hierarchy of menus.

The following example is the path that must be followed in order to connect to the InfoSlug System using this approach. The path begins at the home server's root menu and follows these choices:

*8. Other Gopher and Information Servers/*
*8. North America/*
*4. USA/*
*6. california/*
*4. University of California - Santa Cruz, InfoSlug System/*

When you select this last menu item, you are connected to the InfoSlug System. Once you're connected, press = to find out this server's Internet address. The screen that appears after you press = is shown in Figure 7-7.

Notice that approximately five lines down, the host address is given as *scilibx.ucsc.edu*. If you aren't going to make a bookmark, you can at least record the server's address so next time you want to access InfoSlug, your client can connect to it directly.

```
Press ? for Help, q to Quit, u to go up a menu          Page: 1/1
Link Info (0k)                                          100%
+----------------------------------------------------------------------+
#
Type=1+
Name=About UCSC InfoSlug
Path=1/About UCSC InfoSlug
Host=scilibx.ucsc.edu
Port=70
Admin=Steve Watkins, UC Santa Cruz Science Library <watkins@scilibx.ucsc.edu>
ModDate=Mon Jan 10 22:26:40 1994 <19940110222640>
URL: gopher://scilibx.ucsc.edu:70/11/About UCSC InfoSlug


Size        Language       Document Type
----------  -------------  --------------------------
.10k        English (USA)  application/gopher-menu
.10k        English (USA)  application/gopher+-menu
.10k        English (USA)  text/html


Server Information

+----------------------------------------------------------------------+
[PageDown: <SPACE>] [Help: ?] [Exit: u]
```

**Figure 7-7:** Finding the server's Internet address

## Connecting Directly to Gopher

Connecting directly is quicker and can be accomplished with a simple command:

```
gopher <Internet address>
```

In this case, **<Internet address>** is the server address to which you want to connect. For example, to connect to the InfoSlug System at the University of California, you type

```
gopher scilibx.ucsc.edu
```

and then press ENTER.

## Using Bookmarks Effectively

If you'd like ideas on how best to utilize a bookmark list, I display the Bookmarks menu shown in Figure 7-8.

The first entry is a convenient and quick link to a Veronica server—a handy item to keep readily available. To set this bookmark up, follow the path mentioned earlier for accessing Veronica. When you arrive at the appropriate screen, press uppercase **A**, and then press ENTER to bookmark the entire Veronica search menu. If you want to bookmark just one of the Veronica servers, move the cursor to the appropriate line and press the lowercase a, and then press ENTER.

```
              Internet Gopher Information Client 2.0 p19

                            Bookmarks

   -->  1.  Search gopherspace at PSINet using Veronica <?>
        2.  CancerNet Information/
        3.  Gopher information organized by subject/
        4.  Census/
        5.  U.S. Government Gopher Servers/
        6.  David Riggins' Gopher Jewels/
        7.  Popular FTP Sites via Gopher/
        8.  WAIS Databases sorted by Letter/
        9.  Root gopher server: gopher.tc.umn.edu/
```

**Figure 7-8:**   The Gopher Bookmarks menu

The second bookmark is a link to CancerNet on the Gopher server at *helix.nih.gov*. Offering this information in public libraries would certainly be a worthwhile service. To set this bookmark up, Gopher to *helix.nih.gov* and from the root menu, follow the path */3. Health and clinical Information/1. CancerNet Information*. Then set up your bookmark.

The third bookmark called *Gopher information organized by subject* is a bookmark for a root menu choice at Gopher site *gopher.cc.utah.edu*. Spend some time online with this Gopher server and explore the broad range of topics that are searchable.

The fourth item, *4. Census/*, is a bookmark for one of the subject items listed at this site (*gopher.cc.utah.edu*). The opening screen is shown in Figure 7-9.

To set up this bookmark, begin by connecting with the Gopher server at *gopher.cc.utah.edu*. At the root menu, choose *8. Information Organized by Subject/*, and then choose *14. Census*, and set up your bookmark.

Bookmark five, *U.S. Government Gopher Servers*, takes you to a broad range of government databases as illustrated in the menu in Figure 7-10. To set up this bookmark , Gopher to site *stis.nsf.gov* and follow the path */19.Other U.S. Government Gopher Servers/*.

"Gopher Jewels," created by David Riggins, is a set of Gopher sites organized under various categories depending on their subject concentrations. You can set up this bookmark by connecting to the Gopher site at *cwis.usc.edu* and going to the path */9. Other Gopher and Information Resources/12. Gopher-Jewels*. The root menu is shown in Figure 7-11.

The eighth bookmark points to popular FTP sites via Gopher, as shown in Figure 7-12. This is a good opportunity to experience searching FTP archives through a Gopher interface. You'll find it quite different from the methods you used in Chapter 4. If you'd like to add this resource to your bookmark list, connect to the Gopher server at *gopher.tc.umn.edu* and follow the path to */15. Internet file server (ftp) sites/3. Popular FTP sites via Gopher*.

Bookmark nine connects you to a Gopher site that offers WAIS searching. Databases are sorted alphabetically. Connect to Gopher server *gopher-gw.micro.umn.edu* and follow the path */1.WAISes/3. WAIS Databases sorted by Letter*.

```
                              Census

-->  1.    About this directory.
     2.   1986 Canadian Census Documentation (from SFU)/
     3.   1990 U.S. Census Data (from St. Johns)/
     4.   1990 USA Census Information (from UMN)/
     5.   CANADIAN CENSUS AND ELECTION DATA, 1908-1968/
     6.   CENSUS OF GOVERNMENTS, 1962 AND 1967 (from UPENN)/
     7.   CENSUS OF GOVERNMENTS, 1972: GOVERNMENT EMPLOYMENT AND FINANCE FIL../
     8.   CENSUS OF POPULATION AND HOUSING, 1960 PUBLIC USE SAMPLE: ONE-IN-O../
     9.   CENSUS OF POPULATION AND HOUSING, 1970 [UNITED STATES]: PUBLIC USE../
     10.  Census Information for the United States (from UCSC)/
     11.  Census construction review tables/
     12.  Census-90: 1990 U.S. Census data (from UMd)/
     13.  Other Services (Census, Statlib, etc) (from NCSU)/
     14.  SOCIAL STRUCTURE OF ARGENTINA: CENSUS DATA ON ECONOMIC DEVELOPMENT../
     15.  San Diego Area Census Information/
     16.  The Census Bureau, Building Permits and Data Monopolies: an anecdo...
     17.  U.S. 1990 Census - Selected Cities [PL94-171] (from UPENN)/
     18.  U.S. 1990 Census States (except PA) [PL94-171] (from UPENN)/

                                                            Page: 1/2
```

**Figure 7-9:** The opening Census screen

```
                 Internet Gopher Information Client 2.0 p19

                         U.S. Government Gopher Servers

-->  1.    About this list.
     2.   Extension Service, USDA/
     3.   Federal Info Exchange (FEDIX)/
     4.   Government in General (maintained by UCI)/
     5.   LANL Physics Information Service/
     6.   Library of Congress MARVEL/
     7.   National Aeronautics and Space Administration/
     8.   National Coordination Office for HPCC (NCO/HPCC) Gopher/
     9.   National Institute of Standards and Technology (NIST)/
     10.  National Institutes of Health (NIH)/
     11.  National Oceanic and Atmospheric Administration (NOAA)/
     12.  National Science Foundation (NSF)/
     13.  Oak Ridge National Lab (ORNL) Environmental Sciences Division (ESD../
     14.  Protein Data Bank - Brookhaven National Lab/
     15.  U.S. Dept. of Education (ED) Office of Educational Research and Im../
     16.  U.S. Environmental Protection Agency (EPA)/
     17.  U.S. Geological Survey/
     18.  USDA National Agricultural Library Plant Genome/
     19.  USDA-ARS GRIN National Genetic Resources Program/
```

**Figure 7-10:** Government databases

```
                          Gopher-Jewels

 -->  1.  About Gopher Jewels.
      2.  A List Of Gophers With Subject Trees/
      3.  AIDS and HIV Information/
      4.  Agriculture and Forestry/
      5.  Anthropology and Archaeology/
      6.  Architecture/
      7.  Arts and Humanities/
      8.  Astronomy and Astrophysics/
      9.  Biology and Biosciences/
     10.  Books, Journals, Magazines, Newsletters, Technical Reports and Pub../
     11.  Botany/
     12.  Chemistry/
     13.  Computer Related/
     14.  Disability Information/
     15.  Economics and Business/
     16.  Education and Research (Includes K-12)/
     17.  Employment Opportunities and Resume Postings/
     18.  Engineering/

     19.  Environment/
     20.  Federal Agency and Related Gopher Sites/
     21.  Free-Nets And Other Community Or State Gophers/
     22.  Fun Stuff & Multimedia/
     23.  General Reference Resources/
     24.  Geography/
     25.  Geology and Oceanography/
     26.  Global or World-Wide Topics/
     27.  Grants/
     28.  History/
     29.  Internet Cyberspace related/
     30.  Internet Resources by Type (Gopher, Phone, USENET, WAIS, Other)//
     31.  Language/
     32.  Legal or Law related/
     33.  Library Information and Catalogs/
     34.  List of Lists Resources/
     35.  Manufacturing/
     36.  Math Sciences/

     37.  Medical Related/
     38.  Military/
     39.  Miscellaneous Items/
     40.  Museums, Exhibits and Special Collections/
     41.  News Related Services/
     42.  Patents and Copy Rights/
     43.  Photonics/
     44.  Physics/
     45.  Political and Government/
     46.  Products and Services - Store Fronts/
     47.  Psychology/
     48.  Religion and Philosophy/
     49.  Social Science/
     50.  Weather/
```

**Figure 7-11:** Gopher sites organized by category

```
                      Popular FTP Sites via Gopher

--> 1.   Read Me First.
    2.   Boombox - Home of Gopher and POPmail/
    3.   Case Western Reserve University FREENET/
    4.   Indiana University Mac Gopher Client App (beta)/
    5.   Indiana Windows Archive/
    6.   Interest Group Lists/
    7.   Internet Resource Guide (tar.Z files)/
    8.   Latest Disinfectant (ftp.acns.nwu.edu)/
    9.   Lyrics/
    10.  NCSA - Home of NCSA Telnet/
    11.  National Science Foundation Gopher (STIS)/
    12.  Newton Archives at Johns Hopkins University (bnnrc-srv.med.jhu.edu../
    13.  OCF Document Archives/
    14.  OSS-IS Info Archives (slow)/
    15.  SUMEX-AIM Archives - (Includes Info-Mac: a large collection of Mac../
    16.  Scholarly Communications Project of Virginia Tech/
    17.  Software Archives at MERIT (University of Michigan)/
    18.  Sonata NeXT software archive (sonata.cc.purdue.edu)/

    19.  Supreme Court Rulings (CWRU)/
    20.  UIUC-CSO - Home of the qi server (CSO phonebook software)/
    21.  University of Utah Mac Gopher Client App (beta)/
    22.  Usenet University/
    23.  Washington University Archive (wuarchive)/
```

**Figure 7-12:**   Popular FTP sites

The last item on this sample bookmark menu, *5. Root gopher server: gopher.tc.umn.edu/*, was added automatically. This is my 'home' Gopher server's address at the University of Minnesota. When I invoke Gopher by issuing the command **gopher -b**, this menu choice automatically is offered as a means of connecting to the main server from the Bookmarks screen.

## ≡ For Further Study

If you are interested in obtaining Gopher client applications, explore FTP site *boombox.micro.umn.edu* in the */pub/gopher* directory. Get the *00README* file for details.

You can get image viewers and sound players from FTP site *lennon.itn.med.umich.edu* in the directory */dos/gopher/misc*. These applications are necessary if you want to download and utilize picture and sound files. NOTIS Systems, Inc. released a client called WinGopher, a Microsoft Windows-based front end to Gopher. Along with the more traditional services described in this chapter, WinGopher also downloads sounds and transfers images through a GIF viewer from any Internet application to any Windows application. For more information, contact Robyn McMurray, NOTIS Systems, 1007 Church Street, Evanston, IL 60201. Phone: 708-866-0174, FAX: 708-866-0178.

A great front-end for Mac is TurboGopher v1.3 and it's free. FTP to site *sumex-aim.stanford.edu* and look in the */info-mac/comm* directory. A free Gopher client for Windows is GopherBook. FTP to site *sunsite.unc.edu* and **get** the file *gophbook.zip* in the directory */pub/micro/pc-stuff/ms-windows/winsock/apps*.

To stay abreast of new Gopher developments, subscribe to the gopher-announce mailing list. Email your subscription request to *gopher-announce-request@boombox.micro.umn.edu*. Announcements are archived and available via Gopher. Connect to *gopher.tc.umn.edu* and look under "Information About Gopher."

To obtain a Veronica FAQ, FTP to site *veronica.scs.unr.edu* and go to the */veronica/veronica-faq* directory. For a list of all Veronica servers, Gopher to *veronica.scs.unr.edu* and choose 'Veronica' at the root menu.

# Chapter 8

# Wide Area Information Servers (WAIS)

*WAIS* (pronounced "ways") was originally developed by Thinking Machines Corporation in collaboration with Apple Computer, Inc., Dow Jones & Company, and KPMG Peat Marwick. The name WAIS stands for *Wide Area Information Server*. WAIS enables you to access and do full-text searching in a wide variety of information resources (611, at last count). These sources contain such things as bibliographies; articles; catalogs; indexes; book reviews; various reports, such as agricultural commodity market reports, newsgroup and discussion group message archives; directories, such as the University of North Carolina's telephone directory; or the complete text of books such as the *CIA World Fact Book* and *The Book of Mormon*.

## ≡ WAIS Clients and Servers

Like all of the other services mentioned thus far, WAIS also is based on the client/server model. When you connect to WAIS, you are running a WAIS client program that provides you with your interface, and it is here that you formulate your query using natural language questions to find relevant documents.

The particular WAIS client you use is determined by your method of connecting to the Internet. If you access the Internet through a dial-up service, you will use the WAIS client running on your dial-up host. If a client program is not available, you can TELNET to a public WAIS client. The public clients available for your use are listed in Table 8-1.

**Table 8-1:**  Public WAIS Clients

| Domain Name | IP Address | Login as |
|---|---|---|
| info.funet.fi | 128.214.6.102 | wais |
| swais.cwis.uci.edu* | 128.200.15.2 | swais |
| nnsc.nsf.net | 128.89.1.178 | wais |
| quake.think.com | 192.31.181.1 | wais |
| kudzu.cnidr.org | 128.109.130.57 | wais |
| sunsite.unc.edu | 152.2.22.81 | swais |

*This is a CWIS (Campus Wide Information System) WAIS server.

All these sites are running the *swais* client, which stands for *screen WAIS*. This character-based interface presents three screens:

- The Source Selection screen
- The Search Results screen
- The actual full-text document screen

The opening Source Selection screen is a one-level menu system displaying all of the available sources (databases) for searching.

After the server completes its search, it returns a list of document titles (or *headlines*) and the client displays these on a Search Results screen. The list is arranged in order of relevancy, with the most relevant documents first and the least relevant documents last. The document that contains the most matches is always listed first and given a score of 1000.

Next, you select the document you want to view and WAIS retrieves it and displays a full-text version. At this point, you can save the document to a file, have it mailed to you through the Internet mail system, continue your search by scanning all or part of a particular document (you can use those words for future searches in a process called *relevance feedback*), or discontinue your present line of inquiry and **quit** to another search.

Relevance feedback and saving documents to a file are features that are available only on the more sophisticated clients that run on your personal computer. When TELNETing to a public client/server, you are limited to the mail service, or, if you want to save the document you're viewing, you can use the screen capture feature on your communications software to save the screen.

If you have a direct connection, you can choose your own WAIS client. For example, if you are using a Macintosh, you can use a client program called WAIStation commonly used on that machine. A user's guide for this program is in the */wais/doc* directory at FTP site *quake.think.com* under the filename *waistation_users_guide.txt*. Other sources of software are listed at the end of this chapter.

The client communicates with the server by translating queries into a protocol called *Z39.50*. Z39.50 is an American National Standard protocol and its importance lies in the fact that it provides a uniform procedure for client computers to communicate with computers acting as information servers, no matter what the differences are in their hardware technologies or operating systems. Z39.50, for example, enables a user at one site running MS-DOS on an IBM-PC to view records and retrieve data from a server running on a VAX/VMS super minicomputer without having to know one thing about how that machine works. (For a more thorough introduction to the Z39.50 standard, refer to the file *plain.txt* stored in the directory */wais/wais-discussion* at FTP site *quake.think.com*.)

Although servers don't interpret your natural language queries by decoding human sentences, they do match patterns—the words and phrases you have sent—ranking them based on heuristics. When the server receives a request, it searches a full-text index of one or more databases for relevant documents that match the query. You can search for any kind of information on a WAIS server: plain ASCII text, formatted documents, images, or audio.

Servers search every word contained in a source except for stop words and buzz words. *Stop words* are words that have no value in full-text searching and are ignored in queries sent to the public WAIS server at *quake.think.com*. Stop words include such words as *a, about, above, you, you would, you will,* and others. Another group of words that are ignored are referred to as buzz words. *Buzz words* are words that are considered too common to be helpful in searches and are therefore not searchable. They are extremely common and are weeded out by the database software at the time the database is indexed. Examples include the words *able, access, account, act, street, write, writes,* and *written.*

## ≡ Search Strategies

The success you achieve using WAIS will be determined not only by how well you choose your sources, but also by the words and phrases you choose when formulating your queries. You cannot use proximity operators (request that terms be adjacent, for example) or logical operators (**and, or,** and **not**) to focus your search into a conceptual level. WAIS rates the document's relevancy by how many times the keywords you choose appear in the text no matter where they appear or in what context.

The phrase *cow and farm* retrieves documents with the words *cow* and/or *farm.* The phrase *apple tree* retrieves any document with the words *apple* and *tree,* just the word *apple,* or just the word *tree.*

Truncation, or *wild card,* characters are not available in the WAIS command format. You can search for multiple endings of words only by listing every variation, including different tenses and plural forms of words. For example, if you are looking for articles that cover the topic *censorship in libraries,* you should use the keywords *censor, censorship, censored, censoring, library,* and *libraries.* Include synonyms and other related terms to increase the chances of getting the information you want.

When you choose keywords for your research, consider whether the words you choose are necessary. Certain words are implied by the fact that you are searching a particular source. For example, the word *pets* would be unnecessary in searching *rec.pets.src,* a pet owner's newsgroup that discusses cats, dogs, birds, and horses, etc., and *Simpsons* is redundant in the *Simpsons-episodes* database.

Other factors that affect your success are the speed and efficiency with which swais operates at a particular time and the breadth and depth of information you are given access to when searching. The public client interface runs slowly and is nearly unusable at times. Attempting a TELNET connection to one of the public clients may yield messages like this one:

```
Trying... [128.89.1.178] %MULTINET-F-EHOSTUNREACH, No route to host
```

and

```
Connection closed by Foreign Host
```

Other times, you may connect to the server but the sources you select are not accessible because their format can't be interpreted by the client software you're running.

As with all of the other Internet applications discussed in this book, if you ever achieve a direct link with the Internet, make use of the graphic interfaces that can be run on your personal computer. They are much easier to use and offer more capabilities than the character-based programs.

## ≡ Getting Started

Before you can assess the overall usefulness of WAIS for your library, you must first assess the usefulness of the individual sources that you access through WAIS. Likewise, the first step in conducting a specific search is to determine which of the many sources are most likely to contain relevant information pertaining to your query.

One way of determining the usefulness of WAIS sources is to consult the *directory-of-servers*, a source in itself which is searchable online just like any of the other sources. Maintained by Thinking Machines Corporation, the *directory-of-servers* is a database that contains textual descriptions of all known servers. When you query the *directory-of-servers*, it returns documents in the form of source structures. *Source structures* are files that contain readable text, but they are specially formatted files which look quite different from plain text files. They are recorded in this format so that the documents themselves can be used in a search query statement.

As new sources become available, Thinking Machines registers them. A record is added to the *directory-of-servers* describing what information the new source offers and any fees they charge. One of the WAIS search exercises later in this chapter provides you with practice in searching the *directory-of-servers*.

Another way to familiarize yourself with the content of WAIS sources is by consulting a document called "Brief Description of WAIS Sources," published by Chris Christoff of Bond University. This document consists of two parts: the first part is a list of WAIS sources with brief descriptions arranged by subject, and the second part consists of sources and descriptions listed alphabetically.

These lists are in electronic format and can be found at various sites including the Bond University Archives, Gold Coast, Queensland, Australia. FTP to site *kirk.bond.edu.au* and go to the directory */pub/Bond_Uni/doc/wais*. Once you are in the *wais* directory, you can issue a **dir** command to view a list of the files contained in that directory.

Those beginning with *src-list* are different formats of the first part of Christoff's document. They include the following:

*src-list.txt* is a plain ASCII text file.
*src-list.zip* is a Microsoft Word for Windows version.
*src-list.hqx.Z* is a Microsoft Word version for Macintosh.
*src-list.ps.Z* is a PostScript version.

Filenames beginning with *annex* are various formats of the sources' descriptions, listed alphabetically. These include the following:

*annex.hqx.Z* is a Microsoft Word version for the Macintosh.
*annex.ps.Z* is a compressed PostScript file.
*annex.txt* is a list of sources and descriptions in alphabetical order in plain ASCII text.
*annex.zip* is a Microsoft Word for Windows version.

You also can FTP to *archive.orst.edu,* where you will find copies of these same files in the directory */pub/doc/wais*. There is one additional file located at this site called *list_and_annex.sit.hqx,* which is a Word 5.0 for the Mac file that contains both parts of the file.

Lastly, a file containing the actual source structures for each database (this is what you would see when viewing the files online via WAIS) is available at FTP site *hydra.uwo.ca* in the directory */libsoft* in a file called *WAIS_SERVERS.TXT*. This document offers more descriptive information than the Christoff list, but like that list, it is not as up-to-date as the information you will find by connecting to WAIS server and searching the directory-of-sources online.

One advantage these text files offer, however, is that when you download them, you then have the option of printing them out and making them available in paper format or loading them into a word processor, where you can use text searching facilities to find certain words or phrases.

## ≡ WAIS Search Exercises

The following exercises will help you get acquainted with the logon procedure and searching techniques while using the swais interface. In the first exercise, you connect to the public WAIS client maintained by the Finnish University and Research Network.

## Exercise 1

### *Finding a Thanksgiving Dessert Recipe*

TELNET to *info.funet.fi* and when the *Select service:* prompt appears, type **swais**, and press ENTER. You'll be prompted for the type of terminal you're emulating. Once you've entered this information, the swais client starts running. The login screen is pictured in Figure 8-1.

```
            Finnish University and Research Network FUNET

                    Information Service

The following information services are available:

gopher      Menu-based global information tool
www         World-Wide Web, Global hypertext web
wais        Wide Area Information Server, global databases on
            on different topics
x500        Global X.500 directory
archie      Database of Internet Archive contents
exit        Exit FUNET information services


Select service (gopher/www/wais/archie/exit) ? swais


Supported terminal types are:
      vt100, xterm


Please enter your terminal type (vt220) ? vt100

Starting WAIS ..
```

**Figure 8-1:**   The sdwais client login screen

In a few moments, the client presents you with the Source Selection screen, as shown in Figure 8-2.

This server lists 475 sources in alphabetical order. The source list wraps around, which means that you can display the bottom of the list by moving up one screen. The current screen displays 18 sources. Each line contains the address where the source is located, the source name, and any costs associated with searching it. The first source is highlighted.

To generate a list of basic commands, type **?** at the prompt. The swais help screen, shown in Figure 8-3, appears.

Notice that each time you press the down-arrow key, the highlight bar moves down one line. The highlight tells you which source you are on, but doesn't select the source for searching. To select a source, press the SPACE BAR. An asterisk appears on the line, indicating that it is highlighted.

In this exercise, you conduct a search in the source called *recipes*. You have several options for getting to that source. You can page down by typing J, ^V, or ^D (the ^ represents the CTRL key); you can type the line number of the source and press ENTER (notice that as sources are added or subtracted from the list, line numbers change); or you can search for the source name using the format /<source> where <source> is the name of the source you want to locate. You can enter the exact source name or any length string beginning with the first character. The Source Selection screen where *recipes* appears is shown in Figure 8-4.

Using one of the described methods, move to the line recipes and select it by pressing the SPACE BAR. Note the asterisk (*) that appears at the beginning of that line. (At the time of this writing, the line number for this source was 370.) If you want to select two or more sources to search simultaneously, simply move the highlight bar to each source you want and select it by pressing the SPACE BAR.

**Figure 8-2:** The Source Selection screen

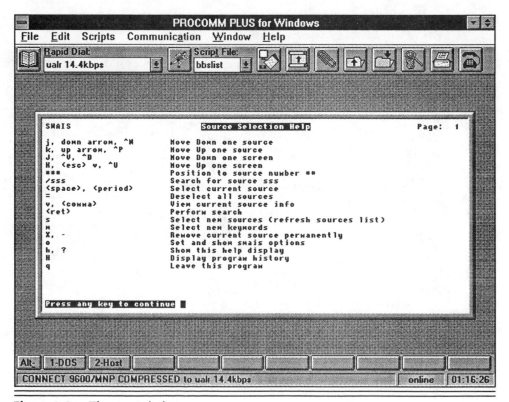

**Figure 8-3:** The swais help screen

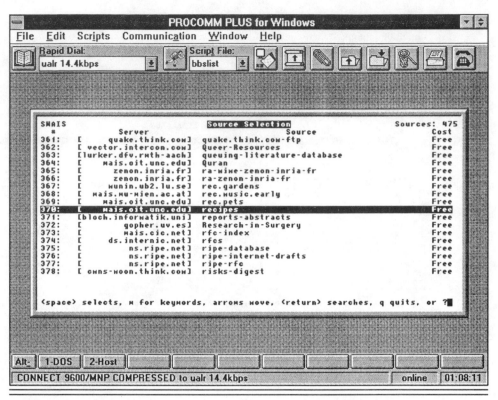

**Figure 8-4:** The Source Selection screen with recipes displayed

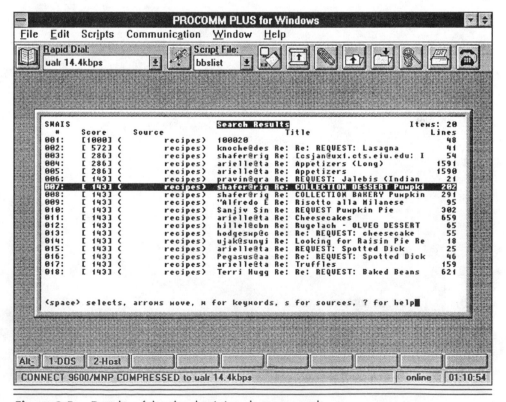

**Figure 8-5:** Results of the thanksgiving dessert search

The search begins when you enter a word or phrase at the *Keywords:* prompt. Type **w** (do not press the ENTER key) and the cursor moves to the *Keywords:* prompt. In this exercise, you search for a Thanksgiving dessert recipe. You can start by typing the phrase *Thanksgiving dessert* or any other words you might like to try. If you make an error while typing, press ^U to clear the text after the *Keywords:* prompt and start again. When you've finished typing the word or phrase that you'd like to search, press ENTER, and the search begins. The results of the search phrase **thanksgiving dessert** are shown in Figure 8-5.

I chose to view line 007: because of the document headline *COLLECTION DESSERT Pumpki* [sic.], not because of it's relevancy rating. Using the arrow key, I moved the highlight bar down to line 007: and pressed the ENTER key. A small part of this file's output is shown here:

```
Getting "shafer@rig Re: COLLECTION DESSERT Pumpkin cheesecake recipes" from recN
ewsgroups: rec.food.recipes
 Path: samba!concert!rock!stanford.edu!ames!news.dfrf.nasa.gov!shafer
From: shafer@rigel.dfrf.nasa.gov (Mary Shafer)
Subject: COLLECTION DESSERT Pumpkin cheesecake recipes
Message-ID: <SHAFER.92Oct21212644@ra.dfrf.nasa.gov>
Keywords: COLLECTION DESSERT
Sender: news@news.dfrf.nasa.gov (Usenet news)
Organization: NASA Dryden, Edwards, Cal.
Date: Thu, 22 Oct 1992 04:26:49 GMT
Approved: shafer@rigel.dfrf.nasa.gov
Lines: 190


[Here are the CHEESECAKE responses to the request for pumpkin recipes.
The others will appear by category. There are a lot of pumpkin
recipes out there. I suspect that the attributions are somewhat
confused, as this got a little jumbled when I started sorting by type.
MFS]

From: gwynn@utkvx4.utk.edu (Evans, Gwynne)
Organization: University of Tennessee Computing Center

                  PUMPKIN CHEESECAKE

1/3 c. margarine
1/3 c. sugar
1 egg
1&1/4 c. flour
2 (8 oz) pkgs cream cheese
3/4 c. sugar
2 c. fresh or canned pumpkin (I like fresh)
1 t. cinnamon
1/4 t. nutmeg
Dash salt
2 eggs

Cream margarine, sugar until light and fluffy. Blend in egg. Add
flour and mix well. Press dough on bottom & 2" high on sides of 9"
springform pan or a high sided cake pan. Bake at 400F for 5 min.
Reduce temperature to 350F.
```

```
Combine softened cream cheese and sugar, mixing at medium speed on
electric mixer till well blended. Blend in pumpkin, spices and salt.
Mix well. Add eggs, one at a time, mixing well after each addition.
Pour mixture into pastry lined pan; smooth surface to edge of crust.
Bake at 350F for 50 min. Take knife and loosen cake from rim of pan.
Cool before removing from pan. Chill. Garnish with whipped cream just
before serving if desired.

Boy, this is good.

Gwynn Evans


----------
```

To move through the file, press the SPACE BAR. To stop displaying the file, press **q** to quit. If you'd like a copy of the file you're reading, press **m** to mail a copy of the text to yourself or someone else. After you've finished reading the document, you are returned to the previous screen where all of the file headings were listed.

To initiate the second search example, press **w** (without pressing ENTER afterwards) and you are returned to the Source Selection screen. Now deselect the *recipes* source by pressing the SPACE BAR. Notice that this removes the asterisk * from the beginning of that line. You can also press = to remove all selected sources at once. Press the up arrow until the highlight bar lands on the source called *rec.gardens* and press the SPACE BAR to select that source for searching.

Once the source is selected, press **w**, and enter the keyword **potato** in the *Keywords:* field; then press ENTER. WAIS conducts a search of the *rec.gardens* database for any occurrence of the word *potato*. The search pulled up the following three files:

```
Press any key to continue
SWAIS                           Search Results                Items:  3
  #    Score     Source                    Title                    Lines
001:   [1000] (    rec.gardens)  klier@cobr Re: Seed catalogs: 3       1737
002:   [ 834] (    rec.gardens)  maynard@fu Re: neato potato growing idea  23
003:   [ 834] (    rec.gardens)  strow@umbc Re: Re: neato potato growing   44
```

The third file listed here called *neato potato growing* is displayed below. Notice that the source of these documents is a USENET newsgroup called *rec.gardens.*

```
Getting "strow@umbc Re: Re: neato potato growing ideas" from rec.gardens.src...F
rom: strow@umbc.edu (L. Larrabee Strow)
 Newsgroups: rec.gardens
Subject: Re: neato potato growing ideas
Date: 26 Mar 1994 03:53:45 GMT

In article <2mv4ak$j30@jethro.Corp.Sun.COM>
maynard@fuzzy.Corp.Sun.COM (Alexandra R. Ohlson) writes:

> Hi.
> My brother-in-law and sister are both into growing potatos.
> They've done so before, but only in the conventional
> turn-the-soil, plant-the-spud, wait and dig method. I know
> I've seen other creative tecniques here before and I'd like
> to surprise them with a list.
```

```
>
> I'm sure I remember seeing one suggestion involving stacking
> of car tires...
>

   I had some left over potaoes[potatoes cut with at least one eye
or sprout and cured] and I wasn't willing to give up any more room in
the garden so I used my winter bird seed metal trash can for an
expeiment. I placed compost with leaf mold, we are the lucky recipiants
of those that bag their leaves, in the bottom and planted the seed
potatoes. as they grew I put more stuff on top untill I got to the top
of the can. When the plants died back , I dumped and dug to get a
fairly nice crop of new potatoes. I have to say, That I think they do
better directly in the ground, but if you don't have the space this is
a good alternative to no potatoes  at all.We are especially excited
over YUKON GOLD and LADYFINGER potatoes.THe first being so very creamy
and buttery tasting , the latter being wonderful for stir frying in
olive oil.
   I remember my mom trying tires when I was little [ I grew up in a car
repair shop] with little sucess. but she did not use good compost so
I,m sure the results would be better with better amendments to the
soil.

use what you can get and recycle what you use...
Van Wensil
```

To quit the WAIS program, press q and your system prompt is displayed.

Note: Shortly before finishing this section of the book, I discovered that the WAIS server at *quake.think.com* had changed its approach slightly. It no longer offered an opening menu of all WAIS sources listed alphabetically as in the above examples. Their new opening screen, which comes up after the login screen shown in Figure 8-6, lists only one source: the *directory-of-servers*.

```
This is the new experimental "wais" login on Quake.Think.COM

As the total number of sources has passed the 500 mark, we've found it's
become virtually impossible to find a source from the 25 screens of
sources.

I have decided that instead of presenting you with all the sources, I'll
just give you the Directory of Servers as a starting point. To find
additional sources, just select the directory-of-server.src source, and ask
it a question. If you know the name of the source you want, use it for the
keywords, and you should get that source as one of the results. If you
don't know what source you want, then just ask a question that has
something to do with what you're looking for, and see what you get.

Once you have a list of results, you should "u"se the result you desire.
You can "v"iew a result before you "u"se it, paying close attention to the
"description".

Please let us know how you like this approach by sending feedback to
"wais@quake.think.com".
```

**Figure 8-6:** The new WAIS opening screen

```
                    DIRECTORY-OF-SERVERS

Server created with WAIS-8 on Fri Mar  8 14:30:57 1991 by
 brewster@think.com
This is a White Pages listing of WAIS servers. For more information on
WAIS, use the WAIS system on the wais-docs server, or add yourself to the
wais-discussion@think.com mailing list, or get the newest software from
think.com:/public/wais.

To server makers: Please make new servers of text, pictures, music
whatever. We will try to list all servers in the directory that get sent
in to: directory-of-servers@quake.think.com (use the -register option on
the command waisindex), but I reserve the right to take servers out if they
are not consistently available. I will send notice to the maintainer
before doing so.

To get a list of all available sources, search for 'source'. This may
limited by the maximum number of results allowed by a client.

Bugs and comments to bug-wais@think.com.
 -brewster@think.com

FIND <keywords>, Back, Up, Quit, or Help: find weather
```

**Figure 8-7:**   The directory-of-servers screen

## Search the Directory-of-Servers via WWW

The *directory-of-servers* can also be searched via World-Wide Web. You may
want to read about World-Wide Web in Chapter 9 before continuing with this
section. If not, proceed by TELNETing to *nxoc01.cern.ch*. When the General
Overview screen appears, select *Servers by type [3]* by typing 3 and pressing EN-
TER. Next, select *Find WAIS index servers using the directory of servers[5]* by
typing 5 and pressing ENTER. This brings you to the screen shown in Figure 8-7.
At the *FIND <keywords>, Back, Up, Quit, or Help:* prompt, type the words **find
<keywords>** where **<keywords>** are the particular keywords you want to search.
For example, enter the words: **find weather**

    After the server completes its search, it returns the following list of WAIS
servers that match the query:

```
              weather (in directory-of-servers)
                        WEATHER

    Index directory-of-servers contains the following 4 items relevant to
    'weather'. The first figure for each entry is its relative score, the second
    the number of lines in the item.

    1000    40  weather.src[1]
     680    18  midwest-weather.src[2]
     240   116  NOAA_Environmental_Services_Data_Directory.src[3]
     200   112  irtf-rd.src[4]
```

To access the first two listed (those with the highest relevancy scores), enter their corresponding numbers. This connects you with the following documents:

```
                                          weather WAIS source file
                        WEATHER DESCRIPTION

    Access links           Direct access[1] or through CERN gateway[2]

    Maintainer             weather-server@quake.think.com

    Host                   quake.think.com


     [End]




                                    midwest-weather WAIS source file
                        MIDWEST-WEATHER DESCRIPTION

    Access links           Direct access[1] or through CERN gateway[2]

    Maintainer             emv@cic.net

    Host                   wais.cic.net

Server created with WAIS release 8 b3.1 on Feb  3 16:41:38 1992 by emv@cedar.ci
c.net


National Weather Service forecasts for the states of
Michigan, Ohio, Indiana, Illinois, Wisconsin, Iowa,
and Minnesota. Updated hourly from the 'gopher' weather
server at the U of Minnesota.

    --Ed


     [End]
```

The Web offers links (see the numbers in square brackets) that will connect you directly to both of these resources. For further details on the Web, see Chapter 9.

### WAIS Search Using Gopher

You also can use Gopher to access WAIS. This offers a much friendlier way to search than using the public client sites described in the first search exercise. You can access WAIS through most Gophers, and in this example, you go to the Gopher server at *gopher2.tc.umn.edu*.

Beginning at the root menu, follow this path:

*/8. Other Gopher and Information Servers*
*/12. WAIS Based Information*

```
              Internet Gopher Information Client 2.0 p19

                   recipes.src: thanksgiving deserts

 1. 100020.101 Re: REQUEST Thanksgiving recipe urgently required.
 2. shafer@rig Re: [csjan@ux1.cts.eiu.edu: Italian Recipes].
 3. shafer@rig Re: COLLECTION BAKERY Pumpkin pie recipes.
 4. "Alfredo E Re: Risotto alla Milanese.
 5. Sanjiv Sin Re: REQUEST Pumpkin Pie.
 6. xeno@iasta Re: REQUEST: Recipes that use Almond Paste.
 7. hillel@cbn Re: Rugelach - OLVEG DESSERT JEWISH.
 8. hodgesmp@c Re: Re: REQUEST: cheesecake.
 9. Bob Jewett Re: RECIPE: Lemon Parfaits.
10. simon@socs Re: REQUEST: Chocolate Mudd Cake.
11. Terri Hugg Re: Re: REQUEST: Baked Beans.
12. news%BBN@u Re: REQUEST: Chocolate-Pecan Pie.
13. arielle@ta Re: Cranberry Radish Sauce.
14. begonia@ha Re: Re: REQUEST: Cranberry Sauce.
```

**Figure 8-8:** The Thanksgiving dessert via Gopher

You now have the choice of viewing all databases, sorted by letter or sorted by subject. Select a WAIS source to search (Gopher allows only one at a time) and type your search statement. Gopher performs the search and returns the results in the form of a menu.

You may find it interesting to note that when the above Thanksgiving dessert search was conducted via Gopher, the search went much faster, the interface was much easier, and the results were somewhat different. Notice also that the collection of pumpkin pie recipes rate number three in relevance on the list shown in Figure 8-8.

## ≡ For Further Study

Consult the sources in this section for additional information on WAIS. *comp.infosystems.wais* and *alt.wais* are Usenet discussion groups focusing on WAIS issues.

The file *getting-started* is a WAIS FAQ that provides useful information on various sources for WAIS clients. To obtain a copy, FTP to site *rtfm.mit.edu* and go to the directory */pub/usenet/news.answers/wais-faq*.

Wais-discussion is a discussion list for users and developers of electronic publishing. Send subscription requests to *wais-discussion-request@think.com*. All postings here go also to the *comp.infosystems.wais* group. Messages are archived at FTP site *quake.think.com* in the file */pub/wais/wais-discussion/issue-\**.

Software sources: The Enterprise Integration Network has developed PC and Mac WAIS clients. FTP to *ftp.einet.net* and go to the directories */einet/mac* or */einet/pc* and view the available files. WAIS, Inc., has developed a freeware WAIS client for the Mac that can be downloaded from the */wais* directory at FTP site *think.com.* Filename is *wais-for-mac-1.1.sea.hqx*. For details on downloading Mac files, see Appendix A.

*Wide Area Information Servers (WAIS) Bibliography* by Barbara Lincoln Brooks (10/26/92). FTP to *qauke.think.com* and go to the directory */pub/wais/wais-discussion* and copy the file *bibliography.txt*.

*Interfaces for Distributed Systems of Information Servers.* by Brewster Kahle, et al. This paper can be downloaded from the archives at *quake.think.comb* in the directory */wais/wais-discussion* as filename *Interfaces.txt*. Includes information on various WAIS client programs.

Commercial versions of WAIS are now being developed and sold by WAIS, Inc., 1040 Noel Drive, Menlo Park, CA, 94025. Contact them by phone: 415-617-0444, fax: 415-327-6513, or email: info@wais.com.

FreeWAIS, a freely distributable version of WAIS, is under development by the Clearinghouse for Networked Information Discovery and Retrieval (CNIDR). Their WWW server is located at *http://cnidr.org/welcome.html*.

# Chapter 9

# World-Wide Web

The *World-Wide Web,* also referred to as *WWW, W3,* or simply *the Web,* started its development at the CERN research center in Geneva, Switzerland, back in 1989. It is now being developed as a collaborative project and currently experiencing phenomenal growth.

The Web utilizes a simple front-end and server protocol to access Internet resources such as FTP, WAIS, Archie, Gopher, and more. It is built around a hypertext system that provides links between different objects: text files, sound files, images, and video. The front-end and server may exist on the same machine or on separate systems that are thousands of miles apart.

To understand the Web, you must understand hypertext. *Hypertext* is a system of managing textual information by creating associations between different documents. A hypertext system is made up of several documents, each of which is called a *node.* One or more words in a document or the entire document itself is *linked* to other words or groups of words in other documents. This linking enables you to move back and forth from the original document to the linked document easily.

Although you can read and talk about hypertext to your heart's content, you won't really understand it until you use it. In 1992, Ernest Perez created an MS-DOS hypertext version of his Ph.D. dissertation *A study of traditional information access models applied in a hypertext information system.* You can retrieve a copy of this document by FTPing to site *hydra.uwo.ca,*going to the */libsoft* directory, and downloading a self-extracting archive called *HYPERDISS,EXE.* If necessary, change the filename before downloading it from the FTP server or your local host so that it conforms to the DOS rule of not exceeding eight characters in length. For example, call the file *hyperdis.exe.*

To unarchive the file once it is on your machine, type **hyperdis** (or whatever filename you have given it), and press ENTER. To view Perez's hypertext dissertation, type **hyplus** and press ENTER. To leave the program, press ALT X and then verify that you want to exit by pressing **y**.

If you already have access to the Internet and a World-Wide Web client, there's an excellent online glossary of hypertext terms you can access by linking to document *URL: http://info.cern.ch/hypertext/WWW/Terms.html.*

## ☰ Accessing and Searching the Web

Ask your service provider whether there is a World-Wide Web client available on your system. If not, you can browse the Web by TELNETing to any one of the public sites listed here. When you visit these sites, you'll encounter two different client programs. The first three sites listed below are running a program called *Lynx*. The last three Web sites listed are running a program called *WWW*.

Public Web Sites

1. *fatty.law.cornell.edu*
2. *ukanaix.cc.ukans.edu*
3. *info.funet.fi*
4. *info.cern.ch*
5. www.*njit.edu* The opening screen for this site looks like this:

```
NJIT INFORMATION TECHNOLOGY ENTRY POINT

    NJIT-IT[1] is based upon HyperMedia technology employed in WORLD-WIDE WEB[2]
    (WWW) software developed at CERN[3] with modifications[4] by NJIT. With
    the NJIT Screen Mode browser use either the cursor keys or the item number,
    followed by the return key to select the topic of interest. Goals[5] of
    the NJIT-IT. HELP[6]


    Test[7] menu EMERGENCY[8]
    University[9] Directory[10] Information Systems NJIT Police 3111
    Calendar[11] Faculty[12] NJIT Library[13] Rutgers Police 648-5111
    Events[14] Staff[15] Other Libraries[16] Newark Police 733-6080
Publications[17] Phone Book[18] Other Info Systems[19] UMDNJ Hospital 456-4300
    News[20] Hours[21] Computing Systems[22] Health Services 3621
    Information Topic:
    Student[23] Academic[24] Administration[25] Facilities[26]

    http://it/


    Next Back Up Find List Recall Top End Go saVe eXit Query Preceding
     Succeeding Home Instructions
    Next page ( ? help, - escape, ++ homebase )
    HYPERTEXT ACTION CHOICE>
```

6. *vms.huji.ac.il* The Hebrew University of Jerusalem Information System. The opening screen of this site looks like this:

```
                /\
                \/
         | |
         | |
         | |    /\ \
         | | / /   \ \/ /
          / /         \ \
          / /           \ \
         / /
        \/
```

```
HEBREW UNIVERSITY zixard dhiqxaipe'd
OF JERUSALEM milyexia
COMPUTATION CENTER miaeyigd fkxn
CAMPUS INFORMATION SYSTEM zinipt rcin zkxrn



<RETURN> for more :
 (iy'x hixtz) zinipt rcin zkxrn milyexia zixard dhiqxaipe'd
THE HEBREW UNIVERSITY OF JERUSALEM CAMPUS INFORMATION SYSTEM


  [1] Libraries in Israel. .ux'a zeixtq [1]
  [2] Libraries out of Israel. .mlera zeixtq [2]
  [3] Databases in Israel (GcG TeX). .ux'a rcin ixb'n [3]
  [4] Databases out of Israel. .mlera rcin ixb'n [4]
  [5] Bulletin boards. .zercen zegel [5]
  [6] Hebrew university information. .i'hiqxaipe' mipt rcin [6]
  [7] Information for the student. .hpcehql rcin [7]
  [8] Municipal information. .("cb'") ipexir rcin [8]
  [9] News groups. .oeic zeveaw [9]
  [10] Recreation. .i'ptd zeryl [10]
  [11] Environmental info. system. .daiaqd zeki' lr rcin - zileg [11]
  [12] Search info. system menus. .rcind zkxrn ihixtza yetig [12]
  [13] Help on the Info. System. .rcind zkxrn lr dkxcd [13]
  [14] Let us know what you think. .rcind zkxrna yeniyd lr zexrd [14]
```

When TELNETing to these public sites, if you're prompted for a login or username, type **WWW** and press ENTER.

## ≡ Lynx Browsers

*Lynx* is a character-based interface for the Web that uses full-screen capabilities. Although some browsers can link you to a variety of resources, Lynx deals only with textual documents.

```
Lynx default home page (p1 of 2)

WELCOME TO LYNX AND THE WORLD OF THE WEB

You are using a WWW Product called Lynx. For more information about
obtaining and installing Lynx please choose About Lynx

The current version of Lynx is 2.2. If you are running an earlier
version PLEASE UPGRADE!

INFORMATION SOURCES ABOUT AND FOR WWW
* For a description of WWW choose Web Overview
* About the WWW Information Sharing project
* WWW Information By Subject
* WWW Information By Type

OTHER INFO SOURCES
* University of Kansas CWIS
* O'Reilly & Ass. Global Network Navigator
* Nova-Links: Internet access made easy
* NCSA: Network Starting Points, Information Resource Meta-Index
-- press space for next page --
Arrow keys: Up and Down to move. Right to follow a link; Left to go back.
H)elp O)ptions P)rint G)o M)ain screen Q)uit /=search [delete]=history list
```

**Figure 9-1:**   The Lynx opening screen

You can try Lynx out by TELNETing to *ukanaix.cc.ukans.edu* Login: **WWW**. After you login, you are asked to specify what type of terminal you are emulating. Enter VT100 because most communication packages can emulate it. The opening screen is shown in Figure 9-1.

The words or phrases that link you to other documents are shown in bold-faced text. The single word or phrase that is shown in reverse highlighting or normal text is the link that is currently selected and if you press ENTER, that link is activated. Use the procedures described in this section when working with Lynx.

Press the ↑ and ↓ keys to move to the next link on the page. You know when you have landed on a particular link when it changes from boldfaced text to normal text or reverse highlighting.

Press the PAGE DOWN key to move forward one page and the PAGE UP key to move back one page.

When you find a link you want to follow, press the → key to connect. If you want to move back to a previous link, press the ← key.

Press **m** to return to the first page.

Press the BACKSPACE or DELETE key to see the path you have followed to arrive at your present location. All of the links that you chose are presented in the form of a history list. (If you'd like to revisit any document presented in this list, simply press the arrow keys to move the cursor to the desired document and then press ENTER.)

Press the = key to display information on the current document and the current link, if you've selected one. (This key works the same way in Gopher.) Here's a sample of this output:

```
Information about the current document

 YOU HAVE REACHED THE INFORMATION PAGE

File that you are currently viewing

 Linkname: Volume 3M: X Window System User's Guide: OSF/Motif Edition:
 Table of Contents
 URL: http://nearnet.gnn.com/mkt/ora/catalog/3m.toc.html
 Owner(s): mailto:market@gnn.com
 size: 805 lines
 mode: normal


No Links on the current page
```

The top part of this screen displays data relating to the current file you are viewing and the bottom portion presents data on the link you have chosen. In this sample, no link was chosen. Notice the field called URL: The data listed in this field is called a *URL,* or *Uniform Resource Locator.*

URLs are the Web's way of identifying the location of a resource anywhere on the Internet. These resources can be text, images, movies, interactive graphics, or sound files.

A URL is a string of text that includes information on the type of resource (Gopher, WAIS, FTP, etc.), the machine's Internet address, and where the item is located on that machine. In the example, the part of the URL before the colon identifies the protocol being used by the server providing the file—in this example, *http,* which stands for Hypertext Transport Protocol. This means that the resource being described is a hypertext document. You will also see protocols such as Gopher, FTP, and WAIS noted in URLs. The second part of the URL (the part after the two forward slashes) gives the Internet address *nearnet.gnn.com* as the host where the item is located. The third and fourth parts provide the directory path and filename.

By pressing **g** (for *go*), you are prompted to enter a specific URL. This is a useful procedure if you are interested in accessing a certain file on the Web and have a specific URL for pointing you directly to that resource.

To see what this is all about, simply connect to a Web site running Lynx and enter the letter **g.** A sample of what appears next is shown in Figure 9-2. Notice the *URL to open:* prompt three lines up from the bottom of the screen. At that point, I entered the URL **http://nearnet.gnn.com/mag/1_94/a.**

You can search two ways using Lynx. When you're viewing a normal document, press / to conduct a keyword search. When you want to search an index, press S.

Although the Web works quite well as a front-end application with some keyword searching capabilities for locating links, resource discovery on the Web is still to some degree serendipitous just as it is with other resource discovery methods, including those used in traditional paper based libraries. If you do begin a journey and several hyperlinks later accidentally stumble upon a useful document or service, the Web offers you the capability of recording your location in a bookmark file much like you did in Gopher.

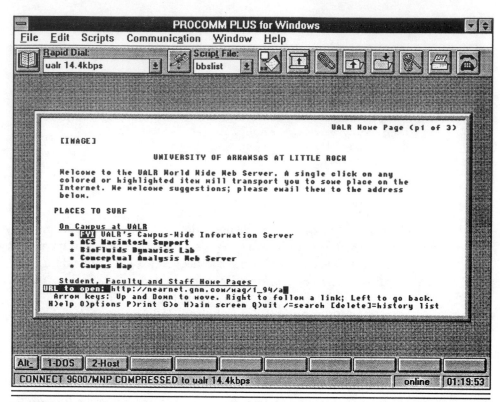

**Figure 9-2:** Running Lynx

To use the bookmark feature, begin by setting up a bookmark file on your local host. To do this, connect with a Lynx client and press o. This enables you to set your options where you tell Lynx the name of the file in which you want to store your bookmarks. The options screen is shown in Figure 9-3.

First I entered **B** to select *B)ookmark file*; and then I entered the filename *lynx.xrc*, pressed ENTER, and then pressed SHIFT >. I then started a search on the Web looking for information on the copyright law at Cornell Law School (a choice on the home screen at the University of Arkansas at Little Rock). When I arrived at a link called *COPYRIGHT ACT* that I wanted to add to my bookmark list, I pressed **a** and the following notice appeared at the bottom of the screen:

```
Do you wish to save this document in your current bookmark file? (y/n)
```

When I pressed **y**, the link was added to my bookmark list. I then pressed **v** to view the bookmark list, which appeared as follows:

```
Bookmark Page


This file may be edited with a standard text editor. Outdated or
invalid links may be removed by simply deleting the line the link
appears on in this file. Please refer to the Lynx documentation or
help files for the HTML link syntax.


COPYRIGHT ACT
```

```
Options Menu

E)ditor : NONE
D)ISPLAY variable : Not available on VMS
B)ookmark file : lynx.xrc
P)ersonal mail address : NONE
S)earching type : CASE INSENSITIVE
C)haracter set : ISO Latin 1
V)I keys : OFF
e(M)acs keys : OFF
K)eypad as arrows
or Numbered links : Numbers act as arrows
U)ser mode : Novice




Select first letter of option line, '>' to save, or 'r' to return to Lynx.
Command:
```

**Figure 9-3:**   Lynx options menu

If you'd like to save the current information you're viewing, type **p** and press ENTER. You are prompted for a filename where the document will be stored on your local host, or you can specify an email address.

To exit Lynx, type **q** and press ENTER. You'll be asked whether you really want to quit, at which point you enter **y** for yes or **n** for no. To quit without verification, enter an uppercase **Q**.

To demonstrate how the Lynx client works, I chose the link called *O'Reilly & Ass. Global Network Navigator* listed in the opening screen. I made the selection by pressing the down arrow key to move the bar to the line that was plain text (all of the other were boldfaced text at that point). Then I pressed the right arrow key and was transported, or "linked," to the GNN Home Page shown in Figure 9-4. I moved to the second screen by pressing the PAGE DOWN key.

Here I chose *GNN Magazine (Issue No. 2)*, pressed the right arrow key, and landed in the table of contents (two pages) shown here.

```
Table of Contents 1


GNN Magazine: Issue Two January 1994 (ISSN 1072-0413)

The Internet -- An Education in Itself

  Remarks by Vice President Al Gore at National Press Club

  Publishing for Professors by Dale Dougherty

  Is the Surf Up? by Mitchell Sprague

  Teaching and Learning in a Networked World by Donna Donovan
```

```
GNN HOME PAGE

The Global Network Navigator (GNN), an Internet-based Information
Center, is a production of O'Reilly & Associates, Inc. and an
appl cation of the World-Wide Web.

Welcome New Navigators! If you are new, please take a minute to learn
more about GNN.

To subscribe to GNN: [GET] the online registration form.

GNN News

GNN Magazine (Issue #2)

The Whole I ternet Catalog

--More-- This is a s archable index. Use 's' to search


2
GNN Marketplace

Navigator's Forum



[GO] to download a copy the GNN Home Page.

COPYRIGHT 1993 O'Reilly & Associates, Inc.
```

**Figure 9-4:**   The GNN Home Page

```
Environmental Education on the Net by Laura Parker Roerden

SchoolNet: Canada's Educational Networking Initiative by Tyler Burns

Academy One Introduces Classrooms to the Internet by Linda Delzeit
--More-- This is a searchable index. Use 's' to search


2

KIDLINK - Global Networking for Youth 10 - 15 by Odd de Presno

Global Lab Project Cultivates Young Scientists by Boris Berenfeld

K-12 Schools on the Internet: One School's Experience by Mike
Showalter

From Littleton to Law on the Net by Peter Martin
```

```
Librarians and the Internet by Mary Ann Neary

GO FIND OUT: EXPLORING THE NET'S RESOURCES

NET HEADS: PRACTICAL ADVICE AND COMMENTARY

HOT AIR: ABOUT GNN MAGAZINE-- FEATURING DOONESBURY CARTOONS
```

I selected the article *Librarians and the Internet* by Mary Ann Neary, a portion of which is shown here.

```
                      LIBRARIANS AND THE INTERNET


by Mary Ann Neary



         _____


Introduction




Librarians have embraced the Internet as a means of enhancing their
information delivery capabilities. As a connector of people, files,
and resources, the Internet is an ideal complement to the librarians'
traditional role, what a former colleague once called, "Bringing
people and books together."

Alert to the potential for linking their campus/institutional systems,
librarians have seen the Internet as a means of expanding their
present system capabilities. Most libraries, whether public, academic,
or corporate (i.e. special libraries) have long had online public
access catalogs, or OPACs, to serve as gateways to the library's
collection. Increasingly, these OPACs offer access to the wider world
and links to the Internet. Many OPACs are themselves searchable on the  .
Internet.

As these system capabilities have grown, so has the role of the
librarian. It is no longer sufficient for librarians to know the
resources of the home institution's library, OPAC, and/or campus
network; it is now considered part of the librarian's role to assist
Internet users in locating those remote sites where key files reside.
Librarians, as information professionals, are trained in organizing
information resources and presenting these resources to users. So, why

Enter a database search string: resource discovery
```

Reprinted with permission from GNN, the Global Network Navigator. Copyright © 1994, O'Reilly and Associates.

While viewing the second page, I pressed s, which brought up the *Enter a database search string:* prompt at the bottom of that screen. For purposes of demonstration, I entered the keywords *resource discovery* and pressed ENTER.

This search brought up a list of citations, the first few of which are shown in the following example. These resources were rated on their relevancy and I could access them by using the arrow keys to move the cursor to the desired line and then pressing the right arrow key to make the selection.

```
Data transfer complete Search response 4
Catalog
* 10: Score: 322, lines: 824 - Volume 3M: X Window System User's
Guide: OSF/Motif Edition: Table of Contents
* 11: Score: 322, lines: 327 - Programmer's Supplement for R5 of the
X Window System: Table of Contents
* 12: Score: 322, lines: 62 -
/gnn/data/mkt/ora/catalog/XResource.series.html
* 13: Score: 322, lines: 329 - /gnn/data/mkt/ora/catalog/r5.toc.html
```

## The WWW Browser

The WWW client is classified as a line-mode browser. Line-oriented, or line mode browsers display output one line after another on your screen. To see what a line-mode browser looks like, TELNET to *info.cern.ch*. No login or password is required. The opening screen looks like this:

```
              Welcome to the World-Wide Web
                  THE WORLD-WIDE WEB

This is just one of many access points to the web, the universe of
information available over networks. To follow references, just type the
number then hit the return (enter) key.

The features you have by connecting to this telnet server are very primitive
compared to the features you have when you run a W3 "client" program on your
own computer. If you possibly can, please pick up a client for your platform
to reduce the load on this service and experience the web in its full
splendor.

For more information, select by number:

A list of available W3 client programs[1]
Everything about the W3 project[2]
Places to start exploring[3]
The First International WWW Conference[4]

This telnet service is provided by the WWW team at the European Particle
Physics Laboratory known as CERN[5]
[End]
1-5, Up, Quit, or Help: 1
```

By typing 3 and pressing ENTER, you select the link called *Places to start exploring[3]*. This takes you to an overview screen, which is shown below:

```
              Overview of the Web
           GENERAL OVERVIEW OF THE WEB

There is no "top" to the World-Wide Web. You can look at it from many points
of view. Here are some places to start.

by Subject[1] The Virtual Library organizes information by subject
matter.
```

```
List of servers[2] All registered HTTP servers by country

by Service Type[3] The Web includes data accessible by many other
protocols. The lists by access protocol may help if
you know what kind of service you are looking for.

If you find a useful starting point for you personally, you can configure
your WWW browser to start there by default.

See also: About the W3 project[4] .
[End]




1-4, Back, Up, Quit, or Help:
```

Unlike Lynx, where you move a cursor to the desired link, you find information on a line-mode browser by following references and by conducting keyword searches. *References* are the numbers enclosed in brackets next to words or phrases. Numbers are placed in square brackets next to a word or group of words signifying that a link exists between that word or group of words and another document. To follow the link, you type the appropriate number and then press ENTER. If you press ENTER without typing something first, the next page is displayed.

You can display the list of available WWW commands by entering the **help** command. The following list shows you the most common commands used with the WWW client program:

```
WWW LineMode Browser version 2.13 (WWWLib 2.15) COMMANDS AVAILABLE


<RETURN> Move down one page within the document.
BOttom Go to the last page of the document.
Top Return to the first page of the document.
Up Move up one page within the document
List List the references from this document.
* <number> Select a referenced document by number (from 1 to 104).
Recall List visited documents.
Recall <number> Return to a previously visited document
as numbered in the recall list.
HOme Return to the starting document.
Back Move back to the last document.
Next Take next link from last document.
REFresh Refresh screen with current document
Go <address> Go to document of given [relative] address
Verbose Switch to verbose mode.
Help Display this page.
Manual Jump to the online manual for this program
Quit Leave the WWW program.
```

The following example demonstrates moving through a series of links using the WWW client. To create this example, I started at the GENERAL OVERVIEW screen shown earlier (where *by Subject[1]*, *List of servers[2]*, and *by Service Type[3]* are listed), I chose *by Subject[1]* and pressed ENTER. That brought up the following page:

```
1-4, Back, Up, Quit, or Help: 1
The World-Wide Web Virtual Library: Subject Catalogue (45/162)
Archaeology[14] Separate list

Asian Studies[15] Separate list

Astronomy and Astrophysics[16]
Separate list.

Bio Sciences[17] Separate list .

Chemistry[18] Separate list

Climate research The Deutsches Klimarechenzentrum[19] (DKRZ, German
Climate Computer Centre)

Commercial Services[20]
Separate list

Computing[21] Separate list.

Conferences[22] Separate list

Earth Science US Geological Survey[23] ; McGill University
1-104, Back, Up, <RETURN> for more, Quit, or Help:20
```

Instead of pressing ENTER several more times and eventually going through the entire alphabet, I stopped here and chose *Commercial Services[20]* and pressed ENTER, which displayed the following screen:

```
The World-Wide Web Virtual Library: Commercial Services
[1]

YELLOW PAGES

Information categorized by subject. See also other subjects[2] . Please
mail WWW-request@info.cern.ch if you know of online information not in these
lists.

This list has just been started. There must be more

Computers Fintronic USA Inc.[3] sell Linux workstations and
notebooks. Linux is a freely available UNIX-like
operating systems.

Electronic Storefronts

Nine Lives Quality Consignment Clothing[4], Located in Los Gatos, CA The
store inventory is available for browsing on the Internet around midday
Pacific Time (US) Monday - Friday. The forms-based interface allows
creation of a "Personal Shopping Assistant" agent to monitor incoming
inventory and send notices viw email when interesting garments arrive.

1-6, Back, Up, <RETURN> for more, Quit, or Help:
```

I pressed ENTER after reviewing this screen, and the following screen appeared:

```
The World-Wide Web Virtual Library: Commercial Services (34/34)
notebooks. Linux is a freely available UNIX-like
operating systems.

Electronic Storefronts

Nine Lives Quality Consignment Clothing[4], Located in Los Gatos, CA The
store inventory is available for browsing on the Internet around midday
Pacific Time (US) Monday - Friday. The forms-based interface allows
creation of a "Personal Shopping Assistant" agent to monitor incoming
inventory and send notices viw email when interesting garments arrive.

Branch Information Services[5] creates electronic storefronts in the
Branch Mall. We advertise all kinds of products - flowers, travel,
magazines, etc. Take a look and give us a call if you know someone who
might benefit from our services.

Publishers Electric Press, Inc.[6] , Commercial publishers and
consumer advisors on the Internet. This server
Includes exemplary hypertext pages of traditional
materials.


1-6, Back, Up, Quit, or Help: 6
```

After viewing page two, I entered the number 6 for more information on the Electronic Press, Inc. This is the output that resulted:

```
6
Electric Press, Inc. Vol. 1, No. 1
"Publishing and public relationson the information superhighway"
_____
Welcome to the Electric Press, Inc. World-Wide Web[1] server. With Electric
Press, you can have your own presence on the Internet[2] in a week. We use
NCSA Mosaic[3] to display your catalogues, brochures, and newsletters in
full-color multimedia format. You can use your existing electronic mail
systems to correspond with customers on the Internet, and we can build you a
custom index to find the information you need, when you need it.



_____

More about Electric Press, Inc and our products.[4]

Why use Electric Press, Inc?[5]

A tasty electronic publishing sampler.[6]

_____

For more information call 703-742-3308 or email info@elpress.com.

1-6, Back, Up, Quit, or Help: 6
```

At this juncture, I chose to explore *A tasty electronic publishing sampler.[6]* and that brought me the following information:

```
Samples of Electronic Publishing
"Publishing and public relationson the information superhighway"


_____


SAMPLES OF ELECTRONIC PUBLISHING IN MOSAIC


_____

The following pages are intended to demonstrate the communication power of
electronic publishing. They represent generic examples of how different
types of publications can be rendered and sometimes even improved through
the use of well-designed hypermedia documents. They are not intended to
advertise particular products or convery particular points of view.

An On-Line Catalogue[1]
Direct mail retail catalogs are costly to produce and
distribute. Electronic catalogs can be produced at
less cost than printed catalogues. More products and
more information about each product can be included.
An electronic catalogue is widely available with no
additional distribution costs. It is always available
1-3, Back, Up, <RETURN> for more, Quit, or Help:

Samples of Electronic Publishing (45/50)
and cannot be lost. In this example, a single
catalogue page is shown containing two products. In
addition to brief descriptions, the instruction
manuals for the products are included.

An Electronic Newsletter[2]
An electronic news letter can carry the same look and
feel as a printed version. Photographs can be
included. A newsletter might be distributed
electronically for several reasons:

As a "teaser," containing only a sample of the printed material, in order
to solicit additional paid subscriptions.

As a service to members or paid subscribers (with restriced access).

As is the case with this example, to reach a larger audience than would
be possible due to the cost of printing and mailing a paper newsletter.

A Product Brochure[3] UNDER DESIGN Particularly for high-tech
organizations, a presence on the Internet is becoming
a usual business requirement. An electronic brochure
can provide more information than its printed
counterpart. It can show a product in use, even
including full-motion video.
```

As previously mentioned, the Electric Press, Inc., provides a sampling of what's possible when you run a Web program called Mosaic on the Internet and apply it to the electronic publishing field. You need a direct Internet connection to run Mosaic and preferably a high-speed link to make it effective. Further details on Mosaic are presented later in this chapter.

One element in the WWW command line syntax is called *options*. You specify options before the argument. For example, the option **docaddress** followed by a hypertext address enables you to connect with and browse a particular document. For a description of all of the various options, see the online help service. You can access this by typing the word **manual** and pressing ENTER. Then select the link called *command line syntax[2]*.

# ≡ Mosaic

Windows-oriented Web browsers are friendlier and capable of doing much more than the less-sophisticated command-line interface browsers. Mosaic is one such program, a popular graphic interface for the Web written by the National Center for Supercomputing Applications (NCSA).

Mosaic is a hypermedia browser. As you browse the Internet, Mosaic can bring up a mix of things such as text and pictures on one screen (known as a "page" of information). Mosaic can also access sound, video, and interactive graphics.

There are NCSA versions of Mosaic for X Windows, Apple Macintosh, and Microsoft Windows platforms. You can find more information about these applications on NCSA's FTP server located at site *ftp.ncsa.uiuc.edu*. Mosaic for the X Windows system can be found in the */Mosaic* directory; Mosaic for Macintosh can be found in the */Mac/Mosaic* directory; and the Microsoft Windows version can be found in the */PC/Mosaic* directory.

## Viewing a Document

Figure 9-5 is the home page for CERN (The European Laboratory for Particle Physics)—the birthplace of the World-Wide Web project. (A *home page* is the main menu of a World-Wide Web site.) By clicking on highlighted or underlined text within CERN's home page, you are linked to some other object (sound, photograph, text, etc.) that relates to that particular topic.

In the preceding example, CERN's home page is displayed in the Mosaic for Microsoft Windows interface. When you start Mosaic, the document window displays the default home page, which is usually NCSA's, but you can change this setting in the *mosaic.ini* file. You may want to consider making this change because NCSA's site receives a lot of traffic and making a connection can be difficult at times.

In the *mosaic.ini* file, you find a line that begins with the words *Home Page=* followed by the URL for NCSA's home page. You can substitute another URL pointing to a different Web site in place of NCSA's. If you do this, the next time you start Mosaic, it will point to the new home page you have designated.

Surrounding the document window are various controls including push buttons and pull-down menus. As you move from one document to the next, Mosaic

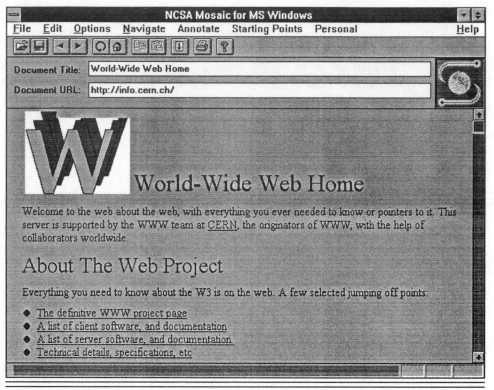

**Figure 9-5:**   The home page for CERN

keeps a history of your moves. You can use the back and forward buttons to move back and forth between previous steps. The Home button moves you directly to your default home page.

The NCSA logo on the upper-right side of the screen is a globe that spins as documents are loading. You can abort a transfer in progress by clicking this logo. You may want to abort the loading process if you find that the file you've linked to is much larger than you expected and/or the loading process is slowing to a halt because of heavy traffic on the Internet.

The Document URL: field shows the URL for the document currently displayed—in this case, CERN's home page, *http://info.cern.ch/*. You move from one document to another by clicking on an anchor. If you have a specific URL to which you want to connect, click on the Open button. This brings up a window in which you type a URL, and then move directly to that document.

### Mosaic Features

Mosaic supports multiple hardware platforms and a special feature called *Hypertext Markup Language* (HTML). HTML is a document format that enables Mosaic to convey more information than the plain text files of text-based browsers like Lynx. HTML provides for features such as inline pictures (pictures embedded into the text), hypertext links to other documents, character formatting (underline, boldface, italic, etc.), and layout formatting (section headings and

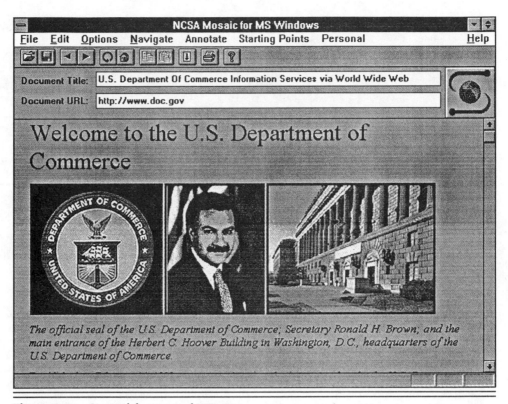

**Figure 9-6:**   Special features of HTML

bulleted lists, etc.). Many of these formatting features are incorporated in the Web document shown in Figure 9-6.

The term *link* refers to a relationship between two entities called *anchors*. Anchor areas are highlighted text—text that has a different color than the text around it, and/or underlined text. An anchor may also be represented by a special symbol. *Links* are references to other documents or objects, such as photographs. These references are made by means of URLs (Uniform Resource Locators).

At one Web site, you'll find a service called the *Virtual Tourist*. Here you are presented with a world map that enables you to link to various resources such as "Virtual Tourist Guides," as shown in Figure 9-7.

If you click on the United States, a more detailed view of the United States appear, as Figure 9-8 shows.

If you then click on the state of Utah, for example, you would be presented with a detailed map of that state. If you choose to delve deeper, you can click on Salt Lake City for detailed information on only that city.

## Running Mosaic

To run Mosaic software, you need a direct link to the Internet or dial-up IP (SLIP or PPP) Internet connection. A SLIP/PPP (Serial Line Internet Protocol/Point to Point Protocol) account turns your computer into a node on the Internet. Your machine is assigned an IP (Internet Protocol) address, and you connect to the Internet by dialing into a service provider's machine.

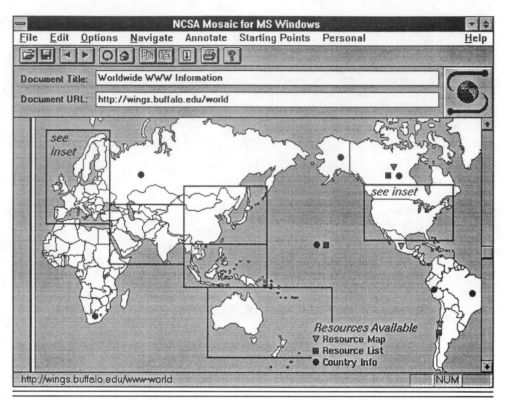

**Figure 9-7:**   The Virtual Tourist

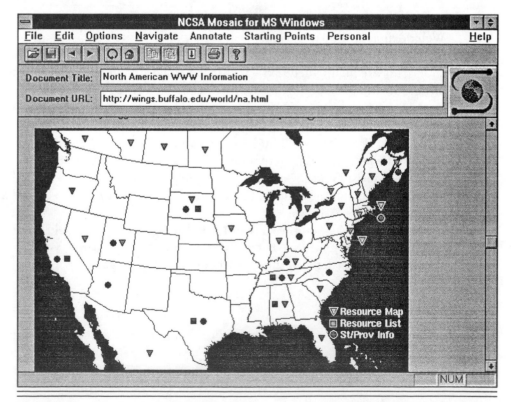

**Figure 9-8:**   Closing in on a destination

To run Mosaic effectively on an IBM compatible PC running Windows 3.1, you need at least an 80386SX-based machine with 4MB of RAM. For best results, use a 33-MHz or faster 80486 with 8MB of RAM.

The most difficult aspect of running Mosaic over a SLIP or PPP connection is establishing the SLIP/PPP connection. If you are accessing the Internet with a stand-alone PC running Windows, you can establish the connection by using a Shareware product called Trumpet Software International Winsock version 1.0, developed by Peter R. Tattam. Trumpet Winsock has an internal SLIP driver and an internal modem dialer. The program also includes a Windows Socket 1.1 compatible TCP/IP stack, which enables your Windows applications to use TCP/IP to communicate with UNIX applications.

Copies of Trumpet Winsock can be found at FTP site *ftp.utas.edu.au* in the */pc/trumpet/winsock* directory as filename *twsk10a.zip* and at FTP site *ftp.ncsa.uicu.edu* in the */PC/Mosaic/sockets* directory as filename *winsock.zip*.

After you have finished installing Trumpet Winsock, run tcpman.exe, select the File pull-down menu and then select Setup. The Network Configuration window shown in Figure 9-9 appears.

Trumpet will need the following information about the SLIP server you are connecting to:

| | |
|---|---|
| IP address | 0.0.0.0 |
| Name server | 0.0.0.0 |
| Time server | 0.0.0.0 |
| Domain Suffix | (The name of your domain) |

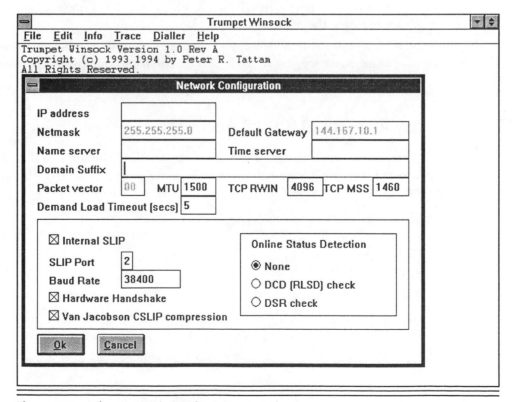

**Figure 9-9:**   The Network Configuration window

This information will be inserted into the Network Configuration Window which is accessed through the File pull down menu. You can get this information from the company that will be providing you with your SLIP service. You will replace the "0.0.0.0" IP addresses shown above with real IP address like 127.35.1.100 and the Domain Suffix field will be filled in with an actual doamin name address such as umdc.edu.

Check Internal SLIP and enter the port number and your modem's baud rate. Save the information by clicking OK, and exit the program. Next, restart the Trumpet Winsock program so that the network setup will take effect. Your system should now be configured properly.

To place the call, select the Dialler (sic) pull-down menu. Here you find several options, but for now you are concerned only with the Manual login command. If you want to create a script file (found under the command Edit Scripts), refer to the Trumpet documentation. After selecting Manual login, enter the following command in the Trumpet window:

```
atdt xxx-xxxx
```

The x's represent the phone number given to you by your service provider.

You can connect to the Internet two ways when running SLIP:

1. Under one method, you are assigned a random IP number each time you log onto the server. After logging on, enter the command **slip**, open the Setup pull-down menu, and enter the new IP number in the IP address field. After entering the new IP number, close the application in order for the number to take effect. Press the ESC key, close Trumpet, and then double click the Mosaic icon.

2. With a static SLIP account, you are assigned an IP number that doesn't change. After logging onto the server, enter the command **slip**, press ESC key, and then double-click the Mosaic icon.

## ≡ Service Providers for SLIP/PPP Accounts

In Chapter 3, you read about companies that provide nationwide SLIP and PPP access to the Internet. Listed below are three more service providers offering nationwide SLIP/PPP services:

Colorado Supernet (*info@csn.org*)
Colorado School of Mines
1500 Illinois Street
Golden, CO 80401

Startup cost is $100.00.

Connection costs:    Monday through Friday:
8 a.m. to 8 p.m.: $3/hour
8 p.m. to midnight: $2/hour

Weekends:
8 a.m. to midnight: $2/hour
midnight to 8 a.m.: $1/hour

Monthly minimum per login is $15/month

Monthly maximum per login is $250/month

800 number surcharge $8/hour. (There is no monthly maximum for 800 users. This is in addition to the above hourly rates.)

JvNCnet (*info@jvnc.net*)
Global Enterprise Services, Inc.
Princeton Corporate Center
3 Independence Way
Princeton, NJ 08540
609-897-7300

Start up cost is $99.00. Connection cost is $29.00/month plus $4.95/hour using the Dialin' Tiger II plan. There is a $6.95/hour surcharge for 800 number access.

ANSRemote (*info@ans.net*)
Advanced Network and Services, Inc.
100 Clearbrook Road
Elmsford, NY 10523
800-456-8267

Start up cost is $25.00. Basic rate is $35.00/month plus $8.50/hour. No surcharge for 800 number access.

## Viewers

Along with Mosaic, you also need to install external applications called *viewers*. These viewer programs enable you to do such things as view GIF and JPEG images and videos, and listen to audio files. The connection Mosaic makes with these external programs is done through statements in the mosaic.ini file. You define viewers in the mosaic.ini file so Mosaic knows which application to call when it comes across a file it can't handle. A selection of viewers and sound players are available in the */PC/Mosaic/viewers* directory at FTP site *ftp.ncsa.uiuc.edu*.

## Mosaic for the Macintosh

NCSA Mosaic for the Macintosh is the client application for Mac users. To run Mac Mosaic, you need at minimum a machine equipped with System 7.0 or later, MacTCP version 2.0.2 or later, and 4MB or more of RAM. You also need a direct connection to an Ethernet line or a dial-up connection using SLIP, PPP, or ARA (Apple Remote Access). For additional information on running Mac Mosaic with a modem, send an email message to *mosaic-mac@ncsa.uiuc.edu*.

You can get the latest version of NCSA Mosaic for the Macintosh from FTP site *ftp.ncsa.uiuc.edu* in the directory */Mac/Mosaic* as filename

*NCSAMosaicMac.103.sit.hqx.* This file is compressed with StuffIt and then Bin-Hexed. Documentation for Mac Mosaic is available from FTP site *ftp.ncsa.uiuc.edu* in the */Mac/Mosaic/Documents* directory.

### The DOS Internet Kit

The DOS Internet Kit is a set of software packages configured for DOS. The kit contains everything you need to set up Mosaic and also includes other useful Internet applications, such as FTP and TELNET for Windows.

To get the DOS Internet Kit, download two files: *disk1.exe* and *disk2.exe* located in the */pub/kit* directory at FTP site *tbone.biol.scarlolina.edu* [129.252.34.45]. Download the *OOREADME.DOC* file for details on how to install the kit software. After you "unpack" *disk1.exe* and *disk2.exe*, refer to the *README.DOC* for further instructions.

### Mosaic Access to FTP Sites

Chapter 4 provided an introduction to FTP and explained how to navigate FTP sites using a command-line interface. By using Mosaic to connect to *URL: http://hoohoo.ncsa.uiuc.edu:80/ftp-interface.html*, you can browse hundreds of FTP archive sites by pointing and clicking. The opening FTP Interface page gives you the option of viewing a monster FTP list or sites broken down into groups with names A to E, F to K, etc. When you click on the line *Sites with names L to O*, the page shown in Figure 9-10 comes up.

From here, you can select a specific FTP site by clicking its name. Mosaic then provides you with a graphic view of the files and directories contained in that site's archives, as shown in Figure 9-11.

### Exploring Commercial Web Sites

CommerceNet is one example of how the Web is being used by commercial enterprises. CommerceNet is an online shopping mall where participating vendors create home pages that function as storefronts. You can visit a company's storefront by clicking on the business's logo located on CommerceNet's home page. If you would like to browse CommerceNet's offerings, you can access the home pages by connecting to *URL: http://www.commerce.net.*

MIT maintains a home page that enables you to connect to several other commercial Web servers. The URL for this home page is *http://tns-www.lcs.mit.edu/commerce.html.*

### Cello

Cello is another WWW browser for Windows that can access several different formats. This browser was developed by Thomas R. Bruce of the Legal Information Institute at Cornell Law School. To learn more about Cello, point your Web client at *http://www.law.cornell.edu/cello/celltop.html.*

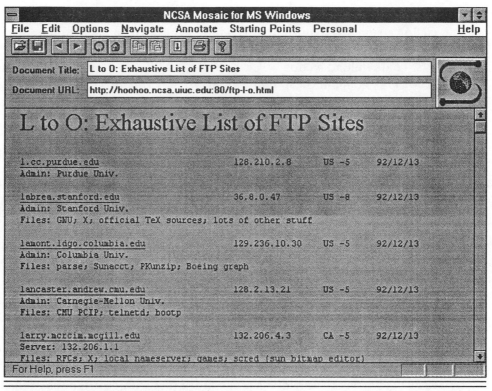

**Figure 9-10:** FTP list of sites L to O

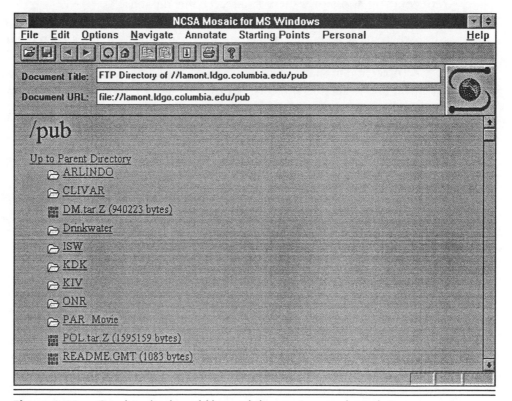

**Figure 9-11:** Graphic display of files and directories at selected site

Cello runs on any IBM-compatible 80386SX or better with 4MB of RAM. Cello version 1.0 requires that you have Winsock-compliant software, such as Peter R. Tattam's Trumpet Winsock.

To download a copy of Cello, FTP to site *ftp.sunet.se* and get the file called *cello.zip* residing in the */pub/www/clients/PC/Cello* directory. This directory also contains viewer software and sound players. Cello software also is available from FTP site *fatty.law.cornell.edu* in the */pub/LII/cello* directory.

Cello's mailing list is *CELLO-L@fatty.law.cornell.edu*.

## ☰ Web Wanderers and ALIWEB

In an attempt to identify all of the information that can be accessed via the World-Wide Web, programs called *Web Wanderers* have been developed. Web Wanderers are automatic programs that start with one Web document and retrieve every document referenced within that document. The Web Wanderer then retrieves every document each succeeding document references and continues this process until the entire Web is indexed. The problem with the Web Wanderer is that it uses a tremendous amount of network resources each time it goes out to create one of these massive databases.

An alternative to the Web Wanderer is ALIWEB (Archie-Like Indexing). ALIWEB is a WWW service that builds and updates a searchable database of indexes to WWW servers. Individuals create index files with descriptions of their services that include keywords, inform ALIWEB that the files exist, and then ALIWEB retieves them and stores them in a searchable database.

ALIWEB retrieves the files automatically on a regular basis so that updated files, when made available, replace older versions, which helps keep the database up-to-date.

At present, emphasis is being placed on building a database of index files on technical and academic subjects, but the range of topics is growing. For additional information on ALIWEB, point your Web client to *http://web.nexor.co.uk/aliweb/doc/aliweb.html*.

## ☰ For Further Study

For ongoing discussions relating to WWW, consult the USENET newsgroup *comp.infosystems.www* or join the mailing list *www-announce@info.cern.ch* by sending the command **subscribe www-announce <your name>** to *listserv@info.cern.ch*.

Manuals explaining World-Wide Web are available via anonymous FTP from *info.cern.ch*. Once logged in, proceed to the */pub/www/doc* directory for a listing of files. Keep in mind that the files are not as up-to-date as online documents.

Neil Larson has written a program called HYPERREZ, a memory-resident shareware hypertext program. If you'd like to experiment with creating your own hypertext document, FTP to site *hydra.uwo.ca*, change to the */libsoft* directory and download a copy of the file called *hyperrez.exe*. Remember to type **binary** at the *FTP>* prompt and then press ENTER before entering the command **get hyper-rez.exe.** Remember also that when you download it from your dial-up host to your personal computer, you must tell your file transfer program that you're transferring a binary file.

HYPERREZ.EXE is a self-extracting archive, so once you've downloaded it to your personal computer, place it in its own directory and enter the command **hyperrez** to unarchive the file. For an introduction, read the READ.ME file first. To install the program, type **hr** at your prompt and press ENTER. *Note*: This program is not an HTML (HyperText Markup Language) editor for creating WWW documents.

For additional help with understanding URLs (Uniform Resource Locators), use a Web client to access *URL: http://WWW.cc.ukans.edu/lynx_help/URL_guide.html*. This will link you with a seven-page guide called *A Beginner's guide to URLS.*

As an alternative to establishing a SLIP connection and running Mosaic, NETCOM On-Line Communications Services offers a special service for connecting individual computer workstations to the Internet by using their proprietary software called NetCruiser. With NetCruiser, you can browse the Web and perform other operations like FTP, TELNET, and email.

NetCruiser runs under Microsoft Windows 3.1 and MS-DOS 5.0 or higher. The software itself is free, but NETCOM charges $25.00 to set up the account. The monthly fee is $19.95/month for up to 40 hours prime time (9:00 a.m. - midnight), unlimited use on weekends, and anytime between midnight and 9:00 a.m. on weekdays. There's a $2.00/hour surcharge when you run over the 40 hours. Depending on whether you call them locally, there may be a long distance phone charge. For additional information, contact

NetCom On-Line Communication Services (info@netcom.com)
4000 Moorpark Avenue
Suite 200
San Jose, CA 95117
800-501-8649

Several companies are now making Mosaic available commercially. Their interest is in enhancing the NCSA version by providing such things as technical support, advanced features and complete documentation. One of these services is provided by Wentworth Worldwide Media, 1866 Colonial Village Lane, Box 10488, Lancaster, PA 17605-0488. Telephone: 800-638-1639. FAX: 717-393-5752.

Email: *orders@wentworth.com*. Wentworth offers a Mosaic Starter Kit for Microsoft Windows and Macintosh which includes Mosaic, TCP/IP, viewer programs, help files, resources, and reference materials. The whole package sells for around $30.00.

The Frequently Asked Questions list for WWW is maintained by Nathan Torkington. You can obtain a copy of this FAQ by FTPing to site *rtfm.mit.edu* and downloading the *www-faq* file located in the */pub/usenet/news.answers* directory. You also can view the file in hypertext by pointing your Web client to *http://www.vuw.ac.nz:80/non-local/gnat/www-faq.html*.

# Chapter 10

# Archie

*Archie* is the name given to an Internet database service that consists of a collection of approximately 21 computers distributed around the world called *Archie servers*. Each Archie server, independently of the others, collects data and stores it for future use. The data it collects is retrieved from anonymous FTP sites. Each Archie server stays in contact with about 1,000 anonymous FTP archive sites and maintains an up-to-date composite index of their holdings. Archie servers do not collect and store the actual files themselves; instead, they index only the directory names and filenames.

Finding a file on the Internet by simply browsing through the directories of hundreds of FTP sites is physically impossible. Herein lies the purpose for learning how to use Archie: Archie servers provide a search mechanism for locating files. Anyone who has access to the Internet can search the indexes. Search results tell you which FTP server stores a particular file or directory and what the pathname is for locating it. Although each Archie server is a separate entity, they all perform the same service and even index close to the same FTP sites.

The following example illustrates how Archie can be an effective resource discovery tool in your library. A patron has just requested a copy of Kehoe's *Zen and the Art of the Internet* and a copy of some software called PKUNZIP. You're confident the files are located on the Internet, but you're not sure where. Because Archie is a directory of text and software resources, Archie is the service you go to for your answer.

You begin by initiating a TELNET session and connecting to one of the Archie servers closest to you. After you log on and the Archie prompt appears, you begin your search using special Archie commands. In less than a minute, your search results scroll across the screen, providing FTP site addresses and pathnames where copies of the files can be found.

You record the information and immediately initiate an FTP session to retrieve the desired files. You give the patron the option of downloading the files to a floppy disk, or, in the case of textual information, printing it out while he or she waits.

This illustrates how Archie can serve a practical purpose by helping patrons locate certain materials on the Internet. The search results Archie provides give you enough information that you can retrieve the necessary files at point of need.

## ☰ How Archie Works

Archie consists of two software tools originally developed by Alan Emtage, Bill Heelan, and Peter Deutsch at the School of Computer Science, McGill University, Montreal, Canada. Archie is now maintained by Bunyip Information Systems (*info@bunyip.com*).

One software tool keeps track of Internet FTP archive sites in a central server and is updated about once a month. Every night, the system executes an anonymous FTP connection to several of the archive sites scattered across the Internet. Archie downloads the directories at each site and then stores them in a searchable database. About one-thirtieth of the total number of sites is done each night so the directories of each site and eventually the entire system are updated once a month.

The other tool is the Archie program itself, and this is the program you will be using. This program allows you to login to an Archie server and query two different databases. One database retrieves directory names and filenames while the other, called *whatis*, retrieves descriptions along with the filenames. You can search these databases for character strings and the system will search all of its filenames and directory names for entries with that string.

## ☰ Accessing and Searching Archie

You can search Archie three ways: on your host computer running an Archie client; interactively using TELNET; and through email. (Using the Internet mail system to contact Archie is discussed in Chapter 11.)

Archie sites are quite popular and during busy times you might see a message that tells you to try back later because all of the lines are full. When this happens, you have three options:

1. Try using a command-line client program if one is available on your host;
2. Use TELNET to access another site on the list; or
3. Submit your request by email (described in Chapter 11). The following search exercises will demonstrate how Archie works.

### TELNET Access

If the host computer you connect to supports TELNET, the remote login program, you can TELNET directly to an Archie server. Before you start your session, it would be wise to open a capture file or log file ( a file in which the text the text that's displayed on your screen is saved) because Archie's output scrolls across the screen quite fast. If your communications software has a scrollback buffer, you can use this instead to pause the display, and then go back and view previously received data.

### Login Procedure

Login to your local host as usual and at the system prompt, enter **telnet <server address>**, where **<server address>** is one of the Archie server addresses listed
later in the chapter, such as *archie.ans.net*. You should see the following response:

```
$ telnet archie.ans.net
Trying... Connected to FORUM.ANS.NET.

AIX telnet (forum.ans.net)

IBM AIX Version 3 for RISC System/6000
(C) Copyrights by IBM and by others 1982, 1991.
login:
```

At the *Login:* prompt, type **archie**, and press ENTER. The system returns with a response similar to this:

```
# Bunyip Information Systems, 1993
# 'erase' character is '^?'.
# 'search' (type string) has the value 'exact'.
archie>
```

When logging into some systems, you may be asked for a password. In these situations, enter your email address and that should give you access to the database. The Archie prompt generally looks like *archie>*, or it may be some variation including part of the host's domain name.

### Finding Help

To retrieve a listing of the specific help topics, enter a question mark (?) at the *help>* prompt. If you enter the command **help** at the *archie>* prompt, you will see a screen that looks something like this one:

```
archie> help

These are the commands you can use in help:

. drop down one level in the hierarchy

? display a list of valid subtopics at the current level

done, ^D, ^C quit from help entirely

<string> help on a topic or subtopic
```

```
help>?

# Subtopics:
#
# about
# autologout
# bugs
# bye
# done
# email
# exit
# find
# general
# help
# list
# mail
# motd
# nopager
# pager
# prog
# quit
# regex
# servers
# set
# show
# site
# term
# unset
# version
# whatis
# whats_new
```

The help topics listed differ somewhat from one archie server to the next. To explore any one of the help topics online, type the topic name at the help> prompt and press ENTER. To return to the Archie> prompt, press the ENTER key without entering any commands at the prompt.

### Locating Servers

When you are back at the *archie>* prompt, enter the command **servers,** and the program displays a list of available servers worldwide. Here is what you should see:

```
$ telnet archie.ans.net
Trying... Connected to FORUM.ANS.NET.

AIX telnet (forum.ans.net)

IBM AIX Version 3 for RISC System/6000
(C) Copyrights by IBM and by others 1982, 1991.

login: archie

# Bunyip Information Systems, 1993

# Terminal type 'vt220' is unknown to this system.
```

```
# 'erase' character is '^?'.
# 'search' (type string) has the value 'exact'.
archie> servers
-----------------< List of active archie servers >---------------

 archie.au* 139.130.4.6 Australia
 archie.edvz.uni-linz.ac.at* 140.78.3.8 Austria
 archie.univie.ac.at* 131.130.1.23 Austria
 archie.uqam.ca* 132.208.250.10 Canada
 archie.funet.fi 128.214.6.100 Finland
 archie.th-darmstadt.de* 130.83.22.60 Germany
 archie.ac.il* 132.65.6.15 Israel
 archie.unipi.it* 131.114.21.10 Italy
 archie.wide.ad.jp 133.4.3.6 Japan
 archie.kr* 128.134.1.1 Korea
 archie.sogang.ac.kr* 163.239.1.11 Korea
 archie.rediris.es* 130.206.1.2 Spain
 archie.luth.se* 130.240.18.4 Sweden
 archie.switch.ch* 130.59.1.40 Switzerland
 archie.ncu.edu.tw* 140.115.19.24 Taiwan
 archie.doc.ic.ac.uk* 146.169.11.3 United Kingdom
 archie.unl.edu 129.93.1.14 USA (NE)
 archie.internic.net* 198.48.45.10 USA (NJ)
 archie.rutgers.edu* 128.6.18.15 USA (NJ)
 archie.ans.net* 147.225.1.10 USA (NY)
 archie.sura.net* 128.167.254.179 USA (MD)

Sites marked with an asterisk '*' run archie version 3.0
```

### Search Commands

You use the **prog** command to search the Archie database for a specified pattern. **Prog** is short for *program* and it tells Archie to run its search program. You can use the command **find** in place of **prog**. At the *archie>* prompt, enter the command **prog** or **find**, followed by a space and the character string you are searching. Capture the results of your search to a disk or make notes on paper to use later for retrieving the desired files via FTP.

## Exercise 1

### Using the prog Command

To practice using the **prog** command, login to an Archie server and try locating a file called *archie_guide.txt*. This is a text file by Richard Hintz called "What is an Archie?". Begin by TELNETing to an Archie server and entering **archie** at the *login:* prompt. Your session will look like this:

```
$ telnet archie.ans.net

Trying... Connected to FORUM.ANS.NET.

AIX telnet (forum.ans.net)
IBM AIX Version 3 for RISC System/6000
(C) Copyrights by IBM and by others 1982, 1991.
```

```
login: archie

# Bunyip Information Systems, 1993

# Terminal type 'vt220' is unknown to this system.
# 'erase' character is '^?'.
# 'search' (type string) has the value 'exact'.
archie>
```

At the *archie>* prompt, enter the command **prog archie_guide.txt**. The database then searches all the FTP sites it tracks for any files or directories called *archie_guide.txt*. In the following output, Archie has found two files with this exact name located at FTP site *sunsite.unc.edu*. The first file listed is located in the directory ***/pub/academic/library/libsoft***.

```
archie> prog archie_guide.txt
# Search type: exact.
# Your queue position: 1
working... /

Host sunsite.unc.edu (152.2.22.81)
Last updated 11:13 22 Dec 1993

 Location: /pub/academic/library/libsoft
 FILE -rw-r--r-- 3091 bytes 00:00 5 Oct 1992 archie_guide.txt

 Location: /pub/docs/about-the-net/libsoft
 FILE -rw-r--r-- 3091 bytes 00:00 8 Sep 1992 archie_guide.txt

archie> quit
# Bye.

Connection closed
```

### Setting Variables

Archie has several variables you can use to modify how searches are performed or to ensure that certain operations take place automatically. Set these variables before you conduct a search.

To control the volume of output a search produces, use the **set maxhits<number>** command, where **<number>** is the maximum number of hits you want Archie to return. For example, if you know you're searching for a piece of software that's probably stored at the majority of FTP sites, it would be wise to use a command something like this before conducting your search:

```
archie> set maxhits 10
```

The results of a **prog** search would then stop after 10 matches are found.

The **set pager** command causes output to be displayed one page at a time. The **unset pager** allows the output to scroll across the screen.

The **set mailto <email address>** command is useful if you want to mail the search results to yourself or others. For example, **set mailto user1@ua1vm.ua.edu** sends the output to user1. The command **set mailto user1@ua1vm.ua.edu,user2@foxhole.com** sends the output to both user1 and user2 at their specified addresses. When mailing to multiple addresses, separate the addresses with commas, but don't use spaces anywhere. After you have set the **mail** variable, conduct your Archie search. When you retrieve results that you'd like to send to your email address, type **mail**. Archie automatically sends the output from the last command you entered. If you didn't set the **mailto** variable prior to your search, you can send the output to yourself by typing the command **mail** followed by your email address and pressing ENTER.

The **sortby** variable organizes the output in various ways. For example, **set sortby time** displays the results of a search in order from newest to oldest; **set sortby filename** organizes the output alphabetically by filename.

The **set search exact** command determines the way Archie searches for matches in its database. For example, when you know exactly what you want, enter the **set search exact** command telling Archie to look for names that are an exact match, including upper- and lowercase. If you ask Archie to search for a file named *Ami-HyTelnet*, it would match *Ami-HyTelnet* but not *ami-hytelnet* or *AMI-HyTelnet*. Notice that in the earlier example of using the **prog** command, an exact pattern search is the default setting when using TELNET to access Archie.

To search for a substring, use the **set search sub** command. This matches any name that contains the substring you specify, upper- or lowercase. For example, if you searched the substring *reference*, Archie matches *REFERENCE*, *reference.txt*, *VMS-reference.zip*, and *test.scr.Reference*. To make this same search case-sensitive, use the command **set search subcase**. Now the name *reference* would match *reference.txt*, but not *test.scr.Reference*.

### Regular Expressions

The regular expression (*regex*) setting is the most complicated mode of searching. Regular expressions are used by UNIX programs to search for a sequence of characters. Regular expressions are similar in purpose to truncation, something many librarians may already be familiar with in searching commercial and other databases. Truncation permits variations in spelling or word length when searching for single words.

After you enter the command **set search regex** at the *archie>* prompt, you can use the following special characters to achieve specific results.

The .. (two dots) are a regular expression that allows the character replaced by the . (dot) to vary. The command **find b..p** would match *bumb*, *burp*, and *blip*—but not *bop* or *bops*.

The $ (dollar sign) is used to find a filename by matching the ending. The command **find $mit** will match *kermit* and *summit*, but not *kermit311.zip*.

The ^ (caret) is used to specify the beginning of a word. The command **find ^kerm** will match anything that begins with kerm—for example, *kerm311.zip*—but it will not find *imbkerm.zip*.

The [ ] (square brackets) are used to find only certain single characters at a certain point in the text. The command **find sl[o a i]p** will match *slop*, *slap*, and *slip* but not *slep* or *slup*. If you used [a-zA-Z], you could match any upper- or lowercase character a through z. The command **find ^pkz11[0-9]** would match *pkz110.exe* and *pkz112.exe*.

*Default Settings*

When you first login to an Archie server, you can see what the default settings are for these and other variables by entering the command **show**. What appears will look something like this:

```
archie> show
# 'autologout' (type numeric) has the value '60'.
# 'collections' (type string) is not set.
# 'compress' (type string) has the value 'none'.
# 'encode' (type string) has the value 'none'.
# 'language' (type string) has the value 'english'.
# 'mailto' (type string) is not set.
# 'match_domain' (type string) is not set.
# 'match_path' (type string) is not set.
# 'max_split_size' (type numeric) has the value '51200'.
# 'maxhits' (type numeric) has the value '50'.
# 'maxhitspm' (type numeric) has the value '100'.
# 'maxmatch' (type numeric) has the value '100'.
# 'output_format' (type string) has the value 'verbose'.
# 'pager' (type boolean) is not set.
# 'search' (type string) has the value 'exact'.
# 'server' (type string) has the value 'localhost'.
# 'sortby' (type string) has the value 'none'.
# 'status' (type boolean) is set.
# 'term' (type string) has the value 'dumb 24 80'.
```

Consult the online help system provided by Archie for any variables that need further explaining.

*Using Archie to Locate FTP Sites*

The **list** command without an argument prints the site names and IP addresses of all FTP sites that Archie knows about. The **list** command also allows you to enter a regular expression as an argument. Some sites return the following response when you enter the **list** command:

```
archie> list
# Sorry, this command has been disabled by the administrator.
```

When this happens, try connecting to another Archie server and issuing the list command.

## Using the "Whatis" Database

Archie supports a software description database, commonly referred to as the *whatis* database. This database contains short descriptions of thousands of programs and related files. You can search this database by typing the command **whatis** at the *archie>* prompt, followed by a space and then any substring you want. No distinction is made between upper- and lowercase letters. When you press ENTER, Archie searches the database and finds lines that contain that substring. The format of the output is the name of a program, software package, or document, followed by a short description.

The following output resulted after I entered the command **whatis sound**:

```
archie> whatis sound
sound2sun Mac to SS1 sound file converter
soundex Various PD programs generating identical tokens for li
ke-sounding names
soundex-spell Spelling corrector using soundex
soundmail Sound mail
sp Soundex spelling-checker
sst SPARCstation Sound Tools
```

If you want to find the location of one of the filenames displayed in your search—for example, *soundmail*—enter the command **find soundmail**.

The contents of a whatis database are somewhat limited. Filenames and descriptions are presented for entry by the Archie administrators or by anyone else who makes a file available on an FTP server and also sends a description of that file to the administrators at Archie.

## ≡ Using an Archie Client

If your host supports an Archie client, logon to your host account and enter the word **archie** at the system prompt. (If your host doesn't support an Archie client, see the "TELNET Session," section, earlier in this chapter.) The response will look something like this:

```
$ archie
Usage: $2$dia0:[sys0.syscommon.][ualr_lib]archie.exe;2 [-[cers][l][t][m#][h host
]["L"]["N"#]] string
 -c : case sensitive substring search
 -e : exact string match (default)
 -r : regular expression search
 -s : case insensitive substring search
 -l : list one match per line
 -t : sort inverted by date
 -m# : specifies maximum number of hits to return (default 98)
 -h host : specifies server host
 -"L" : list known servers and current default
 -"N"# : specifies query niceness level (0-35765)
```

Client programs are the best way to access an Archie database because it takes less time away from the server than a continuous TELNET session. The client links with Archie only when it has information to send or receive. Some Archie clients are menu driven, and others offer a command line interface. If you need assistance in using a particular client, try entering the word **help** at the Archie client prompt.

When you use an Archie client on a UNIX system, you search the Archie database right from your system prompt. The basic format you follow is an expression beginning with the command **archie**, followed by the name of the file or directory you want to look for. For example, the expression **archie pkzip** finds all files and directories called *pkzip* in Archie's database. Archie will print any matches it finds.

**Table 10-1:**   Archie command switches

| Switch | Description |
| --- | --- |
| -c | Searches for substrings (case sensitive); that is, itfiles and directories with the specified string anywhere in their name. |
| -e | Searches for an exact match (this is the default setting). Example: $ **archie -e explorer.zip** will search for files with the exact name *explorer.zip*. |
| -s | Same as -c, but ignores upper- and lowercase letters in the search. |
| -e -s | Allows you to perform a combination search. Archie starts with an *exact* search and if no result is found, Archie widens the search to include a *substring* search. |
| -r | The string that follows this option is treated as a regular expression. |
| -l | Changes how the output is displayed. Rather than the file or directory information being listed on multiple lines, Archie lists the information on a single line, such as<br><br>```19930811060000Z 71 sunsite.unc.edu /pub/academic/library/.cap/libsoft```<br>```19930314000000Z 3584 sunsite.unc.edu /pub/academic/library/libsoft/```<br>```19930305000000Z 3584 sunsite.unc.edu /pub/docs/about-the-net/libsoft/``` |
| -t | Sorts the search results by time and date with the most recent files listed first. This is a useful switch when you're looking for the most recent version of a piece of software. |
| -s -t | Allows you to search for all files with a specified string contained anywhere within them, upper- or lowercase.The output is presented with the newest files shown first. Example: $**archie -s -t internet.libary** |
| -L | Displays a list of Archie server sites. |
| -m# | Sets the maximum number of hits to retrieve. An example of its use would be:<br><br>$ **archie -m2 news.answers**<br><br>This limits the output of the search to two matches. |

You can modify the Archie command by using characters with special meanings called *options* or *switches*. Switches are always given after the **archie** command and before the search string. In the previous example (**archie pkzip**), Archie will find only files and directories that match that exact string. To widen the search to include files and directories that have the string *pkzip* anywhere in their names, follow the command name **archie** with the switch -s, like this: **archie -s pkzip**. The -s switch is a good tool to use if you approach Archie with a subject query rather than a specific filename.

The main switches available are listed in Table 10-1.

## Search Strategies

Although some search strategies take you right to a relevant source, others will not due to the limited scope of the database. Other times, you discover relevant resources quite by accident. Just as you go to the stacks in your library seeking information on a particular topic and find nothing, but then through serendipitous discovery, stumble upon something in the process that is useful in answering an entirely different query, so it is with the Internet.

The following search was done in response to an actual patron query.

The Question: A patron presented a request for an outline of events relating to the Civil War—something in the form of a timeline.

The Search: Using an Archie client to conduct the search, I first entered **archie civilwar** at the system prompt and the search yielded nothing. My reasoning was that there might be a filename with the words *civil* and *war* written in that format.

I refined the search by separating the words and entered the command **archie civil_war**, Archie found the following match:

```
$ archie civil_war

Host cse.unl.edu

 Location: /pub/brady/mosaic
 FILE -rw-r--r-- 2305 May 6 1993 civil_war
```

The filename *civil_war* didn't tell me anything specific about the file's content, so I connected to host *cse.unl.edu* and downloaded the file. The session is shown here:

```
$ ftp cse.unl.edu
athena.ualr.edu MultiNet FTP user process 3.2(106)
Connection opened (Assuming 10-bit connections)
<
< University of Nebraska - Lincoln
< Department of Computer Science and Engineering
< Unauthorized Access to This System or Network is Prohibited
<
<cse.unl.edu FTP server ready.
CSE.UNL.EDU>user anonymous
<Guest login ok, type your name as password.
Password:
<Guest login ok, access restrictions apply.
CSE.UNL.EDU>cd /pub/brady/mosaic
<CWD command successful.
CSE.UNL.EDU>get civil_war
 To local file:
<Opening ASCII mode data connection for 'civil_war' (2305 bytes).
<Transfer complete.
CSE.UNL.EDU>quit
<Goodbye.
```

While the file was still on the local host, I used the **type** command to view the file to determine its relevancy before downloading it to my personal computer:

```
$ type civil_war.
<TITLE>Matthew Brady Pictures Demo</TITLE>
<H1>Matthew Brady Pictures Demo</H1>

These pictures and text come from a CD_ROM for the American Memory Project.
Not all pictures and text are here. This is to demonstrate the features of Mosaic.
<P>
```

"Looks interesting," I thought, but I saw nothing relevant to a Civil War timeline. In the next search, I used the concept *timeline* and entered the following command:

```
$archie timeline
```

This search looked for an exact match and generated the following results:

```
$ archie timeline

Host ftp.cis.ksu.edu

  Location: /pub/Startrek/stories
  DIRECTORY drwxr-xr-x 512 Oct 12 15:36 timeline

Host stsci.edu

  Location: /listserver-archives
  DIRECTORY drwxr-xr-x 512 Nov 6 00:210 timeline
  Location: /observer/weekly_timeline/auto
  FILE -rw-rw-r-- 125155 Nov 4 15:19 timeline
```

At a glance, the two subjects that stood out were "Startrek" and "auto," so I decided to widen the search by adding the -s switch to the same command line. This search produced the following results (only the first two screens of output are presented here):

```
$ archie -s timeline

Host cs.columbia.edu

  Location: /archives/mirror2/israel/jewish-info
  FILE -rw-rw-r-- 74610 Dec 2 1992 timeline.tanach.gz
  Location: /archives/mirror2/world-info/obi/Star.Trek.Stories
  FILE -rw-rw-r-- 21054 Jun 10 1992 timeline.st.universe.gz

Host cse.unl.edu

  Location: /pub/brady/alphabetic
  FILE -r--r--r-- 35291 May 6 1993 timeline.txt
  Location: /pub/brady/mosaic
  FILE -rw-r--r-- 31666 May 6 1993 timeline.txt
  Location: /pub/brady/txt/.cap
  FILE -rw-r--r-- 56 May 6 1993 timeline.txt
  Location: /pub/brady/txt
  FILE -r--r--r-- 35291 May 6 1993 timeline.txt

Host ftp.bio.indiana.edu

  Location: /util/wais/wais-sources
  FILE -rw-r--r-- 3716 Mar 31 1993 hst-weekly-timeline.src

Host ftp.cis.ksu.edu

  Location: /pub/Startrek/stories
  DIRECTORY drwxr-xr-x 512 Oct 12 15:36 timeline
  Location: /pub/mirrors/Doctor_Who/matrix
```

```
         FILE -r--r--r-- 9919 May 19 1993 timeline.Z

Host ftp.iro.umontreal.ca

 Location: /pub/vision/softs/MAEstro/Documentation/UserGuide
 FILE -rw-r--r-- 473747 Nov 24 00:02 Ch7-TimeLine.ps.Z

Host ftp.isi.edu

 Location: /choy/wais/wais-sources
 FILE -rw-r--r-- 3716 Mar 31 1993 hst-weekly-timeline.src

Host ftp.uu.net

 Location: /doc/literary/obi/Star.Trek.Stories
 FILE -rw-rw-r-- 26034 Jun 10 1992 timeline.st.universe.Z

Host ftp.uwp.edu

 Location: /pub/music/classical
 FILE -rw-rw-r-- 3100510 Oct 6 1992 Timeline.ps

Host ftp.wustl.edu

 Location: /graphics/graphics/packages/MAEstro/UserGuide
 FILE -rw-rw-r-- 473747 Jan 11 1992 Ch7-TimeLine.ps.Z
```

Glancing through the output, I decided to limit my search again to textual documents by going back to an exact search for the string *timeline.txt*. This way, I would avoid retrieving all of the compressed files, Postscript files, and source code. That search generated the following results:

```
$ archie timeline.txt

Host cse.unl.edu

 Location: /pub/brady/alphabetic
 FILE -r--r--r-- 35291 May 6 1993 timeline.txt
 Location: /pub/brady/mosaic
 FILE -rw-r--r-- 31666 May 6 1993 timeline.txt
 Location: /pub/brady/txt/.cap
 FILE -rw-r--r-- 56 May 6 1993 timeline.txt
 Location: /pub/brady/txt
 FILE -r--r--r-- 35291 May 6 1993 timeline.txt

Host sunsite.unc.edu

 Location: /pub/academic/history/marshall/general
 FILE -r--r--r-- 49555 Jul 10 04:05 timeline.txt
```

The search found all occurrences of the string *timeline.txt* located in the Archie database, and as you can see, each entry offers basic information for locating particular files. The only way I could determine the exact content of any of these files was to go to the FTP sites and download them. Still focusing on textual sources, I chose to login to *cse.unl.edu* and go to the */pub/brady/txt* directory. The details of this FTP session are shown here:

```
$ ftp cse.unl.edu
athena.ualr.edu MultiNet FTP user process 3.2(106)
Connection opened (Assuming 10-bit connections)
<
< University of Nebraska - Lincoln
< Department of Computer Science and Engineering
< Unauthorized Access to This System or Network is Prohibited
<
<cse.unl.edu FTP server ready.
CSE.UNL.EDU>user anonymous
<Guest login ok, type your name as password.
Password:

<Guest login ok, access restrictions apply.

CSE.UNL.EDU>cd /pub/brady/txt
<CWD command successful.
CSE.UNL.EDU>dir
<Opening ASCII mode data connection for '/bin/ls'.
total 123
drwxr-xr-x 2 122 115 512 May 7 1993 .cap
-rw-r--r-- 1 122 115 165 May 7 1993 README
-r--r--r-- 1 122 115 11741 May 7 1993 biblio.txt
-r--r--r-- 1 122 115 3203 May 7 1993 brady.txt
-r--r--r-- 1 122 115 2124 May 7 1993 ednote.txt
-r--r--r-- 1 122 115 10103 May 7 1993 harvdeth.txt
-r--r--r-- 1 122 115 734 May 7 1993 method.txt
-r--r--r-- 1 122 115 743 May 7 1993 overview.txt
-r--r--r-- 1 122 115 692 May 7 1993 photog.txt
-r--r--r-- 1 122 115 35291 May 7 1993 timeline.txt
-r--r--r-- 1 122 115 4332 May 7 1993 what.txt
```

When I arrived at the *txt* directory and entered a **dir** command, I still didn't have a clue as to whether I had found a relevant resource. I downloaded a copy of the file *README* and read the file while it was still on my local host computer. I then discovered that I had located a directory with information relating to a man named Mathew B. Brady, a Civil War photographer. Making a connection between Civil War and the file called *timeline.txt*, I again initiated an FTP session and downloaded the file called *timeline.txt* and was delighted to find that it was a timeline of the Civil War, drawn largely from the *Encyclopedia of American History* by Richard B. Morris.

## Using the Archie Services via Gopher

You also can connect with an Archie server by way of Gopher. Rather than using cryptic Archie client commands to search an Archie database, Gopher provides you with simple menu choices that lead you to your resources. A Gopher server that allows you to do this is said to have an *Archie gateway*. An example of one of these gateways is on the Gopher server at the University of Minnesota, *gopher.tc.umn.edu.*

To connect with this server, enter **gopher gopher.tc.umn.edu** at your system prompt. Once the root menu appears, look for an item that says *Internet Filer Server (FTP) Sites* or something similar and select it.

```
 1. Information About Gopher/
 2. Computer Information/
 3. Discussion Groups/
 4. Fun & Games/
--> 5. Internet file server (ftp) sites/
 6. Libraries/
 7. News/
10. Other Gopher and Information Servers/
 9. Phone Books/
10. Search Gopher Titles at the University of Minnesota <?>
11. Search lots of places at the University of Minnesota <?>
12. University of Minnesota Campus Information/
```

After you choose the item, a submenu like the following one appears.

```
 1. Read Me First.
 2. Boombox - Home of Gopher and POPmail/
 3. Case Western Reserve University FREENET/
 4. Indiana University Mac Gopher Client App (beta)/
 5. Indiana Windows Archive/
 6. Interest Group Lists/
 7. Internet Resource Guide (tar.Z files)/
 8. Latest Disinfectant (ftp.acns.nwu.edu)/
 9. Lyrics/
10. NCSA - Home of NCSA Telnet/
11. National Science Foundation Gopher (STIS)/
12. Newton Archives at Johns Hopkins University (bnnrc-srv.med.jhu.edu../
13. OCF Document Archives/
14. OSS-IS Info Archives (slow)/
15. SUMEX-AIM Archives - (Includes Info-Mac: a large collection of Mac../
16. Scholarly Communications Project of Virginia Tech/
17. Software Archives at MERIT (University of Michigan)/
11. Sonata NeXT software archive (sonata.cc.purdue.edu)/
19. Supreme Court Rulings (CWRU)/
20. UIUC-CSO - Home of the qi server (CSO phonebook software)/
21. University of Utah Mac Gopher Client App (beta)/
22. Usenet University/
23. Washington University Archive (wuarchive)/
```

The items listed in this directory are gatewayed to the Archie server at *archie.sura.net*. Much of the data accessible from this menu is text, but you'll also run into a number of binary files. If you try to retrieve one of these binary files, Gopher will refuse your request. This is one of the disadvantages of using a Gopher FTP gateway.

## ≡ For Further Study

Explore the Widener University FTP Archive for Archie client software: *ftp.cs.widener.edu* in the directory */pub/archie*. A description of the file list located in this directory looks like this:

```
archie-1.4.1.tar.Z - a command-line client
archie-dos.zip - a CUTCP Archie client for DOS
archie-NeXT.tar.Z - a version of Archie for the NeXT
archie-perl-3.tar.Z - a client written in Perl
```

```
archie-vms.com - Archie 1.3.1 for VMS, in a DCL .com file
archie.el - archie under Emacs; uses ange-ftp
log_archie-p11.tar.Z - log an interactive session with an Archie
server
one-liner.sh - a shell script client
xarchie-1.3.tar.Z - a client for running under Xwindows
```

For additional information similar to that provided by the *whatis* database, refer to the USENET newsgroups *comp.sources.\** and *alt.sources.*

The Archie Group's names and email addresses are:

| | |
|---|---|
| Bill Heelan | *wheelan@cc.mcgill.ea* |
| Peter Deutsch | *peterd@cc.mcgill.ca* |
| Alan Emtage | *bajan@cc.mcgill.ca* |

At some time, you may come across the term *Prospero* when working with Archie clients. In this instance, the Archie client is using the Prospero protocol to search for information. The client is using it to implement a relationship between itself and the server. Prospero, developed by Cliff Neuman, is a tool used for organizing files located on various remote computers as though they were all on your own local computer. For more information, FTP to *prospero.isi.edu* and go to the */pub/prospero* directory.

# Chapter 11

# Resource Discovery with Electronic Mail

This chapter discusses search and retrieval operations you can perform using the Internet mail system. To make this process possible, you connect to computers that function as mail servers—machines that respond to requests they receive via electronic mail. Some of the methods used in performing these searches may seem cumbersome when compared to TELNET and FTP processes, but the system works acceptably well if you don't need your answers in a hurry.

One convenience electronic mail offers is that you can send multiple searches in the same mail message and then continue with other work while you wait for the results to be sent to your mailbox. Also, those organizations with limited budgets will find that service providers offering mail-only connections, like AT&T Mail and MCI Mail, furnish a unique opportunity to connect to the Internet at a very minimal cost. Connect charges and subscription fees are usually less expensive for email-only services than those charged by service providers offering full Internet access.

Even with mail-only access to the Internet, libraries can expand their information resources considerably. CancerNet, a database containing up-to-date information on cancer, is a very valuable resource and its file contents can be searched and downloaded via electronic mail.

## ≡ Archie Mail

Using an Archie client to send requests to an Archie server is the best way to use the Archie service. If you don't have access to a client and you can't TELNET to an Archie server, the next best alternative is to access an Archie server through the Internet mail system.

To use the Archie mail service, send your request via email to one of the TEL-NET Archie server addresses listed in Chapter 10. To access these servers via email, add the word **archie** and an '@' in front of the TELNET address. For example, the email address of the Archie server at *archie.ans.net* becomes *archie@archie.ans.net* when accessed via email.

Leave the subject line of your email message blank and enter the necessary commands in the body of the message. You can use the same commands that were presented in Chapter 10 when accessing Archie via TELNET. No limit is set for the number of commands you can send in a single message, but you can have no more than one command per line. Most of the standard Archie commands can be used in an email request except those that make sense only in an interactive session like **set pager** and **unset pager**.

## Example 1

### *An Email Message that Contains Commands for Retrieving a Help File*

```
MAIL>send
TO: archie@archie.ans.net
Subj:
set mailto acbenson@ualvm.ua.edu
help
quit
```

In the first line of this email message, **set mailto <requester's email address>** ensures that the server's response will be sent to the right address. The last command should always be **quit** because this tells Archie that any text beyond this line is not to be considered part of the command statement. This is important when the sender has a signature automatically added to the end of his/her mail messages. (A signature is text, sometimes nothing more than a user's email address and name. Other times, the signature includes quotes and/or decorative designs made up of various keyboard characters.)

The commands may differ from one site to the next depending on what version of Archie software a particular site is running. For example, one site may accept the **find** command where another site may respond only to the older **prog** command.

Sending the **help** request as your first message is a good place to begin. By requesting a help file at the start, you'll become aware of the commands to which a particular server will respond.

## Example 2

### *Trying to Locate a Particular Software Program*

Here is a sample search in which you ask Archie to find the location of a file called *animals.zip*. When you receive a response from Archie telling you where the file is located, you then can go out and retrieve the file by once again using the Internet mail system. Transferring files via email is explained in the next section.

```
MAIL> send
TO: archie@archie.rutgers.edu
set mailto acbenson@ualvm.ua.edu
set maxhits 10
set search exact
set output_format verbose
find animals.zip
quit
```

The message instructs Archie to do the following:

1. Return the results to me at the email address I specified;

2. Find not more than 10 matches;

3. Search for the exact string *animals.zip*;

4. Print the output in *verbose format* (this is a longer, more detailed format than the output produced by the command **set output_format terse**, *terse* being a shorter output format); and

5. Find FTP sites and corresponding directories where the file *animals.zip* is located.

## ≡ FTP Mail

This section describes how you can access FTP services using *ftpmail*—a program that enables you to download text files and software using the Internet mail system. By typing special commands in the body of an email message and sending them to an FTP mail server, you can accomplish the same tasks you would if you had connected to a regular FTP server (as described in Chapter 4). Even if you have access to an FTP program, you may choose to use an FTP mail server instead. You can send an FTP transaction off in the mail and it will process on its own while you're doing other work. This is especially convenient when the other FTP server allows only 10 simultaneous logins and you are caller number 11.

Two of the better-known FTP mail services are BITftp at Princeton University, *bitftp@pucc.bitnet* (only available to BITNET users), and ftpmail, an application written by Paul Vixie at Digital Equipment Corporation (DEC). Ftpmail is available at the following sites:

*ftpmail@decwrl.dec.com*
*ftpmail@cs.uow.edu.au*
*ftpmail@ftp.uni-stuttgart.de*
*ftpmail@grasp1.univ-lyon1.fr*
*ftpmail@src.doc.ic.ac.uk*

When sending email to a mail server, leave the subject field blank. Place the information necessary for retrieving the file in the body of the message. The basic message format for retrieving text files is illustrated as follows (the message address format may look slightly different, depending on the service provider you're using):

```
MAIL> send
To: ftpmail@decwrl.dec.com
Subj:
connect <host>
ascii
chdir <path>
get <filename>
quit
```

The first command in the body of the message is **connect <host>**, where **<host>** is the site address of the FTP server to which you want to connect. This address should not be confused with the FTP "mail server" address. The mail server address (*ftpmail@decwrl.dec.com* in the above example) is the address to which your request is sent. In the body of your message you list the FTP host address of the archive you'd like to search. The **ascii** command is used for downloading text files as opposed to binary files. The command **chdir <path>** means change the directory to whatever path you designate. The **get <filename>** command serves the same function as the **get** command you use when connected to a regular FTP server where **<filename>** is the name of the file you want to download. The word **quit** tells the mail server that you have finished sending commands. The following example illustrates a specific request:

```
MAIL> send
To: ftpmail@decwrl.dec.com
Subj:
connect naic.nasa.gov
ascii
chdir /files/general_info
get earn-resource-tools.txt
quit
```

At this site (*decwrl.dec.com*), ftpmail is not a supported service. This means that if the system goes down, the system administrators will fix it only when time allows. This could translate into time delays lasting days if things aren't working quite right. Usually, the system administrator will inform you of these conditions by posting a warning in the help file.

The mail server will send you a file with instructions on how to use the system if you simply type **help** on the first line and **quit** on the second line, like this:

```
MAIL> send
To: ftpmail@decwrl.dec.com
Subj:
help
quit
```

Table 11-1 provides a summary of the commands discussed in this help file.

**Table 11-1:** Commands in the FTP Help File

| Command | Description |
| --- | --- |
| **reply <email address>** | Use this command if you want to make sure the mail server returns the information to the correct address. FTP uses the address in the header, but if that's wrong, you won't receive anything back from the mail server. |
| **connect <host>** | Use this command to designate the host to which you'd like to connect. The default FTP server is *gatekeeper.dec.com*. |
| **ascii** | Insert this command when the files you're downloading are printable ASCII files. |
| **binary** | Use this command when you're downloading compressed and/or archived files. |
| **chdir <path>** | Use this command to change to a specified directory. Use only one **chdir** command per ftpmail session. |
| **compress** | Use this command to compress a binary file before sending it. |
| **uuencode** | Use this command to tell ftpmail to convert a binary file into uuencode format before transferring. You must use this command when downloading binary files or they will arrive corrupted. (See Chapter 6 for further details on UUENCODE format.) |
| **chunksize <bytes>** | Use this command to divide the file into chunks, where **<bytes>** is the chunk size you specify. The default size is 64000 bytes. If your dial-up host accepts only mail messages smaller than 10,000 bytes, for example, you would insert the command **chunksize 9,000** on one of the lines in the body of your message. |
| **get <filename>** | Use this command to retrieve the file you specify. You cannot use the **get** command more than 10 times per ftpmail session. |
| **quit** | Use this command to end your ftpmail session. It should be the last command you enter. |

Examples of requests sent to an ftpmail server:

1. Connect to *ftp.eff.org* and get a root directory listing:

```
reply acbenson.ualvm.ua.edu
connect ftp.eff.org
dir
quit
```

2. Connect to *ftp.eff.org* and get the *README* file in the root directory:

```
reply acbenson.ualvm.ua.edu
connect ftp.eff.org
get README
quit
```

3. Connect to *ftp.eff.org* and get the file *patron.behavior.draft.ala* in the directory */pub/academic/library*:

```
reply acbenson.ua1vm.ua.edu
connect ftp.eff.org
chdir /pub/academic/library
get patron.behavior.draft.ala
quit
```

4. Connect to *oak.oakland.edu* and get an educational math game called *animals.zip* in the */pub/msdos/educatin* directory.

```
connect oak.oakland.edu
binary
chdir /pub/msdos/educatin
uuencode
get animals.zip
quit
```

After sending the message in example 4, you may get a return message from the mail server similar to the one I received:

```
We processed the following input from your mail message:


    connect oak.oakland.edu
    binary
    chdir /pub/msdos/educatin
    uuencode
    get animals.zip
    quit


We have entered the following request into our job queue
as job number 766467631.00357:

    connect oak.oakland.edu anonymous -ftpmail/ACBENSON@ua1vm.ua.edu
    reply ACBENSON@ua1vm.ua.edu
    chdir /pub/msdos/educatin
    get animals.zip binary uncompressed uuencode

There are 5127 jobs ahead of this one in our queue.

You should expect the results to be mailed to you within a day or so.
We try to drain the request queue every 30 minutes, but sometimes it
fills up with enough junk that it takes until midnight (Pacific time)
to clear. Note, however, that since ftpmail sends its files out with
"Precedence: bulk", they receive low priority at mail relay nodes.
```

Once the file arrives in your mailbox and you have finished downloading it to your personal computer, use the UUDECODE program to convert the ASCII format back into binary. Before conversion, the file looks like this when it arrives in your mailbox (only the first few lines are shown here):

```
begin 444 ftpmail
M4$L#! H & "2KQPSQ_H)&03D %MC + 04Y)34%,4RY#3TT/ !(#
M)!4V)S@Y:GM,G,G,X?"08!$S3E]I;WT\]>"1ER\]5#W\+-*S?M6;1T0:(<FA)D
```

```
MS)PX:X(4^E0JTZ!.B8),ZG:L0 +G6P5H5P;5 ':"T[-]*Q<DV;1SX;(-FQ<D
M3IAX9=8L"S5CP($ 'QX\"&=8/5X\^-2EXI,*R>>GZW (\@>AHL^-$*M_YG7G
MXQ]>%^#_XP8E G0+T*5Q@Y0# OO-%Z#)_S2$IRM0O\GC!'$'-,F8J<#]ZS5Z
```

See Chapter 6 for details on decoding UUENCODED files.

# ≡ WAISMail

WAISMail, developed by Jonny Goldman of Thinking Machines Corporation, provides a means for accessing the WAIS system via electronic mail. WAISMail is a less sophisticated tool than the one you use when TELNETing to the machine *quake.think.com*, yet it does the job and offers a worthwhile service to those who are limited to using electronic mail for finding and retrieving information on the Internet.

## Basic Commands

Three basic commands are used to communicate with the mail server at Thinking Machines Corporation: **maxres**, **search**, and **DocID**. These commands are explained in the following sections.

### Maxres

The **maxres** command sets the maximum number of matches a search command will generate. For example, **maxres 10** causes the server to stop searching after 10 matches are found. Issue the **maxres** command before any search commands.

### Search

The **search <source-name> {keywords...}** command creates a set of records that contain the specified keyword(s). The variable **<source-name>** determines which WAIS source the server will search. (*Source-name* and *database* are equivalent and are used interchangeably in this chapter.) You can search multiple sources by placing the source-names in double quotation marks. Source-names have .src endings, which may be left on or off.

Here is a sample search statement:

```
search usenet-cookbook apple pie.
```

In this statement, the command is **search**, the source-name is *usenet-cookbook*, and the keywords are *apple pie*.

Messages requesting searches are sent to the WAIS mail server. When the server receives these messages it performs the search and then returns the results. The matches are listed as Result #1, Result #2, Result #3, etc. A sample search statement and the results of that search are shown here.

Search statement sent:

```
maxres 3
search usenet-cookbook apple pie
```

Output returned by WAIS server:

```
Result # 1 Score:1000 lines: 0 bytes: 137987 Date: 0 Type: TEXT
Headline: 91-744.ZO.filt
DocID: 0 137987
/info/pub/wais/wais-data/supreme-court/ascii/91-744.ZO.filt:/info/usr/wais/
wais-sources/supreme-court@archive.orst.edu:9000%TEXT

Result # 2 Score: 788 lines: 0 bytes: 70980 Date: 0 Type: TEXT
Headline: 91-744.ZX3.filt
DocID: 0 70980
/info/pub/wais/wais-data/supreme-court/ascii/91-744.ZX3.filt:/info/usr/wais/
wais-sources/supreme-court@archive.orst.edu:9000%TEXT

Result # 3 Score: 764 lines: 0 bytes: 55646 Date: 0 Type: TEXT
Headline: 89-1391.O.filt
DocID: 0 55646
/info/pub/wais/wais-data/supreme-court/ascii/89-1391.O.filt:/info/usr/wais/
wais-sources/supreme-court@archive.orst.edu:9000%TEXT
```

The first line in each result gives the result number followed by a score. A perfect score of 1000 signifies that WAIS thinks the document is closest to what you are looking for. Other results are listed in descending order from the most relevant (high score) to the least relevant (low score).

The first line also gives the document's size in terms of bytes, the date it was created, if available, and the type of document (TEXT, UUENCODED, or WSRC). The documents that are readable are TEXT documents and WSRC documents. "UUENCODE" documents are binary files converted into ASCII format and they will not be usable until they have been translated, or decoded, back into binary format (see Chapter 6).

The second line of the record gives the headline or document title. Starting with the third line and continuing to the end is the DocID (Document Identification).

By reviewing the various scores and headlines, you choose which records you think are relevant to your search and then send a message to the mail server requesting retrieval of those documents.

### DocID

The DocID: <DOCID> command retrieves specified documents, where <DOCID> is the DocID itself, long and cumbersome as it is. The DocID must be copied exactly as you received it, including upper- and lowercase letters and any white spaces. The DocID can span multiple lines and more than one can be requested at a time. When requesting more than one record in a message, separate each DocID with a blank line.

## Example 1

### Retrieving a List of Searchable Databases

This search retrieves a listing of source-names that can be searched on the server at *quake.think.com*. As with all mail sent to the server, you leave the subject field blank and all communications are typed in the body of the message. Proceed by sending the following message to *waismail@quake.think.com*, the email address for the WAIS mail server:

```
MAIL> send
To: waismail@quake.think.com
Subj:
search directory-of-servers.src help
```

In analyzing the above message, notice that the command **search** is followed by the source-name *directory-of-servers.src,* and this is followed by the keyword *help*. When the server receives this request, it responds by sending a complete listing of source-names. Only the very beginning and ending of this list is shown below:

```
AAS_jobs.src
AAS_meeting.src
ANU-Aboriginal-EconPolicies.src
ANU-Aboriginal-Studies.src
ANU-Ancient-DNA-Studies.src
ANU-Asian-Computing.src
ANU-Asian-Religions.src
ANU-AustPhilosophyForum-L.src
ANU-Australia-NZ-History-L.src
ANU-Australian-Economics.src

wais-docs.src
wais-talk-archives.src
water-quality.src
weather.src
winsock.src
world-factbook.src
world-factbook92.src
world91a.src
wuarchive.src
```

With the complete list of source-names in hand and a basic understanding of the command language discussed earlier, you may begin exploring WAIS via electronic mail. As you read through the list of source-names, you'll notice some that are cryptic, such as **bib-dmi-ens-fr.src**, and others that are more revealing as to their subject content, such as **AskERIC-Helpsheets.src**.

## Example 2

### *Using the* help *Command to Find Out More About a Source-name*

The next search demonstrates how to derive meaning from cryptic source-names by searching the database in question with the keyword **help**. If, for example, you weren't familiar with the contents of the database represented by the source-name *bit.listserv.pacs-l*, you could gain some insight by sending the following message to WAISMail:

```
MAIL> send
To: waismail@quake.think.com
```

```
Subj:
maxres 5
search bit.listserv.pacs-1.think.com help
```

In the above example, the command **maxres** 5 sets the maximum number of matches to 5, **search** is the command, **bit.listserv.pacs-l** is the source-name, and **help** is the keyword. The results of this search are as follows:

```
Result # 1 Score:1000 lines: 0 bytes: 2924 Date: 0 Type: WSRC
Headline: Information on database: bit.listserv.pacs-1
DocID: 0 0 /home/wais/db/bit.listserv.pacs-1.src:bit.listserv.pacs-1@munin.ub2.1
u.se:210%WSRC

Result # 2 Score:1000 lines: 0 bytes: 2613 Date:930415 Type: TEXT
Headline: PA Re: Help Screens on OPACs
DocID: 0 2613 /home/wais/nat/econf/pacs-1/7079:/home/wais/db/bit.listserv.pacs-1
@munin.ub2.1u.se:210%TEXT

Result # 3 Score: 793 lines: 0 bytes: 9494 Date:930930 Type: TEXT
Headline: \"Ernest Pe Re: A WAIS help file
DocID: 0 9494 /home/wais/nat/econf/pacs-1/8214:/home/wais/db/bit.listserv.pacs-1
@munin.ub2.1u.se:210%TEXT

Result # 4 Score: 690 lines: 0 bytes: 809 Date:930127 Type: TEXT
Headline: PA Re: HELP SCREENS
DocID: 0 809 /home/wais/nat/econf/pacs-1/6478:/home/wais/db/bit.listserv.pacs-1@
munin.ub2.1u.se:210%TEXT

Result # 5 Score: 655 lines: 0 bytes: 2679 Date:930712 Type: TEXT
Headline: Walt Crawf Re: Help: Reports of Local PC vendors needed
DocID: 0 2679 /home/wais/nat/econf/pacs-1/7725:/home/wais/db/bit.listserv.pacs-1
@munin.ub2.1u.se:210%TEXT
```

Result #1 appears to be the most relevant, with a score of 1000 and a headline that reads *Information on database: bit.listerv.pacs-l*. The next step is to retrieve the document labeled Result #1 by sending the following message to the mail server:

```
MAIL> send
To: waismail@quake.think.com
Subj:
DocID: 0 0
/home/wais/db/bit.listserv.pacs-1.src:bit.listserv.pacs-1@munin.ub2.1u.se:210%WSRC
```

As explained earlier, you use the DocID: command to retrieve files. Following this command is the document identifier or filename just as it appeared in the original computer output above. Where the line breaks and wraps around to the second line doesn't matter, as long asthe second line begins in the first column. The document type being requested is a WSRC document and the results of this request are shown here:

```
Type: WSRC

(:source
 :version 3
 :ip-address "130.235.162.11"
```

```
:ip-name "munin"
:tcp-port 210
:database-name "bit.listserv.pacs-l"
:cost 0.00
:cost-unit :free
:maintainer "anders@munin"
:keyword-list (
1992
1993
access
available
bitnet
bitnetsubject
cd
cdt
cdtfrom
computer
data
date
edu
electronic
file
ftp
get
information
internet
libraries
library
list
listserv
mail
may
message
network
new
online
original
pacs
please
program
public
re
research
resources
send
services
software
subject
subjectre
system
systems
technology
time
uhupvm1
university
use
users
)
:description "Server created with WAIS rel. 8 b5 DRI 1 on Aug 30 18:18:19 199
```

```
2 by anders@munin.ub2.lu.se
Index of the PACS-L LISTSERV.

Description from mailing-lists.src:
==========
PACS-L%UHUPVM1.BITNET@VM1.NODAK.EDU

 The University Libraries and the Information Technology Division of the
University of Houston have established this list that deals with all
computer systems that libraries make available to their patrons, including CD-ROM
databases, computer-assisted instruction (CAI and ICAI) programs, expert systems,
hypermedia programs, library microcomputer facilities, locally-mounted databases,
online catalogs, and remote end-user search systems. The list is open for general
subscription.

 Archives of PACS-L are stored in the PACS-L FILELIST. To receive a list of files
send the command INDEX LISTNAME to LISTSERV@UHUPVM1.

 To subscribe to PACS-L, send the following command to
LISTSERV@UHUPVM1.BitNet via mail text or interactive message:
SUBSCRIBE PACS-L Your_full_name
For example:
SUBSCRIBE PACS-L Jane Doe
Non-BitNet Internet users can join by sending the above command in the text or
body of a message to LISTSERV%UHUPVM1.BITNET@VM1.NODAK.EDU.

 Coordinator: Charles Bailey <LIB3%UHUPVM1.BITNET@VM1.NODAK.EDU>
 Owner: LIBPACS@UHUPVM1.BitNet
```

As it turns out, this "help" file is more helpful than most you will find. The file not only provides the most basic information, such as who maintains the database and the database's IP address, but it also lists keywords that are descriptive of its contents and includes a description of the Bitnet discussion list called PACS-L.

## Example 3

### *Applications to Reference Service*

The next search example demonstrates the process you might apply when answering a reference question without knowing precisely which database to search or knowing whether an appropriate database even exists. Suppose that a patron has presented you with a request asking which plants can be used for "cover crops." You could begin by sending the following message to the WAIS mailserver:

```
MAIL> send
TO: waismail@quake.think.com
Subj:
maxres 5
search directory-of-servers cover crops
```

By searching the *directory-of-servers*, which is, in effect, a database of databases, you hope to retrieve a list of results giving source-names that contain potentially relevant information. The results sent back from this request, however, ended up being somewhat questionable because the headlines contained source-names that were unrelated to the subject being searched:

```
Headline: eros-data-center.src
Headline: hst-weekly-timeline.src
Headline: smithsonian-pictures.src
Headline: Health-Security-Act.src
Headline: NeXT-Managers.src
```

This result implies that there aren't any databases with a primary concentration in cover crops. At this point, you can do one of three things:

1. Search the directory-of-servers again, but broaden your search by using the keyword *agriculture*;

2. Retrieve the document listed in Result #1 to see whether it will provide some insight into what type of database *eros-data-center.src* is; or

3. Go ahead and assume *eros-data-center.src* has information on cover crops and send a search request using the keywords *cover crops* to that database. The least time-consuming option, and the one most likely to produce the best results, is the first option:

```
MAIL> send
To: waismal@quake.think.com
Subj:
maxres 5
search directory-of-servers agriculture
```

The results from this search are quite promising. Result #1, with a score of 1000, points to a source-name called *sustainable-agriculture* and appears to be relevant.

```
Result # 1 Score:1000 lines: 0 bytes: 934 Date: 0 Type: WSRC
Headline: sustainable-agriculture.src
DocID: 0 934 /proj/wais/wais-sources/sustainable-agriculture.src:/proj/wais/wais
-sources/directory-of-servers@quake.think.com:210%WSRC

Result # 2 Score: 261 lines: 0 bytes: 782 Date: 0 Type: WSRC
Headline: agricultural-market-news.src
DocID: 0 782 /proj/wais/wais-sources/agricultural-market-news.src:/proj/wais/wai
s-sources/directory-of-servers@quake.think.com:210%WSRC

Result # 3 Score: 261 lines: 0 bytes: 1924 Date: 0 Type: WSRC
Headline: usda-csrs-pwd.src
DocID: 0 1924 /proj/wais/wais-sources/usda-csrs-pwd.src:/proj/wais/wais-sources/
directory-of-servers@quake.think.com:210%WSRC

Result # 4 Score: 261 lines: 0 bytes: 1535 Date: 0 Type: WSRC
Headline: usdacris.src
DocID: 0 1535 /proj/wais/wais-sources/usdacris.src:/proj/wais/wais-sources/direc
tory-of-servers@quake.think.com:210%WSRC

Result # 5 Score: 217 lines: 0 bytes: 2544 Date: 0 Type: WSRC
Headline: ANU-CAUT-Academics.src
DocID: 0 2544 /proj/wais/wais-sources/ANU-CAUT-Academics.src:/proj/wais/wais-sou
rces/directory-of-servers@quake.think.com:210%WSRC
```

You decide to send the following keyword search to the first source-name listed: *sustainable-agriculture.src*.

```
MAIL> send
To: waismail@quake.think.com
Subj:
maxres 5
search sustainable.agriculture.src cover crops
```

The results of this request are interesting in that the document with the words *cover crops* in the headline scored only 677, and the two documents scoring 1000 have meaningless titles. (Results #4 and #5 are not included here because they were clearly not relevant.)

```
Result # 1 Score:1000 lines: 0 bytes: 144787 Date: 0 Type: TEXT
Headline: 2.bib
DocID: 0 144787 /pub/academic/agriculture/sustainable_agriculture/general/sust_a
g.bibliography/2.bib:/home3/wais/sustainable-agriculture@sunSITE.unc.edu:210%TEXT

Result # 2 Score:1000 lines: 0 bytes: 176998 Date:930121 Type: TEXT
Headline: Re: WA CB441
DocID: 0 176998 /information/pub/data/market_news/wacb441:/services/wais/wais-so
urces/agricultural-market-news@nostromo.oes.orst.edu:210%TEXT

Result # 3 Score: 677 lines: 0 bytes: 16559 Date: 0 Type: TEXT
Headline: cover.crops.info
DocID: 0 16559 /pub/academic/agriculture/sustainable_agriculture/cover.crops/cov
er.crops.info:/home3/wais/sustainable-agriculture@sunSITE.unc.edu:210%TEXT
```

At this point, you can send a request to the WAISMailer for any of the documents you think are relevant. The request shown below includes the DocID's for Result #1, which had the highest score, and Result #3, which had the words *cover crops* in the headline. Notice that they are properly separated by a blank line. I limited the request to these two because I felt it was important to retrieve a couple of sample documents before downloading everything. The headline in Result #2 wasn't very revealing and at 176,998 bytes, I decided that it was too big a file to transfer without knowing more about it.

```
MAIL> send
To: waismail@quake.think.com
Subj:
DocID: 0 144787 /pub/academic/agriculture/sustainable_agriculture
/general/sust_ag.bibliography/2.bib:/home3/wais/sustainable-agricultu
re@sunSITE.unc.edu:210%TEXT

DocID: 0 16559 pub/academic/agriculture/sustainable_agriculture
/cover.crops/cover.crops.info:/home3/wais/sustainable-agriculture@su
nSITE.unc.edu:210%TEXT
```

As you can see, the command statement **search <source-name> help** can be used to query any source whose purpose is unknown.

## ☰ The Emerging Technologies Portfolio

The Emerging Technologies Portfolio is a collection of 24 draft summaries on emerging technologies prepared by one of the IEEE's Technical Societies/Councils. Each one of these summaries can be retrieved via the Internet mail system. Send a message (the subject line and body of the message can be left blank) to any one of the servers listed in this section. The server will in turn send you a current draft version of the report you've requested. Here are the individual email addresses and areas of interest for each Society/Council:

| | |
|---|---|
| *info.new.tech.aes@ieee.org* | Aerospace and Electronic Systems Society |
| *info.new.tech.ap@ieee.org* | Antennas and Propagation Society |
| *info.new.tech.bt@ieee.org* | Broadcast Technology Society |
| *info.new.tech.chmt@ieee.org* | Components, Hybrids and Manufacturing Technology Society |
| *info.new.tech.ce@ieee.org* | Consumer Electronics Society |
| *info.new.tech.cs@ieee.org* | Control Systems Society |
| *info.new.tech.dei@ieee.org* | Dielectrics and Electrical Insulation Society |
| *info.new.tech.e@ieee.org* | Education Society |
| *info.new.tech.ia@ieee.org* | Industry Applications Society |
| *info.new.tech.ie@ieee.org* | Industrial Electronics Society |
| *info.new.tech.im@ieee.org* | Instrumentation and Measurement Society |
| *info.new.tech.it@ieee.org* | Information Theory Society |
| *info.new.tech.leo@ieee.org* | Lasers and Electro-Optics Society |
| *info.new.tech.mag@ieee.org* | Magnetics Society |
| *info.new.tech.mtt@ieee.org* | Microwave Theory and Techniques Society |
| *info.new.tech.nps@ieee.org* | Nuclear and Plasma Sciences Society |
| *info.new.tech.pc@ieee.org* | Professional Communication Society |
| *info.new.tech.pe@ieee.org* | Power Engineering Society |
| *info.new.tech.r@ieee.org* | Reliability Society |
| *info.new.tech.sit@ieee.org* | Society on Social Implications of Technology |
| *info.new.tech.ssc@ieee.org* | Solid-State Circuits Council |
| *info.new.tech.sp@ieee.org* | Signal Processing Society |
| *info.new.tech.uffc@ieee.org* | Ultrasonics, Ferroelectrics, and Frequency Control Society |
| *info.new.tech.vt@ieee.org* | Vehicular Technology Society |

## ☰ Almanac Servers

*Almanac*, developed at Oregon State University, is a type of information server designed to answer requests through the Internet mail system. You can retrieve reports, newsletters, journals, articles, and sounds. You make requests by sending commands to an Almanac server via email.

What follows is a selective list of primary catalogs, available at four different almanac servers, which may be of interest to librarians. To obtain a copy of the *Almanac User's Guide* from any one of the Almanac sites listed below, send the command **send guide** in the body of an email message addressed to one of the sites.

### Purdue University Cooperative Extension Service at site: *almanac@ecn.purdue.edu*

*Agricultural Computer Network Catalog*: Contains information related to the Agricultural Computer Network Department. Command to retrieve: **send acn catalog**

*Agricultural Communication Service*: Complete listing of educational media (publications, video tapes, slides, and county agent supplies) available from the Media Distribution Center. Files in this catalog cover subjects such as animal disease control, agricultural engineering, animal science, agronomy, entomology, botany and plant pathology, and more. Command to retrieve: **send acs catalog**

*Water Quality*: This catalog contains files on such subjects as salinity control, nitrates and ground water, bottled water, distillation, underground storage tanks, and groundwater contamination, etc. Command to retrieve: **send wq catalog**

*Mailing list archives*: Almanac at Purdue is the server for a number of discussion groups. Here are two examples of these discussion groups, their Internet addresses, and the appropriate command that should be placed in the body of an email message in order to retrieve a list of their archived messages. For a complete list of discussion groups, send the command **send mail-catalog** in the body of your mail message.

- *nae4ha_mg@acn.purdue.edu*: Discussion group for the National Association of Extension 4-H Professionals.
- *dairy_mg@acn.purdue.edu*: Information important to those involved in dairy education.

*Factsheet*: Catalog of the Clemson University Disaster factsheets prepared in 1989 to respond to the cleanup required following Hurricane Hugo. Command to retrieve: **send factsheet catalog**

### University of California, Davis at site: *almanac@silo.ucdavis.edu*

*Information Technology Publication*: Main catalog for instructional Technology. Command to retrieve: **send itincat catalog**

*Information Technology Newsletter*: Main catalog for the Instructional Technology Newsletter. To retrieve a copy, send the command **send itncat catalog** in the body of your mail message.

*Cooperative-Extension*: Contains items related to Cooperative Extension. Command to retrieve: **send extension-db catalog**

*Mining the Internet*: The electronic event "Mining the Internet" and the workshops "Using the Internet" A & B, were introduced at the California Educational Computing Consortium on August 10 through 12, 1991. These training materials are available free of charge in various forms for non-profit purposes by educational institutions. Files can be obtained via anonymous FTP from site *ucdavis.edu* (128.120.2.1) in the */ucd.netdocs/mining* directory. The following files are available:

| | |
|---|---|
| Text versions: | *Mining.txt* |
| | *Internet-A.txt* |
| | *Internet-B.txt* |
| Postscript versions: | *Mining.ps* |
| | *Internet-A.ps* |
| | *Internet-B.ps* |
| Mac versions: | *Mining.hqx* |
| | *Internet-A.hqx* |
| | *Internet-B.hqx* |

The University of California, Davis, found that these workshops and the concept of "Mining the Internet" provided an excellent training course for new Internet users.

## Oregon State University at site:
## *almanac@oes.orst.edu*

*Market News*: Compiled by USDA and sent via satellite to Oregon State University, this catalog contains hundreds of reports on the market prices of various agricultural products. Command to retrieve: **send mn catalog**

*Extension Service*: Contains information relevant to agricultural extension services. Command to retrieve: **send ext catalog**

*MS-DOS*: Papers on MS-DOS, IBMs, and their applications. Command to retrieve: **send ms-dos catalog**

## North Carolina University, Cooperative Extension Service at site:
## *almanac@ces.ncsu.edu*

*Plan-of-work*: N.C. Cooperative Extension Service plan-of-work files. Some of the titles are Sustainable Agriculture, Farm Business Management, and Health and Human Safety. Command to retrieve: **send fs catalog**

*Factsheets*: Computer factsheets available from the almanac server. Command to retrieve: **send fs catalog**

*Training Programs*: Information files on staff development programs related to technology implementation at state Cooperative Extension Services. Command to retrieve: **send tp catalog**

*Crop Science*: A list of available documents relating to crop science, especially corn and tobacco. Command to retrieve: **send cs catalog**

## ☰ FAQs

Frequently Asked Questions, or FAQs, are files that contain answers to questions that are often asked on Usenent news groups. The FAQ files are stored at FTP site *rtfm.mit.edu*. Duplicates of these files are stored at *archie.au* and *archive.orst.edu*. Even if you don't have FTP access to this site, you can still access its holdings by using the Internet mail system. Send the following commands in the body of an email message to *mail-server@rtfm.mit.edu*:

```
help
index
path <your email address>
```

Type each of these commands on a separate line. This email message will retrieve an index of the available files.

## ☰ RFCs and FYIs

RFC-INFO is an email-based service that helps users locate RFCs (Request for Comments) and FYIs (For Your Information)—documents that provide background information on the Internet. Send an email message to *rfc-infoisi.edu*. Leave the subject line blank and enter your request in the body of the message. Sample requests are:

**list: fyi**   will retrieve a list of FYIs
**list: rfc**   will retrieve a list of RFCs

In the second line of the message, you can focus your request on a keyword by entering:

**keyword: <word>**, where **<word>** is the keyword you want to search. For example,

```
list:rfc
keyword: security
```

For further details, enter the command **help:help** in the body of the message.

## ≡ For Further Study

A list of mail servers compiled by Jonathan Kamens can be retrieved from FTP site *pit-manager.mit.edu* in the */pub/usenet/news.answers* directory, filename *finding-sources*.

# Chapter 12

# Directory Services

Directory services, or *white pages,* are directories of Internet users' email addresses, postal addresses, telephone numbers, and other related information. No master directory of Internet email addresses is available, but programs like WHOIS and Netfind can be useful in tracking down someone's address.

Keep in mind that the vast majority of people with Internet addresses are not included in any directory. Email addresses are private and it is usually up to the individual to determine whether they appear in a directory.

If you know someone has an Internet email address, but you're not sure what it is, the easiest way to find out is to call and ask. If they're not sure what their address is, have them send you an email message and when you receive it, note what the From field says at the top of the message.

## ☰ Finger

*Finger* is a service that helps you find someone's email address or tells you who is currently logged in at a particular site. Each site provides its own finger server. The various finger servers distributed around the Internet do not share information, so you must know the server to go to for your answers.

If you use the **finger** command without any argument (just type the word **finger** and press ENTER), the server returns the names of all users currently logged into the local host. If your finger query names a specific user, more detailed information is provided.

Finger servers also offer other information services such as baseball scores *finger jtchern@ocf.berkley* and the week's top musical recordings *finger buckmr@rpi.edu.* Finger even connects you to vending machines attached to the Internet. There are "online" Coke machines, for example, that are automated in such a way that they cna provide status reports telling the inquirer which bins are empty and which bins hold the coldest drinks. Here are a few:

> *finger coke@cs.wisc.edu*
> *finger mnm@coke.elab.cs.cmu.edu*
> *finger drink@csh.rit.edu*

## ≡ WHOIS Database

Several sites on the Internet run WHOIS servers. When you connect to one of these servers, you can query databases of names and email addresses. You can use a WHOIS server two ways. One way is to TELNET to a WHOIS server and login with the username **whois**. You then see a *WHOIS:* prompt, at which point you can enter the name to search. For example, to connect with one of the more famous WHOIS servers at InterNIC, enter **telnet whois.internic.net** at your system prompt.

Another way to connect is by typing the command **whois -h whois.internic.net <username>** at your own system prompt, where <username> is the name of the person you are trying to find.

## ≡ USENET Address Server

A USENET address server is set up on the machine *rtfm.mit.edu*, the main archiver of USENET data. If the person you are looking for has posted an article to a USENET newsgroup in the last year, there's a chance you may find him or her using this service. Using email, type the following command in the body of the message: **send usenet-addresses/<name>**, where <name> is the person for whom you are searching. You also can access the USENET address server through WAIS by searching the source called *usenet-addresses*.

## ≡ Knowbot Information Service (KIS)

The Knowbot Information Service (KIS) doesn't maintain its own database; instead, it goes out and searches other services' databases.

You can access this service by TELNETing to *cnri.reston.va.us 185* or *regulus.bucknell.edu 185*. To learn more about this service, enter ? once you have connected.

## ≡ Netfind

To see how this directory service works, TELNET to a public Netfind server at *redmont.cis.uab.edu*, *mudhoney.micro.umn.edu*, or *netfind.oc.com* and login as **netfind**. Netfind attempts to locate information about a person on the Internet when given a name and a rough description of where the person works. When

```
InterNIC Directory and Database Services (DS) Telnet Interface
                    "White Pages" Menu


    1) User Tutorial
    2) X.500 Person/Organization Lookup
    3) WHOIS Person/Organization Lookup
    4) Netfind Person/Organization Lookup
    5) Exit
```

**Figure 12-1:** The InterNIC main menu

prompted, enter a name followed by keywords relating to location. The name can be a first, last, or login name, but only one name can be used per search. For additional assistance, choose *Help* at the opening menu.

## ≡ InterNIC Directory and Database Services

The InterNIC Directory and Database Services (InterNIC), first introduced in Chapter 1, offers a directory of directories listing FTP sites, library catalogs, white pages directories, and other databases. To access this service via Gopher, connect to the Gopher server at *ds.internic.net*.

To access via TELNET, TELNET to *ds.internic.net* Login: **guest**. If you're looking for an address, select item 3 on the Main Menu, *InterNIC Directory Services (White Pages)*. The next screen that appears is in figure 12-1. Notice that the first menu choice is a tutorial. If you would like to make a copy of the tutorial, turn the screen capture on, and then select that menu item.

## ≡ The Kamens File

Jonathan I. Kamens is the author of a FAQ titled, "How to Find People's E-Mail Addresses." To download a copy, FTP to *stp.sunet.se* and look in the */pub/usenet/comp.answers* directory for a file called *finding-addresses*.

## ≡ For Further Reference

A program called "Hytelnet," introduced in Chapter 15, contains the addresses for directory services that can be accessed via TELNET. Rather than downloading the program and running it yourself to get these addresses, you could access Hytelnet through the Gopher server at Washington and Lee University (*liberty.uc.wlu.edu*).

Information on the current state of email service in various countries can be found in the "International Email Accessibility FAQ." Before seeking out someone's email address in a foreign country, use this guide to determine what level of email service is offered in a particular country.

There are Gopher servers on the Internet that offer access to various directory services. The Gopher server at Notre Dame (*gopher.nd.edu*) for example, can access a large number of sites by using various methods including WHOIS. The Gopher server at *sipb.mit.edu* also offers a gateway to WHOIS servers.

There is a paper called "College Email Address" that's helpful if you're looking for someone's email address at a college. A copy of this document can be downloaded from FTP site *rtfm.mit.edu* in the directory */pub/usenet/soc.college*, filename *College Email Addresses*.

PART **IV**

# GENERAL RESOURCES

Part IV introduces you to a broad range of Internet resources. Chapters 13 and 19 cover people and communications. Here you'll learn about the vast world of USENET newsgroups and find out what discussion lists are and learn how to join them. In Chapter 14, you'll learn about services called Campus Wide Information Systems (CWIS) that provide information about specific universities. Accessing on-line library catalogs is introduced in Chapter 15, where three major systems are discussed. Details are provided on where to find directories and specialized software listing hundreds of accessible catalogs worldwide.

Chapter 16 tells about various electronic publishing formats and explains where to find everything from ejournals to zines on the Internet. Chapter 18 covers special community computing systems called Free-Nets and explores the information resources they offer. This section concludes with a chapter on Bulletin Board Systems (BBSs). Here you'll discover what BBSs are, how to connect to them, and how you might use BBS software in your library to create a community wide information system.

# Chapter 13

# LISTSERV Discussion Lists

*LISTSERV* lists are electronic discussion lists that are supported by a special software application called LISTSERV. LISTSERV, an abbreviation of *list server*, is an automated system that facilitates one-to-many communication and is also a general purpose file server (an application providing users with access to files).

The word *list* refers to a group of people that receive mail distributed by the LISTSERV software. These people give themselves a unique name called a *listname*. For example, the folks that have joined together to discuss Total Quality Management in higher education call themselves TQM-L. Professional writers and those who aspire to write belong to a list called WRITERS. Thousands of these discussion lists are currently on the Internet sharing information on subjects as diverse as potato research, accordions, dentistry, IBM AS/400 computer systems, and fuzzy logic. (See Part V for ideas on how you can make LISTSERV discussion lists a value-added service in your library.)

All lists have a home; that is, a host computer upon which their particular LISTSERV software runs. If you want to join a list, say TQM-L, you have to know where that list originates. You can find the answer by looking at a comprehensive list of discussion lists. These lists are located on various FTP sites around the Internet, some of which are noted at the end of this chapter. Also, several discussion lists relating to libraries are included in the back of this book. (See Appendix B.)

When you want to communicate with the LISTSERV software, you address your email to the LISTSERV at its home address. LISTSERV software serves a special function and can help you with certain tasks. You communicate with it by sending it special commands in the body of email messages. These commands, explained later in the chapter, enable you to take care of details like subscribing to a discussion list, or unsubscribing.

All LISTSERV addresses look basically the same. They begin with the word *listserv*, followed by the @ symbol, and then an Internet address. For example, *listserv@ukanvm.cc.ukans.edu* is the address for the LISTSERV that handles communications for TQM-L. WRITERS communications are handled by *listserv@vm1.nodak.edu*. If you sent a message to *listserv@vm1.nodak.edu* announcing an upcoming writer's workshop, it wouldn't know what you were talking about. Remember, it's just a piece of software that understands and responds to a finite set of commands.

When you want to speak to other members of the list, announcing your upcoming writer's workshop, you address your communications to a different address. You send your email to an address that begins with the listname. These addresses all look basically the same, too. They begin with a listname, followed by the @ symbol, and then an Internet address—the same address as the LISTSERV's. This means that if you want to communicate an announcement to all subscribers of the WRITERS discussion list, you address your email message to *writers@vm1.nodak.edu*.

The first version of LISTSERV was written by EDUCOM and was designed for a relatively small group of people. Its purpose was to bring people together with common interests enabling them to communicate with one another by sharing news and information via the Internet email system. As the number of new lists and subscribers grew, the original version of LISTSERV couldn't function efficiently. To overcome this lack of functionality, the Ecole Centrale de Paris in France developed the more sophisticated Revised LISTSERV, which is now in common use.

## ≡ BITNET LISTSERV Addressing

LISTSERV is one of the services offered by BITNET. BITNET (Because It's Time Network) is a worldwide collection of networks established for the purpose of education and research. If you're sending email to a BITNET discussion list (the list of persons to which LISTSERV distributes email) and you yourself are also on BITNET, you should address your email like this: <listname> at <node> or <listname>@<node> where <listname> is the name of the discussion list and <node> is the BITNET connection point. For example, *ada-law@ndsuvm1* or *ada-lan at ndsuvm1*, where *ada-law* is the listname and *ndsuvm1* is the BITNET node.

If you're accessing BITNET from another network, address email to the BITNET discussion list as <listname>@<node>.BITNET. In this instance, the earlier example would be addressed *ada-law@ndsuvm1.bitnet*.

Remember, email sent to the listname, as illustrated in the preceding examples, is distributed to all subscribers of the discussion list.

## ≡ How to Join a LISTSERV Discussion List

To subscribe to a discussion list, send a message to the LISTSERV software containing the command **subscribe <listname> <your name>**. For example, if I were going to join the discussion list called PACS-L, I would send the message **sub-**

scribe pacs-l allen benson to *listserv@uhupvm1.bitnet*. I should receive a message notifying me that my subscription has been accepted. Notification may come a few minutes—or several hours—later.

Once you're on the list, you'll receive all the email that is sent to the list by other members. When you want to communicate a message to everyone else on the list, send your email to the list itself. (In this example, the correct address would be *pacs-l@uhupvm1.bitnet*.) When you want to send commands to the LISTSERV software, you address your messages to *listserv@uhupvm1. bitnet*. It's important to not get the function of these two addresses mixed up; the address that begins with a listname is used for communicating with people and the address that begins with the word *listserv* is used for communicating with a piece of software.

## LISTSERV Etiquette

After you join a discussion list, you should learn about any rules or customs they may have and abide by them. These rules may vary from one group to the next. You can use the following general guidelines for any discussion list you might join:

- Save the first information file or message you receive for future reference.
- If you use a signature block on the bottom of your email, keep it short. Include your name, email address, postal address, and phone number. Don't exceed more than six lines.
- Never send LISTSERV commands to the discussion list. If you do, your commands will be distributed to every active subscriber. Send your commands to the LISTSERV user ID (*listserv@domain*).
- Avoid flaming (launching personal attacks).
- Before responding to a message, think about whether it would be appropriate to respond privately to the individual who posted the message or publicly to everyone in the discussion list.
- Check your electronic mailbox daily and delete any unwanted messages immediately. Transfer to disk the messages you want to save.
- When you first subscribe to a list, it's a good practice to *lurk* for a while. *Lurking* is when you watch what is going on without actively participating in the discussion. This is a time to observe and understand the audience, determine whether you're interested in what subscribers are talking about, and become aware of any customs or practices that are particular to that list.

## Moderated and Unmoderated Lists

Every discussion list has an administrator, usually one person, that performs daily maintenance by keeping the subscriber address list up-to-date. This person also deals with any network problems that may arise.

Unmoderated mailing lists may distribute a lot of redundant, boring messages. You may have to spend some time looking through every message in order to find a gem.

A list that is *moderated* means that all of the messages go through a *moderator* who decides which messages will be posted to the list. (One person may serve as both the administrator and moderator.) Moderators may pass messages along to the LISTSERV software without modification, they may edit postings slightly, or they may reject an off-topic posting entirely.

Moderators also intervene when things get out of hand and *flame wars* erupt. If an individual subscriber becomes too contumacious, the moderator may ask him or her to unsubscribe or forcibly delete the subscriber from the list.

Moderators also manually bring several messages together creating one neat package called a *digest*. Some even include a table of contents along with the digest. (Digesting can also performed as an automatic function of the LISTSERV software.)

## ≡ LISTSERV Commands

Address any commands intended for the LISTSERV software specifically to the LISTSERV address, not to the 'listname' address. The LISTSERV software takes care of many tasks by responding to a set of special commands. Some of the more useful commands are listed later in this section.

The procedure for sending these commands is simple. Send an email message to *listserv@<node>.bitnet* (or *listserv at <node>*, whichever the case may be). You can send some requests to any BITNET site running LISTSERV software, preferably the one closest to you. Other commands must be sent to a specific LISTSERV site because they relate to a particular discussion list that originates there. Leave the subject line empty, and in the body of the message, insert the desired command. You can send multiple commands, but put each one on a separate line. LISTSERV makes no distinction between upper- and lowercase letters when sending commands.

You can always send commands via Internet mail, but if your facility is a VM/CMS BITNET facility, you also can use the **tell** command to communicate *in real time* with the LISTSERV. For example, if you wanted to send the **list global** command to the host at *yalevm.bitnet*, the command syntax would be **tell listserv at yalevm list global**. You type this at your system prompt and then you press ENTER to send.

## ≡ LISTSERV Commands

**list global**—Sends a list of all LISTSERVs. Each entry in this list includes the listname, full address (*listname@node*), and the list title, which is a brief description of the discussion list. This list may be as long as 4,000 lines of text.

**list global/<string>**—This extension of the **list global** command enables you to specify text to be found in the name or description of the list. If you are looking for a discussion list on a certain topic, such as philosophy, use the command **list global/philosophy**. The results may not be complete because of the eight-letter restriction on LISTSERV names, but it should reduce the search time. The alternative is to use the **list global** command and search the resulting file with a word processor.

list detail—Sends you a list of discussion lists that originate only at the address to which you have written. For example, sending the command **list detail** to *listserv@maine.bitnet* retrieves of all the discussion lists that originate at the University of Maine.

subscribe—Subscribes you to a discussion list. In the body of the message, type **subscribe <listname> <your name>**.

**signoff <listname>**—Unsubscribes you from a list. In the body of the message, type **signoff <listname>**

**signoff * (netwide**—Unsubscribes you from all of the lists you've subscribed to on the Internet.

info—Retrieves a document listing information guides that are available from a LISTSERV at a particular site.

get—Requests a particular file from the LISTSERV file list.

review <listname>—Retrieves a document that lists all of the subscribers to that list and their email addresses. The command has to be sent to the LIST-SERV address where the discussion list originates. If you don't want this information given out about yourself when you join a list, send the LISTSERV the command **conceal**. If you change your mind and you'd like to remove this option, send the command **noconceal**.

**get listserv refcard**—Retrieves a command reference card.

**database list**—Retrieves a list of databases that are available on a particular LISTSERV.

## ≡ Commands for Retrieving Files?

Some discussion lists archive past messages or other files, and an index of these files can be retrieved by sending an email request to the LISTSERV. With a list of specific filenames in hand, you then can send a command to the LISTSERV requesting that a specific file be sent. These commands are explained in this section.

**index <listname>**—Sends you a list of archived files for the list name you designated. Send your request to the LISTSERV site where the list originates. These files are usually monthly notebooks continuing all of the correspondence that has taken place between list members. Each entry on this list includes a filename and filetype.

**get <filename> <filetype>**—Retrieves a specific file.

**get listdb memo**—Retrieves a document called "Revised LISTSERV: Database Functions" by Eric Thomas. This is an introductory manual that discusses the LISTSERV database functions. The purpose of the LISTSERV database functions are to enable a user to extract relevant information from an archive by sending it commands asking it to perform search operations.

**faq**—Retrieves a document called *Frequently Asked Questions about LISTSERV* by Eric Thomas, which explains the process for finding answers to questions by suggesting that you search the discussion list called LISTSRV-L, using LISTSERV's database functions.

**get listserv memo**—Retrieves a document called *What is LISTSERV? What is Revised LISTSERV?* by Eric Thomas.

**set <list name> nomail**—Stops mail delivery without unsubscribing you from the list. When you leave on vacation, this is the command you would send to the LISTSERV to stop mail service temporarily. Upon returning, send the command set <list name> mail to resume delivery.

## How To Search a LISTSERV Message Archive

The only information you need in order to access the message archives of a discussion list are the listname and the LISTSERV address. For example, if you have an interest in agriculture, you might search the archives of AG-EXP-L (listname) at NDSUVM1 (host address). Retrieve a directory of available archive files for AG-EXP-L by sending the command **index ag-exp-l** to *listserv@ndsuvm1.bitnet*. You can type the command in upper- or lowercase letters.

When you receive the index of available files, notice that each entry consists of a **<filename> <filetype>**,followed by who can access the information and the time period covered. If you go to the very bottom of the list, you will see the filename for the most recent messages received by the discussion list. These are usually quite recent—within the last day or two.

For this example, suppose that you've decided to retrieve the first entry listed, which is assigned the filename *ag-exp-l* and filetype *log8901*. Type the command **get ag-exp-l log8901** in the body of an email message and send it to *listserv@ndsuvm1.bitnet*. This completes the procedure for contacting a discussion list, retrieving a list of available notebooks, and then retrieving one of those notebooks.

Your email request may fail if a particular discussion list requires that you subscribe before allowing you access to their database. In those instances, you'll be sent a mail message stating something like this:

```
You are not authorized to GET file <filename> from filelist NOTEBOOK.
```

If you'd still like to search the database, take a moment to subscribe, conduct your search, and then unsubscribe when your work is complete.

## ≡ Advanced Services

You also can search interactively with a user interface called LDBASE, or search in batch mode via electronic mail using the LISTSERV Command Job Language Interpreter (CJLI). (In batch mode, you send several commands all at once in an email message and they are executed one after the other without your intervention.) Eric Thomas designed these LISTSERV database functions so that you could search message archives at their remote host locations rather than downloading them and scanning them locally.

By installing a program called LDBASE, a reference librarian can retrieve relevant information by sending commands to the LISTSERV to perform search operations. To access the LISTSERV interactively, the searcher must obtain the LDBASE user interface by sending the following two commands to a LISTSERV (for example, *listserv@bitnic.bitnet*). Type each command on a separate line in the body of an email message, such as

```
get ldbase exec
get lsviucm module
```

As a reference librarian, you might find this database resource useful when a patron requests general information and would like a response immediately. If the topic is one which has a corresponding discussion list, and you know that list's name and electronic address, you can conduct a search and download the results to a local file while the patron waits.

This process can be illustrated best with an example. Suppose that a patron has requested information on cover crops for gardens that increase the nitrogen content of the soil. You type the command **ldbase** to start the user interface. This word used by itself accesses the home system—that is, the LISTSERV that is set as the default. (To access another node, type **ldbase <node>**.)

With a specific discussion list in mind, in this case *gardens@ukcc*, you enter the command **ldbase ukcc** to gain access to that list's message archives. LDBASE then asks you what the userid is, at which point you would type **listserv**, and press ENTER.

The command statement format is (SEARCH <topic> IN <database-list-name>). The search for an answer to this patron's question will be conducted in the GARDENS' message archives with the following command statements:

```
SEARCH cover crops IN gardens (26 hits)
```

[By omitting the IN keyword, the second search can be applied to the previous hits.]

```
SEARCH sources of nitrogen (1 hit)
SENDBACK PRINT ALL
```

[This is a simple output command requesting that the database output be sent back as a file.]

## The document that was retrieved in this search is shown here:

Mulch

Mulch is a layer of material which is spread over the surface of
a bed or other garden area. It helps keep down grass and unwanted weeds and holds in moisture.

Materials for mulch. Sometimes a black plastic sheet is used for
mulch. Around fruit trees small flat rocks or gravel can be
used. Many gardeners prefer to use organic material like grass,
leaves (preferably shredded), hay, etc. Organic material has the
advantage that it gradually decays to add beneficial humus to the
soil. Pine needles, unshredded leaves, and newspapers decay very
slowly. Oak leaves and pine needles also tend to increase the
acidity of your soil. At one time, we would have been concerned
about possible toxic elements in the ink on newspapers, but most
newspapers now use non-toxic ink.

Sources of mulch. Where can you get materials to use for mulch?
An obvious source is the leaves and grass clippings from your own
property. This may not be enough, especially if you are also
preparing compost. Some of your neighbors probably put out bags
of leaves or grass to be hauled off to the landfill - far better
that you pick them up first and use them. Early in the spring I
was able to get several bags of a wonderful mixture of dead grass
and shredded leaves when at two houses down the street they went
over their yards with a mower. Even if you're not so fortunate,
a plentiful supply of run of the mill leaves and grass should be
easily available. I lost count of how many bags of leaves I
found in the fall within a few blocks of my house, but it must
have been a hundred. Ruth Stout swore by hay as a material for
mulch. If you're in a city and have to buy it there, it's pretty
expensive. If you're in an area where hay is being produced you
can sometimes buy spoiled or old hay very cheaply.

Some gardeners till under the mulch after their crops are har-
vested. Then in the spring, they mulch the garden after their
plants have come up. Others leave it on the garden area year-
round, merely adding to it as the layer becomes less than several
inches thick. Trials at the Rodale Experimental Farm indicate
that there is an advantage to pulling back the mulch and leaving
the planting area bare for a couple of weeks before planting.
This allows the soil to warm up and accelerates production.

Compost

"Good compost is the most important part of the garden. It
aerates soil, breaks up clay, binds together sand, improves
drainage, prevents erosion, neutralizes toxins, holds precious
moisture, releases essential nutrients, and feeds the microbiotic
life of the soil, creating healthy conditions for natural antibi-
otics, worms, and beneficial fungi."
　　　　　　　　John Jeavons in How to Grow More Vegetables...

```
Compost is a natural fertilizer made by allowing kitchen and
garden wastes, grass, leaves, etc. to decay in bins or piles.
Compost is made in piles or bins composed of a mixture of materi-
als. It works better if the pile or bin is at least 3 feet by 3
feet and 3 feet high and if the pile is turned from time to time.
It needs materials which supply carbon and materials which supply
nitrogen. (Leaves, paper, and sawdust are relatively high in
carbon; kitchen wastes, grass clippings, and rotted manure are
relatively high in nitrogen.)  The different materials can be
mixed or layered in the pile. Layering is often suggested and
easier, but the Rodale Institute reports that mixing produces
better compost faster.
Kitchen scraps should be covered with a layer of leaves, grass,
or other material when added to the compost pile. Meat scraps
and dairy wastes should not be used, but almost anything else
from the kitchen can be.
Careful attention to the proportions of different materials in
the pile, maintaining proper moisture, and frequent turning of
the pile speeds the process. (Some claim to get finished compost
in two weeks!)  However, if you're not in a big hurry, a lazier
approach will work just fine. (There is some danger that an
unturned pile may develop an odor as may one with too much nitro-
gen).
```

Copyright © 1992 A.D. by The Ark. Used by permission.

This Note From The Ark sheet is one of a series aimed at providing helpful information. A single copy of any one of these is free. Send a long stamped addressed envelope to The Ark c/o III, Box 4630 SFA Sta., Nacogdoches, TX 75961. A complete set of 8 Notes From The Ark sheets is available for $1.00 and a long stamped addressed envelope with 52 cents postage.

## ≡ For Further Study

To obtain a comprehensive descriptive list of LISTSERV discussion lists, FTP to site *ftp.psi.com* and download the file called *interest-groups* located in the */usenet/new-users* directory. Another source is FTP site *ftp.nisc.sri.com* in a file called *interest-groups* located in the */netinfo* directory.

To search all of the LISTSERV discussion lists online for ones relating to a particular subject, send an email message to any major LISTSERV with the message **list global/<keyword>**, where <keyword> is the subject or topic for which you are looking.

The Law Library at Washington & Lee University also provides an opportunity for searching discussion lists online. TELNET to *liberty.uc.wlu.edu* and login **lawlib.** You'll find a simple menu-driven interface and a wealth of information including searchable lists of discussion lists.

Diane Kovacs maintains a list of academic email conferences. For a copy, FTP to site *ksuvxa.kent.edu* and download the file called *ACADLIST.README* located in the */library* directory. This file provides an introduction to that directory's contents. This directory also can be obtained in paper format or on a 3.5-

inch floppy disk—ASCII text for DOS or Macintosh. Order from the Office of Scientific & Academic Publishing Association of Research Libraries, 1527 New Hampshire Ave. NW, Washington, DC 20036. Email: *cdklein@cni.org*, Telephone: 202-232-2466, or FAX: 202-462-7849.

LSTREV-L is a discussion list that periodically reviews LISTSERV discussion lists. To subscribe, send your request to *listserv@umslvma.umsl.edu*.

To stay informed about discussion lists that are newly created, subscribe to NEW-LIST by sending the message **subscribe new-list <your name>** to *listserv@vm1.nodak.edu* (BITNET: *listserv@ndsuvm1*).

# Chapter 14

# Campus-Wide Information Systems (CWIS)

Many of the major colleges and universities in the world have *Campus-Wide Information Systems* (CWIS) running on their computer networks. These systems make it easy to retrieve campus information from one menu-driven centralized source. If a CWIS is connected to the Internet, you'll be able to access it using TELNET.

As a public information service, CWISs offer several advantages over print information services. You can get and information that's more current; access archived information online around the clock; and if you plan to visit one of these campuses, you can learn something about the institution before you arrive.

In addition to finding calendars of events on a CWIS, you'll find other resources, such as career development services, campus policies, campus phone directories, and local weather information. Some campuses also offer online databases and connections to outside information systems.

One of the more common interfaces used for CWISs is bulletin board system software, but there are others that structure their information around applications like Gopher and Lynx (see Chapter 9 for more information).

This chapter presents three examples of CWISs: *TechInfo*, *Appalachian State University VideoText System*, and *ColumbiaNet*.

## ≡ MIT TechInfo

To connect to TechInfo, TELNET to site *techinfo.mit.edu* [18.72.1.146]. TechInfo's main menu will appears without any special login procedure.

```
      1   TechInfo Feedback Questionnaire
   >  2   About TechInfo
      3   Around MIT - Offices & Services
      4   Classified Ad Listings
```

```
 5  Computing
 6  Courses, Schedules (Spring) & Calendars
 7  Events
 8  Jobs and Volunteer Opportunities
 9  MIT Libraries
10  Ongoing Activities, Notices, & Clubs
11  Policies, Rules & Procedures
12  Potluck
13  Publications
14  Reengineering Updates
15  Weather


=============================================================================:
Main, Return, Find, Outline, Info, Path, Search, Lookup, Advanced, World, Help,
```

TechInfo is a public information service offering such things as job listings, course schedules and descriptions, campus newspapers, and weather reports. This information is provided in the form of text documents, GIF images, and online directories. You can search by using menus, keywords, or an "expand" feature that permits more in-depth searching. A unique function called *Worldwide* lets you browse through documents located on other TechInfo systems connected to the Internet.

## ☰ ColumbiaNet

Connect to ColumbiaNet by TELNETing to *cal.cc.columbia.edu* [128.59.40.130]. This section illustrates the process of finding *On Liberty* by John Stuart Mill. First, you select *13. Misc Info* from the following menu. As you proceed with this exercise, you will be moving through a series of submenus— each one becoming more narrow in focus until you eventually arrive at your destination.

```
 1: Directory Information
 2: AcIS--Academic Computing
 3: CLIO Plus--Library Catalogs, Indexes, Encyclopedia
 4: Calendar, Events, & Schedules
 5: Classes, Finals, Grades, Holds, Bulletins
 6: Student Activities & Services
 7: Faculty & Research
 8: Job Opportunities
 9: Connections to Computers & the Internet
10: University Administrative Services
11: Handbooks, Reports
12: Organization & Governance; The Record
13: Misc Info--News, Weather, Quotations, Books
14: Community Interest
15: ColumbiaNet News: New News: AP, Reuters Available
_____
Select 1-15 or S=scan-all-menus Q=quit
H=help I=info
```

After you select item 13, another menu appears. From this menu—shown below—choose *1. Project Bartleby.*

```
 1: Project Bartleby: Columbia Books, Poetry, Quotations
 2: ColumbiaNet Information
 3: News: ClariNet (AP, Reuters, ...) and UseNet News
 4: Weather Forecast, Local
 5: Metro Area and Other Weather Forecasts
 6: Reference (dictionaries, thesaurus, etc) from U of Minn
 7: Higher Education Forum
 8: Current Events
 9: Government Information Resources
10: Columbia Daily Spectator (campus newspaper)
11: New York City Information
12: Off-Campus: Services outside Columbia
13: Tests & Experiments
```

At the next menu, select *8:Other Books & Poetry.*

```
 1: Project Bartleby: The Art of Copying
 2: Chapman, George, trans. 1857. The Odysseys of Homer.
 3: Inaugural Addresses of the Presidents. 1989.
 4: Keats, John. 1884. Poetical Works.
 5: Wilde, Oscar. 1881. Poems.
 6: Wordsworth, William. 1888. Complete Poetical Works.
 7: Columbia Quotations
 8: Other Books & Poetry
```

After making this selection, you are given opportunity to view any one of 15 works, including *On Liberty* by John Stuart Mill.

```
 1: Baum, L. Frank. 1900. The Wonderful Wizard of Oz.
 2: Conrad, Joseph. 1987. The Nigger of the "Narcissus."
 3: Doyle, Arthur Conan. The Sign of Four.
 4: Dryden, John, trans. 1909. Virgil's Aeneid.
 5: Hume, David. 1910. An Enquiry Concerning Human Understanding.
 6: James, Henry. 1983. Novels 1871-1880.
 7: Jowett, Benjamin, trans. 1901. Plato's Republic.
 8: Kipling, Rudyard. 1899. The Jungle Book.
 9: London, Jack. 1982. Novels & Stories.
10: Marvell, Andrew. 1681. Miscellaneous Poems.
11: Melville, Herman. 1846. Typee.
12: Mill, John Stuart. 1909. On Liberty.
13: More, Sir Thomas. 1901. Utopia.
14: Schwartau, Winn. 1991. Terminal Compromise.
15: Wells, H(erbert) G(eorge). 1898. The Time Machine.
```

## ≡ Appalachian State University VideoText System

To connect with the Appalachian State University CWIS, TELNET to *conrad.appstate.edu,* and when the host asks for a username, type **info,** and press ENTER. Select menu item (V)VIDEOTEXT and you'll be presented with the screen shown in Figure 14-1.

Appalachian State University offers several unique services, one of which is called *Ask Uncle Sigmund.* Uncle Sigmund is an online counselor for students, faculty, and staff who answers questions about relationships and personal problems. Menu item *15.Other Information Systems* offers a gateway to several off-campus systems including North Carolina State, UNC Chapel Hill, UNC Greensboro, UNC Wilmington, Western Carolina, and East Carolina.

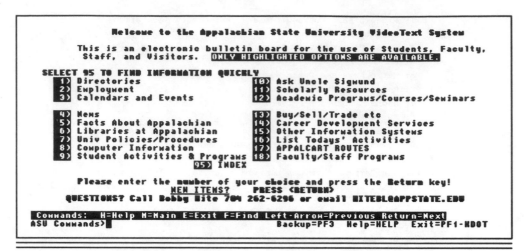

**Figure 14-1:**   Appalachian State University's VideoText CWIS

Under *5. Facts About Appalachian*, you can find statistics like this:

```
CLASS LEVEL          1991    1992    1993

----- -----          ----    ----    ----

Entering Freshmen    1891    2054    1910
Other Freshmen        601     724     642
Sophomore            2542    2479    2795
Junior               2412    2331    2184
Senior               2742    2865    2783
Special/Unclass       357     273     379
TOTAL UNDERGRADS    10545   10726   10693
TOTAL GRADUATES       822     924     948
TOTAL HEADCOUNT     11367   11650   11641
TOTAL FTE           10792   11115   11095
```

Under menu item *11. Scholarly Resources*, you will find, among other things, an introduction to FEDIX and MOLIS. These are online services of Federal Information Exchange, Inc. The FEDIX databases provide current information on such things as agency research opportunities, scholarships, and program contacts. Participating agencies include the Department of Energy (DOE), Department of Commerce (DOC), Department of Education (DOEd), Department of Housing and Urban Development (HUD), National Aeronautics and Space Administration (NASA), Federal Aviation Administration (FAA), National Science Foundation (NSF), National Security Agency (NSA), Office of Naval Research (ONR), U.S. Agency for International Development (AID), and Air Force Office of Scientific Research (AFOSR).

MOLIS, the Minority Online Information Service, provides current information about Historically Black Colleges and Universities and Hispanic-Serving

Institutions. Topics covered include pre-college and education programs, facilities and equipment, scholarships, fellowships, and faculty profiles, etc.

To use these services to access the Internet, TELNET to site *fedix.fie.com* [192.111.228.1] or dial-up to 1-800-232-4879. Modem setup: 8-N-1; Baud rate: 1200, 2400, 9600 (supports V.32,V.42,V.42 bis & MNP 5).

≡ **For Further Study**

If you have access to WAIS, *bit.listserv.cwis-l.src* provides an index to the *CWIS-L* mailing list. This is a good source of information about Campus-Wide Information Systems. Also accessible via WAIS is Judy Hallman's list of CWISs, called *cwis_list.src.*

For a listing of other CWISs you can access on the Internet, FTP to one of the following sites and download the file called *cwis-l: calypso-2.oit.unc.edu* [198.86.40.81] in the directory */pub/docs/about-the-net/cwis* or *sunsite.unc.edu* [152.2.22.81] in the directory */pub/docs/about-the-net/cwis.*

You can access many of the information systems in this list via UNC's laUNChpad, a gateway service that's accessible via TELNET to site *launchpad.unc.edu.* When asked for a username, enter **launch.** At the main menu, choose item 3. *On-line Information Systems (Libtel).*

Another gateway service called LIBS also will give you online access to various CWISs. TELNET to *uncvx1.oit.unc.edu* and enter **libtel** for a username. At the main LIBS menu, select menu item 3. *Campus-Wide Information Systems.* Both of these gateways are described in Chapter 17.

# Chapter 15

# Online Library Catalogs

This chapter introduces three of the best-known computerized library systems you can access on the Internet: The University of California's MELVYL Library System, the Colorado Alliance of Research Libraries (CARL), and the Library of Congress.

You'll also find in this chapter major directories, both software applications and textual documents, that list hundreds of other automated library catalogs, also known as OPACs (online public access catalogs). Most of the libraries described in these directories are accessed using TELNET, but one example of another kind of library, The Virtual Library, is given at the end of this chapter. You access the Virtual Library through the World-Wide Web.

## ≡ University of California's MELVYL Library System

*MELVYL*, the online library of the University of California, offers access to several databases, including online catalogs, periodical databases, and other library systems. As with most campus information systems, access to fee-based databases like INSPEC and PsycINFO is generally restricted to students, faculty, and staff.

To connect with MELVYL, TELNET to *melvyl.ucop.edu*.

At the opening menu, you are presented with two broad classifications of databases: Library databases and Indexes to recent articles. The latter is restricted to University of California users only.

You can access the Library databases by entering the commands **ten**, **cat**, or **pe**. Entering **ten** at the command prompt connects to the Ten-Year MELVYL Catalog which covers the most recent 10 years. Entering **cat** connects you with the full MELVYL catalog. The command **pe** connects you with the MELVYL Periodicals Database.

Here is MELVYL's opening menu:

```
                    MELVYL SYSTEM DATABASES

Library databases:
  TEN      For faster searches, type TEN;
              Ten-Year MELVYL Catalog - materials published from 1984 - 1994
  CAT      Full MELVYL Catalog - UC libraries and the California State Library
  PE       Periodical Titles    - California Academic Libraries List of Serials

Indexes to recent articles:  (for UC users only; password may be needed)
  MAGS     Magazine & Journal   - 1,500 magazines and journals
  NEWS     Newspaper Articles   - five major U.S. newspapers
  CC       Current Contents     - 6,500 scholarly journals
  CCT      Current Contents     - tables of contents of 6,500 scholarly journals
  INS      INSPEC               - 4,000 physics, electronics & computing journals
  MED      MELVYL MEDLINE       - 4,000 medical and life sciences journals
  COMP     Computer Articles    - 200 computer-related magazines and journals
  PSYC     PsycINFO             - 1,300 psychology journals and publications
```

The Ten-Year MELVYL Catalog contains about 1,700,000 titles representing almost 3,600,000 holdings for materials in the University of California libraries and the California State Library. The full MELVYL Catalog database contains, as of 4/11/94, about 7,800,000 titles representing almost 12 million holdings. The Periodicals Database contains 796,796 periodical titles representing 1,277,100 holdings from the University of California and seven other institutions. This database can be searched by title, author, subject, or keywords.

Online help is available for all three databases. At the opening menu of each database, enter **HELP** for information on getting started or **e guide** for a guide to using the database. To move back to the opening menu, type **start** and press ENTER. To end your session, type the command **quit**.

## ≡ The Colorado Alliance of Research Libraries (CARL)

CARL Corporation was established in 1988 as CARL Systems to develop and market the library system used by the Colorado Alliance of Research Libraries. This system offers access to several academic and public library OPAC's, various indexes, and interactive word searching in various information databases.

To connect with CARL, TELNET to *pac.carl.org* and at the *Enter Choice>* prompt, enter **PAC**. You then are asked to enter your terminal type (for example, VT100). Some databases are not accessible without a password or library card number. The opening menu offers you five choices. This menu and the next level of sub-menus follow.

```
CARL Corporation offers access to the following
        groups of databases:

    1. Library Catalogs
          (including Government Publications)
```

```
2. Current Article Indexes and Access
      (including UnCover and ERIC)

3. Information Databases
      (including Encyclopedia)

4. Other Library Systems

5. Library and System News
```

Upon choosing item 1. Library Catalogs, you will connect to the following set of submenus:

```
                        LIBRARY CATALOGS

    6. Auraria Library             17. Regis University
    7. Colorado School of Mines    18. Luther College Network  (IA)
    8. Univ Colo at Boulder        19. Northwest College  (WY)
    9. Univ Colo Health Sciences Center 20. State Department of Education
   10. Univ Colo Law Library       21. Bemis Public Library  (Littleton)
   11. Denver Public Library       22. Government Publications
   12. Denver University           23. Univ Colo Film/Video - Stadium
   13. Denver University Law Library 24. CCLINK -- Community Colleges
   14. University of Northern Colorado 25. MedConnect--Medical Libraries (CO)
   15. University of Wyoming       26. High Plains Regional Libraries
   16. Colorado State University   27. Teikyo Loretto Hts
```

The next item in the main menu, 2. Current Article Indexes and Access, connects to this set of submenus:

```
              CURRENT ARTICLE INDEXES AND ACCESS

       ARTICLE INDEXES                 CURRENT RECEIPTS
   50. UnCover -- Article Access    53. New Journal Issues
       (Article Access & Delivery)
   52. ERIC (Access Restricted as of 11/1/92)
   57. British Library Document              UNION LISTS
       Supply Centre (Article Delivery) 54. Boston Library Consortium
   80. Magazine Index & ASAP
       (full text available)
   81. Business Index & ASAP        NATIONAL SERIALS CATALOGING DATABASE
       (full text available)        55. CONSER
   87. Expanded Academic Index


   86. National Newspaper Index              FULL TEXT
                                    56. Online Libraries
```

The third item in the main menu, 3. Information Databases, leads to the following choices:

```
INFORMATION DATABASES

   60. Choice Book Reviews (access restricted as of 9/1/93)
   61. Encyclopedia
   63. Metro Denver Facts
   64. School Model Programs
```

```
65. Internet Resource Guide
66. Department of Energy
67. Journal Graphics
    (Television/Radio Transcripts)
82. Company ProFile
88. Federal Domestic Assistance Catalog
89. Librarian's Yellow Pages
```

When you choose menu item 4. Other Library Systems, you will be given a choice of two submenus: one leading to a list of CARL libraries in the Eastern half of the United States and the other a list of CARL libraries in the Western United.

```
            OTHER LIBRARY SYSTEMS

41. CARL Corporation Network Libraries - Eastern U.S.
      * Includes public, academic, and school library catalogs,
        and some local information databases.

42. CARL Corporation Network Libraries - Western U.S.
      * Includes public, academic, and school library catalogs,
        and some local information databases.
```

The last item in the main menu, 5. Library and System News, brings you to the following list of news files:

```
LIBRARY AND SYSTEM NEWS

Your first step is to select the NEWS file you wish to consult.
News is currently available for:

 1. Auraria
 2. Univ Colo at Boulder
 3. Denver Public Library
 4. Denver University
 5. Denver University Law Library
 6. Colorado School of Mines
 7. University of Northern Colorado
 8. Regis University
 9. University of Wyoming
10. Univ Colo Health Sciences Center
11. Univ Colo Law Library
12. Government Publications
13. Luther College
14. CCLINK -- Community Colleges
15. Colorado State University
16. High Plains Libraries News
17. GENERAL PAC NEWS -    3/7/94
18. Technos - January 1994
```

Several services are available on CARL and one of the most notable is the Online Libraries system, which offers text-searching capabilities (see *56. Online Libraries* under the heading *Current Article Indexes and Access*). This database presents full-text articles from *Online Libraries and Microcomputers* (9/83 to date), *Online Newsletter* (1980-81 and 1988 to date), and *Online Hotline* (1982 to 1987).

## ≡ Library of Congress

In the fall of 1993, The Library of Congress announced the availability of a new online system called LC MARVEL (Library of Congress Machine-Assisted Realization of the Virtual Electronic Library). LC MARVEL is like the CWIS (Campus-Wide Information System) of the Library of Congress, offering information about the Library, its activities and collections. LC MARVEL also provides information to the U.S. Congress and constituents throughout the world.

Depending on your preference, you can connect to LC MARVEL either by using a Gopher interface or by TELNETing. For Gopher access, enter **gopher marvel.loc.gov** at your system prompt. To access LC MARVEL using TELNET, enter **telnet marvel.loc.gov** and Login: **marvel**. The main menu is pictured here:

```
                        MAIN MENU

        The main menu of LC MARVEL consists of the following
    selections:
         1. About LC MARVEL
         2. Library of Congress: facilities, activities, and services
         3. Research and reference
         4. Library of Congress online systems
         5. The U.S. Congress
         6. Federal government information
         7. Services to libraries and publishers
         8. Copyright
         9. Employee information
        10. The global electronic library (by subject)
        11. Other Internet resources.


                REPORTING COMMENTS AND PROBLEMS

        Since LC MARVEL will be "under construction" for several months, the
    design team is interested in hearing your comments and reports of any
    technical problems that may occur. Send any Internet mail messages to
    LCMARVEL@SEQ1.LOC.GOV.
    ***********************************************************************
```

Here is a brief description of some of the menu items:

2. *Library of Congress: Facilities, Activities, and Services* contains the full-text of LC press releases.

7. *Services to libraries and publishers* offers assistance in how to obtain an ISBN.

11. *Other Internet resources* connects users to a wide variety of Internet navigational tools.

9. *Employee information* offers a full-text view of internal publications, emergency information, job postings, and searchable Library regulations.

To connect with the Library of Congress Information System (LOCIS), take the following path, starting in the main menu of LC MARVEL shown earlier: */Library of Congress Online Systems/Connect to LOCIS (Public Users - No Password Needed) <TEL>.*

You also can connect via TELNET to site *locis.loc.gov* [140.147.254.3]. LOCIS represents more than 28 million records including all LC MARC files, copyright files since 1978, federal bill status files, and public policy citations since 1976. The reference/retrieval system (SCORPIO) and the technical processing/cataloging system (MUMS) are also available. LOCIS can be accessed 8:00 a.m. to 10:00 p.m. Monday through Friday. The opening menu and a few of the submenus follow.

```
       L O C I S :   LIBRARY OF CONGRESS INFORMATION SYSTEM

          To make a choice: type a number, then press ENTER


      1    Library of Congress Catalog      4    Braille and Audio

      2    Federal Legislation              5    Organizations

      3    Copyright Information            6    Foreign Law

  *     *     *     *     *     *     *     *     *     *     *     *

      7    Searching Hours and Basics
      8    Documentation and Classes
      9    Library of Congress General Information
     10    Library of Congress Fast Facts
     11    * * Announcements * *      New Interface for Some Files!



     12    Comments and Logoff
           Choice:
```

Choosing *1. Library of Congress Catalog* brings you to the following screen:

```
                                                     LOCISMENU
                      LIBRARY OF CONGRES   CATALOG
  CHOICE                                               FILE

      1    BOOKS: English language books 1968-, French 1973-, German,     LOCI
           Portuguese, Spanish 1975-, other European languages '1976-77,
           non-European languages 1978-79. Some microforms 1984-.

           BOOKS earlier than the dates above. Some serials, maps,        PREM
           music, audiovisual items.

      3    Combination of files 1 and 2 above  (LOCI and PREM).

      4    SERIALS cataloged at LC & some other libraries since 1973.     LOCS

      5    MAPS and other cartographic items (except atlases) cataloged   LOCM
           at LC 1968- and some other research libraries 1985-.

      6    SUBJECT TERMS and cross references form LC Subject Headings.    LCXR
           NOTE:   Choices 1,4, and 5, depending on commands used, also
                   include ALL catalog files. See HELP screens.
     12    Return to LOCIS MENU screen.
```

Choosing 2.*Federal Legislation* displays a screen containing items that describe Congressional legislation from 1973 to present, as shown here:

```
                                                          C CATALOG
                    FEDERAL LEGISLATION

These files track and describe legislation (bills and resolutions) introduced
in the US Congress, from 1973 (93rd Congress) to the current Congress (the
current Congress is the 103rd). Each file covers a separate Congress.


    CHOICE                                              FILE


    1     Congress, 1981-82      (97th)                 CG97
    2     Congress, 1983-84      (98th)                 CG98
    3     Congress, 1985-86      (99th)                 CG99
    4     Congress, 1987-88      (100th)                C100
    5     Congress, 1989-90      (101st)                C101
    6     Congress, 1991-92      (102nd)                C102
    7     Current Congress, 1993-  (103rd)              C103


    8     Search all Congresses from 1981-->current
    9     Search all Congresses on LOCIS 1973-->current


          Earlier Congresses: press ENTER
    12    Return to LOCIS MENU screen.


          Choice:
```

When you choose 3.*Copyright Information*, you receive the following choices:

```
                                                        LEGISLATION1
                      COPYRIGHT INFORMATION
    CHOICE                                                  FILE


    1    Works registered for copyright since 1978. These include     COHM
         books, films, music, maps, sound recordings, software,
         multimedia kits, drawings, posters, sculpture, etc.
         Serials are in the COHS file.



    2    Serials (periodicals, magazines, journals, newspapers, etc.)  COHS
         registered for copyright since 1978.



    3    Documents relating to copyright ownership, such as name        COHD
         changes and transfers.
```

# ≡ The WWW Virtual Library

To access the Virtual Library, begin by TELNETing to a World-Wide Web server; for example, TELNET to *fatty.law.cornell.edu* and Login: **www**. This connects you with a Lynx browser where you can then type **g** and press ENTER, which allows you to designate a specific Web link. At the *URL to open:* prompt, enter the following URL:

*http://info.cern.ch/hypertext/DataSources/ByAccess.html*

This entry connects you with a page titled *RESOURCES CLASSIFIED BY TYPE OF SERVICE.* The first link on this page is the word **subject** in the sentence "See also categorization exist by **subject**." Make this link by selecting that link name (it becomes unhighlighted) and pressing the right arrow key. This brings you to the following screen, on which you see a list of available subjects arranged alphabetically:

```
            The World-Wide Web Virtual Library: Subject Catalogue (p1 of 10)


            VIRTUAL LIBRARY THE WWW VIRTUAL LIBRARY

This is a distributed subject catalogue. See also arrangement by
service type ., and other subject catalogues of network information

Mail to maintainers of the specified subject or
www-request@info.cern.ch to add pointers to this list, or if you would
like to contribute to administration of a subject area.

See also how to put your data on the web

Aeronautics
        Mailing list archive index . See also NASA LaRC

Agriculture
        See Agricultural info , Almanac mail servers ; the Agricultural
        Genome (National Agricultural Library, part of the U.S.
        Department of Agriculture) ; North Carolina Cooperative
        Extension Service Gopher ; Cornell University - CALS - NYSAES
-- press space for next page --
 Arrow keys: Up and Down to move. Right to follow a link; Left to go back.
H)elp O)ptions P)rint G)o M)ain screen Q)uit /=search [delete]=history list


                                                                    2


            WWW server

Anthropology
        Separate list

Archaeology
        Separate list

Asian Studies
        Separate list

Astronomy and Astrophysics
        Separate list.

Bio Sciences
        Separate list

Chemistry
        Separate list
```

Go to the Ls and locate the linkname *Libraries*. Press the right arrow key to make that link. After making the link, the following screens appear:

```
                              LIBRARIES

   Information categorized by subject. See also other subjects . Please
   mail www-request@info.cern.ch if you know of online information not in
   these lists.


WWW Libraries

     * The National Library of Australia


Other libraries

   You have to log on to most libraries: you can find them in the
   hytelnet lists:
     * On-line Library catalogues
     * Other things to log on to


-- press space for next page --
  Arrow keys: Up and Down to move. Right to follow a link; Left to go back.
 H)elp O)ptions P)rint G)o M)ain screen Q)uit /=search [delete]=history list
                                                                    2
   The BUBL "Bulletin Board for Libraries" contains library-related
   information with a UK bias.

   Other lists are not hypertext and do not allow you to connect directly
   using WWW, but they contain instructions for logging on:
     * Art St.George's index ,
     * "Library" in the internet resource guide ,
     * index of hytelnet .

   See also information by subject , the hytelnet gateway .
```

Accessing this "virtual" online library will take you many places around the globe—hyperlinking you to hundreds of different resources with every path you follow. To move back through the links, press the left arrow key. To move among the various link names, press the up and down arrow keys. To make a selection, press the right arrow key. For additional information on using the Lynx browser program, see Chapter 9.

## ☰ Using OPACs for Subject Searching and Author/Title Verification

The Internet, with its many online catalogs, gives your patrons access to a larger universe of information—one that goes beyond the four walls of your own library. For a small public library with less than 50,000 titles in its collection, the opportunity to access millions of other bibliographic records constitutes a significant increase in services. In this setting, if a library patron presents a subject request that you can't fill locally, you can run a search in another library's online catalog via the Internet. Any relevant materials you find can then be borrowed through interlibrary loan or purchased if that is an option.

If you're working within a large university library system, the advantages of offering access to other library catalogs becomes less apparent because most needs can be met locally. Regardless of your collection's size, however, if you aren't automated, the Internet provides an opportunity to search online at institutions that are automated.

At times, you will find it easier and more advantageous to perform a keyword search in the Library of Congress Information System than to do a subject search in your own card catalog. For example, a patron may ask "Do you have this book? I think the author's name is something like 'Maloan' or 'Stone,' and the title is *The Book of Bicycling*?" If you can't find the title in your card catalog, you could search an online library system with a larger collection to verify the citation. You may get zero hits, or you may pull up *The Complete Book of Bicycling* by Eugene A. Sloan—the book the patron was looking for.

## ≡ For Further Study

For information on locating special library collections on the Internet, Gopher to *riceinfo.rice.edu* and follow the path */9. Library Services/5. Miscellaneous library resources from around the Internet/36. Guides to Library Science Resources on the Internet/4. Special Library Collections Available on the Internet.*

## ≡ Directories and Other Resource Information

Many libraries all around the world make their computerized library catalogs available on the Internet via TELNET.

This section introduces special directories, software applications, and other services that will aid you in locating and connecting to hundreds of these online catalogs.

1. There's a USENET newsgroup that announces new libraries on the Internet and discusses other related topics called *comp.internet.library*. (See Chapter 19 for details on USENET newsgroups.)

2. *UNT's Accessing On-line Bibliographic Databases* by Billy Barron started out as a single indexed document, but now is broken down by continent into separate files. Barron's book describes how to access the university library systems around the world. Each entry includes the library's TELNET address and details on how to login and exit the system. Various library automation systems are described in the appendices. You can obtain copies of Barron's book by FTPing to site *ftp.utdallas.edu* in the directory */pub/staff/billy/libguide*. Filenames are *libraries.africa, libraries.americas, libraries.asia,* and *libraries.europe.*

    You also can find Billy Barron's book by using the Gopher server at *yaleinfo.yale.edu* path */Research and library services/More research & library services at Yale and beyond (Internet)/Library catalogs beyond Yale (via the Internet)/Paper List (BBarrons' Accessing Online Bib Dbases)/.*

3. *AARNet access to Australian and New Zealand OPACs* compiled by Deidre E. Stanton is also available at FTP site *ftp.unt.edu* in the directory */pub/library*. Filename is *AArnet.Library*. If the file can't be found at this site, contact the author : stanton@portia.murdoch.edu.au.

4. *Internet-Accessible Library Catalogs & Databases*, co-authored by Art St. George and Ron Larsen, lists over 100 library catalogs and databases you can access around the world via the Internet or through dial-up connections. To obtain a copy, send the command **get library package** in the body of an email message to *listserv@unmvm.bitnet*.

5. HYTELNET is a software application that provides hypertext access to listings of Internet-accessible library catalogs, Free-Nets, CWISs, BBSs, Gophers, and other TELNET services. You can download the HYTELNET program and run it on your own IBM PC, or you can access it on a remote host. For example, you can access the HYTELNET program via Gopher by connecting to the Gopher server at the University of Saskatchewan by entering this command:

`gopher gopher.usask.ca.`

You also can use interactively a HYTELNET Server at the University of Saskatchewan by TELNETing to *access.usask.ca*. Login: **hytelnet**
The following information then appears on your screen:

```
              HYTELNET version 6.6
               October 10, 1993


This program is distributed as shareware. The author holds all
copyrights. If you find this program to be of use to you, a donation of
$20 would be welcome, to cover my costs and time. See address below.


                  **New in Version 6.6**

Many new site files have been added, and many have been updated or
deleted. Certain files have been renamed to match their domain names.


                    **Operations**

For full keystroke information see <HELP>

Use the cursor keys to move around in Hytelnet. The up and down arrows
move you from one highlighted link to another. Use the right arrow (or
return) to follow a link, and use the left arrow to come back. You
can also use hjkl (vi's cursor keys).

The program notices telnet and tn3270 commands embedded in the files,
and will execute them for the user, if desired. This feature is


            Welcome to HYTELNET version 6.6.x
              Last Update: March 7, 1994


     What is HYTELNET?        <WHATIS>
     Library catalogs         <SITES1>
     Other resources          <SITES2>
```

```
Help files for catalogs    <OP000>
Catalog interfaces         <SYS000>
Internet Glossary          <GLOSSARY>
Telnet tips                <TELNET>
Telnet/TN3270 escape keys  <ESCAPE.KEY>
Key-stroke commands        <HELP>
```

A discussion list called LIB_HYTELNET, moderated by Peter Scott, discusses the HYTELNET program. To subscribe, send a message to *scott@sklib.usask.ca*. Address the messages you want to send to the list to *lib_hytelnet@sas.usask.ca*.

To download your own copy of HYTELNET, FTP to site *midway.uchicago.edu* and go to the */pub/network-clients/dos* directory. Here you will find a file called *hyteln63.zip* (465213 bytes), and if you need it, a copy of *pkunzip.exe* to unzip the file.

6. LIBINET is a hypertext version of L. Farley's guide *Library resources on the Internet: strategies for selection and use*. This is a handbook that gives users strategies for identifying and using library catalogs accessible on the Internet.

The name of the file you should download is called *libinet.exe*. This file is available via FTP from either one of the following sites: *ftp.sunet.se* [130.238.127.3] in the */pub/doc/network/userguides/rasd/libinet* directory, or *calypso-2.oit.unc.edu* [198.86.40.81] in the *pub/academic/library/libsoft* directory.

The *libinet.exe* file is a self-extracting compressed file that when uncompressed occupies about 480K on your hard disk. Before you install this program on your hard disk, first create a subdirectory in which to store it. Then copy the *libinet.exe* file to that directory. Change to the directory, type **libinet**, and press ENTER. When you type **libinet**, you run the self-extracting decompressing program, which creates some 140 disk files. Once the process is complete and everything looks in order, you can then delete the *libinet.exe* file from the subdirectory. To start the program, type **hyplus** and press ENTER. Use the right arrow key to jump from one of the highlighted words or phrases to the next hypertext link. Use the left arrow key to backtrack. Press the F1 key for online help.

A copy of Farley's book can also be accessed via Gopher. Connect to the Gopher server at site *chico.rice.edu* and choose the following menu items: *8. Information by subject/30. Library and Information Science/70. Library Resources on the Internet. Farley (8/91).*

7. CATALIST is an Internet library system guide designed for Microsoft Windows by Richard H. Duggan. The program is a hypertext version of Billy Barron's *UNT's Accessing On-line Bibliographic Databases* that offers assistance in locating library systems that are accessible on the Internet. You can look up a site two ways: alphabetically by institution name or geographically .

CATALIST can run side-by-side with your Windows communications software. When you are connected to an online catalog, you can use CATALIST as a useful source of information on how to search a particu-

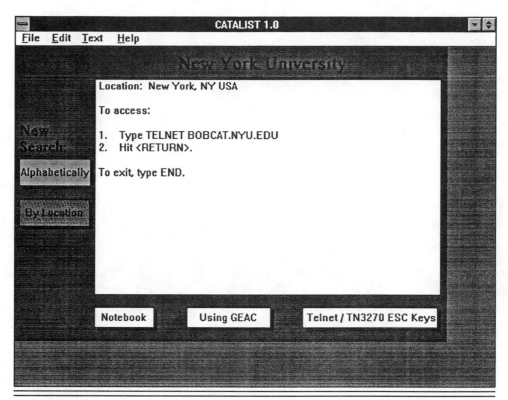

**Figure 15-1:** The CATALIST window

lar catalog. For example, as Figure 15-1 shows, if you've connected with the New York University library and need assistance on the GEAC automation system, you can open the CATALIST window, look up New York University, and click on the button that says *Using GEAC.* CATALIST also offers a notebook function that enables you to save personal notes on a particular site and then call them up whenever you access that site address again.

CATALIST software is available via FTP from site *zebra.acs.udel.edu* in the directory */pub/library.* You must have Asymetrix ToolBook 1.5 or Runtime ToolBook 1.5 to use CATALIST. If you don't have either of these applications, you will need to get the *fullcat.exe* file. Runtime Tool-Book 1.5 is included in the *fullcat.exe* archive. If you already have Tool-Book 1.5 or Runtime ToolBook 1.5, or if you just need the latest version of CATALIST, you need only to download the file called *cat10.exe.*

The *fullcat.exe* and *cat10.exe* files are self-extracting ZIP archives. For instructions on unarchiving these files, download and read the *readme.txt* file. To unarchive the file, you type the filename without the extension (type **fullcat** if you've downloaded the *fullcat.exe* file) and press ENTER. *Then go into Windows and run the install program.*

# Chapter 16

# Electronic Publishing

This chapter introduces you to several new electronic publishing formats that exist online. Many of these publications are available without charge on the Internet and others are available for a fee. Unusual names like cyberzines, ejournals, and etexts are used to describe these new formats whose counterparts exist in the print world as books, magazines, zines, journals, and newsletters.

The very nature of the Internet, with its global coverage and high-speed data transfer rates, makes it an effective distribution channel for these various electronic formats. The spectrum of subjects covered in these publications is as far-reaching as the interests and imaginations of those who subscribe. Some electronic publications are digital versions of publications printed in paper format, while others are exclusively online publications.

Although this new communication medium has many advantages, some concerns in this area are yet to be resolved. One consideration is that electronic publishers currently have no way of preventing online users from making unauthorized copies of materials. Large amounts of data can be downloaded in seconds and in turn, redistributed to a few, or many, within minutes. Another concern is that text in a digitized format can be easily manipulated. Altered documents are difficult, if not impossible, to detect.

If you decide to place an order and purchase a product or service online, you will be asked to supply a valid credit card number. If you question the issue of security when using your credit card to make purchases online, see the FAQ on Internet Commerce where the question "Is it safe to use credit card numbers on the Internet?" explains the risk factors of this practice and tells you what safety measures exist. You can view this FAQ on the Gopher server at site *marketplace.com*. At the root menu, choose menu item */9.Frequently Asked Questions about Internet Commerce*.

## ≡ Ejournals

An *ejournal* is a periodical created and distributed in electronic format. Ejournals cover a wide spectrum of subjects ranging from news items to scholarly refereed articles. Many ejournals are available free of charge on the Internet. Others are produced privately and online users must pay a subscription fee to have them delivered to their electronic mailbox. An advantage that ejournals offer over print journals is the speed with which they can be delivered. The results of new research and news of current events can be published within just days or hours of their occurrence rather than weeks or months. Here are a few samples of what ejournals are like on the Internet. The topics covered here include computing, education, and campus news.

Computing: *The Amateur Computerist* (see Figure 16-1). Access via FTP to site *wuarchive.wustl.edu* in the directory */doc/misc/acn*.

Education: *Academe This Week*. This ejournal can be accessed via the Gopher site for the *Chronicle of Higher Education* at *chronicle.merit.edu*. The root menu is shown here:

```
Internet Gopher Information Client 2.0 p19


Root gopher server: chronicle.merit.edu


     1. NEW IN "ACADEME THIS WEEK".
     2. GETTING TO KNOW OUR READERS.
     3. A GUIDE to The Chronicle of Higher Education, April 6, 1994/
     4. EVENTS IN ACADEME: April 5 to April 19/
     5. BEST-SELLING BOOKS on campuses.
     6. ALMANAC: facts and figures on U.S. higher education.
     7. JOB OPENINGS in Academe from the April 6 Chronicle/
     8. ABOUT THE CHRONICLE: subscriptions, advertising, copyright.
     9. ABOUT "ACADEME THIS WEEK": Search tips and more/
    10. Information provided to ACADEME THIS WEEK by other sources/
```

University Newspapers: *The Gazette* (University of Waterloo's newspaper). Access via Gopher site *watserv2.uwaterloo.ca* path */Events, news, weather/Gazette*. The following output shows the table of contents for the April 6, 1994 issue:

```
     1. Ancillary services fee set at $24.31.
     2. Bicycle helmets vital, researchers say.
     3. Budget gap narrows to $4 million.
     4. Cecilia on Music.
     5. Chemistry students collect awards.
     6. Counselling services gets accreditation.
     7. Income-repayable loans got small tryout.
     8. Music prof develops software package.
     9. NSERC strategic plan still isn't ready.
    10. North campus recreation facility is in use.
    11. Profile: Betti Erb.
    12. Roller blades, skateboards aren't welcome.
    13. Royal Trust donates $100,000 to UW.
```

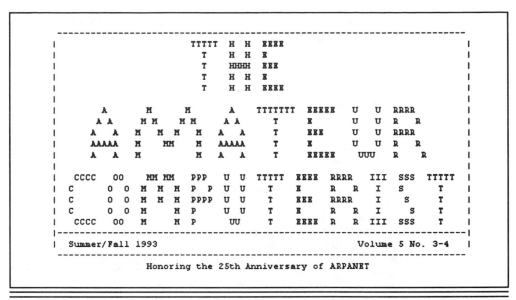

**Figure 16-1:** Screen of the Amateur Computerist

```
14. Safety audits of campus continue.
15. Staff member honoured for crime prevention.
16. Staff numbers down by 59 this year.
17. Welding: little-known specialty in engineering.
18. Wireless access to networks is project's aim.
```

From the Association of Research Libraries (ARL), the *Directory of Electronic Journals and Newsletters* is available on the Gopher server at *arl.cni.org*. You can also access this publication on the Web by pointing your client at *gopher://arl.cni.org:70/11/scomm/edir*. ARL also has created a discussion list called NewJour-L that publishes announcements of new electronic journals as they become available. To subscribe, send email to *listproc@e-math.ams.org* and in the body of the message, type subscribe newjour-l.

## ≡ CICNet's Electronic Journal Archives

CICNet was founded by the member universities of the Committee on Institutional Cooperation. CICNet's network exists for the primary purpose of transmitting and sharing information between academic and research organizations covering a seven state region of the upper Midwest.

The contents of CICNet's Electronic Journal Archives represent a comprehensive collection of all of the public domain electronic journals currently available on the Internet. Originally started by the Library Collection Development Officers of the CIC Universities, the archive is now under the direction of Paul Southworth for CICNet. For further information about this project, contact *pauls@cic.net*.

The archive can be accessed via Gopher at site *gopher.cic.net*. At the root menu, choose */2. Electronic Serials*. From this point, you can explore various avenues. The following output illustrates a sampling of what you'll find when you select menu item */3. Alphabetic List* and then the letter *A*:

```
 1. A-CHAT/
 2. ABLENET Disabilities Studies Group/
 3. AGBU Armenian Info Service/
 4. AIDS Alert/
 5. AIDS Daily Summary/
 6. AIDS News/
 7. AIDS News Service/
 8. AIX Tips News/
 9. AM/FM - UK Radio News/
10. AMSAT News Service/
11. AVS Network News/
12. Abyssinian Prince/
13. Academe This Week (from MERIT)/
14. Academic Exchange Information Center - News Release/
15. Acquisitions Librarians Electronic Network/
16. Action Canada Dossier/
17. Activist/
18. Activist Times Incorporated/
19. Advanced Squad Leader Digest/
20. African Studies Association On-Line/
21. Air Force News/
22. Albert Hoffman's Strange Mistake/
23. Albuquerque NeXT Users Group Newsletter/
24. Alt-167/
25. Alternative Media Alternative Music/
26. Amateur Computerist/
27. Amateur Radio Newsline/
28. Amazine/
29. Amazons International/
30. American Academy of Research Historians of Medieval Spain/
31. American Arab Scientific Society/
32. American Association of Law Libraries - Automatome/
33. American Association of Law Libraries - GOV-LINE Report/
34. American Association of Law Libraries - Legal Info Service/
35. American Library Association Washington Office Newsline/
36. American Medical Association Network/
```

Choosing the path */2. Electronic Serials/9. Other Journal Archives/1. E-Text Archive* brings you to the *E-Text Archive* directory shown here:

```
        E-Text Archive

 1. About The E-Text Archives.
 2. Raw File Listing of Entire Server.
 3. Search Titles On This Gopher <?>
 4. Book.Reviews/
 5. CPSR/
 6. CuD/
 7. Drives/
 8. Factsheet.Five/
 9. Fiction/
10. Gutenberg/
11. Legal/
12. Libellus/
```

```
13. Mailing.Lists/
14. Poetry/
15. Politics/
16. Quartz/
17. Religious.Texts/
18. WELL/
19. Zines/
20. Zines-by-subject/
21. incoming/
22. ls-1R.
```

Starting from this menu, you can explore several different paths. For example, path */8. Factsheet.Five/16. Misc_Zines_A-to-L_48* takes you to a directory filled with descriptions of zines. You'll find the following introductory screen and several entries. Two sample entries are included here.

```
This file/document is ShareRight 1994; you may copy, reproduce, use and/or
distribute this information however and as often as you like as long as
this sentence is included.

Miscellaneous zines from A-L from issue 48.
Miscellaneous zines. Posted January, 1994 by Jerod Pore. This file

is part of FactSheet Five - Electric. Questions or comments regarding
FactSheet Five - Electric should be directed to jerod23@well.sf.ca.us

If you wish to send zines for review in both the electronic and print
versions of Factsheet Five, the snailmail address is

Factsheet Five
PO Box 170099
San Francisco CA 94117-0099


or

Factsheet Five
1800 Market Street
San Francisco CA 94102



************************************************************************
%Title: ARTHURS'S COUSIN Volume 1 Issue 4 April '93
%Descr: In the true spirit of zinedom, Joshua promises to print
    anything. It seems to be taking off but most of the stuff
    is still by him.
A rant against pro-lifers, reprints of The Straight Dope, spare change
comics, and poems.

%Info: $1 Each to
Joshua , 2501 Wickersham Lane #2132, Austin, TX 78741
(24 Pages/D/RSF)
Trades OK/submissions OK/back issues/takes ad
************************************************************************

%Title: BACKWOODS HOME MAGAZINE: A Practical Journal of Self Reliance Issue
%Descr: 21 June '93
    Lots of really fun how-to articles, many of them sent in by
```

```
    the readers. Nicely laid out, well-written, with
    explanatory illustrations. Recipes, guns, gardening,
    business ideas, Americana, letters, and personal essays.
This one has feature articles on using houseplants to improve indoor air
quality, drilling your own well, building your own beehives, using cayenne
pepper sprays for self protection, reusing empty plastic containers, building
your own fence, the truth behind lumber regulations, making soup stock,
buying a dairy goat, choosing a rifle buying a horse, homeschooling, and
homebirthing,                                                    .
Perfect for the home survivalist.
%Info: $4.50 Each , Subs: $17.95 for 6 issues to
Backwoods Home Magazine, 1257 Siskiyou Blvd #213, Ashland, OR 97520
(98 Pages/S/RSF)
No trades/submissions OK/back issues/takes ads.
***************************************************************************
```

*InterText* is a free electronic magazine dedicated to the publication of fiction. Starting from the E-Text Archive menu shown above, follow the path */19. Zines/36. InterText/3. ascii/1. ITv1n1-ascii.* An extract from the first issue follows.

```
INTERTEXT - Volume 1, Number 1 - March-April 1991

    INSIDE THIS ISSUE

  FirstText / JASON SNELL

 A War In the Sand / DANIEL APPELQUIST

 Anticipation of the Night / DANIEL APPELQUIST

  Direct Connection / PHIL NOLTE

  The Sculptor / ANDREA PAYNE

  Mister Wilt / JASON SNELL

 Do You Have Some Time? / MARY ANNE WALTERS

  The Talisman / GREG KNAUSS

  Schrodinger's Monkey / GREG KNAUSS
-----------------------------------------------------------------
   Editor: Jason Snell (jsnell@ucsd.edu)
 Assistant Editor: Geoff Duncan (sgd4589@ocvaxa.cc.oberlin.edu)
 Assistant Editor: Phil Nolte (NU020061@vm1.NoDak.edu)
-----------------------------------------------------------------
InterText Vol. 1, No. 1. Intertext is published electronically on a
bi-monthly basis, and distributed via electronic mail over the
Internet, BITNET, and UUCP. Reproduction of this magazine is
permitted as long as the magazine is not sold and the content of the
magazine is not changed in any way. Copyright (C) 1991, Jason Snell.
All stories (C) 1991 by their respective authors. All further rights
to stories belong to the authors. The ASCII InterText is exported
from Pagemaker 4.0 files into Microsoft Word 4.0. Circulation: 1057
(832 ASCII). For subscription requests, email: jsnell@ucsd.edu
  ->Back issues available via FTP at: network.ucsd.edu<-
-----------------------------------------------------------------
```

```
FirstText / JASON SNELL

  Welcome to InterText, the new net magazine devoted (well, I'd
like to think it will be devoted) to the publication of fiction.
  First off, I'd like to thank Jim McCabe, the man who produced
Athene, for all the work he did on that magazine.
  This magazine takes its place, and I hope that you will all find
the stories we publish to be entertaining and thought-provoking.
Publishing a commercial magazine is a risky business --
electronically publishing a non-commercial magazine is risky and
essentially untried. The only similar magazine that publishes in both
ASCII and PostScript(TM) format in the United States that I know of
is Daniel Appelquist's QUANTA, hich has been published since Fall,
1989. (The other netmagazines are DARGONZINE, which is distributed in
ASCII format only, and the GUILDSMAN, a roleplaying journal.)

                   8
```

This E-text Archive menu can be accessed at other sites, too. In fact, the menu option is in the root menu at Gopher server *etext.archive.umich.edu*.

## ≡ Project Gutenberg

Project Gutenberg is an online database containing numerous electronic texts. Their purpose is to encourage the creation and distribution of English language etexts and they have set a goal of releasing 10,000 titles and distributing them to one trillion people by the year 2001. Due to copyright law, many of the works contained in this etext collection are books written prior to 1920. Titles already released include classic literature such as *A Christmas Carol, Red Badge of Courage, Alice in Wonderland, The Scarlet Letter*, and *The War of the Worlds*.

Individuals that are interested in keeping informed about Project Gutenberg may subscribe to the Project Gutenberg newsletter. Send the following **message to** *listserv@uiucvmd* (BITNET) or *listserv@vmd.cso.uivc.edu*: **subscribe gutnberg <your name>**. (Note: This server only recognizes subscription commands. Other messages should be routed to the Director of Project Gutenberg, Michael S. Hart, at *dircompg@uxi.cso.uiuc.edu*.)

To view the etexts that are available, FTP to site *mrcnext.cso.uiuc.edu*, and go to the */pub/etext* directory. Contained in this directory are files that explain Project Gutenberg and access to the subdirectories where the etexts are stored. Project Gutenberg etexts are also available from FTP sites *nptn.org* in the */pub/e.texts/gutenberg* directory and *wuarchive.wustl.edu* in the */mirrors/msdos/books* directory.

These electronic texts are also available on the Almanac server at Oregon State University. Send the following command via email to *almanac@oes.orst.edu*: **send gutenberg catalog**

You also can access the Gutenberg Collection via Gopher by connecting to the site listed earlier, *gopher.cic.net,* or Gopher site *etext.archive.umich.edu*. Select menu item *10. Gutenberg.*

## ≡ Online Book Initiative

The Online Book Initiative (OBI) collects and distributes freely available material on the Internet. OBI mirrors the Project Gutenberg texts; plus, it includes other public domain materials and materials that the copyright holders have allowed unlimited copying. To explore this resource further, FTP to site *world.std.com* and go to the */obi* directory, or Gopher *world.std.com*.

## ≡ Wiretap

A large storehouse of electronic books reside at Gopher site *wiretap.spies.com*. At the main menu choose */2. Electronic Books at Wiretap*. The first two of a total of 10 pages of titles are shown in the following output. Also at this site you'll find the USENET newsgroups *alt.etext* and *ba.internet*.

```
        Electronic Books at Wiretap

  1. Aesop: Fables, Paperless Edition.
  2. Aesop: Fables, Townsend Translation.
  3. Albert Hoffman: Problem Child.
  4. Ambrose Bierce: Can Such Things Be.
  5. Ambrose Bierce: The Devil's Dictionary.
  6. Andrew Dickson White: Warfare of Science with Theology.
  7. Anglican: Book of Common Prayer.
  8. Anthony Hope: The Prisoner of Zenda.
  9. Anthony Trollope: Ayala's Angel.
 10. Artephius: The Secret Book (Alchemy).
 11. Baroness Orczy: The Scarlet Pimpernel.
 12. Beowulf (F.B. Gummere Translation).
 13. Bible: Elberfelder Ubersetzung Bibel/
 14. Bible: Holy Bible/
 15. Booker T Washington: Up From Slavery.
 16. Bram Stoker: Dracula.
 17. Brendan P Kehoe: Zen and the Art of the Internet.
 18. CIA: Psychological Operations in Guerilla Warfare.


            Page: 1/10

 19. CIA: World Fact Book 1990.
 20. CIA: World Fact Book 1991.
 21. CIA: World Fact Book 1992.
 22. Carl Sandburg: Chicago Poems.
 23. Chaos Industries: The Big Book of Mischief v1.3.
 24. Charles Darwin: The Voyage of the Beagle.
 25. Charles Dickens: A Christmas Carol.
 26. Charles Dickens: A Tale of Two Cities.
 27. Charles Dickens: The Chimes.
 28. Charles Dickens: The Cricket on the Hearth.
 29. Charles G Roberts: The Forge in the Forest.
 30. Charlotte Gilman: Herland.
 31. Christopher Morley: Parnassus on Wheels.
 32. Dale A Grote: Study Guide to Wheelock Latin.
 33. Daniel Young: Scientific Secrets, 1861.
```

34. David Graham Phillips: Susan Lenox, Her Rise and Fall.
35. David Hume: An Enquiry Concerning Human Understanding.
36. Decartes: Discourse on Reason.

2

# ☰ Zines

*Zines, micro-zines, e-zines, fanzines,* and *cyberzines* are online zines ranging in scope from the esoteric and bizarre like *Hi-Rez: Electronic Journal for CyberBeatniks* to more mainstream e-zines like *The Amateur Computerist.* Zines, which were first introduced back in the 70s, are small publications generally created by one person for fun rather than profit. Many thousands of zines currently exist, and each one focuses on a particular subject.

Today, zines are published in paper and electronic format. A good resource for information on paper zines is *The World of Zines* by Mike Gunderloy and Cari Goldberg Janice (Penguin Books, 1992), accessed at various FTP sites.

John Labovitz is the author of the *E-zine List,* a document published in three parts that provides summary information on 167 zines published on the Internet. The *E-zine List* is divided into three files called *part1, part2,* and *part3.* These are located at FTP site *rtfm.mit.edu* in the */pub/usenet/news.answers/writing/zines* directory.

As an aside (and to show you just how esoteric the Internet can be), these files were given widespread accessibility on the Internet due to the efforts of L. Detweiler of the Cyberspatial Reality Advancement Movement (CRAM). Detweiler sponsors compilations like this document (decisions are arbitrary) in an attempt to give "valuable" information broader distribution by making it accessible via automated mail servers, FTP archives, and automated postings. If you have something you'd like him to consider, send inquiries to *1d231782@longs.lance.colostate.edu.*

# ☰ The Oxford Text Archive (OTA)

The OTA is a valuable humanities resource containing over 1,300 articles in 28 languages. A complete index of the texts and a few of the texts themselves are available via FTP to site *black.ox.ac.uk* in the directory */ota.*

# ☰ The Coombspapers Social Sciences Research Data Bank (Australian National University, Canberra)

This is an electronic repository of materials produced by or submitted to the Research Schools of Social Sciences & Pacific and Asian studies, Australian National University, Canberra. In March 1994, the research collection comprised 1,164 ASCII text files on the social sciences and humanities including bibliographies, directories, theses abstracts, and other research materials.

You can access the database via FTP or Gopher to site *cooms.anu.edu.au*. Mirror FTP sites are maintained at *wuarchive.wustl.edu* in the directory */doc/coombspapers*, site *ftp.uunet* in the directory */doc/papers/coombspapers*, and site *uceng.uc.edu* in the directory */pub/wuarchive/ doc/ coombspapers*. For further details, FTP to site *coombs.anu.edu.au* and change directories to */coombspapers/index-files* and download the files called *README* and *INVITATION*.

## ☰ Project Runeberg

Project Runeberg is a database of public domain works written in the Scandinavian language ranging from medieval Swedish texts to Swedish copyright law. This database is accessible via FTP to site *ftp.lysator.liu.se* in the */pub/runeberg* directory or via Gopher to site *gopher.lysator.liu.se*.

## ☰ Catalog of Projects in Electronic Text (CPET)

The CPET database contains a variety of information on electronic text projects from around the world. These etext projects are machine-readable files containing primary source material from the humanities field, including information on several collections of literary works, historical documents, and linguistic data. Housed at the University of Georgetown, these etext projects are either in the form of large corpora for linguistic analysis or major works of major authors for content and style analysis.

For further details, Gopher to site *gopher.georgetown.edu*. From the root menu, choose */4. Catalog of Projects in Electronic Text (CPET)*. This displays the following submenu:

```
        Catalogue of Projects in Electronic Text (CPET)

    --> 1. Information on the CPET Database, 9KB.
        2. How to Access the INGRES On-line Database, 41KB.
        3. Information on the Digests, 3KB.
        4. Digests Organized by Discipline (Directory)/
        5. Digests Organized by Language (Directory)/
```

## ☰ Hot Off the Tree (HOTT)

HOTT is a weekly publication of the Technology Watch Information Group (TWIG) from the University of California at San Diego. HOTT contains excerpts and abstracts of articles from trade journals, online news services, and electronic bulletin boards. You can access HOTT by TELNETing to *melvyl.ucop.edu*.At the command prompt, type **show hott** and press ENTER.

## ☰ Etext Archive at the Well

Gopher to *gopher.well.sf.ca.us*. At the main menu, choose */6. Authors, Books, Periodicals, Zines (Factsheet Five lives here!)/*. This will bring you to the menu shown in the following output:

```
Internet Gopher Information Client 2.0 p19

Authors, Books, Periodicals, Zines (Factsheet Five lives here!)

1. About the Publications area.
2. AIDSwire Digest/
3. Authors/
4. Book Sellers (from gopher.std.com)/
5. The Diamond Sutra.
6. The Economist/
7. Electronic Serials archive at CICNet/
8. The English Server Gopher (Carnegie Mellon, PA)/
9. Factsheet Five, Electric/
10. French Language Press Review/
11. FYI France: the Grandes Ecole, on the Future, by Jack Kessler.
12. Gnosis Magazine - ToC, Back Issues and Guidelines/
13. Incunabula/
14. LOCUS Magazine - Tom Maddox reports on the Electronic Frontier/
15. MicroTimes/
16. Miscellaneous Cyberprose/
17. MONDO 2000/
18. The New Republic/
19. The New Yorker/
20. Online Zines/
21. Whole Earth Review, the Magazine/
22. Wired Magazine/
23. ZYZZYVA: the last word: west coast writers & artists/
```

## ☰ Library Related Ejournals

A few examples of library related ejournals are listed in this section . An excellent source for a comprehensive listing of ejournals is *Library-Oriented Lists and Electronic Serials* by Charles W. Bailey, Jr. You can view this document on the Gopher server at *riceinfo.rice.edu*. Follow the path */9.Library Services/5.Miscellaneous library resources from around the Internet/57.Library-oriented Lists and Electronic Serials*.

At this same Gopher site, you can view some of the ejournals online. To do this, follow the path */9.Library Services/ 5.Miscellaneous library resources from around the Internet/30.Electronic Journals in Library Science* and you will be led to a directory that offers the following ejournals that can be viewed online:

```
1. ALA Washington Online Newsletter/
2. ALCTS Network News/
3. Citations for Serial Literature/
4. College & Research Libraries NewsNet/
5. Conservation Online (CoOl)/
6. Current Cites/
7. Federal Information News Syndicate/
8. HOTT (Hott Off the Tree)/
9. Issues in Science and Technology Librarianship/
10. LITA Newsletter/
11. Library and Information Science Research Electronic Journal/
12. Library of Congress Cataloging Newsline/
13. MC Journal (Journal of Academic Media Librarianship)/
```

14. Newsletter on Serials Pricing Issues/
15. PACS News/
16. PACS Review/

*MeckJournal* is a scholarly journal devoted to new information technologies. To subscribe, send the email message **subscribe meckjournal <your name>** to *meckler@tigger.jvnc.net*.

*ALCTS NETWORK NEWS: An electronic publication of the Association for Library Collections & Technical Services.* Published irregularly, *ALCTS NETWORK NEWS* is available free of charge and is available only in electronic format. To subscribe, send an email message to *listserv@uicvm.bitnet* that reads **subscribe alcts <your name>**. Back issues are available from the LISTSERV. To get a list of available files, send the command **send alcts filelist** to *listserv@uicvm.bitnet*.

You can view the *Library of Congress Cataloging Newsline* by logging onto the Gopher server at *gopher.cic.net* and following the path *Electronic Serials/Alphabetic List/L/LC-Cataloging-Newsline*. The opening screen from the first issue is shown in Figure 16-2. To subscribe, send the command **subscribe lccn <your name>** to *listserv@sun7.loc.gov*.

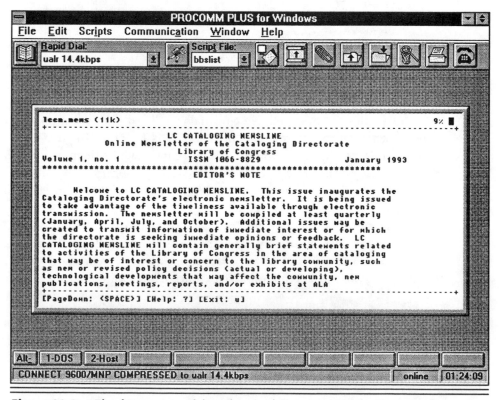

**Figure 16-2:**   The first screen of the Library of Congress Cataloging Newsline

*At Your Service* is a quarterly newsletter for serials librarians, published by EBSCO Subscription Services. To have a copy sent to you via Internet email, send your name, title, institution, mailing address, city, state, ZIP, Internet address, and EBSCO account number to Brian Wilson, User Services Dept., EBSCO Industries, P.O. Box 1943, Birmingham, AL 35201. If you have access to email, address the above information to *ays@ebsco.com*.

The Library and Technology Association (LITA) distributes an electronic version of its *LITA Newsletter*. To subscribe, send the command **subscribe litanews** **<your name>** to *listserv@darmouth.edu* (or, if you're on BITNET, to *listserv@darcms*).

*Matrix News* is a newsletter about cross-network issues. This newsletter doesn't deal only with the Internet, but rather with the Matrix, which is all computer networks worldwide that exchange email. The newsletter is available in paper and online. Paper subscriptions are $30 for 12 monthly issues, and $20 for students. Add $5 to these prices for a subscription to both online and paper, and add $10 for overseas postage. Contact *mids@tic.com*, or MIDS, 1106 Clayton Lane, Suite 500W, Austin, TX 78723. Telephone: 512-451-7602.

You can find online information at **gopher is.internic.net** by following this path: */2.InterNIC Information Services/8.Internet Information for everybody/1. Internet Statistics, Size, and Connectivity/5. Growth and Size Information About various Networks and Services/3. Growth Information About the Internet/2. Matrix Information and Directory Services (MIDS).*

*Net-News*, sponsored by Metronet, is a newsletter devoted to library information resources on the Internet. To subscribe, send the following email message to *metronet@vz.acs.umn.edu*: **sub nnews <your name>**. Back issues of this newsletter are available in the LIBSOFT archive (FTP to site *hydra.uwo.ca* and change to the *LIBSOFT* directory).

## ≡ For Further Study

Many of the books mentioned in this chapter are available in zip format at FTP site *oak.oakland.edu* in the */pub/misc/books* directory.

A large collection of poetry arranged by author resides at FTP site *ocf.berkeley.edu* in the directory */pub/Library/Poetry*. Another source for poetry is the North Dakota State Gopher server *chiphead.cc.ndsu.nodak.edu*. Follow the path */Other Stuff/Fun Stuff/Poems*.

A collection of children's fairy tales including *The Adventure of Aladdin, Beauty and the Beast, Little Mermaid*, and *The Three Little Pigs* are stored at FTP site *world.std.com* in the */obi/Fairy.Tales/Grimm* directory. Enter a **dir** command to view the available files.

# Chapter 17

# Information Systems and Gateway Services

*Gateway* is a generic term that normally refers to a machine that connects two different networks and transfers data between them. A gateway performs such tasks as protocol conversion if the two networks use different protocols. The term *gateway* has also come to mean a computer system that acts as a gateway to other systems.

This chapter introduces various gateway services (or *systems*) that offer pathways to other services. Several of these services exist on the Internet, but I have focused only on a few that offer a large number of pathways and a wide variety of resources.

## ≡ LIBS

TELNET *nessie.cc.wwu.edu*     Login: libs

*LIBS* is a public-domain program that provides a very user-friendly front-end for accessing other Internet services. A main menu leads to several submenus. If you choose to connect to a remote site, the TELNET connection is made for you. LIBS gives you special login and disconnect information just before you connect to the system.

LIBS software is available from FTP site *sonoma.edu*. There is a VAX version called *LIBS.COM* and a UNIX version called *LIBS.SH*. To find out whether LIBS is running on your local host, type **libs** and press ENTER. If it's not, access LIBS by TELNETing to the public site listed previously. The following output shows the welcome screen and root menu:

```
+------------------------------------------------------------------+
|                 LIBS - Internet Access Software v2.0a             |
|                  Sonoma State University, Mar 1993               |
|                                                                  |
|                     Based on data provided by:                   |
|               Art St. George - University of New Mexico          |
|              Chandler Whitelaw - Southern Utah University        |
|                Linda Musser - Penn State University             |
|                         and other sources                        |
|                                                                  |
|                     Technical assistance by:                     |
|              John Campbell - Northern Arizona University         |
|                 Jim Gerland - SUNY Buffalo                       |
|                           and others                             |
|                                                                  |
|        Direct all questions and bug reports to: resmer@sonoma.edu|
|                                                                  |
|                  Copyright (c) 1991-92, Mark Resmer              |
+------------------------------------------------------------------+
                     Press <return> to continue:



                     LIBS - Internet Access Software v2.0a
                  Mark Resmer, Sonoma State University, Mar 1993

              On-line services available through the Internet:

              1 United States Library Catalogs
              2 Library Catalogs in other countries
              3 Campus-wide Information Systems
              4 Databases and Information Services
              5 Wide-area Information Services
              6 Information for first time users

              Press RETURN alone to exit now or
              press Control-C Q <return> to exit at any time
```

## ≡ University of North Carolina LaUNChpad

TELNET *launchpad.unc.edu*    Login: **launch**

The LaUNChpad system provides access to several library systems. Categories are broken down into North American, European, Pacifica, Asian, and Middle-Eastern regions. The LaUNChpad also offers the capability of searching databases, downloading files, and connecting to the local Gopher.

Choosing menu item *3.Online Information Systems* at the main menu provides you with a link to miscellaneous services which include gateways to the Library of Congress Catalog, Ham Radio Call Book, Hytelnet, and other BBSs and Free-Nets.

The LaUNChpad is a bulletin board system and you are required to set up an account before you have access to its services. The registration process is easy.

Simply give your full name, decide on a password, and specify what kind of terminal you're using. After logging in, you'll see this menu:

```
Main Menu

 1. Network News
 2. Electronic mail
 3. On-line Information Systems (LIBTEL)
 4. Topical document search (WAIS)
 5. Download files
 6. Find user
 7. User Options
 8. Pherrit - gopher client
 9. Lynx - WWW client
10. Triangle Free-Net experimental gopher
```

## ≡ Washington University's WorldWindow

TELNET *library.wustl.edu*          No login required.

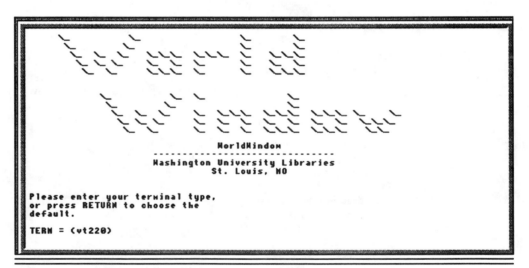

**Figure 17-1:**   Washington University's WorldWindow opening screen

You will be prompted for your terminal type and then presented with the opening screen shown in Figure 17-1. Press return to see this menu:

```
WorldWindow     Washington University Libraries, St. Louis, MO    04/11/94 23:04
qqqqqqqqqqqqqqqqqqqqqqqqqqqqqqqqqqqqqqqqqqqqqqqqqqqqqqqqqqqqqqqqqqqqqqqqqqqqqqqq

--> 1  About WorldWindow
     2  About Washington University Libraries / ...
     3  WU Libraries Online Catalog and Journal Indexes (LUISPLUS)
     4  WU Medical Library Resources / ...
     5  Other Library Collections / ...
     6  Network Resources by Subject / ...
     7  Network Resources by Type / ...
```

```
 8   WU Campus Information (WUINFO) / ...
 9   Internet Tools and Tutorials (Gopher, WWW, etc.) / ...
10   Search WorldWindow Menu by Keyword / <?>
11   New and Trial Resources / ...
```

WorldWindow is a service of Washington University Libraries, St. Louis, Missouri. Choosing /6. *Network Resources by Subject/* takes you to directories on such things as Education, General Science, Medicine and Health Sciences, and Business and Economics. /9. *Internet Tools and*

Tutorials provides online assistance in learning Gopher, WWW, and USENET. Choosing /5. *Other Library Collections* gives you access to the following choices:

```
1   U.S. Library of Congress
2   United States Libraries (by state)
3   Foreign Libraries (by country)
4   National Libraries
5   Medical Libraries
6   Law Libraries
```

## ≡ Information for Maryland (inforM)

Information for Maryland (inforM) is the University of Maryland at College Park Information Service.

Connect via Gopher to site *info.umd.edu.* The root menu is shown here:

```
          University of Maryland at College Park (inforM)

  -->  1. Using This System/
       2. Campus Calendars/
       3. Campus Information/
       4. Educational Resources/
       5. Computing Resources/
       6. Library Information and Resources/
       7. Student Information and Resources/
       8. UMCP Today/
       9. Connections to UMCP Computer Systems/
      10. State of Maryland/
      11. Access to Other Information Resources/
      12. Electronic Newspapers/
      13. Search titles in InforM <?>
```

InforM was designed as a Campus-Wide Information System offering local students the ability to read college catalogs and other department information on computers from home, dorm rooms, or from any computer lab on campus. InforM also provides students with a gateway to all major Internet services. From the main menu pictured previously, choose /4.*Educational Resources* to find services like Ask ERIC, Biotechnology Information Center, Economic Data, and Government. Menu item 6. *Library Information and Resources* links you with LC MARVEL (Library of Congress) and other library systems.

## ≡ Yale University Gopher

Connect to the Gopher server at *yaleinfo.yale.edu*. The main menu looks like this:

```
Root gopher server: yaleinfo.yale.edu

1. YaleInfo (formerly Enterprise) and Gopher/
2. Announcements (updated 4/10/94)/
3. Yale University information/
4. Research and library services/
5. The Internet (additional information and services)/
6. Shortcuts to popular services/
7. Finding information and resources (searching)/
```

From the main menu, choose */9. Special Internet Connections (A–K)* and */10. Special Internet Connections (L–Z)*. This will give you online access to Scott Yanoff's *Special Internet Connections*. The "Yannoff List" contains references to an enormous number of Internet resources. The list is broken down into two parts, with entries listed alphabetically by subject.

## ≡ Washington & Lee Law Library

TELNET *liberty.uc.wlu.edu*    Login: **lawlib**    Password: **lawlib**

Washington & Lee Law Library is a gateway service offering gateways to Gopher servers, Archie, Hytelnet, and over 2,000 libraries worldwide. A view of what you will find after you login is shown in Figure 17-2.

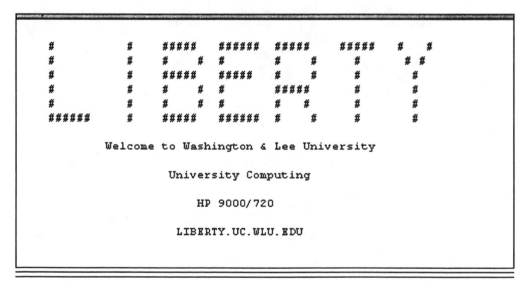

**Figure 17-2:**   Washington & Lee University Law Library opening screen

## ☰ Rice University's Library Resources Gateway

Gopher to *riceinfo.rice.edu* and follow the path */9. Library Services/5. Miscellaneous library resources from around the Internet/*. This brings you to the following submenu:

```
          Miscellaneous library resources from around the Internet

  -->  1. About this directory.
     . **************************************************.
       3. AALL LISP (Legal Info Service to the Public)/
       4. ALCTS Network News/
       5. Acqnet/
       6. American Library Association/
       7. American Library Association Washington Office Newsletter/
       8. Apple Library User Group (ALUG) archives/
       9. Association of Research Libraries (U. of Houston)/
      10. Association of Research Libraries FTP Archives/
      11. Automatome/
      12. Automatome/
      13. Barron's Guide to On-line Bibliographic Databases/
      14. Bodleian Libraries (inc. Radcliffe Science Library)/
      15. Bookstores, Booksellers, & other Commercial Services/
      16. Bulletin Board for Libraries (BUBL) <TEL>
      17. Bulletin Board for Libraries (BUBL) Gopher/
      18. Buslib-l Business Libraries Listserv Archive/

      19. CISE - Directory for Computer and Info. Sci. & Engineering (NSF)/
      20. Clearinghouse of Subject-Oriented Internet Resource Guides (UMich)/
      21. Coalition for Networked Information Server <TEL>
      22. Conservation Online (CoOL)/
      23. Cornell Library Task Force on Electronic Journals: Final Report.
      24. Current Cites/
      25. Current Tables of Contents Library Science Journals (U. Mich.)/
      26. DIMUND Document Information Server/
      27. Data Entries (Texas Woman's University)/
      28. Directory of Electronic Journals and Newsletters (2nd ed.).
      29. Electronic Journals & Newsletters/
      30. Electronic Journals in Library Science/
      31. Electronic Library Literature/
      32. European Chapter of the American Society for Information Science/
      33. Federal Library and Information Center Committee software list/
      34. GO4LIB-L (Library Gopher List) mailing list archive <?>
      35. Go to the top-level of gopher.sunet.se/
      36. Guides to Library Science Resources on the Internet/

      37. ISKO. International Society for Knowledge Organization, FFM/
      38. Information Retrieval List Digest/
      39. Internet Libraries (search catalogs via Yale)/
      40. LC Cataloging Newsline/
      41. LIBRES/
      42. LIBS hierarchical menu for accessing Internet libraries (Ox.) <TEL>
      43. LIBSOFT, an archive of library-related software/
      44. Libraries Collection from PEG (UC Irvine)/
      45. Library Bulletin Boards Systems (from MSU)/
      46. Library Catalogs and Databases/
      47. Library Gophers/
```

```
48. Library Policy Statements/
49. Library Resources on the Internet.
50. Library Resources on the Internet by Laine Farley.
51. Library Resources on the Internet, Farley (8/91).
52. Library Science Collection from U.T. Dallas/
53. Library Science Journals/
54. Library and Information Science Resources from NCSU

55. Library of Congress Information System (LOCIS) <TEL>
56. Library of Congress LC MARVEL/
57. Library-Oriented Lists and Electronic Serials.
58. Library-oriented lists and electronic serials, Bailey (8/18/93).
59. List of Online Library Resources in France (by Jack Kessler).
60. Listservs in Information Retrieval and Information Systems.
61. Listservs in Library and Information Science.
62. Listservs:  What, Why, How.
63. Manuscript and Archives Repositories - at Johns Hopkins/
64. MeckJournal/
65. Meckler's Electronic Publishing Service <TEL>
66. MetroBriefs/
67. Network News/
68. Noonan Guide to Internet Libraries/
69. PACS News/
70. PACS Review/
71. PACS Review/
72. Professional Reading Service (pilot phase)/

73. Public Access Computers List and Review/
74. Public-Access Computer Systems News/
75. Public-Access Computer Systems Review/
76. Publishers' catalogs/
77. Rice University library services/
78. Search Art St. George guide to Internet libraries <?>
79. Search USENET newsgroups concerning libraries and library scien.. <?>
80. Search VPIEJ-L, a discussion list for electronic publishing iss.. <?>
81. Search library-related LISTSERVs (LISTGopher)/
82. Search through the LISTSERV list CWIS-L <?>
83. Sercites/
84. Serials Pricing/
85. Software/
86. The Interpedia Project (Internet Encyclopedia construction effort)/
87. The Wired Librarian/
88. Trip  eports: Fondren Library, Rice University/
89. University Libraries and Scholarly Communication (Mellon Study)/
90. University press catalogs/
```

These directories link you to various sources all around the Internet. For example, by choosing 6. *American Library Association*, you gain online access to current and past issues of ALAWON (ALA Washington Office Newsline: An Electronic Publication of the American Library Association Washington Office), ALCTS NETWORK NEWS (An electronic publication of the Association for Library Collections & Technical Services), and various items relating to LITA (Library and Information Technology Association of ALA), including the *American Library Association Telecommunications and Information Infrastructure Policy Forum Proceedings*.

Menu item *17.Bulletin Board for Libraries* brings you to a number of submenus covering the BUBL Information Services. BUBL (Bulletin Board for Libraries) is primarily a forum for keeping library professionals informed on services and resources on JANET, the Internet, and other networks, but BUBL also offers a wide range of other services that would interest other network users.

Menu item */86. The Interpedia Project* (The Internet Encyclopedia) brings you to a submenu that offers an Interpedia FAQ and four additional subdirectories: Discussion Archives, List Archives, Digest Archives, and a directory that offers the mechanism for searching these archives.

# Chapter 18

# Free-Nets

Free-Nets are computerized civic information systems. Most are linked to the Internet, and, as their name implies, there is no charge for connecting.

The driving force behind the creation of Free-Nets is the National Public Telecommunications Network (NPTN) based in Cleveland, Ohio. Only those civic computer information systems that follow NPTN's principles and standards are allowed to use the name Free-Net.

NPTN is a nonprofit corporation that has established a network of these computerized community information systems. NPTN offers several network services to Free-Net affiliates, including Internet email service and summaries of House and Senate Bills and U.S. Supreme Court decisions.

## ≡ Accessing Free-Nets

Free-Nets organize their information in a hierarchical fashion and make it accessible through menu choices. Each Free-Net contains information relevant to its own community or region, often building the top menu around a city metaphor. For example, Free-Nets may use headings in the top menu named after local buildings or streets.

As with other TELNET services, Free-Nets are limited to a maximum number of simultaneous logons. When you do make a connection, you are given the option of browsing as a guest or becoming a registered member. The opening and login sequence screens for accessing the Cleveland Free-Net are shown in the following output.

```
$ telnet Free-Net-in-a.cwru.edu
Trying... Connected to KANGA.INS.CWRU.EDU, an IBM 486 running UNIX.

BSDI BSD/386 1.0 (kanga) (ttypa)
```

```
                                    /\
          WELCOME TO THE...       _|  |_
                                 _|__  __|_
                __                 |      |
             _|  |_                |  |  |  |
             |    |    /\          |  |  |  |
             |    |   |  |         |  |  |  |___
             |    |   |  |  |      |  |  |  |   |
             |    |   |_|_ |       |  |  |  |   |
             |    |     | |  |     |  |  |  |   |
            _|    |     |_|_  |           |  |_
             |         |       |_|        |    |
             |         |        |_|        |    |
             |                                   |
             |     CLEVELAND FREE-NET            |
             |  COMMUNITY COMPUTER SYSTEM        |
             |_____|

                      brought to you by

              Case Western Reserve University
              Community Telecomputing Laboratory


Are you:
        1. A registered user
        2. A visitor

Please enter 1 or 2: 2

Would you like to:
        1. Apply for an account
        2. Explore the system
        3. Exit the system

Please enter 1, 2 or 3: 2

Copyright 1992, Berkeley Software Design, Inc.
Copyright (c) 1980,1983,1986,1988,1990,1991 The Regents of the University
of California. All rights reserved.

BSDI BSD/386 1.0 Kernel #14: Mon Feb  7 11:26:10 EST 1994

Local time is: Sat Mar  5 22:45:33 EST 1994


WELCOME:

  As a visitor to the Cleveland Free-Net you are allowed to
go anywhere and read anything on the system. However, to
post messages, and send or receive electronic mail, use the
Cafe (chat area) and other features, you must be a REGISTERED
USER. To register, simply use the "Apply for an account"
option from the visitors menu and follow the directions.

  The registration process and all system usage is FREE.
You are limited to one hour per visit but there is no limit
to the number of visits you can have per day.
```

```
     Before you enter the system however, there are two things
we need to tell you.

     First we need to tell you that: By entering this system,
in consideration for the privilege of using the Cleveland
Free-Net and in consideration for having access to the free
information contained on it, that you hereby release Case
Western Reserve University, the National Public Telecomputing
Network, the Cleveland Free-Net Project, its operators, and
any institutions with which they are affiliated for any and
all claims of any nature arising from your use of this system.
(See, aren't you glad we told you that?)

     Second, once you are in the system you may want to try
some of these commands from any arrow ==> prompt:

          who - who is online with you. The Cleveland Free-Net
                handles as many as 12,000 logins a day. You might
                want to see who else is online at the same time
                you are.

         time - tells you the date and time ('case ya don't know),
                how long you have been online, and how much time
                you have remaining in your session.

    go <name> - takes you to the place on the system you name
                (like a building or an area). See the Index in
                the Administration Building for a (more or less)
                complete list of the features available.

            x - logs you off the system from any arrow prompt


     Thank you for visiting the Free-Net. We hope you will become
a registered user and that we'll see you online often.

     Enjoy and Learn!
Press RETURN to continue:


FreePort Software copyright 1991 Case Western Reserve University
        All rights reserved
```

After the above introduction, the following main menu appears. Notice that menu items on the Cleveland Free-Net are named after buildings, such as the library and schoolhouse.

```
<<< CLEVELAND FREE-NET DIRECTORY >>>

    1 The Administration Building
    2 The Post Office
    3 Public Square
    4 The Courthouse & Government Center
    5 The Arts Building
    6 Science and Technology Center
    7 The Medical Arts Building
    8 The Schoolhouse (Academy One)
```

```
 9 The Community Center & Recreation Area
10 The Business and Industrial Park
11 The Library
12 University Circle
13 The Teleport
14 The Communications Center
15 NPTN/USA TODAY HEADLINE NEWS
-------------------------------------------------
h=Help, x=Exit Free-Net, "go help"=extended help

Your Choice ==> 1
```

By choosing *1. Administration Building*, you find the following choices, including such things as *What is the Cleveland Free-Net?* and *Administration Policy*.

```
    <<< THE ADMINISTRATION BUILDING >>>
              <go admin>

 1 What is the Cleveland Free-Net?
 2 About the Free-Net Computers...
 3 User Services
 4 Administration Q & A
 5 Administration Policy
 6 What's New in the Electronic City
 7 Free-Net Menu Outline (quite long)
 8 The Cleveland Free-Net Release Form
 9 Print out the Cleveland Free-Net Release Form
10 Certification for Access to Open Speech Areas
11 The Free-Net Sysops...
12 Submitting a Proposal to Free-Net
13 Obtaining the Free-Net Software
14 The City Plaque  (Thank you for your support)
-------------------------------------------------
h=Help, x=Exit Free-Net, "go help"=extended help
```

## ≡ Big Sky Telegraph

Now we will explore another Free-Net called Big Sky Telegraph. This Free-Net is big on lesson plans, helping rural teachers, and offering online classes. This Free-Net is useful not only to those who are part of Montana's statewide educational network, but also to anyone with a connection to the Internet. After you read the opening screens and complete the login sequence for Big Sky Telegraph, you are presented with the following top menu:

```
        TELEGRAPH'S BBS MAIN MENU

(B)eginner's Bulletins
(M)essages...Conferences and Public Postings
(F)iles...Areas for upload and download
(A)ccess to Additional Services
(I)nterest Groups-Subscribers Only
(Z)ipmail...Read ONLY YOUR messages from ALL conferences
(?)...Help Menu and Advanced Commands
(G)oodbye...Exit this system
```

By selecting menu item *(F)iles...Areas for upload and download,* you are given a submenu showing all of the different topic areas that are available:

```
    Directory      Description                                   Upload Path
    =============  =========================================    ============
 1) NewsArchives   Online News and Info Archives                 NewsArchives
 2) BBS            MT and Nat'l Ed. bbs numbers, and more!  BBS
 3) WMCLibrary     WMC Library Files Transfer Area               WMCLibrary
 4) LessonPlans    Lesson Plans and Curriculum Guides            LessonPlans
 5) Resource       Resource lists, bulletins and files           Resource
 6) Class          Online Class Lessons and Resources       Class
 7) Science        Science Essays, Ideas and Experiments         Science
 8) Networking     Global and National Networking Info           Networking
 9) Kidsnet        Global Penpal Requests and Intros             Kidsnet
10) Internationl   MT Council for International Visitors          Internationl
11) CEC-West       CEC-West Exchange for 15 States          CEC-West
12) CEC-Language   Mini-lesson plans (K-12)                 CEC-West
13) CEC-Math       Mini-lesson plans (K-12)                 CEC-West
14) CEC-Science    Mini-lesson plans (K-12)                 CEC-West
15) CEC-SocStudy   Mini-lesson plans (K-12)                 CEC-West
16) CEC-Misc       Mini-lesson plans (K-12)                 CEC-West
17) Biographies    Post Your Biography Here!                Biographies
18) Reach4Sky      Reach For The Sky/Internet Access Files  Reach4Sky
19) LIT            Library Integration Team Files Area       LIT


Enter Selection ===> 4
```

I then chose category *4) LessonPlans* as a topic to explore further and listed all of the files in that topic area:

```
LessonPlans
Your Uploads and Downloads are going into Files area: LessonPlans

(F)iles...List of all files in THIS topic area
(A)rea...Change to another Files area
(D)ownload...to your computer
(U)pload...from your computer to here
(M)ain Menu...Return to Main Menu
(?)...Help and Advanced file search commands
(G)oodbye...Exit this system

===> f
A control-k will terminate the listing


    HIT CONTROL K TO EXIT TO MENU

    FREE LESSON PLANS FOR YOUR USE


    CHRISTMAS PLAYS!

Animal        11753 Feb-90   Christmas play for nine-plus students
Cheer          9683 Feb-90   Christmas play for ten-plus students
Giant          8184 Feb-90   Christmas play for four-plus students
Goose          6870 Feb-90   Christmas play for eight-plus students
Grand         23972 Feb-90   Christmas play for 11-plus students
```

```
Love            11620 Feb-90   Christmas play for 20-plus students
Xmas             5892 Feb-90   Christmas play for eight-plus students
XmasNight         677 May-91   Poem about Christmas

     INTERESTING LESSON PLANS

Oral.Hist        3563 Mar  4   Outline for Classroom Oral History Project
American        14208 Mar-91   Time of Slavery study
ArchHist         2276 Mar-91   Learn about Local Architecture history


*** Press a key to continue ( control-k for menu ) ........
Art              4253 Feb-90   Art lesson plans from "Computer Learning Month
Autobio          1049 May-91   Autobiography lesson plan
Biographies      2304 Nov-90   Lesson plan for grades 3-8. Developed by
                               Dale Alger, Roundup Central Elem. School.
BusMath          3397 May-91   Business Math Lesson Plan
Camera           2782 Feb-91   Pinhole Camera Instructions & Lesson plan
Dialmail         3200 Apr-91   Project for middle school using DIALMAIL
DOSMac           3817 Feb-91   Lessonplan that compares DOS commands to
                               functions on the Macintosh
Econ             2393 Feb-90   An economics lesson plan -  The School Store

     HIT CONTOL K TO EXIT TO MENU

Egglessn         1588 Mar-91   A lessonplan for Easter
ElemKey          1664 May-91   Elementary Keyboarding
HlthLA           3349 Feb-90   Lesson plans in Health and Language Arts
Cemetary         3968 Apr-91   Cemetary story that can be read in parts
Pascal           1701 May-91   Pascal Lesson Plan
Mathpoem          560 Mar-91   A poem to help teach number skills
LaMathPE        12733 Feb-90   Language Arts, Math, PE, and Health lesson plans
LangArts        14012 Feb-90   Language Arts lesson plans
LArts6-8        12782 Feb-90   Language Arts lesson plans
*** Press a key to continue ( control-k for menu ) .......
```

The list of available lesson plans was quite long, so only the first several lines are shown above. Because Easter was coming up, I decided to download a copy of the file called *Egglessn* using Zmodem. The process of transferring a file from Big Sky Telegraph is as simple as making a series of menu choices. A copy of the downloaded file is shown here:

```
A Delicate Art - Egg Decorating Curriculum areas:  Social Studies,
Reading, Art
Materials: Raw egg
Yellow dye
Red or blue dye
No. 2 pencil
White wax crayon
Small plastic margarine tub filled with crumbled tissue paper.
A fine felt-tip black marker
Objectives:    To expose students to the Ukrainian custom of
decorating eggs. To have students decorate their own eggs with their own creative
designs. Steps to follow:
1. Each student draws a simple design on a piece of paper. They
repeated lines and shapes to make patterns and crate symbols. 2.
Dye each students egg yellow.
3. As the dry egg rests in the nest of tissue, students copy their
design onto the egg with pencil.
```

4. The white crayon is then used to cover any part of the design that was to remain yellow.

5. After three layers of white crayon, the egg is dyed with the second color of dye, red or blue.

6. Two holes are then poked in the ends of the egg and the contents blown out.

7. Place the blown egg in a microwave for 7 to 10 seconds or until the crayon wax began to melt.

8. Wipe the softened was away with paper towels exposing both colors. The designs were taking shape.

9. The students then use a fine-tip permanent marker to outline the shapes and add details.

10. Finally each egg is covered with clear acrylic spray to make it more durable. (in a well ventilated area).

FOLLOW-UP READING:  Patricia Polacco's book titled Rechenka's Eggs is at the third grade reading level and a great lead-in or follow-up to this art activity.

## ≡ Heartland Free-Net

To further demonstrate the depth of information that's available on Free-Net systems, the index to resources found on the Heartland Free-Net System is listed here:

```
        <<< Heartland Free-Net System Index >>>


                -A-

Administration Building     go admin
Alcohol Dependency          go 12step
Amateur Radio               go ham
Audubon Society             go birds
Auto Info/Repair            go auto


                -B-

Banking Info                go bank
Bartonville                 go bartonville
Bel-Wood Nursing Home       go belwood
Bicycling Forum             go bike
Birds                       go birds
Bloom./Normal Calendars     go cal
Board Agendas, Peo. Cnty.   go board
Board Minutes, Peo. Cnty.   go board
Bradley University          go bradley
Brimfield                   go brimfield
Bulletin Board              go public
Business                    go business, go bsns
Business Statistics         go stats


                -C-

Central High School         go central
Change Password             go passwords
Change Terminal Type        go term
Chemical Addictions         go chemical
Chemical Dependency         go chemical
```

```
Children's Events          go children
Computer Forum             go pc, go computer
Conservancy District       go conserve
Craft Show Calendar        go craft
Cultural Events Calendar   go culture


              -D-


Dependency Support         go 12step
Departments, Peo. Cnty.    go pcdirectory
Diabetes Info              go diabetes
Dirksen Congressional Ctr. go dirksen
Drug Abuse                 go drug
Drug Information           go drug


              -E-


Economic Statistics        go stats
Editors                    go editor
Educational Project        go projects
Elected Officials          go elected
Electronic Mail            go mail
email                      go mail
Emergency Preparedness     go esda
Environment Info           go environ
Ethics Discussion          go religion
Eureka College             go eureka
Eye Center                 go eye


              -F-


Festival Calendar          go festival
Fines, Peoria County       go peoria.county
Flight, Space & Airplane   go space
Flea Market Calendar       go flea
Forum, Personal Computer   go pc, go computer
Forum, Public              go forum
Freedom Shrine             go shrine
Fulton County              go fulton


              -G-


Gardening Info             go garden
Genealogy                  go genealogy
Golfing Discussions        go golf
Goodwill Ind. of Cent. IL  go gwill
Govt, Local                go local
Govt, Peoria County        go peoria.county
Govt, State                go state


              -H-


HAM Radio                  go ham
Handicap Info              go gwill
Historical Documents       go shrine
History                    go shrine
Home Repair                go home
```

```
                              -I-

ICC                      go icc
Illinet OnLine           go illinet
Ill. Dept. Employ. Sec.  go ides
Illinois State University  go isu
IDES Jobs                go jobs
Index                    go index
Insurance Answers        go insure
Intervention Resources   go special
Investment Info          go invest


                              -J-

Jobs (Peoria County)     go pcjobs
Journal Star             go pjs


                              -K-

Knox County              go knox


                              -L-

Law                      go law
Lawyer Help              go law
Legal Information        go law
Legal Questions          go law
Letters to Elected Off.  go elected
Library                  go library
Licenses, Peoria County  go license
Lindbergh Middle School  go lind
Link to Other Systems    go link
Literary Discussion      go lit
Local Govt               go local


                              -M-

Mail                     go mail
Mailboxes                go mail
Mailbox List             go users
McLean County            go mclean
Medical, Emergency       go ems
Medicine                 go medical
Medicine, General        go medical
Medicine, Psychology     go mental.health
Mental Health            go mental.health
Movies Discussion        go movies
Museum Events Calendar   go museum
Music Discussion         go music


                              -N-

Nature Conservancy Dist. go conserve
New SIG area             go admin
New Unread BBS           go new
```

-O-

```
Open Bulletin Board      go open
Outer Space              go space
```

-P-

```
Pager                  go pager
Parameters               go parameters
Passwords                go passwords
PC Forum                 go pc
Peoria Calendars         go cal
Peoria, City of          go peoria
Peoria County Depts.    go pcdirectory
Peoria County Govt.     go peoria.county
Peoria Govt Job Listing  go pcjobs
Peoria Journal Star      go pjs
Peoria Park District     go ppd
Personal Computer Forum  go pc
Pest Control             go pests
Pilot, How to Become a   go pilot
Political Discussion Area go politics
Post Office              go mail
Property Assess, Peo Cnty go property
Psychology/Mental Health  go mental
Public Forum             go public
```

-Q-

(No listings under "Q" at the moment.)

-R-

```
Recipes                  go recipe
Recreation Center        go recreation
Recycling                go recycle
Red Cross                go redcross
Registration             go registration
Religion                 go religion
Rockets                  go rockets
```

-S-

```
Satellites               go satellite
Scouting                 go scout
Science                  go science
SciFi Talk               go scifi
Senior Info              go senior
Set Password             go passwords
Set System Parameters    go parameters
Sierra Club              go sierra
Social Services          go ss
Space                    go space
Special Needs            go special
Speeches                 go shrine
Sporting Events Calendar go sportcal
Social Security Q & A    go ssn
```

```
Star Trek                go trek
State Govt               go state
Sweeney, Father (school) go sweeney
System Parameters        go parameters

                  -T-

Tax Clinic               go tax
Taxes                    go tax
Teachers' Area           go teacher
Teen Center              go teen
Terminal Setup           go term
Termite Control          go termites
Theater Events Calendar  go theater
Timeline, Historical     go timeline
Travel Center            go travel
Trek, Star               go trek

               -UVWXYZ-

User Services Menu       go user
Veterinarian, Ask a      go vet
Video Games              go video
Washington School-Peoria go washington
Weather                  go weather
Woodford County          go woodford
Zip Codes                go zip
Zoo, Glen Oak Park       go zoo
```

## ≡ List of Free-Nets

Here is a list of Free-Nets that are easily accessible via the Internet. Each entry provides the name of the Free-Net, its Internet address, and what you must enter at the *Logon:* prompt.

**Big Sky Telegraph**
Login as **bbs**
telnet **192.231.192.1**

**Buffalo Free-Net**
Login as **freeport**
telnet **Free-Net.buffalo.edu**

**Cleveland Free-Net**
Login shown above
telnet **Free-Net-in-a.cwru.edu**

**Columbia Online Information Network**
Login as **guest**
telnet **bigcat.missouri.edu**

**Denver Free-Net**
Login as **guest**
telnet **Free-Net.hsc.colorado.edu**

Heartland Free-Net
Login as **bbsguest**
telnet **heartland.bradley.edu**

Lorain County Free-Net
Login as **guest**
telnet **Free-Net.lorain.oberlin.edu**

National Capital Free-Net
Login as **guest**
telnet **Free-Net.carleton.ca**

Tallahassee Free-Net
Login as **visitor**
telnet **Free-Net.fsu.edu**

Tri-State Online
Login as **visitor**
telnet **cbos.uc.edu**

Victoria Free-Net
Login as **guest**
telnet **Free-Net.victoria.bc.ca**

Youngstown Free-Net
Login as **visitor**
telnet **yfn.ysu.edu**

## ≡ For Further Study

To obtain more information on NPTN, affiliated Free-Nets, or starting your own Free-Net, contact *info@nptn.org* via email, or contact T.M.Grundner, Ed.D., President, NPTN, Box 1987, Cleveland, OH 4406. Internet: *tmg@nptn.org*. Voice: 216-247-5800.

Steve Cisler wrote an essay called *Community Computer Networks: Building Electronic Greenbelts* (6-20-93) that provides an overview of community networks and the kinds of information services they provide. Available via FTP to site *ftp.apple.com*. Various versions can be found in the */alug/communet* directory.

# Chapter 19

# USENET News

*USENET* (User's Network) is a large collection of computers carrying something called *USENET news*—a distributed conferencing system consisting of thousands of discussion groups. Some of these computers are on the Internet; others are not. In a more abstract sense, you could think of USENET as a huge database of conversations—on about 5,000 diverse subjects—between more than two million people worldwide. . You can access and browse USENET directly, or you can access portions of it using WAIS. Subjects range from geophysical fluid dynamics to baking with sourdough.

Because many participants possess a very high level of expertise in their respective fields, USENET news can serve as a useful reference tool in answering certain queries. As a librarian, I sometimes compare this resource with the functionality of *The Book of Associations*. When I'm presented with a highly specialized question for which there doesn't seem to be an answer in any reference source setting on the shelf, I have often consulted a professional association. Many times the members themselves, or some other source to which they have referred me, have the answer I need. Like associations, USENET newsgroups bring together specialists in a particular field.

## ≡ Accessing USENET News

A connection to the Internet does not automatically give you access to newsgroups. In the case of dial-up connections, your service provider must make arrangements to receive USENET files or get a "news feed" from another site that already receives them. When a server at one site provides Usenet articles to a server at another site, it is said to be providing a *news feed* or simply a *feed*.

After your local host sets up a news feed, you can access USENET news. Many commercial providers and university systems already offer this service. You can determine whether your dial-up service, campus, or corporate computing system has a network news feed by asking the system administrator. The host organization determines the number and selection of discussion categories fed to them.

If you don't have access to USENET news through a local feed, try TELNET-ing to one of the following public network news sites:

*etl.go.jp*
*munnari.oz.au*
*quip.eecs.umich.edu*
*sbcs.sunysb.edu*
*sol.ctr.columbis.edu*
*suntan.ec.usf.edu*
*uunet.ca*
*uwec.edu*
*vaxc.cc.monash.edu.au*

## ≡ USENET Newsgroups

Internet sites can choose to subscribe or not to subscribe to a particular newsgroup. One host may carry 3,395 newsgroups, while another may carry only 2,500.

Each newsgroup specializes in a particular subject. They're organized in a tree structure, or hierarchy, with various levels of topics and subtopics. For instance, one newsgroup hierarchy called *soc* posts articles relating to social issues. The newsgroup *soc.culture. indian.telugu* is a social newsgroup concentrating on the culture of the Telugu people of India.

One collection of newsgroups, termed "World" Newsgroups, are usually distributed around the entire USENET worldwide. These newsgroups are divided into the following seven broad classifications and each of these classifications is organized into groups and subgroups according to topic: *rec* (recreation), *sci* (science), *comp* (computers), *soc* (social), *talk*, *news* (newsgroups), and *misc* (miscellaneous).

### The World Newsgroups

Under the classification of *rec* (groups oriented towards the arts, hobbies, and recreational activities) there are a number of music groups which are further divided into subgroups such as classical, folk, and afro-latin. Following are three examples of music newsgroups in the "rec" hierarchy.

| | |
|---|---|
| *rec.music.classical* | Discussion about classical music |
| *rec.music.folk* | Folks discussing folk music |
| *rec.music.afro-latin* | Music w/ African and Latin influences |

Other broad topics in the *rec* classification include arts, audio, aviation, food, games, sport, travel, etc. As with music, these groups are broken down into more specialized subgroups.

Under the classification sci (discussions relating to research in or applications of the established sciences) are medical groups with subgroups in AIDS and nutrition.

*sci.med*
*sci.med.aids*
*sci.med.nutrition*

Other groups in this classification concentrate on topics such as aeronautics, anthropology, space-related news, and virtual-worlds.

The *comp* newsgroups discuss topics of interest to both computer professionals and hobbyists, including topics in programming language, software, hardware, and operating systems, etc.

The *soc* groups address social issues; for example, religion, politics, and culture.

The *talk* classification consists of groups that are debate-oriented and contain very little useful information.

The *news* groups discuss issues relating to newsgroups (network and software).

The *misc* groups address subjects that can't easily be classified under any of the other headings.

## Specialized Newsgroups

You will notice several other newsgroup classifications listed on the main menu that are not part of the traditional or mainstream hierarchy of newsgroups. These are classified as "alternative" newsgroups hierarchies. Alternative newgroups are organized into groups and subgroups similar to the traditional newsgroups. They are called "alternative" because they don't conform to USENET standards. The formation of a new mainstream newsgroup is strictly controlled. An announcement must be made followed by a dicussion and a request for people to vote. The alternative newsgroups are less strict. Anyone who knows how to start one can do so.

Some of the classifications that are included in the alternative hierarchy include "alt," "bionet," "bit," and "biz." Examples of newsgroups in the "alt" classification inlude alt, bionet, bit, and biz. Examples of newsgroups in the alt classification include *alt.sport.bungee, alt.hypertext, alt.my.crummy.boss, alt .conspiracy*, and many hundreds more that are bizarre and weird.

*Bionet* is a newsgroup hierarchy for topics of interest to biologists.

*Bit* newsgroups are redistributions of the Bitnet LISTSERV mailing lists. This offers another means for reading mail distributed by, for example, PACS-L (which is listed under the name *bit.listserv.pacs-l*). Before you subscribe to a LISTSERV discussion list, you might want to see whether it's echoed (duplicated) on USENET news, especially if you find it hard to manage the volume of email arriving daily in your mail box.

*Biz* carries information about business products, especially computer products and services. The *Clari* hierarchy of newsgroups is gatewayed from Clarinet News, a commercial electronic publishing service which provides UPI, AP, and satellite news services. Groups under this classification include *clari.biz.economy* (economic news and indicators), *clari.news.law.civil* (civil trials and litigation), and more. Librarians may be interested in *K12*, which is a collection of school-based or school-oriented newsgroups.

## ≡ Reading the News

News articles look like email messages, but they're delivered in a very different way. The following example shows a news article posted to the *soc.libraries.talk* newsgroup:

```
X-NEWS: ualr.edu soc.libraries.talk: 2
Path:
gould.ualr.edu!news.ualr.edu!news.uoknor.edu!constellation!convex!convex!cs.utexas.e
du!howland.reston.ans.net!europa.eng.gtefsd.com!library.ucla.edu!csulb.edu!csus.edu!
netcom.com!noring
Newsgroups:
comp.bbs.misc,comp.os.ms-windows.misc,comp.os.ms-windows.nt.misc,comp.os.ms-windows.
programmer.misc,comp.os.os2.misc,comp.text,misc.misc,no.multimedia,rec.arts.books,so
c.misc,soc.libraries.talk
Subject: Now Available! The Hypertext "The Devil's Dictionary". Demo Version.
Message-ID: <noringCMoIsl.30z@netcom.com>
From: noring@netcom.com (Jon Noring)
Date: Tue, 15 Mar 1994 00:02:25 GMT
Followup-To: poster
Organization: Netcom Online Communications Services (408-241-9760 login: guest)
Summary: Written in Windows 3.1 Help Format; Condensed Version; From OmniMedia
Lines: 66
Xref: gould.ualr.edu comp.bbs.misc:8 comp.os.ms-windows.misc:26
comp.os.ms-windows.nt.misc:13 comp.os.ms-windows.programmer.misc:22
comp.os.os2.misc:55 comp.text:3 misc.misc:11 rec.arts.books:80 soc.misc:3
soc.libraries.talk:2

[Followups set to 'poster'. If you must publicly post a followup, please do
so to rec.arts.books. Thank you.]

Hello everybody,

A free Demo of the hypertext "The Devil's Dictionary" (Condensed Version),
produced by OmniMedia, is available for download on the Internet,  It is
written in Windows 3.1 Help format.

This document should be viewable by Windows 3.1, Windows NT, and OS/2 2.x
(and possibly other operating systems with the appropriate special software).

Here's the description from the accompanying text file:
-----------------------------------------------------------------------
This is the Demo for the latest electronic book published by OmniMedia, "The
Devil's Dictionary," (Condensed Version) by Ambrose Bierce. It is in Windows
3.1 Help format, so it can be viewed under Windows 3.1, OS/2 2.x, Windows NT,
Excel for the Macintosh, and possibly some other operating systems that have
software to read Windows Help files. "The Devil's Dictionary" is considered
Bierce's most famous work, and is exceptionally entertaining and humorous --
it is best described as the "Cynic's Bible" par excellence. The full
commercial version (containing 623 total definitions, the Demo has 92) is
quite attractively priced and can be purchased from OmniMedia. This Demo is
freeware and can be distributed far and wide;  please upload it to your
```

```
favorite BBS sites and distribute it among all your friends  -- everyone will
be glad you did!  It is appropriate for all ages.
------------------------------------------------------------------------


You can freely download the Demo from anonymous ftp site:

ftp.netcom.com    /pub/noring/books/devdict.zip

Be SURE to type 'binary' before issuing the 'get' command!


I encourage you to redistribute this document far and wide - upload it to your
favorite BBS and distribute copies to your friends and acquaintances. Please
upload only the original zip file.

I'm sure you will enjoy the Demo of "The Devil's Dictionary" (Condensed
Version).


Jon Noring
OmniMedia

(p.s., if you don't have anonymous ftp access, I will e-mail a uuencoded
version of the zip file. Of course, you will need to be able to uudecode it,
which I can't help you with. And I'm not sure on this, but the file
devdict.zip MIGHT be accessible from Netcom via mail server -- I just don't
know how to do it, if possible at all -- any help here from my fellow
Netcom'ers?)


--

Join the INFJ mailing list!  Ask for the 46Kb file describing what INFJ is!
============================================================================
Jon Noring          | Famous literary works in Windows 3.1 Help format are
Omnimedia           | available via anonymous ftp from ftp.netcom.com
1312 Carlton Place  | /pub/noring/books. Current titles include "Fanny
Livermore, CA 94550 | Hill", "Aesop's Fables", and the "Devil's Dictionary",
510-294-8153        | with more coming!
============================================================================
Subscribe to the Windows Help / Multimedia Viewer Authoring Mailing List
```

With USENET, messages are not sent to individuals the way they are in the LISTSERV discussion groups. Instead, a user sends, or *posts*, an article to a newsgroup on one site and the local system collects its articles and sends them as a file to adjoining USENET sites. In a LISTSERV discussion group, when one subscriber mails a message to the LISTSERV, all subscribers to that list receive the same mail message. Rather than sending many copies of one message, USENET provides a single central copy that all subscribers can read.

Like most of the Internet services described in this book, USENET news makes use of a client/server model. The server program manages the news feed. The client pr-ogram in this arrangement is called a *newsreader* and it provides you with your interface to USENET. Many newsreaders operate on various platforms, including *nn, xrn, tin, vn, rn, trn, INN*, and others. Also available are *GNUS* and *Gnews,* which can be used with the GNU Emacs text editor.

The following sections provide simple reference guides for three newsreaders. For more detailed information on these or other newsreaders, consult the online help service at your site.

## Quick Reference Guide for *nnr*

*nnr* is an NNTP (Network News Transfer Protocol) newsreader for IBM VM/CMS.

1. Enter the command **nnr** to invoke the program and display the first screen, called the PHLI/Main Screen (Primary High Level Index). This is an index of three-letter codes that fills the first screen and subsequent screens, depending on the number of newsgroups to which your host subscribes. Select a newsgroup classification by moving forward with the PF8 key.

2. When you find a newsgroup classification in the high level index that you'd like to explore, move the cursor to its name and press PF2 (ALL_NEWS). The next screen displayed is the SHLI/Groups (Secondary High Level Index). This index presents all of the related groups and subgroups that are available under the selected classification.

3. Move the cursor to the desired group and press PF4 (HEADERS). This brings you to the next screen ( called the Header Screen)which provides you with a list of headers or subject lines that look similar to a list of email messages you may be used to seeing.

4. Move the cursor to any header that looks interesting and press PF2 (ARTICLE) to read a specific article. This displays the Article Screen. The PFKeys you're most likely to use at this stage are these:

| | |
|---|---|
| PF2 (Next) | Read next article in sequence |
| PF3 (Quit) | Exit article screen |
| PF4 (Previous) | Read the previous article in the sequence |
| PF9 (Print) | Sends the article to a printer |
| PF11 (Log) | Logs article in NNRLOG NOTEBOOK |
| PF12 (NxtGroup) | Moves to the next group in the SHLI list |

Note that the documents you select for printing won't actually print until you exit **nnr**. If you select two or more documents during a single session, they will be combined into one print job. Logging a document in a NOTEBOOK before printing it gives you the opportunity to edit it in your file list, using xedit.

## Quick Reference Guide for *trn*

*trn* is a Usenet newsreader that runs on UNIX platforms.

1. Type **trn** and press ENTER to start the newsreader.
2. The program creates a file called *.newsrc* in which all of the newsgroups you subscribe to are placed. This file also keeps track of the messages you have read.

3. The program goes through all of the newsgroups fed to your site. You have three choices for each newsgroup: view that group's articles now (press **y**), skip it for now and go to next newsgroup with unread articles (press **n**), or "unsubscribe" so you never see that newsgroup again unless you resubscribe to it at some future date (press **u**).

4. If you pressed y, you are presented with the first unread article. Press the SPACEBAR to move down one page, **n** to go to the next unread article, or **q** to leave the newsgroup and go to the next newsgroup.

5. To save an article, press **s** followed by the name of the file in which you want the article saved.

6. Press **x** to unscramble a *rot13* message (see below for explanation of *rot13*).

7. Type the letter **h** to bring up help at any point.

8. Type **q** to quit the program.

## Quick Reference Guide for ANU-NEWS

ANU-NEWS is a newsreader for VMS Systems.

1. Enter **news** at the **$** prompt.

2. You are presented with one long list of newsgroups.

3. Use the down and up cursor keys to scroll through the list.

4. When you see a newsgroup you'd like to access, place the cursor on that line and press ENTER. You are presented with a list of headers for all the articles presently posted to that group. Scroll through these to choose which article you'd like to read.

5. To read an article, move the cursor to the desired line and press ENTER. To scroll through the article, press ENTER again or use the cursor keys.

6. Enter **dir/all** at the *NEWS>* prompt to return to the long list of newsgroups.

7. To register (subscribe to) a particular newsgroup, move your cursor to the appropriate line and enter the word **register** at the *NEWS>* prompt. The next time you enter the newsreader, the groups you registered will be highlighted for easier identification.

8. Enter the command **dir/reg** at the *NEWS>* prompt to view your directory of registered groups.

9. To remove a group from this list, place the cursor on the appropriate line and enter the word **deregister** at the *NEWS>* prompt.

10. When you want to leave the program, type **exit** and press ENTER. The system creates a file called NEWSRC.;1 which will contain information on the groups you are registered to receive.

## ≡ Downloading Binary Files

Although most newsgroups are platforms for discussion, some are distribution points for software and other binary files. Transferring binary files to or from USENET news is a little trickier than transferring files from an FTP site because USENET is a system based on ASCII text and is capable only of transmitting AS-CII text files. Because images are software binary files, they first must be transformed into ASCII files before they can be transferred to or from USENET successfully. The same holds true for binary files transferred through the email system.

A program called UUENCODE, explained fully in Chapter 6, encodes these files into ASCII format for transferring. Once UUENCODEd files arrive on your personal machine, you transform them back into binary format using a program called UUDECODE. These programs enable people to send files such as spreadsheets, WordPerfect documents and executable files.

Two examples of newsgroups that distribute encoded binary files are *comp.binaries.ibm.pc* and *comp.binaries.mac*. To retrieve software from one of these newsgroups, first save the software to a file on your personal computer. Then run it through the UUDECODE program to transform it back into a usable state.

### Rot13 Cipher

Some files on USENET will look like gibberish and they are not encoded files. These files have likely been transformed with a program called *rot13*, which replaces each letter in the text of the document with the letter that is 13 places ahead of it or behind it (rotates 13 positions in the alphabet). For example, A becomes N, N becomes A, B becomes O, and so on. rot13 is not really meant to create an undecipherable code; it's more a matter of politeness. Articles that may be offensive or that might give away the ending to a book or movie are encoded in rot13. There may also be a warning given in the article's subject line such as " Offensive to Native Americans," or " Offensive to Germans," etc.

## ≡ For Further Study

One newsgroup called *news.announce.newusers* posts documents that are of particular interest to users that are new to USENET. Lists of active newsgroups are posted to *news.announce.newgroups*. To help prevent newcomers from asking the same questions that newcomers before them have already asked, individual newsgroups periodically post FAQs (Frequently Asked Questions). These are text files that new users should read before attempting to post any messages.

For more information on newsreader software, email the command **send usenet/news.announce.newusers/usenet_software:_history_and_sources** to *mail-server@rtfm.mit.edu*.

Some newsgroups of interest to watch include these:

- *misc.activism.progressive*: press releases from organizations such as the American Indian Movement and Greenpeace.

- *biz.clarinet.sample*: digest of U.S. and international news primarily from UPI.

- *m.a.progressive*: articles on abortion rights, South Africa, labor and environment issues.

- *sci.space.news*: news from NASA.

- *alt.news.media*: press releases from the White House.

Before exploring the picture files residing on the various *alt.binaries.pictures* newsgroups, download a copy of the FAQ that explains all of the idiosyncrasies of posting and downloading files in this format. FTP to site *bongo.cc.utexas.edu* and get the files called *FAQ.abp.1* and *FAQ.abp.2* residing in the */gifstuff* directory.

# Chapter 20

# Computer Bulletin Boards

A bulletin board system, better known as a *BBS*, is a kind of private telecommunications service typically set up by a computer hobbyist, but also by large corporations government institutions. A hobbyist generally sets up a BBS for his or her own enjoyment and for the enjoyment of others in the same region with similar interests. Corporations and government institutions set up BBSs that reach a much larger audience.

Usually, a BBS enthusiast dialing up to a local BBS reads messages already posted, posts new messages, uploads or downloads some software, does some conferencing (real-time chatting), and then plays a little Trade Wars 2002 (a BBS game). Online users that access corporate and governmental BBSs are usually seeking resources to satisfy specific information needs.

Although some BBSs do have email links with the Internet, they are not hosts on the Internet *per se*. Still, some of them play a very significant role in the area of online information service and anyone with a computer, modem, telephone, and communications software can call a computer BBS.For this reason, BBSs are being introduced here. The hardware and software requirements for connecting to BBSs are the same as those introduced in Chapter 2 for connecting to the Internet.

## ≡ What Is a BBS?

A Bulletin Board System has traditionally been a personal computer that runs bulletin board software— specialized software that provides an interface for performing various tasks such as answering the phone and logging callers into the system. With the advent of the Internet, BBSs are also found on Internet hosts, as will be pointed out later in this chapter. The following example illustrates the opening screens and the top menu for the Small Business Administration's BBS. Information on connecting to this free BBS is given later in the chapter.

```
    SSSSSSSSSSS     BBBBBBBBBB       AAAAAAAAAA
  SSSSSS            BB       BB      AA        AA
  SSSSSS            BB       BB      AA        AA
    SSSSSSSSSSS     BBBBBBBBB        AAAAAAAAAAAA
           SSSS     BB       BB      AA        AA
      SSSSSSSS      BB       BB      AA        AA
  SSSSSSSSSSSSS     BBBBBBBBBB       AA        AA
         +--------------------------------+
         |    ALL UNVALIDATED NEW USERS   |
         +--------------------------------+
```

We are setting up temporary procedures to speed up validations. If your mail writing access is still restricted, you have read the guidelines and provided the information requested in item number 7 on the main mail menu, and you have been waiting longer than 3 weeks for contact by us, you may call for validation during the following times:

```
         +-------------------------+
         | PHONE:  (202) 205-7009  |
         | Monday - Friday         |
         | 0900 - 11:00 am  EST    |
         |                         |
         | Monday - Thursday       |
         | 1:00 - 3:00 pm   EST    |
         +-------------------------+
```

```
First Name? allen
Last Name? benson
Calling From BENTON, AR
Is this correct? Y
Enter Your Password: ******

Calling From BENTON, AR
You are caller number 767338
Welcome Allen!  You are authorized 75 minutes this call.
```

```
                    SBA ONLINE NUMBERS
                     1-800-697-4636
    DIRECT DIAL: (202) 401-9600          900 SERVICE:  1-900-463-4636
                    COMPLIMENTS OF...
SSSSSSSSSSS    PPPPPPPPP   RRRRRRRRRR   III   NNNN     NNN   TTTTTTTTT
SSS            PPP    PPP  RRR     RRR  III   NNNNN    NNN      TTT
SSSSSSSSSSS    PPPPPPPPP   RRRRRRRRRR   III   NNN NN   NNN      TTT
        SSS    PPPP        RRRRRRRR     III   NNN  NN NNN       TTT
        SSS    PPPP        RRR   RRRR   III   NNN   NNNNN       TTT
SSSSSSSSSSS    PPPP        RRR    RRRR  III   NNN    NNNN       TTT
```

```
         Press 'S' to stop or any other key to continue...
```

```
+---------------------------------------------+
|- On January 26, 1994 SBA Online changed to a  |
|   combination 1-800/1-900/Direct Dial Svc. See |
|   selection #8 on the Top Menu for details.  |
|- Eff Feb 1, 1994, all access times are changed |
|      to 75 mins (1-900, 1-800, Direct Dial).  |
|- Choose #7 on the Mail Menu for Offline Mail   |
|   Reader Information and Help.               |
|- NEW USERS:  Please go to #7 of the Main Mail  |
|   Menu if you wish to write mail to the public |
+---------------------------------------------+


  -Press Any Key-


  +-----------------------------------+    +----------------------------+
  |            MAIN MENU              |    |        Welcome to          |
  +-----------------------------------+    |        SBA Online!         |
  | [1]   General Information         |    +----------------------------+
  | [2]   Services Available          |
  | [3]   Local Information           |
  | [4]   Outside Resources           |
  | [5]   Quick Search Menu           |
  | [6]   White House Information      |
  | [7]   Talk to Your Government!     |
  | [8]   SBA Online Access Changes: '94|
  | [9]   New Items                   |
  +-----------------------------------+



  +--------------------------------------------------------------------+
  |   [H]elp                    [M]ail                  [G]oodbye       |
  +--------------------------------------------------------------------+
```

Some bulletin board systems support only one telephone line and allow one person to call in at a time, while others support many telephone lines allowing several people to call in simultaneously. The person who runs a bulletin board is called a *sysop,* which stands for *system operator.*

## ☰ What Can You Find on BBSs?

Many BBSs are specialized and focus on a variety of topics from aviation and Zmodem to exotic bird raising and home renovation. To expand your library's reference services, you might start keeping a record of BBSs that focus on subjects of interest to you or your patrons.

Five basic services are offered on most BBSs:

1. Reading and posting messages
2. Uploading and downloading files
3. Doors
4. Chat
5. Email

When you read or post a message on a bulletin board, you're tapping into the human resources that are available—the people who are often specialists in a particular field of interest. Most BBSs have a general message area and then an area for messages on special topics that are either called *conferences* or *message areas*. Everyone participating in a conference can read all messages that are posted to that conference.

The *files* section of the bulletin board is where information files are stored. This section also provides the tools for copying files from the BBS to your computer.

*Doors* are programs that are separate from the BBS software. A menu choice links you to one of these special purpose programs, such as a game or online shopping. When you want to leave the specialized program, you close it and return to the BBS software.

*Chat* is a service that enables two or more callers to carry on a conversation with each other in real time.

*Email* is offered on many BBSs and it works on the same principle as Internet email. Messages are addressed to specific individuals or groups of individuals.

## ≡ How Do You Connect to a BBS?

When you have your computer, modem, telephone line, and communications software all set up and running, the only other thing you need to access a BBS is a telephone number. Using whatever communications software you have, dial a BBS number and wait for the remote computer to answer.

Once you're connected, some of the first things the BBS tells you may include the brand of software being used (common brands are PCBoard, MAJOR BBS, Wildcat, and Spitfire), the modem speed at which you are connecting, and any important announcements. You'll also be made aware of any costs associated with using the service. Most BBSs are free (except for long distance telephone charges if they apply); others have modest monthly or annual membership fees.

The BBS then prompts you for your name and password. If this is your first login, be prepared to answer a lot of questions as part of the registration process. The next time you call in, you can just enter your name and password.

If you want to save any part of your session, you must use a similar process to the one you used withTELNET: Use the *capture* feature of your communications software to record on disk what transpires during your session.

Bulletin boards come and go, so you may want to test the number on a telephone first to make sure it's really connected to a modem and not to a human being who knows nothing about BBSs. Beware, too, that some bulletin boards require users to be at least 21 years old to logon.

## ≡ Sampling of Bulletin Boards

If you don't have a local bulletin board to call and explore, here are a few bulletin boards with 800 numbers that offer information that may be of particular interest to librarians. All boards are 8-N-1 (eight data bits, no parity bit, one stop bit; for further details on the 8-N-1 setting, see Chapter 2, Serial Port Settings) unless stated otherwise.

Name:    Economic Research Service
Tele:    800-821-6229
Subject: Agricultural economics and statistics

Name:    National Education BBS
Tele:    800-222-4922, or **telnet nebbs.nersc.gov**  login: **guest**
Subject: As part of the Office of Educational Research and Improvement, they state as their mission, "... to collect and interpret data, assess student achievement, support basic and applied research, ...promotes the use of educational technology, advances innovative school improvement projects, strengthens library services, and disseminates information."

Name:    Labor News (Department of Labor)
Tele:    800-597-1221
Subject: Labor statistics, relevant Acts of Congress, testimony, and speeches.

Name:    SBA BBS (Small Business Administration)
Tele:    800-697-4636

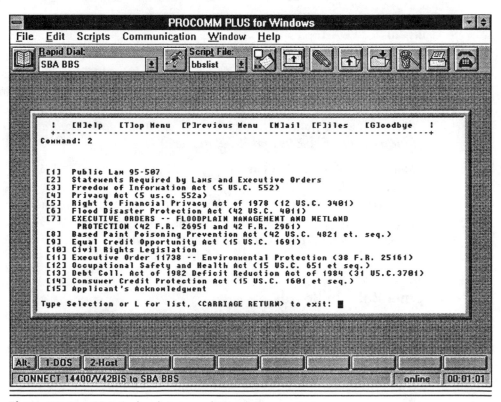

**Figure 20-1:**   SBA Federal Acts and Regulations menu.

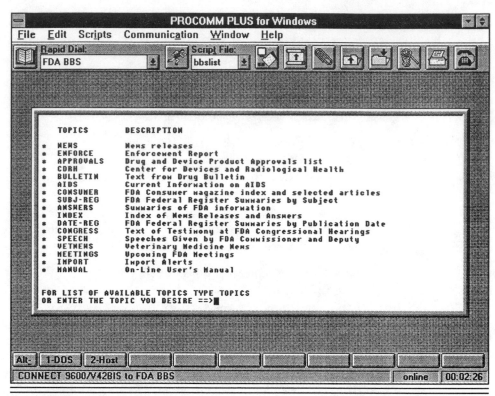

**Figure 20-2:**   FDA Topics

Subject: Several topics including information on NAFTA, census, and business-related resources. A sampling of the kind of information contained in this database is shown in Figure 20-1. To arrive at this particular menu, start at the Main Menu and choose: */2.Services Available/5. Legislation and Regulations/2. Federal Acts and Regulations.*

Name:   FDA BBS (Food and Drug Administration)
Tele:      800-222-0185
Subject: Information on the FDA including FDA testimony and speeches. Set your modem parameters to 7E1 and login with **bbs**. Once logged on, entering the command **topics** at the ==> prompt gives the list of topics shown in Figure 20-2, accompanied by brief descriptions.

## Internet Bulletin Boards

Science educators might be interested in a space-related BBS called SPACEMET INTERNET which can be accessed via TELNET to site *space-met.phast.umass.edu*. To login, register by entering your first and last name.

| | |
|---|---|
| KIDS BBS: | TELNET to site *kids.kotel.co.kr*. Login: **kids**. |
| IDS World Network: | TELNET to *idsvax.ids.risc.net* Login: **guest** |
| Quartz: | TELNET to *quartz.rutgers.edu*. Login: **bbs** |
| Endless Forest BBS: | TELNET to *forest.unommaha.edu 2001*. |

For a list of BBS services on the Internet, send an email message to *bbslist@aug3.augsburg.edu*. Don't place any text in the subject field or body of the message. Upon receiving this email message, the server will return three lists of resources.

## ≡ The Future of BBSs in Libraries

Bulletin boards can provide a unique service in libraries. Bulletin board systems can be used to create a central focal point for information exchange in a neighborhood, city, or in an entire county. In fact, bulletin board systems can be used as a mechanism for creating an electronic "community information system."

For instance, your library could act as a central depository for various local, state, and federal government documents. The main menu of this community information BBS could guide users to "virtual" government offices such as the mayor's office, where citizens could access often-requested documents.

You could include a choice on the main menu titled "Newcomers to our area" that might lead citizens to a submenu listing the Chamber of Commerce. This choice could in turn lead to another submenu where the choices might be local area maps, apartment rental guides, local entertainment, or child care services.

The advantage of offering this information in a digital format on a BBS is that the information becomes accessible from anywhere in your service area where a citizen has access to a personal computer with the necessary software and hardware for communicating with your BBS. The individual requesting information can either view the document on screen or download the file to a disk. This kind of system would enable citizens to access information from one location that would otherwise be stored in a variety of locations.

Not only could a bulletin board serve as a permanent framework for an ongoing community-wide information system, but it could also serve as an inexpensive and effective Internet training ground by introducing library users to concepts such as uploading, downloading, and decompressing files. After these operations become familiar to library users, you can then provide a gateway to the Internet. The interface offered by the Internet may not be as friendly as a BBS, but the library BBS users will at least be somewhat familiar with the basic concepts like file transfer and email.

## ≡ For Further Study

A good place to begin looking for BBS lists is in *Computer Shopper*, a monthly periodical to which your library may already subscribe. If not, it is readily available at newsstands, or you can find out about subscription information by calling 1-800-274-6384. Another good source is *Boardwatch Magazine*, also available on most newsstands, or you may subscribe by sending an email message to *subscriptions@boardwatch.com*. Each month these magazines publish nationwide listings of bulletin boards and online services.

*Online Access* is a magazine that contains information about online services around the world and it includes a list of BBSs arranged by area code. For subscription information, write to 920 N. Franklin St. Suite 203, Chicago, IL 60610.

The *ONLINE ACCESS BBS Phone Book* contains thousands of BBS numbers and can be obtained via Internet email by sending a request for the file *Online.BBS* to *online.access.syslink@mcs.com*. If these sources don't lead you to some local BBSs, try contacting local computer stores or local colleges with computer science departments for possible leads.

Another online source for bulletin board lists is the Small Business Administration's BBS introduced earlier. This bulletin board offers a list of Federal Government Bulletin Board Systems. You can capture this file to a disk for future reference. Dial up to the SBA's bulletin board, log in, and choose *[7]Talk to Your Government* at the top menu and *[2]Listing of Federal Bulletin Boards* at the next menu.

As an alternative to buying commercially distributed BBS software, you can explore software archives on the Internet for appropriate applications. For example, publicly distributed BBS software is available via FTP to site *oak.oakland.edu* in the directory */pub/msdos/bbs*. Two other directories that may be of interest at this site are */pub/msdos/bbsdoors* and */pub/msdos/bbslists*.

# INTEGRATING THE INTERNET INTO TRADITIONAL LIBRARY SERVICES

Part V addresses several issues that pertain specifically to libraries including the issue of how and why Internet affects the kind of services libraries can deliver.

Chapter 21 discusses the librarian's role in terms of training, public relations, and adding value to Internet services. Chapter 22 offers practical suggestions for applying Internet services in the areas of technical services, acquisitions, and collection development. Chapter 23 concentrates on the reference department and how it can integrate Internet services into its day-to-day practice.

# The Librarian's Role

Resource sharing on a national scale is already commonplace in most libraries. Inter-library loan services link the smallest libraries with the largest, rural libraries with metropolitan libraries, public libraries with academic libraries. The alliances they form with one another improve local services by providing greater access to more information. These alliances are also a benefit to library operations because they reduce acquisitions costs, the need for additional shelf space, and demands on staff time. Of course, ILL services aren't free and the expense per item can sometimes be quite high.

Increasingly, however, the focus is shifting to timelier delivery of information through the use of CD-ROM databases and online services. Many libraries are concluding that an Internet connection offers one of the most effective means of linking up with remote Online Public Access Catalogs, commercial database services, product vendors, and colleagues. Once connected to the Internet, librarians discover that it is the only means of linking up with several thousand other information resources—resources that are accessible only via the Internet.

The National Cancer Center Database in Japan (Gopher site *gan.ncc.go.jp*) makes cancer screening guidelines, news, and general information on cancer treatments available free-of-charge on the Internet. With a computer, modem, communications software, and telephone line, you can access this cancer database from any continent on the globe. The fact that this information originated in Japan and was subsequently made available on a worldwide basis has an impact not only on what information librarians deem useful to the communities they serve, but also on what information is being requested by their community.

Just as the resource itself is made available world-wide, so is the news of its existence. This fact then makes it necessary for librarians to also stay abreast of new information resources and services on a global scale. Librarians must also be proactive in introducing these global resources to the public.

As you can see, the librarian's role is an important one in implementing Internet services. In this chapter, I've identified three areas that are key to establishing and maintaining a successful Internet system whether you are part of a corporation, university, city, or county: training, public relations, and adding value to services. The sections that follow explore each of these items more closely.

# ≡ Training

This book was designed so that it could serve not only as a tool for self-teaching, but also as a training tool for library staff and patrons. Internet instructors can use any one of the search examples included in this book for hands-on training when introducing a particular Internet service. These exercises were designed to teach broad principles, not to make you proficient at finding a specific text file at a specific site. You can create new exercises by expanding on the ones presented here.

## Presenting an Overview of the Internet

Before getting into the actual hands-on training itself, you should begin with a general overview of the Internet. You can use a format such as the one used in the flyer presented at the end of this chapter, or, if the audience is already familiar with the Internet on this level, you could develop something more detailed.

The following sample introduction covers three important Internet features and explains what their benefits are to libraries. This exercise would be an appropriate opening for a training session directed towards librarians who have access to the Internet, but who are not yet integrating it into their day-to-day services.

## Why Should the Internet be Made an Integral Part of Our Services?

**Access to more information:** The Internet can improve library service by making more resources available to library users. Some Internet resources, such as the various archives that store discussion list messages, electronic journals, and other textual documents, were previously non-existent. Only now have they become available in electronic format on the Internet. For those library patrons who seek this kind of information, a library with Internet access becomes a more viable resource to them.

**Access to new services:** Services like electronic publishing on a global scale were unheard of prior to the existence of the Internet. Now, one person can state his or her opinions and have them published world-wide via LISTSERV discussion lists and USENET Newsgroups. One or more people can create an electronic journal or zine and place it in an online archive, making it available to millions of other Internet users. While publishing and distribution in print format are measured in weeks and months, publishing on the Internet is measured in seconds and minutes.

**Time and location are irrelevant:** Other resources that existed previously, such as online library catalogs, were accessible to library patrons, but only locally and during limited hours. The Internet removed the limitations of time and geographic location, making these same resources accessible every hour of the day from every continent on the globe.

## Security and the User's Responsibilities

As part of the introduction, you should also include a few words on security. This is an important issue and one that must be introduced to anyone who will be given access to the Internet. The following explanation is offered as a guide for presenting this topic to individuals who access the Internet through a host computer.

### Security

There is a direct relationship between your level of concern for security and the value of the information you're trying to protect. While the responsibility for security against system crackers (a person who breaks into other people's computer systems) lies with the system manager in charge of the host system itself, your concern might be for individual files that you're storing on that system.

In most instances, you use storage space on a host computer as a temporary holding place for files before downloading them to your personal computer. You may decide that protecting these files isn't that important, and it's not likely that you'll be sending sensitive information through email that requires encryption. What still remains an issue, however, is your responsibility to help protect the system as a whole.

In this respect, there is a security mechanism that is of concern to you and that is your password. Passwords are an important first line of defense against intruders and it's in everyone's best interest to give this principle mode of protection some serious thought. You don't want to be the weak link in a chain because of a poorly chosen password. If an intruder can break into your host's system using your password, he or she may then be able to find other security holes in that system or use it as a means of entry into other systems on the Internet.

### Choosing a Password

When you establish an Internet account, you should follow some basic ruleswhen choosing a password. You'll make it easy for a cracker to decipher your password if you choose one that's easy to remember, like your first name, your spouse's first name, or a pet's name. To help make your account more secure, consider the following principles when creating and using your password:

1. Don't use your name or a modification of your name for your password.
2. Don't use a word or modification of a word that occurs in any dictionary.
3. Don't use an acronym.
4. Once you've created an account password, don't share it with anyone.
5. Change your password often, at least every six months.
6. Don't leave your terminal unattended when you're logged in.

# ≡ Copyright and Digital Information

There appears to be an unlimited potential for copying digital works on the Internet. New Internet users will soon recognize the ease and speed with which data can be transferred all around the world; how a file can be easily downloaded from one computer and redistributed to another or many hundreds of other computers with no degradation in the quality of successive generations of copies; and how easy it is to manipulate a digital work by deleting or modifying copyright notices or other portions of text.

It is important for librarians to be aware of and help safeguard intellectual property rights on the Internet; to be familiar with the exclusive rights held by copyright owners and what constitutes "fair use" when reproducing digital works. These key issues are dealt with in the following paragraphs and should be given careful consideration when librarians add value to Internet services by repackaging existing information, creating Community Wide Information Systems or online Local History Archives—ideas which are presented later in this chapter.

## The Importance of Intellectual Property Rights

While most Internet users believe in the free flow of information, questions have been raised about the importance of copyright protection and how it applies in a a network environment. It is clear that in a free-market economy such as ours the elements of compensation and/or permission stimulate the creation and organization of information. For some people, producing information is a livelihood and they take risks and invest time and money to produce their information. If their intellectual property rights go unprotected on the Internet, they will be less likely to contribute. They believe that it's just as important in a network environment to preserve the protections that copyright affords as it is in a traditional print environment.

There are others, especially in the field of education, that make their information freely available and grant unlimited redistribution of their works over the Internet. Their primary interests are the widespread distribution of their work and the personal recognition that results. Due to an increasing amount of unauthorized modifications and reproductions without proper credit, many of these authors are now attaching a notice to their digital works with the proviso that they be redistributed in full, without modification, and with proper credit given to the author.

Under current copyright law, the moment a work is created, it is copyrighted even if it is distributed without a copyright notice. (Exceptions are works created by the Federal Government or when the owner of a work expressly states that it is dedicated to the public domain.) To prevent people from making a false assumption that a work is public domain, it makes sense for anyone claiming copyright protection to include the notice.

## Exclusive Rights of Copyright Owners

In 1993, the Information Infrastructure Task Force (IITF) was formed to articulate the purpose of President Clinton's National Information Infrastructure (NII).

The IITF is organized into various committees and working groups and one of these working groups deals with key issues relating to intellectual property rights.

When considering what impact the latest innovations in digital technology have had on copyright protection, the Working Group on Intellectual Property Rights concluded that, "...with no more than minor clarification and amendment, the Copyright Act, like the Patent Act, will provide the necessary protection of rights—and limitations on those rights—to promote the progress of science and the useful arts." (For information on how to obtain a copy of this document, see the list of resources found at the end of this section.)

To better understand the impact of computer and communications technology on the creation, reproduction and distribution of copyrighted works in a network environment, it is important to review the list of exclusive rights currently granted to copyright holders in Section 106 of the copyright law:

- to reproduce the copyrighted work in copies or phonorecords;
- to prepare derivative works based upon the copyrighted work;
- to distribute copies or phonorecords of the copyrighted work to the public by sale or other transfer of ownership, or by rental, lease, or lending;
- in the case of literary, musical, dramatic, and choreographic works, pantomimes, and motion pictures and other audiovisual works, to perform the copyrighted work publicly; and
- in the case of literary, musical, dramatic, and choreographic works, pantomimes, and pictorial, graphic, or sculptural works, including the individual images of a motion picture or other audiovisual work, to display the copyrighted work publicly.

When working with computers, digital information, and online services, unless authorized or specifically exempt, infringement of the reproduction right can occur, for example, when:

- a printed work is scanned into a digital file;
- a digital file is uploaded to a server or downloaded from a server;
- a digital file is transferred from one computer to another;
- an email message posted to a discussion list is captured to a disk.

## The Fair Use Doctrine

Just as there are exclusive rights granted to copyright owners, there is also a "fair use" provision in the 1976 law (17 U.S.C., Section 107) which places certain limitations on the rights of copyright owners. The following excerpt from Section 107 presents some of the guidelines for determining whether a copyrighted work may be used without gaining permission from the copyright holder:

"Notwithstanding the provisions of sections 106 and 106A, the fair use of a copyrighted work, including such use by reproduction in copies or phonorecords or by any other means specified by that section, for purposes such as criticism, comment, news reporting, teaching (including multiple copies for classroom use), scholarship, or research, is not an infringement of copyright."

In addition to these guidelines, courts evaluate the following four factors in detail when determining whether the use made of a copyrighted work in any particular case is a fair use:

1. the purpose and character of the use;
2. the nature of the copyrighted work;
3. the amount and substantiality of the portion used in relation to the copyrighted work as a whole; and
4. the effect of the use upon the potential market for or value of the copyrighted work.

## The Rights of Libraries and Archives

Additional exemptions of the Copyright Act are provided specifically for libraries and archives under Section 108. Here libraries are given the right to reproduce or distribute one copy of a copyrighted work. Before libraries can exercise this right, certain conditions must be met:

1. the reproduction or distribution is made without any purpose of direct or indirect commercial advantage;
2. the collections of the library are open to the public or available not only to researchers affiliated with the library, but also to other persons doing research in a specialized field; and
3. the reproduction or distribution of the work includes a notice of copyright.

To avoid infringing on the rights of the copyright owner, there are certain circumstances under which libraries may reproduce or distribute copyrighted works and these are explained under Sections 108(b) through 108(g):

- a facsimile copy of an unpublished work can be made if the sole purpose is preservation or security and if the reproduced copy is housed in the library's collection.

  As the law is currently written, the NII Working Group believes that this exemption does not include the right to reproduce works in digital format.

- a facsimile copy of a published work may be made if the original copy is damaged or has been deemed lost or stolen and it can be shown that an unused replacement copy priced a fairly cannot be found. Again, it is not expressly stated that this exemption allows for copies to be made in digital format.

- if a user requests a copy of an article from a periodical issue or a small part from any other copyrighted work.

- a copy may be made and distributed of an out-of-print work if the library can show that the copyrighted work cannot be obtained elsewhere at a fair price.

These last two exemptions require that three conditions must be met:

1. the copy must become the property of the user;

2. the library must not receive any notice that its intended use will be for anything other than private study, research, or scholarship; and

3. a warning of copyright must be displayed where the library takes orders and on any order forms that are used.

   - a limited number of copies of an audiovisual news program may be distributed by lending.

   - single copies of copyrighted works may be made for interlibrary loan purposes.

## Online Resources Relating to Copyright

For additional information on copyright issues and how they may relate to the Internet, consult the following resources:

A copy of the report, "Intellectual Property and the National Information Infrastructure" can be obtained via FTP from site *ftp.uspto.gov* in the */pub/nii-ip* directory or on the IITF Bulletin Board by using Gopher to connect to site *iitf.doc.gov* or by TELNETing to site *iitf.doc.gov* and logging in as **gopher**. It can also be viewed via the Web by connecting to URL http://www.uspto.gov/

The Coalition for Networked Information (CNI) supports a discussion list dedicate to copyright issues. To subscribe, send the following email message to *listserv@cni.org*: **subscribe cni-copyright <your name>**. You can search their message archive interactively by TELNETing to *a.cni.org*. Once connected, login with **brsuser** and look in the "Copy" database for messages from the CNI-Copyright list.

Several interesting text files from the CNI-Copyright forum can be viewed and downloaded via Gopher by connecting to *gopher.cni.org*. Choose menu item *3.Coalition FTP Archives (ftp.cni.org)/6. (CNI-Copyright) Copyright and Intellectual Property Forum.*

"Frequently Asked Questions about Copyright," a FAQ maintained by Terry Carroll, is available via FTP from site *rtfm.mit.edu* in the directory */pub/usenet/news.answers/law/Copyright-FAQ*, files part1 through part6.

Much of the copyright law can be viewed online through a World Wide Web interface by TELNETing to *fatty.law.cornell.edu 8210*. (As mentioned in Chapter 5, on VAX/VMS systems, specify the port number as */port=8210*.) Login with **www.**

## ≡ Internet Use Policies

The Library will need to draft an Internet Use Policy and use it in conjunction with their in-house training program. Issues that should be covered include security, library policy on use of shareware, public domain software, and other data and network etiquette. There should also be guidelines for library related and personal use of the Internet as it relates to email, the downloading and uploading of files, managing disk space, joining discussion lists, and special considerations that may apply when multiple users share a single account.

To view sample policies pertaining to library use of the Internet, search the PACS-L message archives by sending the following query in the body of an email message to *listserv@uhupvm1.uh.edu*:

```
//search job echo=no
database search dd=rules
//rules dd    *
search library internet policies in pacs-l
index
/*
```

You will receive a return message in the form of an index listing all of the relevant hits. From this index, select the message files that look interesting and note what their index numbers are. These numbers should be listed after the **print** command. Send another email message to the LISTSERV using the following job control language:

```
//search job echo=no
database search dd=rules
//rules dd    *
search * in pacs-l
print <insert index numbers here separated by commas>
/*
```

(For more information on querying LISTSERV message archives using job control language (JCL), see Chapter 13.)

To view a sample Computer Ethics Policy, consult the Gopher server at Virginia Commonwealth University at site *hibbs.vcu.edu* and follow the path *4. VCU Information Takeouts//1.Computer Ethics Policy/1.Ethics Policy Statements* and */2.Ethics Policy Guidelines*. At this same site, follow the path */1.Gopher Development Project/6.University Information/6/University Policies/1.Policies Maintained by Student Affairs/4.Ethics Policy on Computing*.

If you are interested in locating additional ethics policies, laws, copyright policies, and some data access policies, FTP to site *ariel.unm.edu*, and go to the */ethics* directory and download the file called *00-Index*.

## ☰ Designing Training Sessions

You can use the table of contents for this book, beginning with Chapter 4, as an outline for designing training programs. The materials presented in Chapters 4, 5, and 6 must be learned before the concepts in Chapters 7 through 23 can be applied. The outlines presented below are examples of how you can use the table of contents outline for Chapter 4 and the related material in Appendix A as a guide in creating training sessions. Some chapters, such as Chapter 18, "FreeNets," can be covered in one session, and others will require more time.

### Sample Training Session 1

Title:    Resource Sharing Using File Transfer Protocol, Part I.

Topics:   Introduction to Internet Protocols in General
          Introduction to File Transfer Protocol (FTP)
          Exercises in Downloading ASCII Text Files

### Sample Training Session 2

Title:    Resource Sharing Using File Transfer Protocol, Part II.

Topics:   Exercises in Downloading Compressed Files
          Exercises in Downloading Executable Files
          Exercises in Downloading Picture Files

### Sample Training Session 3

Title:    File Types and the Software That Creates Them
          (Adapt this to either Macintosh or IBM compatible machines,
          whichever is appropriate.)
Topics:   Compressed Files
          Archived Files

An entire training session could also focus on a particular FTP archive or Gopher server that is of special interest to librarians. Any one of the subjects covered in Part VI can be used as a theme for a training session. If, for example, you are going to give a training session to law librarians, you could focus one entire session on Internet resources relating to law. Other resources of interest to librarians that have been mentioned elsewhere in this book are Rice University's Library Resources Gateway introduced in Chapter 17 and LIBSOFT, a library software archive located at ftp site **hydra.uwo.ca** in the *libsoft* directory, introduced in Chapter 4.

One interesting resource that hasn't yet been introduced and that may fit nicely into a training session on policies is the Library Policy Archive, a collection of textual documents residing on the Electronic Frontier Foundation's FTP server.

The Electronic Frontier Foundation (EFF) believes that a new community is forming that has computer-based communication media as its basis. Their purpose is to make this electronic frontier useful to everyone and to help maintain a free and open flow of information within it. To this end they created an extensive collection of documents to help raise public awareness about civil liberties including First Amendment rights.

One such collection is called the Library Policy Archive. This is a collection of library policy statements including the ALA's *Freedom to Read Statement* and *The Library Bill of Rights*. Other papers that are relevant to computers include, *Computers and Academic Freedom* and *Citizen's Rights and Access to Electronic Information*. The advantages of information like this being made available to librarians via the Internet can be pointed out in your training session. Only one copy of each of these files is stored electronically and you can access them quickly and share them withby many at anytime of the day, from any place on earth where an Internet connection exists. Because these files are stored in a digitized format, you can easily search them for certain character strings using a word processor. Also, using the cut and paste features of a word processor, extracting quotations and inserting them into a policy or speech becomes a simple matter.

All of these documents are available via FTP to site *ftp.eff.org* in */pub/academic/library* directory. For a complete listing of available files, see Appendix C.

## ≡ Online Training Resources

Along with the training opportunities that exist in this book, you can also consult various online resources. One to consider is the Network Training Materials Gopher server. To connect, Gopher to site *trainmat.ncl.ac.uk*. A view of the root menu follows:

```
        Root gopher server: trainmat.ncl.ac.uk

   1. About the Network Training Materials Gopher.
   2. Network Training Pack/
   3. Other network training materials/
   4. Training aids/
   5. Networking guides/
   6. Resource lists/
   7. Network Trainers/
   8. Bibliography/
```

The Trainmat Gopher was set up to encourage Internet training and is operated jointly by Mailbase and ITTI (Information Technology Training Initiative) at the University of Newcastle upon Tyne, UK. The materials contained in their database may be used and adapted by anyone, provided that the source is acknowledged, and that the materials are not sold or used for commercial gain.

The Network Training Pack is also available at FTP site *ftp.ncl.ac.uk* in the directory */pub/network-training/trainpack*. Files are available in a number of formats, and they are designed in such a way that they allow for the insertion of local text and comment.

A software application that you might want to make available to the public as an Internet self-training tool is Merit's *Cruise of the Internet*. This is a computer-based tutorial for learning to get around the Internet. Versions are available for Macintosh, IBM, and IMB-compatible computers. For more information, FTP to site *nic.merit.edu* and get the *READ.ME* file first. Although there isn't very much information contained in this program, it is somewhat of a novelty and may prove interesting to new Internet users because of its graphic interface.

Patrick J. Suarez has written an interactive tutorial for DOS users called *The Beginner's Guide to the Internet*. The tutorial includes basic information on Internet access, TELNET, FTP, email, mailing lists, and newsgroups. To get your copy, FTP to site *oak.oakland.edu*, go to the */pub/msdos/info* directory, and look for a file called *bgi13A.zip*. The shareware registration fee is $25.

## ☰ Public Relations

Librarians who use the Internet and hope to continue using it and improving its accessibility will need the support of the community they serve. This support can be gained by making the community aware of the Internet's existence and informing others of its features and benefits through demonstrations, press releases, flyers, and speaking engagements.

## ☰ Demonstrating Internet Services

One of the best ways to gain support for the Internet is by offering a hands-on demonstration. One or more individuals on the library staff should always be prepared to present a demonstration of the services that are available on the Internet. Plan the demonstration carefully so that it presents the Internet as a viable resource for the majority of people in the audience. Always be thinking about what their information needs might be and how the Internet can be used to satisfy those needs.

If your goal is to introduce the Internet as a useful health information resource, don't connect to the National Center of Biotechnology Information and discuss genetics. Instead, prepare a demonstration where you connect to a resource such as the Albert Einstein College of Medicine Gopher server (**gopher gopher.aecom.yu.edu**). Follow the path *Internet Resources/Medical/Health Information* and explore, for example, the documents residing in the CancerNet database. Once you've connected to the CancerNet, ask your audience if anyone has a topic in mind that would be of particular interest and then retrieve the appropriate document and print it. As you explore the Internet, keep a notebook of useful resources and services that you think would be appropriate for demonstration purposes.

Learn what time of day is best for logging onto the Internet. If you find that file transfer speeds almost grind to a halt at 3:30 p.m., that's probably a bad time to demonstrate FTP by downloading a 500Kb text file. Choose a client/server program that consistently functions well such as Gopher or FTP. Design a search and practice it until it is committed to memory and be ready at any time to provide a demonstration of the Internet service you've chosen.

### Sample Demonstration: Adult Services

The following demonstration shows how to download a GIF file, a text document, and an executable file. The files chosen here should prove interesting to a broad range of adults. I also introduce some fun things you can do if your time is limited.

1. Downloading a GIF file: A colorful rendition of a parrot is available for downloading from several sites. Try FTPing to site *ftp.clarkson.edu* [128.153.4.2], go to the */pub/simtel20-cdrom/msdos/gif* directory, and download the file called *parrot.gif*. If you can't get the file there, try site *freebsd.cdrom.com*, go to the */.2/simtel/msdos/gif* directory, and down-

load the file called *parrot.gif*. If you have a communications software program like Procomm Plus for Windows that shows the image as it's being downloaded, all the better.

An impressive image of the Shuttle can be found at FTP site *ftp.nau.edu* in the */graphics/gif/digi* directory, filename *shuttlelaunch.gif*.

GIF files of works by famous authors such as Monet, Renoir, and Manet can be found at FTP site *uxa.ecn.bgu.edu* in the */pub/fine-art/temp* directory.

These demonstrations work best if you have a viewer program already mounted on your hard drive that enables you to demonstrate other image files downloaded previously in addition to the parrot image. See Chapter 4 on FTP for sources of GIF files.

2. Downloading a textual document: Downloading a copy of the *Declaration of Independence* or the *Constitution of the United States* is interesting because of the link you can create between early historical documents and modern telecommunications. Both of these documents are at FTP site *ftp.eff.org* in the */pub/academic/civics* directory. Their filenames are *constitution.us* and *dec_of_ind*. You might even prepare in advance a query of one of these documents for a word or phrase whose existence has been questioned.For example, download the *Declaration of Independence* and pull it into a word processor (such as Microsoft Word) that offers the capability of finding the occurrence of a combination of any characters. State a hypothetical question, such as "Does the word 'taxes' occur anywhere in the text?" Perform the search and demonstrate the wonders of working with digitized information.

3. Downloading an executable file: FTP to site *oak.oakland.edu*, go to the */pub/msdos/info* directory, and download a copy of the file called *bkache56.zip*. This is a shareware program called Backache Relief Now! Version 5.6 (1992) from Jim Hood & Seattle Scientific Photography (introduced in Chapter 4). Be sure to practice the downloading, unzipping, and installation procedure from beginning to end so that the whole operation becomes second nature.

4. Food Recipes Database: To visit the Food Recipes Database, Gopher to *gopher.accom.yu.edu* and choose *Internet Resources/Miscellaneous/About the Food Recipes Database/Search the Food Recipes Database*.

5. If you are giving a demonstration after a Shuttle mission is announced or is in progress, you can finger NASA for information on crew members and the status of the mission. Type **finger nasanews@space.mit.edu** and press ENTER.

6. If you'd like to demonstrate Gopher, the server at *cns.cscns.com* in Colorado has a very rich selection of menu items.

## Sample Demonstration: Youth Services

Demonstrating Gopher: This demonstration illustrates to children in the 10- to 15-year-old range that the Internet isn't just for grownups. You might begin by telling the children that there are two kinds of gophers in the world: one that burrows through the earth and another that burrows through information. In fact, there's one information gopher that especially likes kids called the KIDLINK GOPHER. This one lives in Pittsburgh, Pennsylvania, but it burrows all around the world linking kids together from several nations.

What do kids in Estonia, the Netherlands, or Romania want to do when they grow up? How would they change the world if they could? Where does the KIDLINK GOPHER meet with these kids when they want to talk? The KIDCAFE, of course.

Here's how you reach the KIDLINK GOPHER: Have one of the kids sit down at the computer and type **gopher gopher.duq.edu** at the system prompt and then press ENTER. If you don't have access to a Gopher client, have the student TELNET to *kids.ccit.dua.edu* and login as **gopher**. Here's the root menu of the KIDLINK GOPHER:

```
 1. _.
 2. About the KIDLINK Gopher
 3. About the KIDLINK Projects/
 4. Finding and Using KIDLINK Services/
 5. KIDLINK in the Classrooms/
 6. KIDLINK People/
 7. KIDART Computer Art Gallery/
 8. Research, Reports, Papers, and Newsletters/
 9. Directly Access The KIDLINK Archive LOG Files/
10. Hot Path to KIDLINK Annual Celebration Info Menu!/
11. Other Resources About Kids/
12. Search all *Menu Titles* on This Server (fast) <?>
13. FULL TEXT Search of *All Files* on This Server (slow) <?>
```

Explore various paths ahead of time and you'll discover lots of interesting things children will enjoy. For example, follow the path *8. Research, Reports, Papers, and Newsletters/1. KIDLINK Newsletters/18. KIDS-92 Newsletter No.1.* Here you can show them an issue of the KIDLINK Newsletter. Have one of them read aloud what life is like for Gilberto Nieves Ruiz, a 14-year-old living in Puerto Rico.

You might like to explain to teachers and parents that the kids meet to talk using electronic mail on four different discussion lists running on a computer in North Dakota. First, children introduce themselves by answering the following four questions when they join:

1. Who am I?
2. What do I want to be when I grow up?
3. How do I want the world to be better when I grow up?
4. What can I do now to make this happen?

Discussions take place on four different discussion lists which were described in *The KIDS-92 Newsletter*, Issue number 1, Jun 10 1991 issue, as follows:

```
RESPONSE   is where the children send their responses to the four
           questions. This is the *only* purpose of this list.
           When this is done, we invite them to send messages to
           KIDCAFE and KIDS-ACT.
```

```
KIDCAFE    is for kids aged 10 - 15. Here, they can talk about
           whatever they like, find new  friends in other count-
           ries, discuss the future, school, hobbies, environment,
           or whatever. Only those at the correct age can write
           messages to KIDCAFE, and they need to send their per-
           sonal introductions to RESPONSE before starting.

KIDS-ACT   is for kids aged 10 - 15. Here, they can talk about
           what THEY can do NOW to achieve their future visions.
           The rules for participation is as for KIDCAFE.

KIDS-92    is for teachers, coordinators, parents, social workers,
           and others interested in KIDS-92. This is where we post
           information about important developments, exchange ex-
           periences, report media coverage, news, etc.

KIDS-91    is where KIDS-91 is currently being reviewed. Later
           this year, KIDS-91 will be closed and turned into a
           read-only history database. The archives of KIDS-91
                    contains interesting information for teachers and others.
```

If any of the children would like to participate online in any of these discussions, you can explain LISTSERV subscriptions to the teachers and parents. In this case, send the command **sub <listname> <kid's name>** to *listserv@vm1.nodak.edu.*

You might also point out to the teachers that there is valuable information pertaining just to them on this server in a document called *Answers to Commonly Asked 'Primary and Secondary School Internet User' Questions* by J. Sellers (February 1994). To find it, start at the main menu and follow the path *11. Other Resources About Kids/5. Internet Resources - Primary/Secondary Ed (RFC 1578).*

Demonstrating a new look at history: FTP to site *ftp.eff.org*, go to the */pub/academic/civics* directory, and download a copy of a Windows application called *wtp.zip.* If the purpose of your demonstration is to show a group of children how to transfer a file, you might want to have one of the children go through the process of downloading and unzipping it. Otherwise, you can download the file ahead of time and get it running before the children arrive. Assuming you do the latter, once the file is unzipped, use the File Manager to find *wtp.hlp* and double-click it. For additional help, read the *wtp.txt* file.

Tell the children that you went to Cambridge, Massachusetts to get a book for them—an electronic book called *We the People.* (Maybe you can go into the fact that you didn't really leave town and that it only took a couple of minutes to get it.)

How many of them have ever seen an electronic book or heard the word *hypertext*? Holding up a book on American history, you could say "Imagine that you're reading along and you come to the word *democracy*. What if you'd like to read more? How would you find other text in the book that talks about democracy? That's right, you'd go to the index, like this. Then you'd find where the word *democracy* is listed, see on which other pages it's discussed, and then go to the text on those pages."

"An electronic book works differently." Holding the mouse in one hand and pointing to the computer monitor you say "When you come to the word *democracy* in an electronic book, you use a mouse to click it and you'll suddenly jump to a new place in the electronic book that tells you more about democracy." Demonstrate while you speak and then let the children try it.

*We the People* is Shareware produced by LeftJustified.

A payment form is included with the software. If you'd like to register it, fill in the form, and send it in along with $15.00. We the People explores democracy through famous documents such as the U.N. Declaration of Human Rights, a translation of the Magna Carta, and excerpts from the constitutions of ten nations.

Demonstrating an educational program: "So, you don't like fractions?" I remember saying this to a young boy named Chris, about 10 years old, whose mother had just finished telling me that her son wasn't doing well in math. She asked whether we had any books on fractions. While his mother was talking, Chris interjected, telling me that he didn't like fractions. All of our books on fractions were out, so I asked him if he liked computers. Looking up, he smiled, tugged on his baseball cap, and said, "Sure do!" I told him I'd be back in five minutes with something he might like.

You might begin your demonstration by asking how many of the children in your group enjoy fractions (assuming they're old enough to know what fractions are). Tell them you'll take them on a quick trip to Michigan where there's a math game you know they'll like.

Use FTP to download a file called *thmath12.zip* (194333 bytes), an elementary math (grades 1 through 6) arcade-style game that resides at FTP site *oak.oakland.edu* in the */pub/msdos/educatin* [sic] directory. In the real-life situation described earlier, I had some of this information memorized ahead of time, and it helped make the operation go quickly. I knew about the FTP site at *oak.oakland.edu* and I also knew that the *educatin* directory contained educational software. (The longer you use the Internet, the Oakland software depository and certain other resources will become more familiar to you, just as materials in your reference collection become more familiar to you with continued use.) What I didn't know was whether the educational software directory contained any software applications dealing with fractions. Even after viewing the filenames in the *educatin* directory, I still wasn't sure. I did guess right, however, but I still downloaded the *00_index.txt* file while I was logged into that site just in case I had to go back again. The *00_index.txt* file provided brief one-line descriptions of all the files residing in that directory.

Download a copy of the index file yourself and see whether you think there's another program that would prove more effective for your demonstration. The application called *animals.zip* is a nice math program for younger children and it's small (28824) so it should download quickly.

## Sample Demonstration: High School/College Students

The following examples are meant to be entertaining and easy to execute. You can begin each section with a brief explanation of the protocol being used.

1. TELNET
   - Start out with a quote of the day. TELNET to *astro.temple.edu 12345* [129.32.1.100]. This machine displays a quote when ever you TEL-NET to this address.
   - Check out major league baseball schedules by TELNETing to *cu-line.colorado.edu 862* (On VAX machines, type *culine.colorado.edu /port=862*). Once connected, you will be given a list of teams and their corresponding codes. At the *<mlb>* prompt, enter the appropriate code for the schedule you'd like to see.
   - Is anyone leaving on a vacation sometime soon? Get up-to-date weather reports anywhere in the world by TELNETing to *down-wind.sprl.umich.edu 3000*. Find the elevation, population, and other statistics for the U.S. city they plan to visit by entering **gopher go-pher.gsfc.nasa.gov** and following the path */Other Resources/US geographic name server*.

2. FINGER
   - Visit a coke machine by entering the command **finger coke@cmu.edu** or **finger coke@cs.wisc.edu**.
   - Visit a candy machine by entering the command **finger mnm@coke.elab.cs.cmu.edu**.
   - Trivia fans might like trying Cyndi William's Trivia Time by entering the command **finger cyndiw@magnus1.com**. Each Monday, a new quiz is made available and answers to the previous week's quiz are given.

3. FTP
   - Any *Cheers* fans in the audience? If so, take them to FTP site *nic.funet.fi* and go to the */pub/culture/tv+film/series/Cheers* directory where they'll find files containing Norm sayings, episode guides, and other trivia.
   - The Star Trek archives at FTP site *ftp.coe.montana.edu* may also prove popular. Once logged in, go to the */pub/mirrors/.star-trek/Tim_Lynch_stuff/misc* directory and download a short ASCII text file called *encyc.rev*. This is a review of the Star Trek Encyclopedia by Michael Okuda, Denise Okuda, and Debbie Mirek.
     (To decompress the Cheers and Star Trek files, you need a copy of the program GUNZIP. See Appendix A for details.)
   - For thousands of song lyrics, FTP to *ftp.sunet.se* and change directories to */pub/music/lyrics*.

4. GOPHER
   - Demonstrate what an electronic library is like by giving them a tour of CICNet's Electronic Journal Archives at Gopher site *gopher.cic.net*. Beginning at the root menu, follow the path */2. Electronic Serials/9. Other Journal Archives/1. E-Text Archive/20. Zines-by-subject/*.
   - Star Trek fans will have fun exploring all of the information available on the Gopher server at *wiretap.spies.com*. Choose */Mass Media/StarTrek*.

## ≡ Introducing a New Service

This section presents ideas for integrating a new Internet service into your existing information system. It also offers suggestions on how you might make the availability of a new Internet service known to the public.

The first Internet service our library introduced to the public was CancerNet. We chose this Internet database because it offered easy and convenient access to authoritative cancer information, the patron's requests could be satisfied at point of need, and the information was more up-to-date than any print source could possibly be. It has proven to be a perfect example of how convenience and the timely delivery of information are more important to the patron than the "box" in which the information is delivered. From the patron's point of view, it is irrelevant that this information exists as digitized files outside the four walls of the library and that these files are delivered through the telephone lines.

To make the service operational, we first created a notebook containing three items:

1. An information form that could be used if the reference librarian wasn't available to make the connection with the National Cancer Institute. This form, shown here, also briefly explains the CancerNet service.

```
                        C a n c e r N e t

CancerNet is a quick way to obtain, through electronic mail, cancer informa-
tion statements from the National Cancer Institute's Physician Data Query
(PDQ) system. Most of the information is available in both English and
Spanish.

The topics listed in this notebook are arranged alphabetically and each en-
try is followed by a 6 digit code which is used when ordering.

Bladder Cancer................. cn-101206
Bladder Cancer................. cn-201206

Document numbers beginning with the number "2" are intended for patients.
Those beginning with the number "1" are intended for doctors and other
health care professionals. Two sample printouts are included in the back of
this notebook.

Depending on the reference librarian's availability, documents will be re-
trieved while the patron waits, or they will be retrieved not later than 24
hours after the patron's request.

The following information is needed for ordering:

Title:_____Code Number:_____


_____
Patron's Name          Address                Tele No.

Information can be downloaded to a floppy disk or printed out on paper.
Patrons must provide their own formatted floppy discs. There is no fee
charged for this service.

Branch Libraries:  Send this completed form to the main library via FAX and
the document you requested will be sent back to you via FAX in 24 hours or
less. Patrons also have the option of having the information downloaded to
a floppy disk, but they must come to the main library for that service.
```

2. Next we included a printed copy of the index listing all of the documents that are available. An excerpt from this alphabetical listing follows.

```
DIAGNOSIS. . . . . . . . . . . . . . . . . . . . PHYSICIANS . . PATIENTS


Adrenocortical Carcinoma . . . . . . . . . .cn-101198 . . cn-201198
AIDS-Related Lymphoma. . . . . . . . . . . .cn-103779 . . cn-203779
Anal Cancer. . . . . . . . . . . . . . . . .cn-100022 . . cn-200022
Bile Duct Cancer - see Extrahepatic Bile Duct Cancer
Bladder Cancer . . . . . . . . . . . . . . .cn-101206 . . cn-201206
Brain Cancer
        Adult . . . . . . . . . . . . . . . .cn-101143 . . cn-201143
        Childhood . . . . . . . . . . . . . .cn-100047 . . cn-200047
Breast Cancer . . . . . . . . . . . . . . . cn-100013 . . cn-200013
Carcinoid Tumor - see Gastrointestinal Carcinoid Tumor
Carcinoma of Unknown Primary . . . . . . . . cn-103331 . . . .N/A
Cervical Cancer. . . . . . . . . . . . . . . cn-100103 . . cn-200103
Choriocarcinoma - See Gestational Trophoblastic Tumor
Colon Cancer . . . . . . . . . . . . . . . . cn-100008 . . cn-200008
Endometrial Cancer . . . . . . . . . . . . .cn-101176 . . cn-201176
Esophageal Cancer. . . . . . . . . . . . . .cn-100089 . . cn-200089
Extrahepatic Bile Duct Cancer. . . . . . . .cn-101191 . . cn-201191
Ewing's Sarcoma. . . . . . . . . . . . . . .cn-100021 . . cn-200021
Eye
        Intraocular Melanoma. . . . . . . . .cn-101279 . . cn-201279
        Retinoblastoma. . . . . . . . . . . .cn-100993 . . cn-200993
Gallbladder Cancer . . . . . . . . . . . . .cn-101186 . . cn-201186
Gastric Cancer . . . . . . . . . . . . . . .cn-100025 . . cn-200025
Gastrointestinal Carcinoid Tumor . . . . . .cn-101064 . . cn-201064
Germ Cell Tumors
        Extragonadal Germ Cell Tumors. . . . .cn-103773 . . . N/A
        Ovarian Germ Cell Tumor . . . . . . . .cn-103125 . . cn-203125
        Testicular Cancer . . . . . . . . . . .cn-101121 . . cn-201121
Gestational Trophoblastic Tumor. . . . . . .cn-101163 . . cn-201163
Head and Neck Cancer
        Hypopharyngeal Cancer . . . . . . . . .cn-101500 . . cn-201500
        Laryngeal Cancer. . . . . . . . . . . .cn-101519 . . cn-201519
        Lip and Oral Cavity Cancer. . . . . . .cn-102840 . . cn-202840
```

3. In the back of the notebook, we included two sample printouts showing examples of both the patients and physicians statement.

In addition to this, we inserted a subject card in our card catalog and a "dummy" book on the shelf, directing patrons to the reference desk for information on CancerNet.

The following press release was then issued announcing this new service to the community.

```
LIBRARY MAKES FIRST CONNECTION TO GLOBAL NETWORK

Allen Benson, Director of the Saline County Library, is pleased to an-
nounce that they are now offering a special service to patrons who are
seeking information on cancer. On July 19th, the Saline County Library es-
tablished an Internet connection to the National Cancer Institute via a
computer terminal in the library. This service, called CancerNet, provides
an easy way to obtain cancer information statements from the National Can-
cer Institute's Physician Data Query (PDQ) system.

The library keeps a list of all the documents that the National Cancer In-
stitute makes available and the library can get copies usually while the
patron waits. The process works like this:  A reference librarian connects
to the computers at the National Cancer Institute and queries their data-
base for a particular file. When he/she finds the one that the patron has
requested, he/she brings it back across the telephone lines to the library
here in Benton, Arkansas. The file that's retrieved isn't like a paper
file that you might find setting on the shelf in the library, but rather
an electronic file and it only takes a few seconds to retrieve it. Once
the document is on the library's computer, a reference librarian prints it
out in paper format which takes one or two minutes, depending on the size
of the document.

CancerNet offers additional information on other products and services
that are made available at the National Cancer Institute, including a list
of patient publications that are available from the Office of Cancer Commu-
nications. The information on CancerNet is updated monthly. For most dis-
eases, two statements are available for each diagnosis: one for physicians
and another for patients and most are available in both English and Span-
ish.

This service is also available to patrons at the Bryant branch library.
The branch library will be FAXing their requests to the main library and
they will in turn FAX the results back.
The Saline County Library will continue to make new resources available to
the citizens of Saline County by tapping into this information "super high-
way" called the Internet. Benson believes that geographic location should
not be a limitation when it comes to accessing information housed in other
locations around the world. As a result of computers and new advances in
telecommunications, geographic location has become irrelevant.
```

## Introductory Flyer

The following flyer is offered as an example of what can be distributed near your public access computers as a general introduction to the Internet. The issues you cover will of course vary depending on the community you serve. This particular flyer was designed for public library use.

# Questions and Answers About the Internet

1. *What is the Internet?*

   The Internet is a large computer network made up of more than 10,000 smaller networks that exist worldwide. These smaller networks are owned by countless businesses, governmental and educational organizations, research institutions, and individuals. All of the networks are interconnected and can communicate and share information with one another almost instantly.

2. *Just how big is the Internet?*

   The Internet spans every continent on the globe including Antarctica. It is estimated that there are over 4 million people using the Internet in over 100 countries. Its growth is staggering. In the U.S. alone, its size increased by 96% from December 1990 to December 1991. It is estimated that 100 million people will be using the Internet by the year 1998.

3. *What is the Internet used for?*

   The Internet is used for finding and retrieving information. It's a place where you can store your own information and make it available to others. It's also a place where conversations take place—conversations between children in grades K-12, teachers, researchers, librarians, government officials, and private citizens from all walks of life.

4. *What kinds of resources are available on the Internet?*

   Users can find information on such things as the most recent Supreme Court decisions, hourly updates on earthquake activity around the world, search university libraries all over the world, view satellite weather photos, read press releases from the White House, leave personal messages at NASA, find out about food recipes, baseball scores, pruning apple trees, raising ostriches, and thousands of other topics. It is truly a global community—a way of working and living.

5. *How do you connect to the Internet?*

   You need a computer, a modem, a telephone line, and a special piece of software called *communications* software. The modem is a device that enables you to send and receive information over the telephone lines and the communication software enables your computer to talk with other computers.

6. *What are the benefits of using the Internet in the Library?*

   The Internet expands the resources of the library dramatically by making many resources from all over the world available to patrons. It can be used for bringing information, data, images, and even computer software into the library that would otherwise be impossible to get. Having access to these resources provides tools for our citizens that are unavailable in libraries without Internet access. The Internet also brings people together with common interests and it's blind to class, race, ability, and disability. The Internet enables individuals living in one geographic location to share their ideas with others around the globe.

7. *I've heard that there are files on the Internet that some would deem objectionable. Can access to these files be restricted or denied?*

   Just as we cannot restrict an individual's access to printed information, we cannot refuse anyone service because they have asked us to provide them with a specific item on the Internet that someone else may deem objectionable. The principles of intellectual freedom that apply to the traditional library also apply to this new "electronic" library.

## ≡ Adding Value to Internet Services

As you explore the ideas presented in this section, keep in mind the various issues covered earlier regarding copyright ownership. When downloading files, look for and read copyright notices and be aware of the rights, if any, being granted by the copyright owner. In the case of shareware, it is common for the owner to grant an express license to use the software on a trial basis and to distribute it to others for the same purpose.

Contact the copyright owner directly for permission to reproduce or distribute a copyrighted work when your reproduction or distribution doesn't fall under "fair use" exemptions or some other exemptions.

## ≡ Using a Word Processor To Add Value to Internet Services

Much of the data available online is textual and can be downloaded from its original source and then loaded into a word processor for full text searching. Word processors like Microsoft Word have the capability to find each occurrence of a combination of any characters, whole words, or parts of words in a textual document.

You will find many situations in which this implementation will be useful. For example, if a patron wants to join a LISTSERV discussion list that talks about horror fiction, download the file that describes all of the various discussion lists on BITNET (see "For Further Study" in Chapter 13) and save it to disk. To answer this question, or others like it that will come up in the future, load the file into a word processor and use the Find" feature(in Word for Windows click on the Edit pull-down menu and choose Find) to search for the appropriate string—in this case, *horror*. Even with a file this large (over 700,000 bytes), a modern computer can finish the search in a matter of seconds. If you find any relevant entries, cut and paste them to a new document and print it out for your patron.

This is a good example of how librarians can add value to an Internet service that is essentially useless in its raw state on an FTP server. Although it's unrealistic to expect an individual library patron to download and manipulate a file this size for what may end up being 200 bytes of useful information, the librarian can justify retrieving and managing this file because it is potentially useful to many.

Save the *List of Discussion Lists* file to a disk and make it readily accessible to your community. If you're running Windows, create an icon for the file. Be prepared to show interested patrons how to use a word processor to search the file for keywords and have help sheets ready for assisting patrons with message archive searching and LISTSERV subscriptions.

## ≡ Libraries as Publishers of Electronic Documents

Libraries now have the opportunity to become involved in the online publishing process by setting up World-Wide Web servers and writing home pages, setting up Gopher servers, establishing FTP archive sites, creating and maintaining LISTSERV discussion lists, and publishing electronic journals.

## Local History Archives

Libraries can also become information publishers in the area of local history. Materials that might be appropriate for archiving would include writings on local history, club newsletters, family histories, cemetery records, photographs, and sound recordings of story tellers and musicians, etc. Much of this information isn't indexed and could be quite useful if it were keyword searchable—something that's possible in digital form.

An application like Mosaic can serve as an interface for all the different file formats required for storing this wide range of materials. With a direct connection to the Internet, local historical information could be made available to researchers anywhere in the world with access to the Internet. Even when local citizens move away, they can still access their hometown library via the Internet for local historical information, regardless of their geographic location.

Libraries might consider forming cooperatives with local historical associations and museums, pooling resources and creating one comprehensive electronic historical archive that benefits everyone. The library could make their hardware, software, and expertise in converting materials into digital formats available to others. The library would of course be instrumental in organizing and archiving the information for public use.

## Locating and Repackaging Information

The same skills that librarians have applied in traditional library settings can also be applied in a global network environment. Academic librarians can monitor specific resources that relate to their subject specialties such as LISTSERV discussion lists, electronic journals, newsgroups, and FTP archive holdings. They could go out onto the Internet and obtain appropriate items, organize and assemble these materials into one package, and archive them in a menu-driven system like Gopher.

Librarians around the world with similar interests could cooperate via the Internet and share in the creation and maintenance of the database. Through a public relations program, faculty and students could be made aware of the availability of this information as a service of the library.

Public librarians can locate and archive materials that are being demanded locally. For example, if a local school teacher has made a Supreme Court decision or some recent federal legislation part of his or her curriculum, the librarian can retrieve it from the Internet, save it on disk, and make it available in a word processing program with text searching capabilities. (See the "Goverment" section in Part VI for resources relating to these two topics.)

If students are writing reports on different countries, a school media specialist can introduce them to the *CIA World Fact Book* online via the Internet through a WAIS (see Chapter 8) or Gopher interface (Gopher to site *wiretap.spies.com* and choose menu item */2.Electronic Books at Wiretap*). Both WAIS and Gopher offer text searching capabilities.

The media specialist could also download the entire *CIA World Fact Book* file from an FTP site and mount it locally in a word processor with text searching capabilities (FTP to site *nptn.org* and change to the */pub/e.texts/gutenberg* directory).

Some reference materials that exist in paper format may also be available in digital format on the Internet. The *Catalog of Federal Domestic Assistance* is one such example. This document can be accessed through the Library of Congress Gopher and is much more usable in this format than in its paper counterpart.

You could research a topic that is of particular interest in your community—for example, "business loans for Vietnam vets"—and download relevant documents and load them into a local database. You could add a table of contents and an index and install the entire package under a menu item on your local area network.

To try this particular example, connect to the Gopher server at *marvel.loc.gov* and choose */9.Government Information/1. Federal Information Resources/1.Information by Agency/1. General Information Resources*. The *General Information Resources* menu follows.

```
General Information Resources

 1. U.S. Government Manual, 1993-94 (Via UMich)/
 2. Budget FY 1995 (Proposed)/
 3. Budget FY 1995 (Proposed):  How To Obtain Copies
 4. Catalog of Federal Domestic Assistance (Search) <?>
 5. Code of Federal Regulations (Partial, Via Counterpoint)/
 6. Constitution/
 7. FedWorld (NTIS Gateway to Federal Bulletin Boards) <TEL>
 8. Federal Bulletin Boards (List)
 9. Federal Information Exchange/
10. Federal Register/
11. FinanceNet (NPR/NSF Gopher on Government Financial Management)/
12. Freedom of Information Act (FOIA): Guide to Use
13. Government Gopher Servers (From NSF)/
14. Government Gopher Servers (From UC Irvine/PEG)/
15. Government Printing Office (GPO)/
16. Government Publications Catalogs and Services via Bernan <TEL>
17. Guide to Internet Government Resources (Gumprecht, 2/2/94)
18. Guide to Internet Government Resources (Parhamovich, 7/94)
19. Guide to Internet Government Resources in Bus. and Econ. (2/94)
20. Historical Documents of the U.S./
21. Job Openings in the Federal Government/
22. Monthly Catalog (Govt. Pubs. Via CARL:  choose PAC, 1, 22, 83.. <TEL>
23. National Performance Review Report/
24. National Social Statistics:  Surveys, Census (Via UPenn)/
25. Open Source Solutions, Inc. (OSS Gopher)/
26. The Legal Domain Network/
27. Wiretap Gopher/
```

After choosing menu item 4.*Catalog of Federal Domestic Assistance (Search)* <*?*>, I entered the following search terms: **business loans Vietnam veterans**. This search resulted in 75 hits covering five screens of output, the first of which follows.

```
-->  1.  59.038 Veterans Loan Program.
     2.  64.010 Veterans Nursing Home Care.
     3.  17.804 Local Veterans Employment Representative Program.
     4.  64.120 Post-Vietnam Era Veterans' Educational Assistance.
     5.  17.801 Disabled Veterans Outreach Program (DVOP).
     6.  45.157 Promotion of the Humanities_Dissertation Grants.
     7.  64.125 Vocational and Educational Counseling for Servicemembers.
     8.  27.002 Federal Employment Assistance for Veterans.
     9.  17.802 Veterans Employment Program.
    10.  64.011 Veterans Outpatient Care.
    11.  64.126  Native American Veteran Direct Loan Program.
    12.  64.119 Veterans Housing_Manufactured Home Loans.
    13.  17.301 Non-Discrimination and Affirmative Action by Federal.
    14.  84.022 Fulbright-Hays Training Grants_Doctoral Dissertation.
    15.  64.124 All-Volunteer Force Educational Assistance.
    16.  64.114 Veterans Housing_Guaranteed and Insured Loans.
    17.  64.022 Veterans Hospital Based Home Care.
    18.  53.001 Employment Promotion of People with Disabilities.
```

At this point, you can access any one of these text files and conduct a full text search by entering a forward slash (/) followed by a text string. The string must match the term or terms you are searching for exactly—including case sensitivity. You can use the asterisk (*) for truncation at the end of a word. The first part of the *1. 59.038 Veterans Loan Program* document is presented here:

```
59.038 Veterans Loan Program

(Veterans Loans)

FEDERAL AGENCY: SMALL BUSINESS ADMINISTRATION

AUTHORIZATION: Small Business Act of 1953, Section 7(a), as
amended, Public Law 97-72, and 97-377.

OBJECTIVES: To provide loans to small businesses owned by
Vietnam-era and disabled veterans.

TYPES OF ASSISTANCE: Direct Loans.

USES AND USE RESTRICTIONS: To construct, expand, or convert
facilities; to purchase building equipment or materials; for working
capital. Excludes gambling establishments, publishing media, radio and
television, nonprofit enterprises, speculators in property, lending or
investment enterprises, and financing of real property held for
investment; also excludes funds to indiscriminately relocate the
business. Fund  must not otherwise be available on reasonable terms,
nor used to pay off a loan to an unsecured creditor who is in a
position to sustain loss. Guaranty loans under the regular Business
Loan Program must be used if available before a direct loan can be
considered.

ELIGIBILITY REQUIREMENTS:

Applicant Eligibility: Must be a small business concern as
described in SBA regulations. Small business concerns must be owned (a
minimum of 51 percent) by an eligible veteran(s). Management and daily
operation of the business must be directed by one or more of the
```

```
veteran owners of the applicant whose veteran status is used to qualify
for the loan. Vietnam-era veterans who served for a period of more than
180 days, any part of which was between August 5, 1964, and May 7,
1975, and were discharged other than dishonorably. Disabled veterans of
any era with a minimum compensable disability of 30 percent or a
veteran of any era who was discharged for disability. Veterans status
may be used only once to obtain a loan under this program.

Beneficiary Eligibility: Small business concerns.

Credentials/Documentation: Statement of personal history,
personal financial statement, company financial statement, summary of
collat  al, resume, and evidence of discharge on other than
dishonorable basis. Loan must be of such sound value or so secured as
to reasonably assure repayment.

APPLICATION AND AWARD PROCESS:

Preapplication Coordination: None. This program is excluded from
coverage under E.O. 12372.

Application Procedure: Applications are filed in the field office
serving the territory in which the applicant's business is located.
(See listing of field offices in Appendix IV of the Catalog.)

Award Procedure: Applicant is notified by authorization letter
from district SBA office, or participating bank.
```

To move this document or another document to your local machine, press **m** and a window will appear where you are asked to enter your Internet email address. Type the address, press ENTER, and the document will be mailed to your account.

## Partnerships with Traditional Publishers

Another publishing service that libraries may one day provide involves the forming of partnerships with traditional publishers. At the time this book was being written, the Advisory Board of the Scholarly Communications Project (University Libraries, Virginia Polytechnic Institute and State University) put forth an interesting proposal—a co-publication plan that places libraries in a role of managing and providing access to electronic publications along with publishers.

The Advisory Board suggested that scholarly journals be published in two versions: One version would be a full text electronic version archived and made available at no cost by a library. A second version would be a summary version published by a traditional publisher in paper format and/or in an electronic database with access charges.

Their belief was that scholars would be interested in subscribing to and browsing the publisher's summaries. Then, if the scholar found something of interest, he or she would access the full text version archived by the library in electronic format at no cost. The library would be doing what it does best—acquiring, organizing, and archiving information for public use. The publisher would be concentrating in its area of expertise—copy editing, sorting, and verifying information. It is possible that as time evolves, co-publishing arrangements such as this may become a reality.

## ≡ For Further Study

For further information relating to security issues, see the FAQ maintained by Alec Muffett that answers regularly asked questions in the USENET newsgroups *comp.security.misc* and *alt.security*. To access a copy of this document, Gopher to *arthur.cs.purdue.edu* and follow the path */5. Purdue Computer Emergency Response Team (PCERT) Archives/2. Assorted security-related documents and papers/*. Once in this directory, begin by reading */5.README*, then go to menu item */6.alt.security.faq*, which is the document itself.

System managers or anyone interested in setting up or operating a network will find the *Site Security Handbook*, edited by P. Holbrook and J. Reynolds, an essential document. It can be retrieved from FTP site *nic.ddn.mil* in the */rfc* directory, filename *rfc1244.txt*.

A complete copy of the *Electronic Communications Privacy Act of 1986* (ECPA) can be obtained by sending the command **GET PRIVACY LAW F=MAIL** to *listserv@bitnic.educom.edu*.

More online training information is available through NETTRAIN, a moderated discussion group that talks about Internet/BITNET network training. Search their message archives (see Chapter 13) or subscribe by sending the message **subscribe nettrain <your name>** to *listserv@ubvm.cc.buffalo.edu*.

To reach the American Library Association (ALA) Gopher, connect with the Gopher server at *gopher.uic.edu* and follow this path: */9. The Library/12. American Library Association (ALA)*. The root menu appears as follows:

```
     American Library Association (ALA) (Under Construction)


    1. I.   About this gopher.
    2. II.  About ALA/
    3. III. ALA and Division Conferences/
    4. IV.  Publications (Electronic and other)/
    5. V.   ALA's Council and Executive Board/
    6. VI.  ALA, Division, and Round Table Elections/
    7. VII. ALA, Division, and Round Table Committee Charges and Rosters/
    8. VIII. ALA Policy Manual and Constitution & Bylaws/
    9. IX.  ALA and Division Standards & Guidelines/
   10. X.   ALA Intellectual Freedom Statements/
   11. XI.  Legislation Affecting Libraries/
   12. XII. Awards and Scholarships/
   13. XIII. ALA's Divisions/
   14. XIV. ALA's Round Tables/
   15. XV.  ALA's Offices and Other Units/
   16. XVI. ALA Chapters and Affiliates/
```

# Chapter 22

# Implementing Internet Services In-House

As a librarian, you should view the Internet as a strategic resource for your entire operation, not just as a single, technical resource. While the Internet functions well as a reference tool and its primary use will be in that department, it can also serve as a consulting resource and communication tool in other departments. Email, for example, can be used for ordering books and other materials, requesting reference assistance from colleagues, and sending claims to subscription agents for missing journals. Acquisitions librarians can use the Internet to verify bibliographic data, place orders, and explore the holdings of online bookstores. Catalogers can access other library's online catalogs for copy cataloging. The Internet makes it possible for those involved with collection development to study other librarys' holdings, read book reviews online, and create bibliographies.

New ideas for Internet implementations should be continuously solicited from all employees in every department. These ideas can be evaluated not just in terms of how they will benefit the overall operations of the library, but also in terms of how they will benefit the community.

## ≡ Technical Services

This section introduces three LISTSERV discussion lists that discuss issues relating to cataloging. Examples are given of how you can browse the contents of their message archives. (See Chapter 13 for more information on searching message archives.) Resources relating to technical services are also available on the Gopher server maintained by the Library of Congress.

## Discussion Lists

AUTOCAT is a library cataloging and authorities discussion list. To subscribe, send the message **subscribe autocat <your name>** to *listserv@uvmvm.bitnet*. To retrieve a listing of the files contained in their message archive, send the message **get autocat filelist** to *listserv@uvmvm.bitnet*. An excerpt from the output resulting from this command is presented in the following example. To retrieve any one of the files listed, send the command **get <filename> <filetype>** to *listserv@uvmvm.bitnet*. For example, if you'd like to retrieve the first one listed, send the command **get autocat log9010**.

```
* filename filetype   GET PUT -fm lrecl nrecs   date     time   Remarks
* -------- --------   --- --- --- ----- ----- -------- -------- ----------------
----------------
  AUTOCAT  LOG9010    ALL OWN V    80    464 90/10/31 18:42:16 Started on Wed,
24 Oct 90 13:37:49 EST
  AUTOCAT  LOG9011    ALL OWN V    80   3652 90/11/29 17:49:55 Started on Thu,
1 Nov 90 08:16:00 EDT
  AUTOCAT  LOG9012    ALL OWN V    80   3807 90/12/31 13:47:18 Started on Fri,
30 Nov 90 11:54:51 EST
  AUTOCAT  LOG9101    ALL OWN V    80   5160 91/01/31 23:30:11 Started on Wed,
2 Jan 91 10:24:52 EST
  AUTOCAT  LOG9102    ALL OWN V    80   8084 91/02/28 19:14:34 Started on Thu,
31 Jan 91 07:52:52 EST
  AUTOCAT  LOG9103    ALL OWN V    80   6546 91/03/31 06:49:42 Started on Fri,
1 Mar 91 08:16:58 EST
  AUTOCAT  LOG9104    ALL OWN V    80   6403 91/04/30 22:49:36 Started on Mon,
1 Apr 91 08:18:32 EST
  AUTOCAT  LOG9105    ALL OWN V    80   7429 91/05/31 21:37:33 Started on Wed,
```

COOPCAT is a cooperative cataloging arrangements discussion list. To subscribe, send the message **subscribe coopcat <your name>** to *listserv@nervm.bitnet*.

NOTRBCAT is a discussion list for people interested in rare book and special collections cataloging. To subscribe, send the message **subscribe notrbcat <your name>** to *listserv@indycms.bitnet*. To obtain a list of their archived message files, send the command **get notrbcat filelist** to *listserv@indycms.bitnet*. An excerpt from the output resulting from this command is shown in the following example. This filelist includes brief explanations of the contents of each file.

```
* List of EXLIBRIS members by institution, A-R
  EXLIBRIS MEMBERS1   ALL OWN V    72    639 92/06/19 08:31:33
* List of EXLIBRIS members by institution, S-Z
  EXLIBRIS MEMBERS2   ALL OWN V    76    579 92/06/19 08:31:46
* NOTRBCAT and EXLIBRIS members combined, alphabetically by surname
  EXCAT    MEMBERS    ALL OWN V    76    715 92/08/16 21:33:15
* Guide to the use of the cooperative authority files
  AUTHORTY GUIDE      ALL OWN .    .      0 ........ ........
* Index to the authority files
  AUTHORTY INDEX      ALL OWN V    62     21 92/02/20 22:51:56
* Printer authority file (cooperative project)
  PRINTER  FILE       ALL OWN V    79     86 92/02/20 22:52:26
* Name authority file (cooperative project): all except printers
  NAME     FILE       ALL OWN V    79     33 92/02/20 22:52:11
```

```
* List of libraries with areas of specialty in which expertise can be
* shared
  CO-OP      FILE      ALL OWN .    .   0 ........  ........
* Handlist of Writings on Nineteenth-Century British and American
* Handcraft Binding, Bindings, and Binders, by Donald Farren
  BIND19  FILE      ALL OWN V    80   769 92/06/10 20:26:14
```

If you'd like to retrieve a copy of the last file listed, "Handlist of Writings on Nineteenth-Century British and American Handcraft Binding, Bindings, and Binders" by Donald Farren, simply send the command **get bind19 file** in the body of an email message to *listserv@indycms.bitnet*.

# ☰ LC Marvel

LC Marvel is a Gopher server maintained by the Library of Congress that will be of particular interest to catalogers. To connect, Gopher to site *marvel.loc.gov* or TELNET to *marvel.loc.gov* and login as **marvel**. At the main menu, choose *4. Libraries and Publishers (Technical Services)/ 6. USMARC Standards/ 1.The US-MARC Formats: Background and Principles*. This brings you to a document that discusses the background and principles for content designation in the USMARC formats.

A paper titled *Access to Online Information Resources within USMARC* by Rebecca S. Guenther is also available from the Library of Congress Gopher. After logging into LC Marvel, choose *4.Libraries and Publishers (Technical Services/ 6. USMARC Standards/2.The USMARC Listserv (Archives and Documents)/1.Access to Online Information Resources in USMARC*. The opening paragraph of this document is presented here:

```
Introduction

        The Network Development and MARC Standards Office of the
Library of Congress has been exploring the description of online
information resources as well as access information using the
USMARC formats. Librarians and information professionals, as well
as other users, operate in increasingly networked and
internetworked environments. Librarians see it as their role to
organize information. In the case of online information resources,
it is highly desirable to create order out of the chaos of
networked information. Many different kinds of online information
resources, whether they are numeric databases, computer forums,
discussion groups, mailing list servers, online public access
catalogs (OPACs), full-text databases, or other varieties of
information resources, are available to users over one or more
networks such as the Internet, BITNET, etc. Many libraries are
providing access to their catalogs through the networks.
```

Many other items are of interest to catalogers at this site, such as *LC Cataloging Newsline: Online Newsletter of the Cataloging Directorate*. Back issues of this newsletter can be viewed online or mailed to your local machine and printed out.

# ≡ Acquisitions

This section lists various Internet resources that may be of interest to acquisitions librarians. These include lists of bookstores that ship their merchandise world-wide, bookstore reviews, lists of book catalogs and book clubs, and publisher's catalogs that can be accessed online.

Bookstores that ship world-wide: Evelyn C. Leeper has compiled a selective list of bookstores that ship world-wide and organized the list into the following categories:

General
Academic
Science Fictionand Mystery
Gay/Lesbian/Bisexual
Children's
Computer
Religion

A sample listing from the General category is presented in the following example. Notice that three of the four entries include email addresses.

```
===============================================================================
General (see also Academic):

WordsWorth Books (30 Brattle Street, Cambridge MA 02138-3761,
        800-899-2202 or +1-617-354-4223, FAX +1-617-354-4674,
        info@wordsworth.com). The flag-ship of Harvard Square book
        shops with 100,000+ titles. Has been offering their book store
        service through e-mail for quite a while. "Their staff have
        managed to locate and send many books for me (in Sweden) via UPS
        Express at costs equal or less than buying at a real store
        (hardcovers especially). What's more, the book search costs only
        one dollar. Their collection is really huge, too." Mon-Sat
        8:30AM-11:30PM, Sun 10AM-10:30PM). GMT-5h

The Tattered Cover (2955 East First Avenue, Denver CO 80206, [mail address
        is Tattered Cover Bookstore, 1536 Wynkoop, Denver CO 80202],
        800-833-9327 or +1 303-322-7727, TT/V (303) 320-0536,
        FAX +1 303-399-2279, books@tatteredcover.com [for individual
        ordering], corporate@tatteredcover.com [for corporate ordering]).
        Huge--4 floors. Over 400,000 books in stock. Considered to be
        the best independent bookstore in the U.S. Also ships worldwide.
        Free gift-wrapping. Hours: 9:30AM - 9PM M-Sat; 10-6 Sun. GMT-7h

Powell's City of Books (main store) (1005 W Burnside, Portland OR,
        +1 503-228-4651, FAX +1 503-228-4631). Truly a national treasure,
        one of the wonders of Portland. Powell's has new and used books by
        the millions. Its depth and coverage exceeds most large-city
        libraries. Ships worldwide. To receive an automated reply on how
        to browse the technical books database via email, send any message
        to ping@technical.powells.portland.or.us. GMT-8h

Cody's (2454 Telegraph, Berkeley CA +1 510-845-7852). "One of the two
        stores in the Bay area I hold up as the definition of the
        term 'bookstore.' (The other is Kepler's in Menlo Park.)"
```

```
A very large selection of just about everything
(foreign-language books on Dwight just west of Telegraph).
"Cody's is the only book store in the Bay Area with a
significant selection of books on various subjects that
interest me (including Judaica, system dynamics and whitewater
maps). It is true that it isn't as good as it was when Fred Cody
was alive ... but it's still a damn good store." There is even a
book about Cody's: CODY'S BOOKS: THE LIFE AND TIMES OF A BERKELEY
BOOKSTORE, 1956-1977, by Pat and Fred Cody (it was described in
an article in the August 3, 1992 issue of "Publishers Weekly").
Will ship worldwide. Sun-Thu 9:15AM-9:45PM, Fri-Sat
9:15AM-10:45PM. GMT-8h
```

You can retrieve the complete listing of stores by FTPing to site *rtfm.mit.edu* in a file called *ship-by-mail* stored in the */pub/usenet/news.answers/books/stores* directory. Other bookstores listed by geographic location can be found on the same FTP server in these directories:

```
/pub/usenet/news.answers/books/stores/asian.Z
/pub/usenet/news.answers/books/stores/european.Z
/pub/usenet/news.answers/books/stores/north-american/bay-area.Z
/pub/usenet/news.answers/books/stores/north-american/eastern.Z
/pub/usenet/news.answers/books/stores/north-american/northern.Z
/pub/usenet/news.answers/books/stores/north-american/nyc.Z
/pub/usenet/news.answers/books/stores/north-american/western.Z
```

Book catalogs and book clubs: Cindy Tittle Moore has compiled a list of bookseller's catalogs and book clubs. For a copy of this file, FTP to site *rtfm.mit.edu* and download the file called *catalogues* located in the */pub/usenet/news.answers/books* directory. Book seller's entries include mailing addresses and descriptions of holdings. Book club entries give terms of membership and subject concentrations. A few sample entries follow:

```
* A K Press  [UK]              Tel: 031-667-1507 (24hr answerphone/fax)
  22 Lutton Place
  Edinburgh, EH8 9PE Scotland

  Carries a 64 page catalogue of 'radical left' books, many
  difficult to get hold of. Well over 1,000 titles on anarchism,
  feminism, situationism, surrealism, etc. Various catalogues.
  Cheque/postal order/International Money Order, or US dollars (at
  own risk).


* Harry E. Bagley Books Ltd. [CANADA]

  PO Box 691                   Tel: 506-459-3034
  Fredericton, NB E3B 5B4      Fax: 506-452-9292
  Canada

  General booksellers in business for 23 years. They deal with any
  and all used or out of print and antiquarian books. A free search
  service is provided and they welcome new customers on the mailing
  list as well as catalogues from fellow dealers. Business is
  world-wide, usually transacted in US funds (or cheques sterling)
  outside of Canada.
```

* Books of the Big Outside (Dave Foreman's) [US]

   Ned Ludd Books          Tel: 602-628-9610 (credit card orders)
   P.O. Box 85190
   Tucson, AZ 85754-5190

"The purpose of this catalog is to make important books [on
conservation] available to wilderness defenders. Our focus in on
Wilderness, Biological Diversity, Eco-philosophy, and
Anti-Modernism. Many of the books included here are little-known
or difficult to find elsewhere." So writes Dave Foreman,
associated with Earth First!, who reviews each book. Politics
aside, this is a valuable, fascinating, and sometimes depressing
collection of books (due to the numbing odds set before those
interested in wilderness conservation.) Catalog contains "over 400
Books, Maps, Cassettes & CDs."


* Cambridge Architectural Books, Inc.

   12 Bow Street, 1st floor
   Cambridge, MA 02138
   + 1 617 354 5300
   Fax + 1 617 354 1932

An excellent 63-page catalogue of selected books. Includes
architecture (history, theory, individual architects), gardens and
landscape architecture, urbanism and geography, construction
(relatively small section), furniture, industrial design,
typography and graphic design, photography (small section, mostly
architectural), interior design and decoration. Many direct
imports unavailable elsewhere.


* China Books & Periodicals, Inc. [US]

   2929 Twenty-fourth Street     Tel: 415-282-2994
   San Francisco, CA 94110       Fax: 415-282-0994

An entire catalogue about China and Chinese culture. Checks
or credit cards accepted. UPS or Bookpost shipping. Overseas
shipping OK (additional charge).


* Classic Motorbooks / Zenith [Aviation] Books [US]

   P.O. Box 1          Tel: 1-800-826-6600 or 1-715-294-3345
   Osceola, WI 54020   Fax: 1-715-294-4448

These two are actually the same company. and you can combine books
from both catalogues in the same order although they don't
advertise the fact. Motorbooks is THE source for automotive
books, both histories and shop manuals, including some imported
books. They are also a publisher and a distributor. Zenith is one
of the larger sources for aviation-related books. They take credit
cards and overseas orders.

```
    * Columbia Trading Co., Nautical Books [US]

        504 Main Street (Rte 6A)      Tel: 1-508-362-8966
        West Barnstable, MA  02668    Fax: 1-508-362-3551

      Rare and used books on nautical subjects. Catalogue comes out
      about every two months. It is a small catalogue (about 23 pages).
      Good selection, prices not too bad.

    * Common Reader, A [US]

        141 Tompkins Avenue
        Pleasantville, NY 10570
        1-800-832-7323

      A wonderful selection of obscure, hard-to-find and plain good
      books. An excellent variety of topics, a range of prices (tends
      toward moderate-to-expensive). Credit cards accepted. Ships UPS.
      Money-back guarantee within 30 days. A monthly catalogue, free.
```

Publisher's catalogs online: Steve Brock (*sbrock@teal.csn.org*) has compiled a listing of book publishers that make their catalogs available online. Examples include: Meckler Publishing Company, O'Reilly and Associates, Johns Hopkins University Press and Harvard Business School Publishing Corporation. Many of the publishers listed also have the capability of taking orders online. For the complete file, FTP to site *rtfm.mit.edu* and download the file called *reviews-faq* found in the */pub/usenet/news.answers/books* directory.

You also can access Brock's list through a Gopher server at *gopher.usask.ca*. At the root menu, follow the path */5. Library/7. Useful non-U of S Library Information/14. Publisher's Catalogues.*

Bookstore Reviews: Reviews of bookstores can be found on the Gopher server at *consultant.micro.umn.edu* in the path */Fun & Games/Games/Bookstores.*

O'Reilly and Associates: For news, ordering information, and book descriptions, FTP to site *ftp.ora.com* and go to the */pub* directory for a list of files. You can also access these files via Gopher to site *ora.com* in the path */Book Descriptions and Information.*

Viewing *ACQNET* Online: *ACQNET* (The Acquisitions Librarians Electronic Network) is an ejournal that "aims to provide a medium for acquisitions librarians and others interested in acquisitions work to exchange information, ideas, and to find solutions to common problems." To access, Gopher to *gopher.cic.net* and follow the path */2. Electronic Serials/3. Alphabetic List/1. A/15. Acquisitions Librarians Electronic Network/.* In the next submenu, there will be several pages listing back issues starting with first issue *acq-v1n001*. For background information on *ACQNET*, read */1. acq-about.*

## ≡ Collection Development

This section describes Internet resources that would be of interest to those who are involved with making decisions about what to add to their collections. Topics include online sources for lists of books that can be purchased directly from their authors, sources of online book reviews, and searching other librarys' online catalogs for assistance in creating bibliographies.

Basement Full of Books: Vonda N. McIntyre has compiled a list of new books that are available by mail directly from their authors. The list is available via FTP to site *rtfm.mit.edu* in a file called *basement-full-of-books* in the */pub/usenet/news.answers/books* directory. This list offers a unique opportunity for book purchasers to request inscriptions and signatures in the books they purchase. In some cases, authors can be contacted by email for more information; otherwise, it is recommended that individuals send stamped return envelopes to the individual authors. Works by the following authors were listed in the 31 January 1994 update:

| | |
|---|---|
| Diane de Avalle-Arce (Pilar de Ovalle), | Victor Koman, |
| Lee Ballentine | David Kopaska-Merkel, |
| Todd Barton & Ursula K. Le Guin, | John M. Landsberg (ed), |
| William Barton & Michael Capobianco, | Edward M. Lerner, |
| Nancy Varian Berberick, | Vonda N. McIntyre, |
| Bruce Boston, | Thom Metzger, |
| David Brin, | Janice Miller & Russ Miller, |
| Jeff Carver, | Hank Nuwer, |
| Valerie Nieman Colander, | Jerry Oltion, |
| Juanita Coulson, | Jonathan Ostrowsky-Lantz (ed.), |
| Joel Davis, | Alexei & Cory Panshin, |
| Dayle A. Dermatis, | Bill Ransom, |
| Gene DeWeese, | Mary Rosenblum, |
| Phyllis Eisenstein, | Robert J. Sawyer, |
| Harlan Ellison, | J. Neil Schulman, |
| M.J. Engh, | Richard Seltzer, |
| Sheila Finch, | Dave Smeds, |
| Colin Greenland, | John E. Stith, |
| James Gunn, | L.A. Taylor, |
| Joe Haldeman, | Gene Wolfe, |
| Gwenyth Hood, | Jane Yolen, |
| Norman F. Joly, | and George Zebrowski. |
| Eileen Kernaghan, | |

Book Reviews: The USENET newsgroup called *alt.book.reviews* is a forum for posting reviews of books that may be of interest to school and public librarians, bookstores, publishers, teachers, and professors. The reviews are archived at FTP site *csn.org*. Go to the */pub/alt.books.reviews* directory and view the available files.

Book reviews on Native American topics can be found at FTP site *ftp.cit.cornell.edu* in the */pub/special/nativeprofs/nativelit* directory.

Book reviews collected from NativeNet are archived on the Gopher server at *cscns.com*. From the root menu, follow the path */11. Inter-Tribal Network/1. Book Reviews*.

Book reviews from the *Whole Earth Review* magazine can be accessed on the Gopher server at *gopher.well.sf.ca.us* by following the path */Art and Culture/Book Reviews.*

Book-Talk is a LISTSERV discussion group that talks about books and other formats that will be published soon. Join by sending the email message **subscribe book-talk <your name>** to *listserv@columbia.ilc.com.*

Viewing other online catalogs to aid in collection department: TELNETing to other libraries on the Internet and accessing their catalogs can provide interesting insight into what other libraries are collecting in a particular subject area, how many copies of a particular title they have cataloged, and how many are circulating at a particular point in time. The following example helps illustrate this use of online library catalogs.

In this example, you are be connecting with the Atlanta/Fulton Public Library, which is a CARL library. Begin by TELNETing to *pac.carl.org.* At the *Enter Choice>* prompt, enter **PAC**. From the main menu, choose *4. Other Library Systems* and then *41. CARL Corporation Network Libraries - Eastern U.S.* Upon choosing this, you are presented with a list of OPACs. The search example presented below uses the first one on the list, *Atlanta/Fulton County Public Library.* By typing that item's line number (**160**) and pressing ENTER, you are automatically connected to that library's computer via TELNET. At the opening screen shown below, menu item **1** was entered.

```
PPPP     A     SSSSS  SSSSS  PPPP   OOOOO  RRRR    TTTTTT
P  P    A A    S      S      P  P   O   O  R   R     TT
PPPP   AAAAA   SSSSS  SSSSS  PPPP   O   O  RRRR      TT
P      A   A        S      S P      O   O  ·R   R    TT
P      A   A   SSSSS  SSSSS  P      OOOOO  R   R     TT


         WELCOME to PASSPORT -- Your On Line Connection

   Atlanta-Fulton Public Library
       1. Library Catalog
       2. Auburn Avenue Research Library Catalog  (coming January 1994)
       3. Community Information and Referral Database
       4. Library News - Hours, Policies


   Reference Databases
       10. Academic American Encyclopedia
       11. Facts on File
       12. Company Profiles
       13. Catalog of Federal Domestic Assistance


   Other U.S. Libraries
       20. CARL Libraries


    Type the number of your choice and press <RETURN>
    1
    WORKING...
```

When you choose *1. Library Catalog*, you are presented with the following screen:

```
SELECTED DATABASE:  AFPL Library Catalog

    The computer can find items by NAME or by WORD

    NAMES can be authors, editors, or names of
    persons or institutions written about in the book

    WORDS can be words from the title, or subjects,
    concepts, ideas, dates etc.

    You may also BROWSE by TITLE, CALL NUMBER, or SERIES.

    Enter   N   for   NAME search
            W   for   WORD search
            B   to    BROWSE by title, call number, or series
            S   to    STOP or SWITCH to another database


    Type the letter for the search you want.
     and press <RETURN>,   or type  ?  for <HELP>


            SELECTED DATABASE:  AFPL Library Catalog

ENTER  COMMAND (use  //EXIT  to return HOME)>>      w
```

## Exercise 1

### *Word Search*

When developing a certain subject area in your collection, you might consider doing this type of online searching to complement data you've collected from other more traditional resources. Naturally, the library catalogs you choose to search will be for reasons particular to your own goals and objectives.

To initiate a word search at the Atlanta/Fulton Public Library, enter the letter **w** at the prompt. On the next screen, you see a prompt where the search word(s) can be entered. The subject of this search is *pregnancy*.

```
        SELECTED DATABASE: AFPL Library Catalog


REMEMBER -- WORDS can be words from the title, or can be subjects,
concepts, ideas, dates, etc.

        for example --  GONE WITH THE WIND
                        SILVER MINING COLORADO
                        BEHAVIOR  MODIFICATION

Enter word or words (no more than one line, please)
separated by spaces and press <RETURN>.

>pregnancy
```

As you can see from the following screen, the term was too broad and the result set was too large, so the search was narrowed by adding another search term, *health*. To add this word to the previous result set, simply press ENTER and the *NEW WORD(S):* prompt appears.

```
WORKING...
PREGNANCY             461  ITEMS

Result sets larger than 300 items will not be sorted.


You may make your search more specific  (and reduce
the size of the list)  by adding another word
to your search. The result will be items in
your current list that also contain the new
word.


  to ADD a new word, enter it,

  <D>ISPLAY to see the current list, or

  <Q>UIT for a new search:


NEW WORD(S): health
```

Combining the terms *health* and *pregnancy* resulted in 37 hits. To display the results of this search, enter option **d**. The first page of output follows.

```
PREGNANCY  + HEALTH    37 ITEMS

You now have: PREGNANCY  + HEALTH    37 ITEMS

You may make your search more specific  (and reduce
the size of the list)  by adding another word
to your search. The result will be items in
your current list that also contain the new
word.


  to ADD a new word, enter it,

  <D>ISPLAY to see the current list, or

  <Q>UIT for a new search:


NEW WORD(S): d


  1 Shapiro, Howard I. 1                    AFPL see record    1993
      The pregnancy book for today's woman  618.24 SHAPIRO

  2 Mehren, Elizabeth.                      AFPL see record    1991
      Born too soon the story of Emily, our premature  362.19892 MEHREN
```

```
  3 Peterson, Gayle H.                         AFPL COL PK ADLT    1991
    An easier childbirth a mother's workbook for hea 618.24 PETERSON

  4 Avraham, Regina.                           AFPL see record     1991
    The reproductive system                      J 612.6 AVRAHAM

  5 McMillen, Sally G. 1                       AFPL see record      1990
    Motherhood in the Old South pregnancy, childbirt 306.874 MCMILLEN

  6 Finger, Anne Simmons                       AFPL STEW-L ADLT     1990
    Past due a story of disability, pregnancy, and b 618.2 FINGER

  7 Walker, Bruce E.                           AFPL see record      1989
    Pregnancy, diet and cancer a high fat diet durin 641.563

 <RETURN> To continue display
 Enter <Line number(s)> To Display Full Records (Number + B  for Brief)
 <P>revious For Previous Page OR <Q>uit For New Search 1
```

Notice that at this level each entry provides author, title, Dewey Decimal classification numbers, and year of publication. When you type the number **1** and press ENTER, the following pages appear displaying the full record.

```
------------------------------------------------AFPL Library Catalog-------
AUTHOR(s):      Shapiro, Howard I., 1937-
TITLE(s):       The pregnancy book for today's woman /  Howard I. Shapiro.

                2nd ed.

                New York : HarperPerennial,  c1993.
                xiv, 530 p. :  ill. ;  23 cm.
                Includes bibliographical references (p. 475-515) and index.


OTHER ENTRIES:  Pregnancy  Popular works.
                Childbirth.
                Pregnant women  Health and hygiene.

Format:         Book

LOCN:   ADMS P ADLT      STATUS: Checked out --
CALL #: 618.24 SHAPIRO


Author: Shapiro, Howard I. 1
Title:  The pregnancy book for today's woman


LOCN:   EAST A ADLT      STATUS: Not Checked Out --
CALL #: 618.24 SHAPIRO


LOCN:   FAIRBN ADLT      STATUS: Not Checked Out --
CALL #: 618.24 SHAPIRO


LOCN:   HAPEVL ADLT      STATUS: Not Checked Out --
CALL #: 618.24 SHAPIRO
```

```
LOCN:   KIRKWD ADLT      STATUS: Checked out --
CALL #: 618.24 SHAPIRO


----1 of 37---------------------------------AFPL Library Catalog------
<R>epeat this display, <Q>uit,
<X> for Express,  <H> for Search History, ? for HELP >
```

Checking the STATUS: field is interesting from a collection development standpoint when you compare this item's circulation status with another work by Hales that is listed next. Out of a total of six copies, four of Hales' are checked out.

```
---------------------------------------------AFPL Library Catalog------
AUTHOR(s):       Hales, Dianne R., 1950-
TITLE(s):        Pregnancy and birth /  Dianne Hales ; introduction by C.
                    Everett Koop.

                 New York :  Chelsea House Publishers,  c1989.
                 106 p. :  ill. ;  24 cm.
                 The Encyclopedia of health. The life cycle
                 Includes index.
                 Bibliography: p. 95-96.
Summary:         Examines pregnancy and childbirth, from the beginning of a
                    new life to changes in the family after delivery.

OTHER ENTRIES:   Childbirth  Popular works.
                 Pregnancy  Popular works.
                 Encyclopedia of health. Life cycle.

Format:       BOOK

LOCN:   A-COLL ADLT      STATUS: Not Checked Out --
CALL #: 618.2 HALES

more follows -- press <RETURN> (Q to quit)


Author: Hales, Dianne R. 195
Title:  Pregnancy and birth


LOCN:   CENTRL 2ND FL    STATUS: Not checked out --
CALL #: 618.2 HALES

LOCN:   CENTRL 2ND FL    STATUS: Checked out --
CALL #: 618.2 HALES

LOCN:   EAST A ADLT      STATUS: Checked out --
CALL #: 618.2 HALES

LOCN:   ROSWEL ADLT      STATUS: Checked out --
CALL #: 618.2 HALES

LOCN:   SDY SP ADLT      STATUS: Checked out --
CALL #: 618.2 HALES
```

```
LOCN:    SWEST  ADLT       STATUS: Not Checked Out --
CALL #: 618.2 HALES

more follows -- press <RETURN> (Q to quit)
```

The bibliographic records in this catalog can also be accessed by author and title. This makes online library catalogs useful tools for copy catalogers, too.

## ≡ For Further Study

This chapter introduced several different ideas for implementing Internet services in-house. To reinforce the usefulness of maintaining an Internet connection for library operations, I offer the following list of Internet services that I have found beneficial in my own work. At one time or another, each of these services has contributed to the overall improvement of our library's operations. They have also directly or indirectly expanded the services we've been able to offer others in our community.

### Other Useful Internet Services

1. Placing orders with vendors for software, books, and other materials.
2. Getting user support for computer software and hardware.
3. Searching for and advertising employment opportunities.
4. Corresponding with other librarians via email.
5. Accessing and searching library catalogs world-wide for author/title verification, copy cataloging, and the creation of bibliographies.
6. Keeping abreast of current events and new innovations in the library profession through ejournals and LISTSERVs.
7. Accessing any one of millions of public domain, shareware and freeware programs, text files, image files, and sound files via FTP.
8. Interactively searching dozens of free online databases world-wide via TELNET.
9. Connecting with government agency bulletin boards that cover topics ranging from environment and health to business and law.

# Chapter 23

# Reference Services

Reference librarians who are responsible for locating Internet resources often view the Internet as a complex information structure and for good reason. Finding the right information at the right time in a world-wide network like the Internet is more difficult than it is in a single online system. Most of this difficulty evolves from the fact that there isn't a centralized catalog offering controlled access to the Internet's resources and services.

The purpose of this chapter is to present the Internet in such a way that, in spite of this difficulty, it becomes as practical and accessible to you as any other resource sitting on your ready reference shelf. All the various Internet resource discovery tools, services, and sources of information introduced in this book are interesting in themselves, but what do you do with it all when you're out there facing the public at the reference desk? Two closely related issues come into play here:

1. Within the context of the reference question itself, what's the best way to approach locating and accessing information on the Internet? and

2. What should your role as a reference librarian be in providing these services?

## ≡ Problems Associated with Locating and Accessing Information

Issues relating to locating and accessing information on the Internet were being addressed early in 1991 when OCLC (Online Computer Library Center, Inc.) initiated a project investigating the nature of electronic information stored on the Internet. OCLC's goal was to locate and identify the various types of electronic information available on the Internet, produce a descriptive taxonomy of this information, and assess the problems libraries face in handling this information. In

**319**

their final research report[1], and in other leading articles on this subject, it's apparent that Internet resources are not yet an integral part of existing reference department infrastructures for two reasons:

1. Because of the difficulty in locating and accessing network information, and

2. Because the reference librarian's role in a global network environment is unclear

Two fundamentally different approaches address the problem of locating and accessing information on the Internet. One approach, which is based on knowledge, seeks to improve access to files by determining the meaning and content of the files as they exists on the Internet. Once this structure is imposed on the data, access is improved. This is a familiar process to librarians, one that catalogers have been applying for years. Catalogers create bibliographic records that "fill in" for the information itself. These *surrogates*, which contain author, title, publisher, and indexing terms, etc., are joined together into a single database called a *card catalog* (unautomated) or *OPAC* (automated). An information seeker searches this database, locates what he or she wants, and then goes out and retrieves the document itself.

The other way of providing access to information is through sheer computing power—employing powerful search engines that go right to the documents themselves to determine relevancy. Many of the Internet resources and services are based on this model. Currently, one of the best examples of this brute force approach is WAIS, introduced in Chapter 8. WAIS consists of a set of software programs that enables you to search out and retrieve information from more than 600 different databases distributed around the Internet. The software includes a user interface called a *client* and another application called a *server* that automatically indexes the contents of each database and responds to requests sent by the client. WAIS doesn't search a centralized database of bibliographic records. It goes right to a full-text database that you specify and conducts a keyword search on every document contained therein.

Peter Deutsch presents a concept that combines both methods of accessing information in a thesis that examines systems for locating and accessing distributed databases on the Internet. "Resource discovery," he explains, "is the act of discovering the existence of classes of resources in an Internet environment, locating specific instances of such resources, and accessing those resources."[2] He proposed using a method of universal encoding to identify resources on the Internet. Special resource identifiers would contain the physical information needed to actually access an item and a Unique Resource Serial Number (URSN) would be assigned identifying the item's contents. Software applications called *Information Brokers*, the mechanisms for handling this process, would manage the user's resources and control access to their information.

Some of what Peter Deutsch had in mind has become reality with the creation of the Uniform Resource Locater—or *URL*, for short. This is a draft standard for identifying any item on the Internet by means of a single expression that describes what the object is and where it is located on the Internet. URLs are an integral part of the World-Wide Web which is discussed in Chapter 9.

Someday there may be a central database containing a bibliographic record for every resource existing on the Internet. Resource discovery tools may someday use a common interface, search language, and communication protocol. Or, as it was described in *View from the Edge: The Cyberpunk Handbook* (R. Talsorian Games, Inc., 1988), "...in 2013, the Net can be entered directly using your own brain, neural plugs and complex interface programs that turn computer data into perceptual events."[3] In the interim, there are distributed database systems like Gopher and WAIS, numerous online resource guides like Strangelove's "Directory of Electronic Journals and Newsletters," hypertext directories like Hytelnet, and of course, intelligent librarians.

## ≡ Integrating Internet Services

The second issue mentioned at the outset of this chapter relates to the role of reference librarians in integrating Internet services into their current reference practice. With the addition of the global Internet as yet another reference resource, librarians must make a decision at the reference question level whether or not to use it; it is at this level that they must decide whether the Internet is appropriate for a particular user or question.

### The Reference Question

In *Gorgan's Case Studies In Reference Work, Vol.I*, Gorgan describes three types of questions based on the complexity of the information required:

1. Author/title questions
2. Factual or fact-finding questions, and
3. Subject questions (material-finding queries).[4]

The Internet can be used to answer author/title questions by connecting to any one of several OPACs worldwide. Fact-finding questions can be answered by consulting textual documents such as the Social Security Administration Phone Book (see Part VI under the heading "Government") or by TELNETing to an online database such as *culine.colorado.edu 862* to find the game schedule for a major league baseball team. Subject requests can be handled a number of different ways: By utilizing Internet resource discovery tools like Veronica, WAIS, or WWW; or by using word processors to conduct full-text searches on electronic books and journals.

William Katz points out in his *Introduction to Reference Work, Volume II*, that the search process for these types of questions "is more a matter of familiarity with the reference collection and the typical question than with any sophisticated process."[5] He goes on to say that when questions require more than semiautomatic reasoning coupled with memory; when they require real searching, then the structure is normally in terms of isolating the most likely sources. When information is found, it's analyzed for relevancy. If the result is satisfactory, the search is over. If it's not, the referenece librarian begins searching again by exploring other sources.

This same process can be applied in a network environment. At the outset, you should decide whether or not the patron's question can be answered by using the Internet. Starting at the top of the decision tree, decide whether you are familiar with a specific Internet resource that's relevant to answering the question. If you are, then proceed by going online and connecting to the appropriate resource. It might be a textual document stored at an FTP site, a database that can be searched online via TELNET, or a Gopher or WAIS source that specializes in a particular subject.

## Example 1

### *The Author/Title Question*

A patron approaches you with a question that requires bibliographic verification of an author or title. Using your best judgement, you might look in one or more of the following resources held locally: *Books in Print*, *Forthcoming Books*, your online catalog or card catalog, etc. If you don't find what you need locally, the Internet provides another option. You can use TELNET to connect with another library's online catalog. The type of library you work in and the clientele you serve will help determine which remote catalogs you should become most familiar with and learn to access from memory just as you've memorized where certain other resources are located in your stacks.

As an example, at the public library in which I work, I've found CARL to be a convenient point of entry. The Internet address is easy to remember, *pac.carl.org*, and the login process is intuitive. It provides a gateway to many other library systems that are divided into two broad categories:

- Eastern U.S.
- Western U.S.

All the libraries accessed through *pac.carl.org* use the same automated system (CARL) which means that you have to learn only one interface for searching the various library catalogs. Because it's a gateway service, you won't have to initiate a separate TELNET session every time you switch to a different library. That process is done transparently for you.

You could also mount a library directory program like CATALIST or HYTELNET (see Chapter 15) on your personal computer, which allows you to search the directory for the information you need to access any one of the hundreds of different online catalogs that are available.

Another option is to keep close at hand a printed copy of the Art St. George list or one of the other directories mentioned in Chapter 15. Because these directories contain hundreds of OPACs from which you can choose, the issue still comes down to selecting one or two ahead of time and becoming familiar with their holdings and their automation systems before you need to use them—before a patron approaches you with an author/title question.

One last alternative is to use a program like Infopop which is described later in this chapter. You can use this program to maintain an online record of a few select OPACs that have automation systems you're familiar with and that you find especially useful. You can customize the Infopop database to include special notes about library holdings, how to connect, searching strategies, etc.

## Example 2

### *The Fact-Finding Question*

Several opportunities exist on the Internet for answering factual questions. Factual questions about the Internet itself are easiest to answer. Examples include "Is there a Gopher site that specializes in law?", "Can you use the Internet to search the United States Military Academy's library at West Point?", "I'd like to join this LISTSERV I heard about called WOODWORK. What's their address?", and "Where do I subscribe to the *China News Digest?*."

To answer these questions and other questions like them, you should keep some basic Internet resources on your ready reference shelf and stored on disk to be accessed via a personal computer (see this chapter's section "Adding Value to Internet Services"). In addition to the book you're now holding in your hands, the following 10 resources should form the basis of your collection:

1. Electronic book list: Gopher to site *wiretap.spies.com*. At the main menu, choose */2. Electronic Books at Wiretap*. While using screen capture, page down through the 10 pages of titles. (Remember, in Gopher you use the SPACE BAR to page down.) Data in Gopher doesn't scroll across the screen, so in order to capture the first screen, you must "dump it" into the capture file by pressing ALT C. To move to the next page, press the SPACE BAR once again. To capture the new screen, press ALT C and continue the process until you have gone through all 10 pages. Print it out and store it in a notebook titled "Electronic Books."

2. Discussion lists: To obtain a comprehensive list of LISTSERV discussion lists, FTP to site *ftp.psi.com* and download the file called *interest-groups* located in the */usenet/new-users* directory. This list includes detailed descriptions of each discussion group. Print it out and keep it in a ring binder labeled *Discussion Lists*.

3. Software: FTP to site *oak.oakland.edu* and download a copy of the file called *simlist.zip* (text format list of all MS-DOS files with descriptions) located in the *SimTel/msdos/filedocs* directory. Label this notebook *Software*.

4. Libraries: If you're going to keep directories in paper format on the ready reference shelf, I would recommend having both the Art St. George list (send the command **get library package** in the body of an email message to *listserv@unmvm.bitnet*) and the Billy Barron list (FTP to site *ftp.utdallas.edu* and go to the */pub/staff/billy/ libguide* directory to

download the files *libraries.africa, libraries.americas, libraries.asia, libraries.europe*, etc.). You might want to label these resources *Libraries: Art St. George List* and *Libraries: Billy Barron's List*.

5. Ejournals: For a comprehensive list of ejournals and newsletters, send electronic mail to *listserv @acadvm1.uottawa.ca*. In the body of the message, type

```
GET EJOURNL1 DIRECTRY
GET EJOURNL2 DIRECTRY
```

This notebook could be labeled *Ejournals*.

6. Zines: To assemble a Zine list, FTP to site *ftp.netcom.com*, and go to the */pub/johnl/zines*, and download the file called *e-zine-list*. Place this file in a ring binder labeled *Zines*.

7. Newsgroups: For a comprehensive list of active USENET Newsgroups, FTP to site *pit-manager.mit.edu*, go to the directory */pub/usenet/news.announce.newusers*, and download the file *List_of_Active_Newsgroups*. Label this resource *Newsgroups*.

8. WAIS Sources: Download a copy of the Christoff list which consists of two parts: the first part is a list of WAIS sources with brief descriptions arranged by subject; the second part consists of sources and descriptions listed alphabetically. FTP to site *kirk.bond.edu.au* and go to the directory */pub/Bond_Uni/doc/wais*. Once you are in the *wais* directory, you can issue a **dir** command to view a list of the files contained in that directory. The plain ASCII text files are named *src-list.txt* and *annex.txt*. The notebook containing these files could be called *WAIS Sources* or *WAIS Databases*.

9. Gopher Sites: The most practical way to access the various names and addresses of Gopher servers is by going online and connecting to a Gopher server. At the main menu, follow the path */Other Gopher and Information Servers*, and proceed from there. You can either view all the Gopher servers in the world at once, or you can view them broken down by continent, country, or state, etc. To create a paper copy of all the Gopher servers in the world, choose that menu item and capture the screen output to a disk; then print it out. Label this notebook *Gopher Sites*. Depending on your own particular situation and the amount of use a resource such as this gets, you should update it at least once every six months or as often as once a month.

10. FTP Sites: Because Archie is available, it isn't as essential to have a list of FTP sites available in print. However, if you see the need for such a list, FTP to site *ftp.shsu.edu*, and download a copy of the file *sites.Z*. (Note that this is a compressed file. The uppercase Z means you will need a copy of GUNZIP or UNCOMPRESS to uncompress the file. See Appendix A for details.) A far less practical way to get a listing of FTP sites is to log into an Archie server and issue the command **list** and press ENTER. Have your screen capture turned on to capture the output to a

file as it scrolls across the screen. Because there are thousands of FTP sites, this is a time-consuming process and a drain on Internet resources. For this very reason, some sites that have disabled this command.

Factual questions that pertain to issues other than the Internet itself are more difficult to answer. Resources are available, but they're scattered all around on thousands of different information servers. It depends upon the nature of the question whether you choose Veronica, WAIS, or Archie, etc., but if you aren't sure where to begin, you might start with an Archie exact_sub search. This search first looks for filenames and directory names that match your specified string exactly. If that doesn't work, then Archie looks for files where the specified string occurs anywhere in the filename or directory name. It is the broadest search possible of the tens of thousands of FTP filenames indexed by Archie and it is case insensitive. (For more details, see Chapter 10.)

The following example illustrates the command syntax used in an **exact_sub** search and it might be worthwhile to commit it to memory:

```
telnet archie.ans.net (or whatever site you prefer)
Login: archie   <ENTER>
archie> set search exact_sub   <ENTER>
archie> prog <search string>
```

Where **<search string>** is the string of characters you want to search. The same search using an Archie client would look like this:

```
$ archie -e -s <search string>
```

If my Archie search resulted in zero hits and I was given a chance to try another strategy, I'd get my Gopher client running and execute a Veronica search. I may try broadening or narrowing the search terms, but essentially I'd stick with these two resource discovery tools and go no further.

The other possibility that might exist is that you know just where to go to get an answer to your question. You may have to consult an online directory or manual on your ready reference shelf to get a specific address, but essentially you know how to locate and access the resource. Developing your knowledge of resources on the Internet that answer factual questions will come with time. Creating an online database that organizes your resources by subject and that allows you to create hyperlinks to related subjects is discussed later in this chapter.

## Example 3

### The Subject Question

When a patron approaches you with a subject-related question, you would again start at the top of the decision tree by asking the question "Do I know of a resource on the Internet that's relevant to answering this patron's question?" With both subject and fact-finding questions, I'm sure you won't be surprised when I tell you that the answer you'll come up with most often is "no" or "not sure."

While introducing the various Internet resources and services throughout this book, I have tried to avoid over-exageration of their usefulness in answering reference questions in libraries. Certainly email and FTP have proven themselves useful tools for certain types of communication and for acquiring resources that would otherwise be unavailable. Yet, the fact remains that most of the information needs expressed by library patrons cannot be met by accessing non-commercial databases on the Internet. The majority of answers will still be found in online commercial databases (though they may be reached via the Internet), microfilm, microfiche, CD-ROMs, and print format materials such as books, magazines, and newspapers, etc.

In those instances, where you do know of an appropriate Internet resource for answering a subject question, you should go to that resource and utilize it. If you're not aware of anything relevant existing on the Internet, you might begin by exploring your local holdings and services which offer the convenience of controlled access points such as your library catalog, CD-ROM databases, and commercial online services.

If you decide to extend your search onto the Internet, remember the frame of mind with which this has to be approached. There is no centralized database, so avoid the frustration of looking for and not finding this kind of access to Internet information. You're going to utilize computers running powerful search engines that are designed to go right to the heart of the data itself.

It would be nice if I could tell you that searching for information on topics relating to artificial intelligence, virtual reality, snake bites, and furniture building you will get excellent results, but if you search for information on volcanos, volleyball, and Volvos you will get zero hits. But the fact is, you don't really know what you'll find until you try.

As time passes, and with continuous contact, you will learn more about the strengths and weaknesses of the Internet. I have utilized the Internet to answer reference questions relating to all seven topics listed above. With the first two listed, artificial intelligance and virtual reality, I was very confident at the top of the decision tree that an Internet excursion would reap plentiful returns. With the other five, I was less confident, and with two of the items, it was only through serindipitus discovery that I found anything at all.

It helps to understand at the outset that there are certain broad subject categories that are well represented on the Internet. Knowing what these subject categories are will help guide you when you're trying to decide whether you should even approach the Internet as a resource for answering a particular reference question. I would consider the following 12 subject areas as the most heavily represented on the Internet:

1. Agriculture
2. Astronomy
3. Biology
4. Computers (computer culture, software, hardware, networks, technology, and literature)
5. Education

6. Electronic texts of all kinds (zines, ejournals, etc.)

7. Government & Politics

8. Health

9. History

10. Internet

11. Law

12. Libraries

The decision tree presented in Figure 23-1 provides you with a basic framework upon which you can begin building your own personal philosophy of how and when to utilize the Internet for reference questions.

## Providing Reader's Advisory Service

To service patrons in the area of reader's advisory, you might try thinking in terms of formats rather than resource discovery tools. For example, if patrons have expressed an interest in computers and you know they haven't explored the Internet, you might begin by offering them a list of LISTSERVs that discuss issues relating to computers plus help sheets explaining how to subscribe and how to search LISTSERV message archives (see Chapters 13 and 21 for more information).

Other formats that deal with the subject of computers include electronic ejournals such as *The Amateur Computerist* (see Chapter 16). Newsgroups are a great source of news and information on dozens of different topics relating to computers (see Chapter 19). Remember, too, that some FTP sites maintain large repositories of information relating to specific subjects. You might recommend to the patrons that they visit the Oakland software archive (FTP to site *oak.oak-land.edu*) and explore the various directories contained there.

Appendix D of this book may prove helpful in some subject areas, but the list is fairly selective and you may have to consult other print or online resources for additional guidance. A useful print resource that can assist you in this area is *The Internet Directory* by Eric Braun (ISBN: 0-449-90898-4). This book provides an index to thousands of resources including discussion lists, Newsgroups, OPACs, FTP archives, Gopher servers, electronic journals, RFCs, and more. If you look in the index under the heading *psychology*, for example, you'll find references to mailing lists, Gopher servers, Newsgroups, and electronic journals. It is by no means an exhaustive list of Internet resources, but it would serve nicely as another ready reference tool.

You could introduce fiction readers to the Internet by recommending some of the online zines and electronic journals listed in Chapter 16. Also, there are LISTSERV discussion groups and USENET Newsgroups that provide forums for discussing literature.

It's not unusual to hear patrons ask "Where's your travel section?", "Where's *Value Line*?", or "Where's the *Reader's Guide*?" but it would be very unusual to hear the question "Where's the EFF Gopher server?" or "Where's the

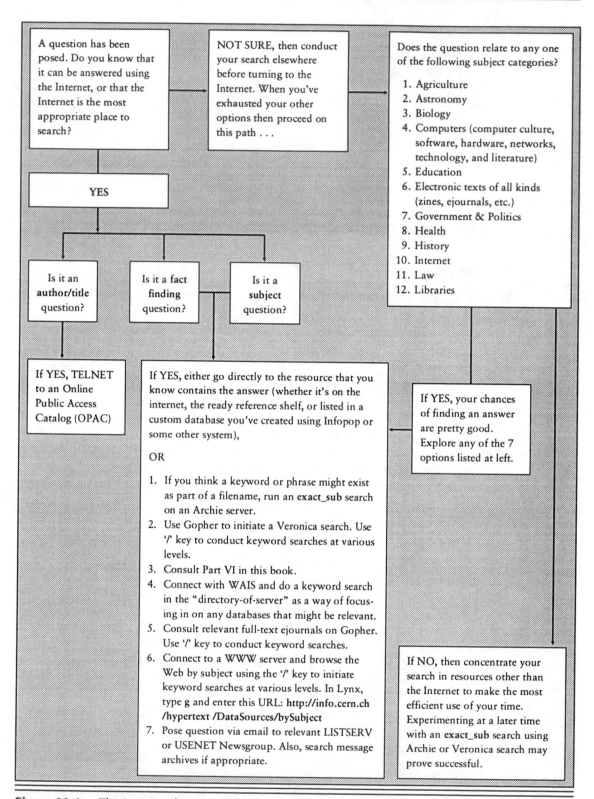

**Figure 23-1:** The Internet decision tree

zine archives?" When you get a question that includes the word *Internet*, be sensitive to the fact that the person asking may know nothing about the Internet, but it's away of asking for a general introduction to the global network, and what better place to come than to the library?

The kind of service reference librarians provide newcomers will vary depending on what that person's perception is of the Internet. Some will see the Internet as a source of entertainment. They'll browse Gopher servers and the Web just for fun; something to do to pass the time. It would be equivalent to coming into the library and paging through *The Guiness Book of Records* or browsing the stacks, not because they have a specific question that needs answering, but because they want to be entertained. Other individuals view the Internet as a reference tool; a mechanism for document delivery; a means of communicating via email. They'll access it only when they have a question that needs to be answered, a specific task that needs to be performed, or because they have an idea that needs to be communicated. If you offer public access to the Internet and it's your responsibility to train new users, keep these different view points in mind.

## ≡ Introduction to Infopop Software

In the traditional search process, if sources don't come readily to mind, you consult various access points to information like bibliographies, indexes, and catalogs, or subject sources such as vertical files. In an Internet environment, these choices don't yet exist. To some degree, you can circumvent this lack of having controlled access pointsby creating your own index and online help system.

This section introduces a Windows application called Infopop that provides this capability. The purpose of introducing this application is not to imply that you should create a comprehensive catalog of every resource on the Internet; instead you should use it to create a personalized system built over time; one that meets your own needs and interests and one that focuses on local needs, preferences, and clientele.

Infopop is freeware from GMUtant Software and it exists in two versions: a TSR (terminate-and-stay-resident program) and a non-TSR program. *TSR programs* are programs that are designed to stay in the computer's RAM (random-access memory) at all times and can be activated by the user with a keystroke. Infopop isn't public domain software, but it can be used, distributed, and copied freely. To obtain a copy, FTP to one of the following sites:

Host: *freebsd.cdrom.com*
Path: *l.2/simtel/msdos/hypertxt*
Filename: *infpop27.zip*

Host: *plaza.aarnet.edu.au*
Path: */micros/pc/oak/hypertxt*
Filename: *infpop27.zip*

Host: *rigel.acs.oakland.edu*
Path: */pub/msdos/hypertxt*
Filename: *infpop27.zip*

## How Infopop Works

Assuming that you use a microcomputer with a communication program that uses the serial port to access the Internet, loading the TSR version first will enable you to call-up Infopop at anytime during your session and use it as an online help system.

Every time Infopop is loaded, a file called INFOPOP.HLP is automatically loaded, too. Clyde W. Grotophorst, the software's designer, created this default database for those who may be interested in searching for a specific class of service providers. For example, a user might want to browse miscellaneous TELNET sites or locate sites offering access to library catalogs. In the main menu, the choices are clear. However, creating a hierarchy of information based on service-types makes it difficult to organize and to locate information. Like HYTELNET, what appears at the top of the hierarchy in the main menu has no relation to specific topics.

Although users cannot change the existing INFOPOP.HLP file as Grotophorst wrote it, they can create an auxiliary database that can be called into the Infopop search engine at any time by pressing F3. This feature gives you the opportunity to build a database that is modeled around subjects rather than service-types. Two sample databases are presented in the following example that incorporate this principle. The agricultural database shows how you can build your own online directory where information is organized by subject, going from general to specific headings.

Suppose that you want to assist a patron by searching an agricultural database. You could create an Infopop file that leads you from the general subject "agriculture," to the specific resource "PENpages" and also includes help sheets on how to use PENpages. Or, you may need quick access to ready reference sources on the Internet that you've decided are relevant to your patron's needs. Infopop works well for either of these applications and the accompanying sample databases demonstrate this.

Features of the software include the capability of creating *hyperlinks*, a program feature that allows you to jump from one place in the database to another by simply pressing a key or clicking a mouse button. The TSR version (IP.EXE) allows you to cut and paste Internet addresses from Infopop's information window onto your underlying application. Another feature is a text searching function where the user can type a character string, press a hotkey combination, and a window pops up containing any matches that are found.

## Creating an Infopop Database

To create an Infopop database, also termed a *supplemental file*, you need to use a text editor or word processor that is capable of creating pure ASCII text files. If you use Microsoft Word to create the supplemental file, remember to save the file using the Text-only-with-line-breaks setting. If you're using WordPerfect, use CTRL-F5 rather than F7 or F10.

MAKEINFO is the utility you use to create additional databases for the Infopop search engine. Use an ASCII editor to create your database. Save the document as *<filename>.txt*. Now, at the DOS prompt, type **MAKEINFO** followed by **<filename>.txt** to create a new database with the name you specify.

Next, activate Infopop and then press F3. To load a new database, type the filename (without the extension) you assigned it and press ENTER.

Use the following directives at the beginning of any supplemental files you create:

| | |
|---|---|
| `!WIDTH 77` | This sets the width of the text in the window. If your line goes over that, MAKEINFO will wrap it. |
| `!NOWRAP` | If you'd like your text to appear just as you type it, specify !NOWRAP. |
| `!SCROLLING` | This means you allow the user to scroll the window to display text that won't fit in the window. |

## ≡ Creating An Infopop Database

### Step 1

First determine a topic name and assign it a topic number. Use the following format to make an entry:

```
!TOPIC <topic number> <topic name>
```

Example:

```
!TOPIC 10 Agricultural Resources
```

The ! in the first position indicates to MAKEINFO that a compiler directive follows. Group topics by number range to make editing easier. Don't leave a gap larger than 50 or more unused numbers, or it will have a negative impact on the size of your final *.HLP file.

### Step 2

The next line down is:

```
!INDEX
```

This directive places the topic name on the opening index or main menu. If you don't want the topic to appear in the opening index, type the following:

```
!NOINDEX
```

If you want a topic to be listed first in the index, type:

```
!INDEX 1
```

If you want it to be last, type:

```
!INDEX 100
```

This places it in last position, assuming there are no more than 100 topics. (MAKEINFO defaults to an alphabetical listing; however, if you don't assign !IN-DEX a number, MAKEINFO will report an error and request that you assign one.)

## Step 3

The next line(s) constitute the text that will appear in the window associated with TOPIC 10. When you select the main topic heading in the main menu and press ENTER, this is the text that will appear in the next window. The text that would normally follow the heading in the main menu would be a list of topics; that is, a submenu. These menu items would then be hyperlinked to the actual textual matter.

*Making hyperlinks:* Hyperlinks are made by inserting certain ASCII characters into the text. These will include the diamond ♦ (decimal value 4), club ♣ (decimal value 5), and smiley face ☺ (decimal value 2). Begin inserting an ASCII diamond character into the text. Follow this with the TOPIC number you want to reference. Follow this number with an ASCII club character. Next, type the text you want to use to reference the linked topic. (The wording can be anything; it doesn't have to follow the wording that follows the !TOPIC directive for the topic you're linking to.) Then follow with another club.

Example hyperlink:

```
♦1♣Sustainable Ag♣
```

Example of linked topic:

```
!TOPIC 1 Sustainable Ag
!NO INDEX
<Insert the text here>
```

Notice that in the above example, that the word !NOINDEX is used to prevent this topic from appearing in the main menu.

## Step 4

The input file must be plain ASCII text, so use an ASCII editor to create your database. Save the file as *<filename>.txt*. It is essential that you use the *.txt extension.

*Special features:*

1. If you'd like a string of text to appear bold, use the ASCII character that looks like a smiley face (decimal value 2). Place one at the start of the text you'd like to boldface and one at the end of the text string.

   Example:  ☺Journalism education☺

2. You can comment the file by placing a semicolon ; in the first character position of the text. No single topic can exceed 64K.

# A Sample Agricultural Online Database Using Infopop

```
!NOWRAP
;By designating !NOWRAP things such as centering headings or
;indenting sentences will remain as they are here.
!SCROLLING
!TOPIC 20 Agriculture
!INDEX 1
;The word "Agriculture" above appears in the root menu. All
;files relating to agriculture must have a number between 1
;20.
Resources:
♦1♣Sustainable Ag♣
♦2♣PENpages♣
♦3♣CUFAN♣
♦4♣Email lists♣
♦5♣Almanac Servers♣
♦6♣Bulletin Boards♣
♦7♣Etext Resources♣
♦9♣OPACs♣

;The above text beginning with the word "Resources:" appears
;in the second window. Those strings with ♣ preceding and
;following them are hyperlinked to another window.

!TOPIC 1 Sustainable Ag
!NOINDEX

;The ☺ symbol is used to mark bolded strings.

Access: ☺ftp ftp.oit.unc.edu☺
Directory:  pub/docs/sustainable_agriculture/
newsgroup.archie/org.ag.bib
File:  Part1.bib through Part7.bib

!TOPIC 2 PENpages
!NOINDEX
Access: ☺telnet psupen.psu.edu☺
Access: telnet 128.118.36.5
Login: Type 2-letter state abbreviation

!TOPIC 3 CUFAN
!NOINDEX
CUFAN (Clemson University Agricultural and Forestry Net)
Access: ☺telnet eureka.clemson.edu☺
Access:  130.127.8.3

!TOPIC 4 Email lists
!NOINDEX
Agricultural email lists and services.
Access: ☺ftp ftp.sura.net☺
Directory: pub/nic
File: agricultural.list

North Carolina State University Library gopher:
gopher dewey.lib.ncsu.edu
submenus   /NCSU's "Library Without Walls /Reference Desk
/Guides to the Internet /Directory of Scholarly Electronic
Resources/ /Biological Sciences
```

```
!TOPIC 5 Almanac
!NOINDEX
        Almanac at North Carolina State
Access: ☺mail almanac at ces.ncsu.edu☺

        Almanac at Oregon State
Access:☺mail almanac at oes.orst.edu☺

        Almanac at Purdue University
Access: ☺mail almanac at ecn.purdue.edu☺

        Almanac at University of California
Access: ☺mail almanac at silo.ucdavis.edu☺

        Extension Service - USDA
Access: ☺mail almanac at esusda.gov☺


!TOPIC 6 Bulletin Boards
!NOINDEX
CSU Fresno ATI-NET (Advanced Technology Information
  Network)
Access: ☺telnet caticsuf.csufresno.edu☺
Access: 129.8.100.15


!TOPIC 7 Etext Resources
!NOINDEX
♦8♣Internet Documents♣


!TOPIC 8 Internet Documents
!NOINDEX
        Drew, Wilfred. Not just cows: A guide to
Internet/Bitnet resources in agriculture and related
sciences. SUNY at Morrisville College of Agriculture and
Technology, 5/8/92.

This document is available from three sources:

Access: ☺ftp ftp.sura.net☺
Directory: pub/nic
File: agriculture.list

Access: ☺ftp hydra.vwo.ca☺
Directory: libsoft
File: agguide.txt

Access: ☺ftp ftp.unt.edu☺
Directory: pub/library
File: AGRICULTURE-INTERNET.TXT


!TOPIC 9 OPACs
!NOINDEX
Miami University
telnet watson.lib.muohio.edu
at login type: library

;THIS MARKS THE END OF THE SECTION ON AGRICULTURE.
```

# Sample Ready Reference Online Database Using Infopop

```
!NOWRAP
!SCROLLING
!TOPIC 20 Ready Reference
!INDEX 1



                                    Resources:
♦1♣Archie addresses♣
♦2♣Auroral activity♣
♦3♣Book Reviews♣
♦4♣Books (Etext)♣
♦5♣Earthquakes♣
♦6♣Elements (Periodic Table)♣
♦7♣Geography♣
♦8♣Hurricanes♣
♦9♣Internet Addresses♣
♦11♣NASA press releases♣
♦12♣Newsletters♣
♦13♣Oceanographic Information♣
♦14♣Singles (US Top Pop Singles for the Week)♣
♦15♣Time♣
♦16♣Weather♣

!TOPIC 1 Archie addresses
!NOINDEX
US Servers:
telnet archie.ans.net
telnet archie.sura.net
telnet archie.rutgers.edu
telnet archie.unl.edu

!TOPIC 2 Auroral activity
!NOINDEX
Reports of auroral activity made available hourly at 30
minutes past each hour between 22:30 UTC and 17:30 UTC
daily.

gopher xi.uleth.ca

!TOPIC 3 Book reviews
!NOINDEX
Search Choice Book Reviews via Carl
telnet pac.carl.org

At main menu choose: 3. Information Databases.
At next menu choose: 60. Choice Book Reviews.

!TOPIC 4 Books (Etext)
!NOINDEX
1. Interactive communication:

tell almanac@oes.orst.edu get gutenberg catalog
```

```
2. gopher dewey.lib.ncsu.edu

subdirectory /NCSU's "Library Without Walls"/Reference Desk/
/Guides to the Internet


!TOPIC 5 Earthquakes
!NOINDEX
gopher geophys.washington.edu


!TOPIC 6 Elements (Periodic Table)
!NOINDEX
University of California Santa Cruz, Infoslug System
gopher scilibx.ucsc.edu
In subdirectory /The Library/Electronic Reference Books/
Periodic Table of Elements

!TOPIC 7 Geography
!NOINDEX
Geographic Name Server
This server provides online information about known
geographic locations including latitude, longitude, zip
code, area code, population, and altitude.

telnet martini.eecs.umich.edu

Type help for instructions.

!TOPIC 8 Hurricanes
!NOINDEX
gopher typhoon.atmos.colostate.edu


!TOPIC 9 Internet Addresses
!NOINDEX
"White Pages"
telnet wp.nyser.net
username: fred
For help retrieve file named: hswp.txt from site ftp.syr.edu
in subdirectory /networks/doc

NETFIND:  This service attempts to locate information about
a person on the Internet when given their name,
organization, or school. When prompted, enter a name
followed by keywords relating to location, such as: acbenson University of
Alabama. The name can be first, last,
or login name, but only one can be specified.

telnet bruno.cs.colorado.edu     Login: netfind
See menu item "1. Help" for additional information.


!TOPIC 11 NASA Press Releases
!NOINDEX
Daily press release from NASA.
gopher space.mit.edu
```

```
!TOPIC 12 Newsletters
!NOINDEX
1. gopher dewey.lib.ncsu.edu

Subdirectory /NCSU's "Library Without Walls"/Reference
Desk/Guides to the Internet/Directory of Electronic Journals
and Newsletters

!TOPIC 13 Oceanographic Info
!NOINDEX
telnet nodc.nodc.noaa.gov

Login: noaadir

!TOPIC 14 Singles
!NOINDEX
US Top Pop Singles for the Week.
gopher aix.rpi.edu 79

!TOPIC 15 Time
!NOINDEX
High percision time service/National Bureau of Standards.
telnet india.colorado.edu 13

!TOPIC 16 Weather
!NOINDEX
"The Weather Machine."
gopher wx.atmos.uiuc.edu
```

## ≡ For Further Study

There is a monthly competition called the Internet Hunt for competitive-minded reference librarians who like to test their skills at locating information on the Internet. Rick Gates, the creator of the Hunt, can be contacted at *rgates@ccit.arizona.edu*. If you're interested in seeing previous hunts—what questions were asked and how they were answered—connect to the Gopher server at *gopher.cic.net* and select */6. The Internet Hunt* at the main menu. This leads you to miscellaneous information about the Internet Hunt, questions, results, rules, and history, etc.

In addition to the book by Eric Braun mentioned earlier, two other books that will aid in answering subject questions are *Internet Yellow Pages* by Harley Hahn (ISBN: 0-07-882023-5, Osborne-McGraw) and *Internet Yellow Pages* by Christine Maxwell (ISBN: 1-56205-306-X, New Riders Pub.).

## ≡ References

1. Dillon, Martin, et al. *Assessing Information on the Internet: Toward Providing Library Services for Computer-Mediated Communication*. Dublin, OH: Online Computer Library Center, Inc., 1993. Downloaded from FTP site *zues.rsch.oclc.org* in directory */pub/internet_resources_ project/report* as file *report.ps.tar.Z* (312328 bytes).

2. Deutsch, Peter. *Resource Discovery in an Internet Environment*. Masters Thesis. School of Computer Science, McGill, June 1992, [p.1]. Downloaded from FTP site *archives.cc.mcgill.ca* in directory */pub/peterd/thesis* as files *cover.june30.txt* (4858 bytes) and *thesis.june30.txt* (113945 bytes).

3. Birch, David G.W. and Peter Buck. *What is Cyberspace?* (n.d.) Downloaded from FTP site *ftp.eff.org* in directory */pub/EFF/papers/cyber* as file *what-is-cyberspace* (18319 bytes).

4. Gorgan, Denis Joseph. *Gorgan's Case Studies in Reference Work, Vol.1: Enquiries and the Reference Process*. London: Clive Bingley, 1967.

5. William A. Katz, *Introduction to reference work, Volume II: Reference services and reference process* (New York: McGraw-Hill Book Company, 1974), p.99.

# APPENDIXES

Part VI consists of four appendixes. Appendix A discusses the various file types that are found on the Internet and it explains how to convert these file types into usable form. Appendix B contains a selective list of discussion lists relating to libraries. Details on joining these lists are given in Chapter 13. Appendix C lists the documents that are available for downloading from the Electronic Frontier Foundation's Library Policy Archive. Appendix D is a selective list of Internet resources arranged by subject.

# File Types and the Software that Creates Them

When viewing filenames on the Internet, you'll see several different file extensions. Each extension provides a clue as to the type of format in which a particular file has been saved. It is important to note that these extensions also tell you what processes, if any, must be performed before a file can be made usable. There are several different binary formats that, once you've downloaded them, have to be converted into other formats before they're usable. Most of the file formats that you'll encounter at FTP sites, and were not explained in chapter 4 and 6, are introduced here.

## ≡ Compressed Files (.Z and .gz)

One compression program found on UNIX systems is called *compress*. When compress is used to make a file smaller it also creates a new file name by adding the extension .Z to the end of the original filename (note this is an uppercase "Z"). If you retrieve a file whose name ends with a .Z extension, you will have to uncompress it before you can use it. To uncompress it you use a program called *uncompress*. Thus, if you have retrieved a file called *<filename>*.Z and you are working on a machine running the UNIX operating system, the following UNIX command will uncompress the file:

```
uncompress <filename>
```

where **<filename>** is the name of the file you wish to uncompress. The .Z extension may be left on or off.

If you are on a UNIX machine, it is likely that compress for UNIX is already running on it. If you intend to download a .Z file to your PC or Mac and then uncompress it, you will need one of the following programs: To obtain a copy of compress that is compatible with MS-DOS, FTP to *oak.oakland.edu* in directory */pub/msdos/compress* and download the file *comp430s.zip*. The syntax for uncompressing a file with this program is:

```
A:\> comp430d -d <filename>.Z
```

where **<filename>.Z** is the name of the file you wish to uncompress. The .Z extension must be included with the filename. To obtain a copy of compress for Macintosh, FTP to *sumex-aim.stanford.edu* and download the file *maccompress-32.hqx* which is located in the */info-mac/util* directory.

Files with a .gz extension are files created with another UNIX system compression program called *gzip*. Its counterpart, *gunzip*, uncompresses files. The gunzip program can also uncompress .Z files and .zip files. For a version of gzip for MS-DOS, FTP to *garbo.uwasa.fi* and download the file *gzip124.zip* in the */pc/unix* directory (a self-extracting file). For a version of gzip for Macintosh, FTP to *sumex-aim.stanford.edu* and go to the directory */info-mac/tmit* and download the file called *gzip.hqx*.

## Archive Files (.arc)

The difference between an archiver and other compression programs is that an archiver compresses several input files and then collects them together into one single archive file. To "archive" a group of files is to compress and combine several related files into a single, easy-to-manage file and to do it in such a way that the individual files may later be recovered intact. *PKPAK* is a program that is used to compress files when adding them to an archive. *PKUNPAK* will expand them upon extraction. When downloading files with the .arc extension you will need a copy of PKPAK version 3.61 to extract the component files. To retrieve a copy of this program FTP to site *oak.oakland.edu* and download file *pk361.exe* in the directory */pub/msdos/archivers*. This is a "self-extracting archvie." When you run this program, it will create nine files:

| | |
|---|---|
| *PKPAK.EXE* | Main archiving program |
| *PKUNPAK.EXE* | Main extraction program |
| *PKPAKJR.EXE* | Archiving program for limited memory |
| *PKUNPAKJR.EXE* | Extraction program for limited memory |
| *MAKESFX.COM* | Starts the process of creating self-extracting files |
| *README.DOC* | Read FIRST ! |
| *ORDER.DOC* | Registration information and order form |
| *MANUAL.DOC* | Reference manual for PKware File Compression Programs |
| *APPNOTE.TXT* | Technical background material |

You can use the PKUNPAK.EXE to extract files. The following example shows how to use the PKUNPAK.EXE program to unpack an archived file called *callback.arc*:

```
a:\ pkunpak callback
```

You can drop the .arc extension when typing the filename. To obtain a copy of *arcmac* for Macintosh, FTP to *mac.archive.umich.edu* and download the file *arcmac.hqx* in directory */mac/utilities/compressionapps*.

## ARJ Files (.arj)

*ARJ* is a program that creates archive files and automatically compresses the files when adding them to an archive. For files with an .arj extension you will need a copy of ARJ241.EXE to extract the files. ARJ241.EXE is a self-extracting archive. When you run the program it will create ARJ.EXE and other related documentation. Once you have a copy of ARJ.EXE you can use it to extract files. To unpack an ARJ archive called *foo.arj*, you would type the command:

```
a:\> arj e foo
```

It isn't necessary to supply the .arj extension when typing the file name. To obtain a copy of ARJ for MS-DOS, FTP to *wuarchive.wustl.edu* and download the file *arj24la.exe* in directory */mirrors/msdos/archivers*. For a Macintosh copy of ARJ, FTP to *mac.archive.umich.edu* and download the file *unarjmac.cpt.hqx* in directory */mac/util/compression*.

## LHA Files (.lzh)

*LHA* is another program used to create and maintain file archives. To extract files that have the .lzh extension you will need a copy of LHA213.EXE. This is a self-extracting file, so when you simply run the program it will produce LHA.EXE and other related documentation. To unpack a file with the .lzh extension type: a:\> lha e <filename>

You don't have to specify the .lzh extension on the filename. To obtain a copy of LHA for MS-DOS, FTP to *wuarchive.wustl.edu* and download the file */mirrors/msdos/archivers/lha213.exe*. For a Macintosh copy of LHA, FTP to *mac.archive.umich.edu* and download the file *maclha2.0.cpt.hqx* in directory */mac/utilities/compressionapps*.

## Zoofiles (.zoo)

*ZOO* is an archiving program similar in function to PKPAK and ZIP, however, it cannot be used to unpack files created with PKPAK and ZIP. A unique feature of ZOO is that it can produce archives with long pathnames in them and it can store comments about each file. If you want to unarchive a ZOO file you will need a copy of ZOO.EXE. Following is an example of the ZOO syntax for extracting a file:

```
a:\>zoo e <filename>
```

The .ZOO extension does not have to be specified. To obtain a copy of ZOO for Macintosh, FTP to *mac.archive.umich.edu* and download the file *maczoo.sit.hqx* in the directory */mac/utilities/compressionapps*. ZOO for

MS-DOS can be found at FTP site *wuarchive.wustl.edu*. Look in the */mirrors/msdos/zoo* directory for a file called *zoo210.exe*.

### Squeezed Files (_q_)

Nusq110.com is a program used to squeeze and unsqueeze files that have a "Q" as the middle letter of the file extension. Files with this letter in the extension were squeezed with sqpc12a.com, or something similar. If you download a file that has been squeezed you will need a copy of NUSQ110.COM to unsqueeze it before it can be used. The syntax to unsqeeze a file would be:

```
a:\>nusq110 <filename>.tqt
```

where <filename>.tqt is the name of the file you want to unsqueeze. Here it is important to supply the full file name and the type of file (the extension).

To obtain a copy of this program for MS-DOS, FTP to *oak.oakland.edu* and download the file *sqpc12a.com* (squeeze) in the */pub/msdos/starter/* directory and *nussq110.com* (unsqueeze) in the same directory.

Files with the extension .sqz are also "squeezed" files, but are different from the above file types. For a version of this squeeze program for MS-DOS, FTP to *wuarchive.wustl.edu* and download the file *sqz1083e.exe* in directory */pub/msdos/archivers*.

### Tarfiles (.tar)

These are archived files that must be unpacked by using the *tar* program. Tarfiles usually consist of multiple files and sometimes directories. To obtain a copy of tar for MS-DOS, FTP to *oak.oakland.edu* and download the file called *tar4dos.zip* located in the */pub/msdos/filutl* directory. For a Macintosh version, FTP to *sumex-aim.stanford.edu* and download the file called *tar-30.hqx* located in the */info-mac/util* directory.

### Compressed Tarfiles (.tar.Z)

Sometimes compression programs are combined with tar to create compressed archives. Files that are packed into an archive and then compressed will have two file extensions. On UNIX systems, files with the format *filename.tar.Z*

have been archived by tar and then compressed. Tar is not a compression program. It just combines several files creating one. The tarfile is then compressed with another program like compress which creates a tar.Z file. When you retrieve files like this you must first uncompress them and then untar them.

Let's say, for example, that you have downloaded the UNIX version of Hytelnet from the archive site at the University of North Texas (*ftp.unt.edu* in directory */pub/library/hytelnet* filename *unix*.) This file consists of multiple files that have been packed together into one file called hytelnet.tar.Z. First you create a directory and move the compressed tarfile into that directory. Once it is there you uncompress the file and then you unpack it. If, after viewing the directory, you see that the process worked and all of the files were converted properly, you can then delete the original tarfile.

If you FTP a file *ka9qbin.8.tar.Z* from a site and it arrives at your computer as *ka9qbin.8*, it is still a compressed and tarred binary file. The file name has just been truncated to meet DOS filename standards. You must still uncompress the file first, and then untar it. The name change does not change the filetype.

If you try to uncompress the file and it doesn't work, try renaming the file by adding the .Z extension again.

## ≡ Miscellaneous Other File Types

### PostScript files (.ps)

The file extension .ps stands for PostScript. *PostScript* is a programming language that is used to generate images on a printer. To view these text files they must be printed on a PostScript printer.

### Btoa files

Btoa (binary to ASCII) is another program that converts binary files to ASCII text. To obtain a copy of btoa for MS-DOS, FTP to *wuarchive.wustl.edu* and download a copy of the file *atob11.zip* located in the */mirrors/msdos/archivers/filutl* directory.

### .exe

Although this looks like a normal executable program, it sometimes represents a self-extracting MS-DOS file. Simply run these to unpack the archive.

### MPEG

MPEG (Moving Pictures Expert Group) is a subcommittee of the ISO (International Standards Committee) and their purpose is to develop standards for digital video and audio compression. MPEGLPLAY v1.0 can be downloaded from FTP site *ftp.wustl.edu* in the */systems/ibmpc/win3/desktop* directory. The filename is *mpegwin.zip* (WARNING: 736,425 bytes).

## ≡ Macintosh File Formats

### Introduction to Compression Programs

The most common Macintosh compression tools include StuffIt, StuffIt Lite, and StuffIt Deluxe which create files with .sit extensions, and Compact Pro which creates files with .cpt extensions. The above utilities also create self-extracting archives—files with .sea extensions. Another Macintosh compression program called PackIt creates files with .pit extensions.

As a Mac user, if you would like to compress files for uploading or decompress files created by DOS or UNIX computers, StuffIt Deluxe is a commercial program with very versatile file-handling capabilities. It also will convert files from BinHex format. It is produced by Aladdin Systems, Inc., 165 Westridge Dr., Watsonville, CA 95073 408-761-6200; FAX 408-761-6206; email *aladdin@well.sf.ca.us*.

### StuffIt Files (.sit)

StuffIt files usually appear with the .sit extension. Stuffit is a Macintosh program that performs an operation similar to a PC archiver; it compresses and collects several files together into a single file. Files with .sit extensions may also be created with compression programs called StuffIt Lite and StuffIt Deluxe.

A copy of StuffIt for Macintosh can be obtained by FTPing to *sumex-aim.stanford.edu* and downloading the file called *stufit-lite-30.hqx* located in the */info-mac/util* directory. If you need to unstuff a file using an MS-DOS utility, FTP to *garbo.uwasa.fi* and download the file *unsit30.zip* located in the */pc/arcers* directory.

### PackIt files (.pit)

For a copy of PackIt for Macintosh, FTP to *sumex-aim.stanford.edu* and download the file *stuffit-151.hqx* in the */info-mac/util* directory.

### Compact Pro files (.cpt)

For a copy of Compact Pro for Macintosh, FTP to *sumex-aim.stanford.edu* and download file *compact-pro-133.hqx* in the */info-mac/util* directory.

### Self Extracting files (.sea)

To extract a file with the .sea extension, you simply run the file. To practice this procedure, FTP to site *ftp.unt.edu*, go to the directory */pub/library/hytelnet/mac* and download the file *hytelnet.mac.sea.hqx*. This file consists of multiple files that have been packed into a self-extracting archive (.sea) and then converted into BinHex format (.hqx). The .hqx at the far right tells you the first thing you must do before you can use this file is convert it from BinHex format. (Run it through one of the BinHex programs mentioned earlier.) The second thing you must do is unpack the resulting *hytelnet.mac.sea* file. The .sea extension indicates that you can accomplish this by simply running the program.

## ≡ MacBinary

Macintosh files consist of two parts: a data fork and a resource fork. In some instances the data fork contains the main part of the file—text if it is a document, or the actual image if it is a GIF file—and the resource fork contains the icon and other data relating to the main file. In other instances, such as applications, the main part of the file is stored in the resource fork and the data fork is usually empty. Individuals who want to store Macintosh files on non-Macintosh computers have to convert them to a MacBinary format before transferring them.

*MacBinary* is the name of a program used for converting files to and from MacBinary format. The newer Macintosh telecommunications programs have a built in feature capable of converting and unconverting these files. Files with the extension .bin are binary images of Macintosh files in MacBinary format. These files will only be useful to you if you are using a Macintosh computer. It isn't necessary to use MacBinary to transfer GIF images because GIF files don't contain any information that's specific to Macintosh computers. Encoding them in MacBinary format would just make it impossible for non-Macintosh users to use them.

### BinHex files (.hqx)

Most of the Macintosh files you'll find on the Internet are stored in BinHex (Binary/Hexadecimal) format. These are ASCII text files containing an image of a Macintosh file. There is a common practice of labeling such files with .hqx extensions. The BinHex process does what MacBinary does plus it converts binary files into ASCII text. This enables you to transfer the file via the Internet mail system or as USENET news.

To download .hqx files and use them on a Macintosh computer, you must first run them through a program that converts them from .hqx format into a regular Macintosh file. If you do this conversion process on a Unix system before transferring the program to your Macintosh, you can use the MCVERT program, stored at *sumex-aim.stanford.edu* in directory */info-mac/info/cmp* as filename *mcvert.shar*.

If you've transferred the BinHex files to your Macintosh, then you'd run a de-binhexing utility to convert the .hqx files into either real Macintosh files or compressed files. If they are compressed, then use one of the decompression programs to decompress it.

Some of the popular programs that allow you to convert BinHex files into applications and documents right on your Macintosh are StuffIt, BinHex 4.0, and Compact Pro. For a copy of BinHex 4.0, FTP to *sumex-aim.stanford.edu* and go to directory */info-mac/info/cmp* and download a copy of the file *binhex4.bin*. This file is a MacBinary version of BinHex 4.0. Make sure you issue a "binary" command on the FTP server before downloading or you'll get a corrupted file. You can also FTP to *mac.archive.umich.edu* and go to the directory *mac/utilities/compressionapps* and download the file *binhex4.0.bin*.

For a very thorough discussion of telecommunication issues relating to Macintosh, see the "Frequently Asked Questions (FAQ) list for *comp.sys.mac.comm*" edited by Eric Rosen. This document can be retrieved via FTP from site *rtfm.mit.edu* (18.70.0.224) in the directory *pub/usenet/news.answers/macintosh/comm-faq*. The document is divided between four separate files with the names: *part1*, *part2*, *part3* and *part4*.

# Library Discussion Lists

This is a selective list of discussion lists relating to libraries. A few have been added that are technically not LISTSERV based discussion lists. These lists use an application called Kotsikonas's List Processor, but their addresses still use the word 'listserv' in them. Where the word 'listserv' is not included in the email address, you will be communicating with a person, not list server software, when mailing in a subscription request. An example is the list called CONSERVATION DISTLIST which is run by *whenry@lindy.stanford.edu*. Still send the basic information regarding who you are, why you are writing, and the name of the list to which you'd like to subscribe.

## ≡ Library Related Discussion Lists

| | |
|---|---|
| Acqnet | Acquisitions librarians list <br> email to: *cri@cornellc.bitnet* |
| ACRLNY-L | Library jobs & events <br> *listserv@nyuacf.bitnet* |
| ADVANC-L | The Geac Advance Library System for online services <br> *listserv@idbsu.bitnet* |
| AFAS-L | African American Studies & Librarianship <br> *listserv@kentvm.bitnet* |
| AJCUIL-L | Law Librarians/Interlibrary Loan <br> *listserv@guvm.bitnet* |
| ALA | ALA File List <br> *listserv@uicvm.bitnet* |

| | |
|---|---|
| ALACOUN | ALA Council <br> *listserv@uicvm.bitnet* |
| ALF-L | Academic Librarians Forum <br> *listserv@Yorkvm1.bitnet* |
| ARACHNET | Discussion of 600+ Electronic Scholarly Journals, Digests, etc. <br> *listserv@uottawa.bitnet* |
| ARCHIVES | Archives & Archivists List <br> *listserv@indycms.bitnet* |
| ARIE-L | Users of RLG Ariel Document Transmission System <br> *listserv@idbsu.bitnet* |
| ARLIS-L | Art Libraries Discussion List <br> *listserv@ukcc.bitnet* |
| ATLAS-L | Data Research ATLAS Users <br> *listserv@tcubvm.bitnet* |
| AUTOCAT | Library Cataloging & Authorities Discussion <br> *listserv@uvmvm.bitnet* |
| BI-L | Bibliographic Instruction <br> *listserv@bingvmb.bitnet* |
| BIBLIST | Topics in Research Library User Services <br> *listserv@searn.bitnet* |
| BIBSOFT | Bibliographic Databases & Formatting Software <br> *listserv@indycms.bitnet* |
| BLACKLIB | Conference of Black Librarians <br> *listserv@guvm.bitnet* |
| BRS-L | Full Text Retrieval Software Discussion <br> *listserv@uscvm.bitnet* |
| BUSLIB-L | Business Library Issues <br> *listserv@idbsu.bitnet* |
| CALL-L | Canadian Law Librarians Discussion <br> *listserv@unbvm1.bitnet* |
| CARL-L | Carl Users Forum <br> *listserv@uhccvm.bitnet* |
| CDROM-L | CD-Rom User List <br> *listserv@uccvma.bitnet* |
| CDROMLAN | CD-Rom Use on a Network <br> *listserv@idbsu.bitnet* |
| CDS-ISIS | Unesco's Text Retrieval Software <br> *listserv@hearn.bitnet* |
| CIRCPLUS | Circulation Department Issues <br> *listserv@idbsu.bitnet* |

| | |
|---|---|
| COLLDV-L | Collection development list<br>*listserv@uscvm.bitnet* |
| CONSALD | Committee on South Asian Libraries & Documentation<br>*listserv@utxvm.bitnet* |
| CONSERVATION DISTLIST | preservation<br>email to: *whenry@lindy.stanford.edu* |
| COOPCAT | Cooperative Cataloging Arrangements List<br>*listserv@nervm.bitnet* |
| DLDG-L | Dance Librarians Discussion List<br>*listserv@iubvm.bitnet* |
| DYNIX-L | Dynix Users List<br>*listserv@oyster.smcm.edu* |
| ELDNET-L | Engineering Libraries<br>*listserv@uiucvmd.bitnet* |
| ELEASAI | Open Library/Information Science Research forum<br>*listserv@arizvm1.bitnet* |
| ELLASBIB | Library Automation in Greece<br>*listserv@gearn.bitnet* |
| ELN-L | Electronic Library Network Project List<br>*listserv@ubvm.bitnet* |
| EMAILMAN | Learning About Accessing Electronic Information<br>*listserv@vtvm1.bitnet* |
| EXLIBRIS | Rare Book & Special Collections Forum<br>*listserv@rutvm1.bitnet* |
| FIRSTSEARCH-L | FirstSearch and Other OCLC Offerings<br>*listserv@oclc.org* |
| FISC-L | Fee-based Information Services in Academia<br>*listserv@ndsuvm1.bitnet* |
| FLIPPER | Florida Libraries Interested in Preservation<br>*listserv@nervm.bitnet* |
| GAY-LIBN | Gay/Lesbian/Bisexual Librarians Network<br>*listserv@uscvm.bitnet* |
| GEONET-L | Geoscience Librarians & Informmation Specialists<br>*listserv@iubvm.bitnet* |
| GOVDOC-L | Federal Deposit Libraries<br>*listserv@psuvm.bitnet* |
| GTRTI-L | Research & Teaching in Global Information Technology<br>*listserv@gsuvm1.bitnet* |
| GUTNBERG | Electronic Texts<br>*listserv@uiucvmd.bitnet* |
| IIRS | Israeli Information Retrieval Specialists list<br>*listserv@taunivm.bitnet* |

| | | |
|---|---|---|
| ILL-L | Interlibrary Loan Discussion Group | *listserv@uvmvm.bitnet* |
| INDEX-L | Indexer's Discussion Group | *listserv@bingvmb.bitnet* |
| INFO+REF | Discussion of Information & Referral Services | *listserv@indycms.bitnet* |
| INFOSYS | Info Systems List | *listserv@hdetud1.bitnet* |
| INNOPAC | Innovative Interfaces OPAC & Related | *listserv@maine.bitnet* |
| IR-L | Information Retrieval List | *listserv@uccvma.bitnet* |
| IS-TQM | TQM Implementation in Information Science | *listserv@mitvma.bitnet* |
| INT-LAW | Foreign & International Law Librarians | *listserv@uminn1.bitnet* |
| IRLIST | Any Topic Related to Information Retrieval & Computer Use | *listserv@irlearn.bitnet* |
| KUTUP-L | Discussion Among Turkish Libraries | *listserv@trmetu.bitnet* |
| LAW-LIB | Law Librarians List | *listserv@ucdavis.edu* |
| LIBADMIN | Issues of Library Administration and Management | *listserv@umab.bitnet* |
| LIBER | Library/Media Services | *listserv@uvmvm.bitnet* |
| LIBEVENT | Library Information Services List | *listserv@uscvm.bitnet* |
| LIB_HYTELNET | Discussion of the Hytelnet Application. To subscribe, send message to *scott@skilib.usask.ca.* Messages sent to the list should be addressed to *lib_hytelnet@sas,.usask.ca.* | |
| LIBMASTR | Library Master Bibliographic Database Program List | *listserv@uottawa.bitnet* |
| LIBNET-L | Libraries & Networks in North Carolina | *listserv@ncsuvm.bitnet* |
| LIBPER-L | Library Personnel Issues | *listserv@Ksuvm.bitnet* |
| LIBPLAN-L | University Library Planning | *listserv@qucdn.bitnet* |

| | | |
|---|---|---|
| LIB-REF-L | Changing Environment of Reference Services | *listserv@kentvm.bitnet* |
| LIBRARY | Libraries & Librarians | *listserv@indycms.bitnet* |
| LIBRES | Library and Information Science Research | *listserv@kentvm.bitnet* |
| LIS-L | Forum for Library and Information Science Students | *listserv@vmd.cso.uiuc.edu* |
| LM_NET | School Library/Media Services | *listserv@suvm.bitnet* |
| MAPS-L | Map Librarians List | *listserv@uga.bitnet* |
| MEDLIB-L | Medical & Health Science Libraries | *listserv@ubvm.bitnet* |
| METALIB | Metal Library | *listserv@jpntuvm0.bitnet* |
| MLA-L | Music Library Association | *listserv@iubvm.bitnet* |
| MLARES-L | Music Library Research Support | *listserv@iubvm.bitnet* |
| NASIG | North American Serials List | *listserv@uvmvm.bitnet* |
| NISO | National Information Standards Organization | *listserv@nervm.bitnet* |
| NNEWS | Library & Information Resources on the Internet | *listserv@ndsuvm1.bitnet* |
| NOTIS-L | NOTIS Users List | *listserv@tcsvm.bitnet* |
| NOTISACQ | NOTIS Acquisition List | *listserv@cuvmp.bitnet* |
| NOTMUS | NOTIS Music Library List | *listserv@ubvm.bitnet* |
| NOTRBCAT | Rare Book & Special Collection Catalogers | *listserv@indycms.bitnet* |
| OCLC-NEWS | Discussion of OCLC Service News | *listserv@oclc.org* |
| OffCAMP | Off-campus Library Services | *listserv@waynest1.bitnet* |
| OCLC-JOURNALS | Information About OCLC Electronic Journal Publishing | *listserv@oclc.org* |
| PACS-L | Public Access Computer Systems forum | *listserv@uhupvm1.bitnet* |

| | | |
|---|---|---|
| PACS-P | PACS-L Publications Only | *listserv@uhupvm1.bitnet* |
| PRO-CITE | ProCite Bibliographic Software Users List | *listserv@iubvm.bitnet* |
| PUBLIB | Use of the Internet in Public Libraries | *listserv@nysernet.org* |
| PUBYAC | Youth Services in Public Libraries | *listserv@nysernet.org* |
| RLGAMSC | RLG Archives, Manuscripts & Special Collections | *listserv@rutvm1.bitnet* |
| RLGART-L | RLG Art & Architecture | *listserv@yalevm.bitnet* |
| RLGLaw-L | RLG Law Library List | *listserv@uminn1.bitnet* |
| RLGPSCD | RLG Public Service & Collection Development | *listserv@brownvm.bitnet* |
| RLGTECH | RLG Technical Services list | *listserv@rutvm1.bitnet* |
| Sercites | Citations for serial literature | *listserv@mitvma.bitnet* |
| SERIALST | Serials in Libraries—user discussion | *listserv@uvmvm.bitnet* |
| SHARP-L | History of the Printed Word | *listserv@iubvm.bitnet* |
| SLAJOB | Job Board International for Special Librarians | *listserv@iubvm.bitnet* |
| SLIS-L | Indiana University School of Library and Information Science | *listserv@iubmv.bitnet* |
| SLIS-L | University of Alabama School of Library and Information Studies | *listserv@ua1vm.ua.edu* |
| SPILIB | Spires Library Discussion List | *listserv@suvm.bitnet* |
| USMARC-L | USMARC Advisory Group forum | *listserv@maine.bitnet* |
| VIRTUAL | Libraries of the future | *listserv@indycms.bitnet* |
| VISIONS | Forum on the Future of Libraries | *listserv@library.sdsu.edu* |

# Documents Stored in the EFF Library Policy Archive

The following is a list of online documents available from the Electronic Frontier Foundation's Library Policy Archive. Each citation includes a brief description and ends with the document's corresponding filename. All of the files listed here reside in the */pub/academic/library* directory at FTP site *ftp.eff.org*.

1. Abernathy, Joe. *Houston Chronicle article.*

   This is the original article upon which Carl Kadie wrote his parody "Houston comical slams public libraries as 'pornography ring'." [See entry below by Carl Kadie.]

   *library.porn.real*

2. *Access for children and young people to videotapes and other nonprint formats.*

   An interpretation by the American Library Association of the "Library Bill of Rights".

   *access.children.nonprint.ala*

3. *Access to resources and services in the school library media program.*

   ALA's policy on grade and high school libraries. States that the principles of the Library Bill of Rights apply to school libraries.

   *school-libraries.ala*

4. *ALA ordering information.*

   1991 information on how to order intellectual freedom material from the American Library Association. Much of the material is free.

   *order.form.ala*

5. *ALA policy on meeting rooms.*

   In part, it says that facilities should be made available to the public served by the given library "on inequitable basis, regardless of the beliefs or affiliations of individuals or groups requesting their use." It is an interpretation by the American Library Association of the "Library Bill of Rights".

   *meeting-rooms.ala*

6. *The American Library Association's definition of "censorship" and related terms.*

   *censorship.def.ala*

7. *The American Library Association's "Policy on Confidentiality of Library Records".*

   *confidentiality.1.ala*

8. *The American Library Association's "Statement Concerning Confidentiality of Personally Identifiable Information about Library Users".*

   *confidentiality.2.ala*

9. Bennett, Rich. *Guidelines for the development of policies regarding patron behavior and library usage (a draft).*

   Deals with how libraries must approach the regulation of user behavior within the framework of the law. Provides guidelines based upon constitutional principles.

   *patron.behavior.draft.ala*

10. *Canadian Library Association Statement on Intellectual Freedom.*

    *int-freedom.can*

11. *Challenged materials.*

    An interpretation by the American Library Association of the "Library Bill of Rights".

    *challenged-materials.ala*

12. *Computers and academic freedom.*

    In the directory */pub/academic/books*, the README file contains a directory of book references relating to Computers and Academic Freedom. Some of the titles cited are available in full text in the *pub/academic/books* directory.

    Available via FTP to site *ftp.eff.org* in the directory */pub/academic/books* filename *README.*

13. *Diversity in collection development.*

    An interpretation by the American Library Association of the "Library Bill of Rights".

    *diversity.ala*

14. *Evaluating library collections.*

    An interpretation by the American Library Association of the "Library Bill of Rights".

    *evaluating-collections.ala*

15. *Exhibit spaces and bulletin boards.* An interpretation by the American Library Association of the "Library Bill of Rights".

    *bulletin-boards.ala*

16. *Expurgation of library materials.* An interpretation by the American Library Association of the "Library Bill of Rights".

    *expurgation.ala*

17. *Free access to libraries for minors.*

    An interpretation by the American Library Association of the "Library Bill of Rights".

    *access.minors.ala*

18. *The "Freedom to Read Statement" of the American Library Association and Association of American Publishers.*

    *freedom-to-read.ala*

19. Halbert, Martin. "Copyright, digital media, and libraries." *The Public-Access Computer Systems Review* 2, no. 1 (1991): 164–170.

    Available via anonymous FTP to site *ftp.eff.org* in the directory */pub/EFF/legal-issues* filename *copyright-libraries*

20. *Intellectual freedom statement.*

    An interpretation by the American Library Association of the "Library Bill of Rights".

    *int-freedom.ala*

21. Kadie, Carl. *Houston Comical slams public libraries as "pornography ring".*

    Parody of a real newspaper article published in the Houston Chronicle by Joe Abernathy. Parody opens: "Library Porno: a card catalog away. Top-flight, tax-aided research centers also home to the sexually explicit."

    *library.porn*

22. *The Library Bill of Rights from the American Library Association.*

    *bill-of-rights.ala*

23. *Library initiated programs as a resource.*

    An interpretation by the American Library Association of the "Library Bill of Rights".

    *library-programs.ala*

24. *Regulations, policies, and procedures affecting access to library resources and services.*

    An interpretation by the American Library Association of the "Library Bill of Rights".

    *access.policies.ala*

23. *Restricted access to library materials.*

    An interpretation by the American Library Association of the "Library Bill of Rights".

    *access.restrictions.ala*

26. Reynolds, Dennis J., ed. *Citizen rights and access to electronic information: A collection of background essays prepared for the 1991 LITA President's Program.*

    A printed booklet distributed at the American Library Association conference in July 1991.

    *elec.rights1-4*

27. *Statement on labeling.*

    An interpretation by the American Library Association of the "Library Bill of Rights." This document presents three reasons why labeling is bad. The first is that "Labeling is an attempt to prejudice attitudes and as such, it is a censor's tool."

    *labeling.ala*

28. *The universal right to free expression.*

    An interpretation by the American Library Association of the "Library Bill of Rights".

    *free-expression.ala*

29. *Workbook for selection policy writing.*

    Primarily aimed at textbook and library book selection in grade and high schools. Includes information on how to create a selection policy and how to handle complaints. Also includes a sample selection policy.

    *selection-workbook.ala*

# Internet Resources Arranged by Subject A–Z

This section contains a selective list of Internet resources arranged by subject. It is meant to be a place for browsing and a point of departure for discovering other Internet resources. It is by no means comprehensive and was not meant to be an index to the tens of thousands of information servers located on the Internet. If your goal is to determine whether a specific subject is covered in some form on the Internet, check here first and then turn to the various resource discovery tools introduced in previous chapters. If you'd like to browse the Internet by subject, one of the best ways to do this is by TELNETing to the Web server at *info.cern.ch*. (See also Chapter 15.)

The items presented in this section utilize resource sharing services like TEL-NET and FTP, and resource discovery services like Gopher, WAIS, and World-WideWeb. Special formats are used for listing resource locations and for the sake of expediency, they differ slightly from the formats used in previous chapters. One or more of the following components will be included in each entry:

ACCESS METHOD: This component tells you which Internet service is used to access an item. If the resource is found at an FTP site, the Internet address will be preceded by 'ftp' in lowercase letters like this: ftp ftp.eff.org. At your system prompt you would enter **ftp ftp.eff.org**. This would invoke your FTP client which would in turn connect to the FTP server at site *ftp.eff.org*.

ADDRESS: This component provides the Internet address where the item, person, or organization is located (IP address, domain name address, or electronic mail address).

PATHNAME: Once you've logged into a remote host, this component will provide directions for finding an item within that computer's file structure. The pathname tells you what path to follow for locating a particular file or menu item. The different levels of the directory or menu tree are separated by forward slashes '/'.

For example, a Gopher resource might be listed as: gopher is.internic.net /North America/United States/Arkansas/Evening Star. First you enter **gopher is.internic.net** to connect to the Gopher server at InterNIC. The first '/' represents the root menu. The text "North America" is a menu item listed in the root menu pointing to a submenu called "North America." Choosing "North America" will take you to the "North America" submenu which includes "United States" as one of its menu items. Choosing "United States" will take you to the "United States" submenu where there will be a menu item called "Arkansas" and so on.

Citing resources stored at FTP sites also involves the use of pathnames. For example, the reference: ftp ftp.unt.edu /pub/library/hytelnet/vms means that you should FTP to site *ftp.unt.edu*. Once logged in, you would enter the following command at the *FTP>* prompt: **cd pub/library/hytelnet/vms**. (Note that in the original reference to this resource, "pub" is preceded by a '/'. After logging into the FTP server you drop the first forward slash when using the **cd** command. This is because you are, at that point, already in the root directory.)

**FILENAME:** This item will be provided when a file is the resource being sought. A complete FTP citation will look something like this: ftp ftp.unt.edu /pub/library/ hytelnet/vms; vma_make.com. In this example, the pathname /pub/library/hytelnet/vms ends with a semicolon ';'. The next string that follows is the filename. To retrieve the file in the above example you would type **get vms_make.com** and press ENTER.

**MESSAGE:** When sending an email request to a computer, the precise wording of the command that should be inserted in the body of the message will be presented in boldface type.

## Sample Entries:

1.  FINGER—finger quake@geophys.washington.edu

2.  GOPHER—gopher cln.etc.bc.ca /Government of British Columbia/BC Ministry of Tourism and Culture/Royal British Columbia Museum.

3.  EMAIL—Subscribe to ROOTS-L by sending the message **subscribe roots-l <your name>** to listserv@vm1.nodak.edu.

4.  TELNET—telnet martini.eecs.umich.edu 3000 (On VAX/VMS, designate the port number as follows: telnet martini.eecs.umich.edu /port=3000.)

5.  FTP—ftp ftp.sura.net /pub/nic; agricultural.list

6.  USENET—USENET newsgroup: *rec.aviation*

7.  WAIS—WAIS source: *agricultural-market-news*

8.  THE WEB—http://fatty.law.cornell.edu:80/usr2/ wwwtext/nasdaq/nasdtoc.htm1 (See chapter 9 for explanation of how to use this Uniform Resource Locator)

**Note:** Throughout this section a number of Internet addresses, FTP paths, Gopher menus, and other directories are given. Be aware that many of these will change over time, especially Gopher menus and the location of files in FTP archives.

# ☰ Internet Resources

## Agriculture

1. 4H Project Manuals: gopher.ucdavis.edu /Community Outreach/U.C. Cooperative Extension/4h-youth.

2. List of Agricultural Internet Services: ftp ftp.sura.net /pub/nic; agricultural.list.

3. On-Line Databases Accessible via Telnet:

    Penn State PENPages: telnet psupen.psu.edu

    For username, enter your 2-letter state code (MN for Minnesota, AR for Arkansas, etc.).

    CSU Fresno: Current market information, weather forecasts and news relating to agriculture.
    telnet caticsuf.csufresno.edu   Login: **super.**

    Clemson University Forestry and Agricultural Network (CUFAN): telnet eureka.clemson.edu   Login: **public.**

    Purdue: telnet hermes.ecn.purdeu.edu   Username: **cerf**
    Password: **purdue.** Also access via gopher hermes.ecn.purdue.edu.

    Cornell Extension NETwork: telnet empire.cce.cornell.edu
    Login: **guest.**

4. University of Delaware for the College of Agricultural Sciences: gopher bluehen.ags.udel.edu.

5. Beekeeping: ftp sunsite.unc.edu /pub/academic/ agriculture/sustainable_agriculture/beekeeping. View directory for available files.

6. Agricultural Commodity Market Reports: WAIS source: *agricultural-market-news*

7. Drew, Wilfred. *Not Just Cows: A Guide to Internet/Bitnet Resources in Agriculture and Related Sciences.* Morrisville, NY: Morrisville college of Agriculture and Technology; May 8, 1992. ftp ftp.sura.net /pub/nic; agricultural.list

## Arts

1. Bibliography of Arts-related Resources on the Internet. ftp nic.funet.fi /pub/doc/library; artbase.txt.Z

## Astronomy

1.  Documents, Pictures, News, Applications Relating to Astronomy: ftp nic.funet.fi /pub/astro; see directory for listing of files.

2.  NASA Spacelink: telnet spacelink.msfc.nasa.gov

    NASA Spacelink is a space-related informational database operated by the Marshall Space Flight Center in Huntsville, Alabama. Includes information on space history, shuttle, and satellite news. When you connect, you'll be asked to provide a Username and a Password. If it's your first time, enter **newuser** as your Username and enter **newuser** as your Password. There is an introduction for users who logon as NEWUSER. After the introduction you'll assign yourself a personal Username and Password.

3.  NASA/IPAL Extragalactic Database (NED): telnet ned.ipac.caltech.edu Login: **ned**

    NED is operated by the Jet Propulsion Laboratory, California Institute of Technology. Its purpose is to make literature on extragalactic objects available over computer networks. The NED Interface connects you to an object-oriented database that assists you in accessing objects by name, around a name, or around a position.

    Included with this database is a literature search screen that enables you to retrieve bibliographic references, published notes, abstracts of papers, and images of catalog entries. NED can be searched interactively or in Batch mode.

4.  NASA News: finger nasanews@space.mit.edu

    After entering the above finger command, several screens will scroll by. Turn your screen capture on to save this daily bulletin.

5.  NASA Lunar and Planetary Institute: telnet lpi.jsc.nasa.gov Login:**lpi**.

    Main Menu includes such items as "Lunar and Planetary Bibliography" and "Mars Exploration Bulletin Board."

6.  Archive of Space Shuttle Images: ftp sseop.jsc.nasa.gov. Get README files.

7.  Space related USENET newsgroups: *sci.space*, *sci.astro*, *sci.aeronautics*, *sci.space.shuttle*.

8.  National Space Science Data Center: telnet nssdca.gsfc.nasa.gov Login **nodis**

    Archive for space and earth science researchers.

9.  Space related BITNET discussion lists:

    Send message **subscribe space-request <your name>** to listserv@isu.isunet.edu

    Send message **subscribe elements-request <your name>** to listserv@telesoft.com

Send message **subscribe gps-request <your name>** to listserv@esseye.si.com

10. Goddard Space Flight Center: gopher stsci.edu /Astronomical Internet Resources.

11. Ames SPACE Archive: ftp explorer.arc.nasa.gov /pub/SPACE. View directory for available files.

## Automobiles

1. Automotive Archive Containing FAQs, Mailing Lists, Information on Products and Laws, etc.: ftp rtfm.mit.edu /pub/usenet/rec.autos. See directory for available files.

## Aviation

1. USENET newsgroup: *rec.aviation*.

2. Humor and Trivia: ftp rascal.ics.utexas.edu /misc/av.

3. Northwestern University Aviation Gopher: gopher av.eecs.nwu.edu.

## Biology

1. Center for Scientific Computing: The Gopher server at this location offers information on Internet resources of interest to biologists. gopher finsun.csc.fi /Finnish EMBnet.../FAQ Files/A Biologist's Guide...

## Books

1. *CIA World Fact Book 1992*. gopher dewey.lib.ncsu.edu /6. NCSU's Library Without Walls/3. Reference Desk/1. Almanacs/1. CIA World Fact Book 1992/

2. Dictionaries and Thesauri: gopher dewey.lib.ncsu.edu /6. NCSU's Library Without Walls/3. Reference Desk/2. Dictionaries and Thesauri/

```
              Dictionaries and Thesauri

1.  Acronym Directory (WWW) <HTML>
2.  American English Dictionary <?>
3.  Computer Jargon (search) <?>
4.  Dictionary of Acronyms (search) <?>
5.  Internet User's Glossary (search) <?>
6.  Jargon File, Access by Searchable Index <HTML>
7.  Roget's Thesaurus (1911)/
8.  Unofficial Smilie Dictionary.
9.  Webster's Dictionary (San Francisco State University) <?>
```

3. gopher dewey.lib.ncsu.edu /6. NCSU's Library Without Walls/3. Reference Desk/4. Guides (to subject literature, to Internet resources, etc.)/

## Bookstores

1.  University of California, San Diego, Bookstore: telnet ucsdbkst.ucsd.edu [132.239.83.66] Login: **ult**.

    A sample of the logon screen output is shown below:

```
                Welcome to the University of California, San Diego


    UUUU       UUUU   /CCCCCCCCCCCCCC   /SSSSSSSSSSSSSS   DDDDDDDDDDDDDD\
    UUUU       UUUU   CCCC              SSSS             DDDD        DDDD
    UUUU       UUUU   CCCC              \SSSSSSSSSSSSS\  DDDD        DDDD
    UUUU       UUUU   CCCC                         SSSS  DDDD        DDDD
    \UUUUUUUUUUUUUU/  \CCCCCCCCCCCCCC   SSSSSSSSSSSSSS/  DDDDDDDDDDDDDD/


    BBBBB\ /OOOO\ /OOOO\ K   K  /SSSSS TTTTTT /OOOO\ RRRRR\ EEEEE
    B   B O    O O    O  K K   S        T     O    O R   R E
    B   / O    O O    O  KK    S        T     O    O R   R E
    BBBBB O    O O    O  KK    \SSSS\   T     O    O RRRRR/ EEEE
    B   \ O    O O    O  K K        S   T     O    O R   R E
    B   B O    O O    O  K K        S   T     O    O R   R E
    BBBBB/ \OOOO/ \OOOO/ K   K  SSSSS/  T     \OOOO/ R    R EEEEE




    Welcome to the UCSD Bookstore
    To login to the system, please enter 'ult' in lower case and press return.
    login: ult




    ***********************************************************************

    *
    *
    *
    *
    * Welcome to the UCSD Bookstore.
    *
    *
    *
    *
    * To continue with the login process, please enter 'BOOKSTORE' and press
    *
    * return.  To exit the system, enter 'BYE' and press return.
    *
    *
    *
    *
    *
```

```
*****************************************************************************
Last login: Sun Mar  6 15:13:27 PST 1994 on pts/1 from gremlin.ucsd.edu
Ultimate PLUS line 99 is assigned to /dev/pts/2.

UCSD Bookstore
06 MAR 1994 15:42:07 Logon please: bookstore

<<<   Copyright 1992, The Ultimate Corp., as an unpublished          >>>
<<<   work.  All Rights Reserved.  This work is the property of       >>>
<<<   and embodies trade secrets and confidential information         >>>
<<<   proprietary to The Ultimate Corp., and may not be reproduced,   >>>
<<<   copied, used, disclosed, transferred, adapted, or modified      >>>
<<<   without the express written approval of The Ultimate Corp.      >>>




                 Welcome to the UCSD Bookstore BiblioFile.
    BiblioFile is your desktop link to the UCSD Bookstore.  You can
 browse our book database, find out about upcoming events, and even see
 which books are on the New York Times Best Seller List.

         At this time, we can only support VT100 emulation.

 We have gone through a system upgrade recently.  The information you
 see in our database is outdated.  We are currently working on upgrading
 BiblioFile and should be completed by the end of December.




 Press any key to continue.

 [1.00]                  UCSD Bookstore  BiblioFile                   [BK]
 qqqqqqqqqqqqqqqqqqqqqqqqqqqqqqqqqqqqqqqqqqqqqqqqqqqqqqqqqqqqqqqqqqqqqqqqqqqq

       1 - Browse Book Database

       2 - Special Request

       3 - Best Seller Lists

       4 - Special Events




 qqqqqqqqqqqqqqqqqqqqqqqqqqqqqqqqqqqqqqqqqqqqqqqqqqqqqqqqqqqqqqqqqqqqqqqqqqqq
                         OFF - Logoff

      Please enter Menu Selection and press <return>.

      ENTER MENU SELECTION: 3

 [1.00]                  New York Times Best Sellers                [BK-03]
 qqqqqqqqqqqqqqqqqqqqqqqqqqqqqqqqqqqqqqqqqqqqqqqqqqqqqqqqqqqqqqqqqqqqqqqqqqqq
```

Choosing selection *3 - Best Seller Lists*, you are given the following six choices:

```
*** Hardback Listings ***          *** Paperback Listings ***

1 - Fiction                        4 - Fiction

2 - Non-Fiction                    5 - Non-Fiction

3 - Advice, How-to, and Misc.      6 - Advice, How-to, and Misc.
```

Upon choosing number *1 - Fiction*, the following information is provided:

```
         Display New York Times Best Seller Listing        BK.300.B
         For the Week of March 06 through March 12, 1994
                       Hardback ** Fiction
                                                     List    Our
         Author        Title                         Price   Price
    1    Steel         Accident                      23.95   15.56
    2    Crichton      Disclosure                    24.00   15.60
    3    Waller        Bridges Of Madison County     14.95    9.71
    4    Waller        Slow Waltz In Cedar Bend      16.95   11.01
    5    Spencer       Family Blessings              22.95   14.91
    6    Esquivel      Like Water For Chocolate      17.50   11.37
    7    Cook          Fatal Cure                    22.95   14.91
    8    Braun         Cat Who Came To Breakfast     19.95   12.96
    9    Crispin       Star Trek : Sarek             22.00   14.30
   10    Kellerman     Bad Love                      22.95   14.91
   11 *  Sanders       Mcnally 's Caper              22.95   14.91
   12    Clancy        Without Remorse               24.95   16.21
   13    Clarke        Rama Revealed                 22.95   14.91
   14    Griffin       Honor Bound                   22.95   14.91
   15 *  Redfield      Celestine Prophesy            17.95   11.66
```

2.  Book Stacks Unlimited, Inc., 200 Public Square, Suite 26-4600, Cleveland, OH 44114. telnet books.com 900 [192.148.240.9].

    Online bookstore and reader's conference system searchable by author, title, ISBN, or keyword. You can also browse the shelves (with over 650,000 titles) by subject online, place your order and have the books shipped to you. The conferencing system gives you an opportunity to share reviews with other readers. Modem # (216) 694-5732 (9600 Baud).

3.  Basement Full of Books, Vonda N. McIntyre, P.O. Box 31041, Seattle, WA 98103-1041.

    This service provides a list of books available by mail directly from their authors. A copy of this list can be obtained one of the following ways:

    FTP: ftp rtfm.mit.edu /pub/usenet/news.answers/books; basement-full-of-books.

    EMAIL: Email to mail-server@rtfm.mit.edu with the message **send usenet/news.answers/books/basement-full-of-books** in the body of the message.

A sample entry from this list is presented below:

```
//\//\//\//\//\//\//\//\//\//\//\//\//\//\//\//\//\//\//\//\//\

AUTOGRAPHED NEW FIRST EDITIONS BY JOE HALDEMAN

THE HEMINGWAY HOAX, William Morrow, Inc., 1990.

A scholar with a taste for larceny is pursued by an
inter-dimensional literary critic with a license to kill.

BUYING TIME, William Morrow, 1989.

In a future where you can live forever if you have the right friends and a
fortune, Dallas Barr is running out of money, friends, and time.  Men with
guns want to make his life even shorter.

We have a few copies of the British first edition, with my original title --
THE LONG HABIT OF LIVING New English Library, 1989.

ALL MY SINS REMEMBERED.  St Martins, 1977.

An undercover agent travels from planet to planet, working in disguise.

MINDBRIDGE.  St. Martins, 1976.

The first exploration team to a nearby star
discovers an alien race that may be the salvation of
humanity--or its destruction.

TOOL OF THE TRADE.  William Morrow, 1987.

A Soviet agent lives quietly in the U.S. for most of his life,
waiting to be contacted by his government.  His discovery of a
mechanism that controls people's behavior earns him more attention
than he bargained for.

WORLDS APART.  Viking, 1983.

The second book in the WORLDS trilogy, this
book follows Marianne O'Hara from her home in an orbiting
space station to the ruins of Earth and then back to aim for
the stars.

For further information, please send SASE or email to:

          Joe & Gay Haldeman
          5412 NW 14th Ave.
          Gainesville, FL 32605

          GEnie:  J.HALDEMAN1
```

4.  Laura Fillmore's OBS (Online Bookstore) is based in Rockport, Mass. telnet marketplace.com.

    Payments are handled by typing in a credit card number. Customers can have books delivered electronically to their home computers.

5.  Online Bookstore: gopher.tic.com OR email obs@tic.com.

### Business

1.  *Commerce Business Daily*: gopher cscns.com /12. SPECIAL- Commerce Business Daily.

    Gopher provides interactive searching of this full-text database. The opening screen is presented below:

    ```
                 COMMERCE BUSINESS DAILY ON THE INTERNET
                 ----------------------------------------


    Softshare Information Systems: 1-800-346-6703 ext 233  or sshare@cscns.com
           CNS On-line Systems: 1-800-748-1200  or service@cscns.com


    CNS and Softshare Government Information Systems is excited about
    making this gopher area available to the users of the Internet.

    The Commerce Business Daily is a publication that announces invitations to
    bid on proposals requested by the US Federal Government. This gopher is
    updated every business day.

    The CBD information is also available via newsgroup or uucp. For
    information about this, please email service@cscns.com or call 1-800-748-1200.

    If you are serious about your CBD needs, we can arrange to send you
    invitations via internet email that apply only to your company. Softshare
    will work with you in setting up a company profile.  Based in this
    profile, you will receive articles in your email that pertain to your
    company. Matches will automatically include the details of previous awards
    that have been granted in similar procurement requests. For more
    information concerning automatic email, please contact:

        by phone: 1-800-346-6703  ext 233 (Melissa Allensworth)
        by email: sshare@cscns.com
    ```

2.  A Hypermedia Version of the *Nasdaq Financial Executive Journal*. http://fatty.law.cornell.edu:80/usr2/wwwtext/ nasdaq/nasdtoc.htm1.

3.  University of California San Diego Business Gopher: gopher infopath.ucsd.edu /7. News & Services/8. Economic Bulletin Board.

    The menu choices in the Economic Bulletin Board directory appear as follows:

    ```
                        Economic Bulletin Board


    -->  1.   IMPORTANT! About the EBB and UMich.
         2.   Current Business Statistics/
         3.   Defense Conversion Subcommittee (DCS) Info/
         4.   EBB and Agency Information and misc. files/
         5.   Eastern Europe trade leads/
         6.   Economic Indicators/
         7.   Employment Statistics/
         8.   Energy statistics/
         9.   Foreign Trade/
        10.   General Information Files/
        11.   Industry Statistics/
    ```

```
12. International Market Insight (IMI) reports/
13. Monetary Statistics/
14. National Income and Products Accounts/
15. Press releases from the U.S. Trade Representative/
16. Price and Productivity Statistics/
17. Regional Economic Statistics/
18. Social and Environmental Files/
```

```
                                                         Page: 1/2
19. Special Studies and Reports/
20. Summaries of current economic conditions/
21. Trade Opportunity Program (TOP)/
22. U.S. Treasury Auction Results/
23. USDA Agricultural leads/
```

4.  Company ProFiles: telnet pac.carl.org.

At the *Enter Choice>* prompt enter **PAC**. From the main menu, choose
*3. Information Databases* and then *82. Company ProFile.* This will
bring you to the following two screens where, in this example, a word
search on the string **ids** was entered. In the first screen, **w** was entered at
the command prompt to designate a word search and in the second
screen, **ids** was entered as the word to search.

```
04/06/94
03:02 P.M.      SELECTED DATABASE:  Company ProFiles


                     COMPANY proFILES


               c Information Access Company


The COMPANY ProFILES database gives directory listings from over
100,000 private and public companies, including addresses, phone
numbers, SIC codes, revenues, and numbers of employees.  COMPANY
ProFILES are updated monthly.



             Enter    W    for  WORD search

                 S    to    STOP or SWITCH·to another database

        Type the letter for the kind of search you want,
        and end each line you type by pressing <RETURN>

                 SELECTED DATABASE:  Company ProFiles

ENTER  COMMAND (use  //EXIT  to return HOME)>>      w




             SELECTED DATABASE: Company ProFiles


REMEMBER -- WORDS can be words from the title, or can be subjects,
concepts, ideas, dates, etc.
```

```
                        for example --  GONE WITH THE WIND
                                        SILVER MINING COLORADO
                                        BEHAVIOR  MODIFICATION

Enter word or words (no more than one line, please)
separated by spaces and press <RETURN>.




    >ids
```

The next screen shows how many hits occurred and gives you the option of revising your search, displaying the results, or quitting. By entering **d**, the first page of hits is displayed. The first item listed, *1. IDS Financial Services, Inc.*, was chosen to demonstrate a full record display.

```
WORKING...
IDS                    17  ITEMS

You may make your search more specific  (and reduce
the size of the list)  by adding another word
to your search. The result will be items in
your current list that also contain the new
word.


  to ADD a new word, enter it,

 <D>ISPLAY to see the current list, or

 <Q>UIT for a new search:


NEW WORD(S): d



  1                                                          -

      IDS Financial Services Inc.


  2                                                          -

      North American Container Corp.


  3                                                          -

      Interior Design Services Inc.


  4                                                          -

      IDS Financial Services Inc. Dennis M. Gurtz and

  5                                                          -

      IDS Bank and Trust. IDS Trust


  6                                                          -

      IDS Deposit Corp.


  7                                                          -

      IDS Life Insurance Company of New York
```

```
  <RETURN> To continue display
  Enter <Line number(s)> To Display Full Records (Number + B for Brief)
  <P>revious For Previous Page OR <Q>uit For New Search
  1




                           -------------Company ProFiles-----------
  COMPANY NAME:    IDS Financial Services Inc.
  Also known as:   IDS Financial Services
  Mailing add.:      IDS Financial Services Inc.
                     IDS Tower 10
                     Minneapolis
                     MN
                     55440
  Telephone:       612 671-3131
  Established:     1894
  Designation:     Private subsidiary
  Parent Company:  American Express Co.
  Parent Company:  IDS Financial Corp.
  Labor force:     1800 Employees
  Revenue/Source:  $367.0 M
                   OPERATING REVENUE
  Fiscal year:     911231
  Description:     Finance: Financial planning services.
  Primary SIC:     6282_Investment Advice
  Management:      Chief Executive Officer
  more follows -- press <RETURN> (Q to quit)
                   Stiefler, Jeff
                   Chief Executive Officer and President
                   Jeff Stiefler
                   Chief Executive Officer and Pres
                   Chief Financial Officer
                   Hubers, David
                   Senior Vice President, Finance Officer
                   David Hubers
                   Senior Vice President, Finance O
                   Head of Marketing, Sales
                   Saunders, Reid
                   Senior Vice President, Marketing
                   Reid Saunders
                   Senior Vice President, Marketing
                   Personnel Director
                   Kinder, Susan
                   Director of Human Resources
                   Susan Kinder
                   Director of Human Resources
                   Updated as of: 930810
```

## Careers

1. Online Career Center: gopher gopher.msen.com.

   The Online Career Center database was formed by forty U.S. corporations in 1993 as a non-profit employer association for recruiting, outplacement, career assistance, and communications via the Internet. For additional information, contact William O. Warren, executive director,

Online Career Center, 3125 Dandy Trail, Indianapolis, IN 46214; email occ@mail.msen.com, or for an automated reply, email to occ-info@mail.msen.com.

## Chemistry

1. Chemistry Information: ftp ucssun1.sdsu.edu /pub/chemras. See directory for list of available files.

   Reference sources are listed for nomenclature, compound identification, properties, structure determination, toxicity, synthesis, registry numbers, and synthesis.

## Childcare

1. Childcare Newsletters: ftp nigel.msen.com /pub/newsletters/Kids. See directory for list of available files.

## Communications

1. COMSERVE: Send commands via email to Comserve@vm.its.rpi.edu.

   COMSERVE is a network resource that was designed to provide a wide range of information services to individuals engaged in studies relating to communication (mass communication, rhetoric, journalism, speech). Its creators wanted to form an "electronic site" where the exchange of information could take place 24 hours a day, 7 days a week at no charge to users.

   COMSERVE is technically a large collection of text files and computer programs. It functions as a server acting on commands that it receives from users via the Internet mail system. Communication with COMSERVE can also be accomplished by running a program on your local machine called "Easycom." Users working on machines running the CMS operating system can get the program by issuing the following CMS command:

   **tell Comserve at Rpitsvm Send Easycom Exec.**

   With the Easycom program in your computer account, you can begin a conversation with COMSERVE by typing **Easycom** at the *ready;* prompt and pressing ENTER. Easycom presents you with menus that describe COMSERVE's principal functions.

   If you don't use this Easycom menu-driven system to interact with COMSERVE, then you must send your requests via email to the address listed at the beginning of this section. Command statements may contain any mixture of upper- and lowercase letters. Insert the commands in the body of an email message. To retrieve a list of all valid commands, send the command **help**. By sending the command **help topics** you will retrieve a list of topical help packages. Each one describes a group of related commands in detail.

## Computers and Computing

1. Bibliography of Current Journal Articles Relating to Computers and Information Technology: telnet melvyl.ucop.edu. Enter the words **show current cites** at command prompt.

3. *PC Magazine*: ftp wuarchive.wustl.edu/mirrors/ msdos/pcmag. View directory for list of available files.

4. *VAX Manual* by Joe St. Sauver: ftp decoy.uoregon.edu /pub/vaxbook; README. See README file for details relating to the contents of this directory.

5. High-Performance Computing Daily News & Information Service (HPCwire): telnet hpcwire.ans.net Login:**hpcwire.**

   HPCwire is a news, information, and services exchange for the High-Performance computing industry. Made available at no charge by several commercial organizations, it operates as an information-management and retrieval system under the host *hpcwire.ans.net* and can be reached using telnet.

   When you connect for the first time, it will ask you if you are a registered user. If you're not, it will lead you through the registration process.

   The news service is divided into General News, Financial and Management/People. All sections are updated on a daily basis. HCPwire also offers a forum for exchanging ideas, Internet information such as general resource guides, FTP sources, accessible library catalogs, a job bank, newsletters, research register, and software. Documents can be downloaded via email or FTP. All data is fully indexed and is available for full content retrieval. Examples of some of the feature stories that were listed on their news service 10 March 1993 include:

   > *Using Hydrodynamics to Understand the Bay.*
   > *New Software Makes Parallel Systems Sharable.*
   > *Human Speech and the Brain: Teaching a Computer to Read.*
   > *Nature's Light Show: Origins of the Auroras.*
   > *Virtual Computing and the Virtual Computer.*
   > *Japanese Companies Downsize, Buy U.S. Workstations.*

6. Virtual Reality Archive: ftp ftp.u.washington.edu /public/VirtualReality. View directory for a list of available files.

7. Proper Publishing's Internet Computer Index: The Gopher server is located at site ici.proper.com. To connect with Internet Computer Index via WWW, point your WWW client to http://ici.proper.com.

   Proper Publishing's Internet Computer Index offers index searching of hardware and software reviews. It also lists several information resources for PC, Macintosh and Unix such as FTP sites, Gopher directories, FAQa and more. The service is free and can be searched via Gopher and World Wide Web.

## Earth Sciences

1.  Thoen, Bill. *Internet Resources for Earth Sciences*. gopher dewey.lib.ncsu.edu /6. NCSU's Library Without Walls/3. Reference Desk/4. Guides (to subject literature, to Internet resources, etc.)/17. Internet Resources for Earth Sciences, Thoen (5/92).

    This document lists Internet resources relating to earth sciences including Usenet Newsgroups, Bitnet Discussion Lists, Earth Science Anonymous FTP Sites, Groundwater Modeling Software, National Geophisical Data Center, and more.

## Earthquakes

1.  Earthquake Reports: For reports on recent earthquakes including the longitude and latitude of the activity, magnitude and time of occurrence, finger quake@geophys.washington.edu. You can also send an empty email message to this Internet address to retrieve details about recent earthquakes.

## Economics

1.  Goffe, Bill. *Resources for Economists on the Internet*. gopher dewey.lib.ncsu.edu /6. NCSU's Library Without Walls/3. Reference Desk/4. Guides (to subject literature, to Internet resources, etc.)/30. Resources for Economists on the Internet, Goffe.

    This document lists various resources related to economics including Gopher servers such as the University of Michigan Economics Department and the National Bureau of Economic Research Gopher, databases like the Economic Bulletin Board (EBB) and the New England Electronic Economic Data Center, working paper archives, bibliographical services, and more.

## Education

1.  AskERIC Gopher: gopher ericir.syr.edu

    The root menu on this Gopher server is shown below:

```
            Root gopher server: ericir.syr.edu

    1.  Information About the AskERIC Electronic Library/
    2.  The Map of the Library/
    3.  Library of Education Resources/
    4.  Information on Vocational Education/
    5.  Access and Search Other Information Sources/
    6.  Network Guides and Directories/
    7.  AskERIC Electronic Library Reference Tools/
    8.  ERIC Clearinghouse on Assessment and Evaluation/
```

2. ERIC Resources in Education (RIE) and Current Index to Journals in Education (CIJE) 1983-: telnet sklib.usask.ca [128.233.1.20]. Path: /4: Education Databases/1: ERIC (CIJE and RJE), 1983-.

   This menu option brings you to the ERIC indexes. This is a database that can be searched to locate references to journal articles and documents relating to the field of education. There are three basic commands: **find** (or **f**) to search for terms, **scan** (or **s**) and **list** (or **l**) to display your search results, and **help** (or **h**) to obtain information about the system.

3. CNN News Classroom Guides: Send an email message to **majaordomo@tenet.edu**. In the body of your message type **subscribe cnn-newsroom**.

4. EDNET: This is a BITNET discussion list dedicated to the discussion of using the Internet as an educational tool. Send the message **subscribe ednet <your name>** to listserv@nic.umass.edu.

5. National Education BBS: telnet nebbs.nersc.gov Login:**guest**.

   A Bulletin Board System for educators.

6. Newton: telnet newton.dep.anl.gov Login:**newton**.

   A Bulletin Board System for science, math, and computer science educators.

7. The Global Schoolhouse Project: This project connects students around the world via the Internet through collaborative research and video conferencing. The projects scheduled for 1994 will include 17 schools from 11 states and several international schools. For more information, contact Greg Fitzgerald, Global Schoolhouse Project, 7040 Avenida Encinas #104-281, Carlsbad, CA 92000. Tele: 619-931-5934. Email: gfitz@eis.calstate.edu.

8. Test Information: gopher gopher.cua.edu

   This Gopher server at Catholic University of America provides a wide range of information about educational and psychological testing. It features a comprehensive collection of full text articles about the latest in alternative assessment. It also hosts the Educational Testing Service (ETS) Test Collection database and the Buros Test Review Locator. Once connect to the Gopher server, look under Special Resources.

9. Kidsnet: Send an email message with the command **get kidlink filelist** to listserv@vm1.nodak.edu.

   This project is intended to foster networking between children ages 10-15 worldwide. The above document will provide information on the Kidsnet project and their archives.

10. McAnge, Thomas R., Jr., et al. (Virginia Cooperative Extension; Virginia Polytechnic Institute and State University). *A Survey of Educational Computer Networks*; June 1990: ftp ariel.unm.edu /library; networks.survey.

    This is a survey of the current (1990) and planned computer networking activities in K12 education.

11. Apple Computer Higher Education Gopher Server: gopher info.hed.apple.com.

    This service promotes communication with the higher education community. It offers information on Apple Products, Disability Solutions, NetNews Groups of Interest, and more. Users can participate in discussions on seven academic disciplines by sharing information in "Dialog Folders" on subject like Medical and Health Sciences and Library and Information Systems.

12. Duquesne University Gopher: gopher kids.duq.edu.

    Focuses on projects that get kids ages 10-15 involved in using Internet.

13. EDUCOM: gopher educom.edu.

    This entire Gopher server is dedicated to EDUCOM which helps higher education use computer technology in all areas of operations.

14. OERI Gopher Server: gopher gopher.ed.gov.

    This Gopher site is devoted to sharing statistical data and research and development information that relates to teaching and learning.

## Engineering

1. The University of Saskatchewan Engineering Info System: gopher gopher.usask.ca /U of S Engineering Gopher.

## Environment

1. EPA Gopher Server: gopher futures.wic.epa.gov.

    The Environmental Protection Agency established this gopher to provide information about the agency's work on future research. This server provides pointers to all other government gopher servers available.

```
            Internet Gopher Information Client 2.0 p19

                USA Environmental Protection Agency


    1.  ** Welcome to EPA's Future Studies Gopher! **.
    2.  Contacts within EPA.
    3.  **********************************************.
    4.  Agriculture/
    5.  Articles/
    6.  PARTICIPATION INVITED -- VIRTUAL WORKSHOP ON ENVIRONMENTAL TECH /
    7.  Air Water Land/
    8.  U.S. Climate Change Action Plan/
    9.  Energy Graphics/
    10. Guides and Locators/
    11. Industrial sector /
    12. The MegaTrends Report/
    13. Newsletters and Items of Regional Interest/
```

```
14. Population/
15. Sustainable Development/
16. Technology Issues/
17. The Milennium Project/
18. *********************************************.
```

```
This Gopher+ server was conceived and developed by the Future Studies
Group within the Office of Strategic Planning and Environmental Data.
This server is still being developed, so check back often if you don't see
what you're looking for.  We add new files fairly regularly.  For those who
are interested, the server runs on a Mac IIsi with 8 megabytes of memory
and a 500 meg hard drive.
```

```
If you are looking for something specific, the entire contents of this
server are available through WAIS (Wide Area Information Servers).  The
name of the WAIS database is epafutures.src, and it can be accessed via
the WAIS directory of servers.  The directory is
/Proj/Wais/Indexes/epafutures on Server.wais.com (port 210).
```

## Gardening/Horticulture

1.  Royal British Columbia Museum, Vancouver, Canada: gopher cln.etc.bc.ca /Government of British Columbia/BC Ministry of Tourism and Culture/Royal British Columbia Museum.

    This gopher server offers a taxonomic database of the plants in this museum's Native Plant Garden.

2.  Missouri Horticulture Guides: gopher bigcat.missouri.edu /references/guides-h.

3.  Texas A&M Master Gardener Project: gopher taex-gopher1.tamu.edu.

    A view of this Gopher's root menu is presented below:

```
           Internet Gopher Information Client 2.0 p19


                  Gardening- The Master Gardener


-->  1.  About this Gopher.
     2.  Introduction to Master Gardener files.
     3.  Fruits and Nuts/
     4.  Flowering Plants, Annual and Perennial/
     5.  Ornamental Trees and Shrubs/
     6.  Turf Grasses/
     7.  Vegetables/
     8.  TAMU Main Gopher Server/
```

4.  WAIS Source: *rec.gardens.src*

## Genealogy

1.  Subscribe to ROOTS-L by sending the message **subscribe roots-l <your name>** to listserv@vm1.nodak.edu.

## Geography

1.  Geographic Name Server: telnet martini.eecs.umich.edu 3000.

    This server is a menu-driven database that provides information on such things as population, elevation, latitude, longitude. The program asks for the name of a city or zip code.

## Government

1.  *Federal Information Resources Management (Circular A-130), Revision*: ftp nis.nsf.net /omb; omb.a130.rev2.

    In the summer of 1993, the federal Office of Management and Budget issued these policies assuring public access to computerized public records, and public federal records in all forms. A copy of this 19-page document can also be obtained via email: Send the command **send omb.a130.rev2** in the body of an email message addressed to info@nis.nsf.net.

2.  Government Accounting Office DayBook: telnet cap.gwu.edu Login:**guest** Password **visitor.**

    Lists reports and testimony issued each day by the U.S. General Accounting Office. To view current issues of the DayBook, type **go federal** and look in the Legislative Branch Information area.

3.  The FDA Electronic Bulletin Board: telnet 150.148.8.48.

    This bulletin board, provided as a service of the Food and Drug Administration, offers searching capabilities in several databases including:

    *The FDA Electronic Bulletin Board News:* FDA news releases relating to public health, safety and interest.

    *Enforce:* This file contains a list of FDA-regulated products under recall.

    *Import:* Import Detention Summaries reporting on items that have been detained because of violation of the law.

    *Consumer:* This file contains a table of contents and selected articles from the current issue of FDA Consumer (FDA's official monthly magazine).

    *CDRH:* Contains the Centers for Devices and Radiological Health (CDRH) Bulletins.

    *Approvals:* Contains the complete text of the Drug and Device Product Approvals list.

    *Date-Reg:* This file contains summaries of all FDA Federal Register announcements arranged by publication date.

    *Subj-Reg:* A file containing the summaries of all FDA Federal Register announcements arranged by subject.

4. U.S. Senate: gopher gopher.senate.gov, or via WWW at ftp://ftp.senate.gov.

5. Supreme Court Decisions: ftp po.cwru.edu /hermes/ascii. Documents relating to the Supreme Court can also be accessed via gopher marvel.loc.gov. Choosing /9.Government Information/1. Federal Information Resources/1.Information by Agency/3. Judiciary/4.Supreme Court Decisions and Documents/ will bring you to the following menu:

```
         Supreme Court Decisions and Documents (Via U.Md.)

1.  Search the Supreme Court Files <?>
2.  PROJECT HERMES.
3.  Justices of The Supreme Court Biographies/
4.  Cases Decided In 1989/
5.  Cases Decided In 1990/
6.  Cases Decided In 1991/
7.  Cases Decided In 1992/
8.  Cases Decided In 1993/
9.  Cases Decided In 1994/
10. Index of Supreme Court Cases.
11. search for supreme court nominee to replace justice blackmun.
12. nomination of judge steven breyer to supreme court.
13. clinton's statement on judge breyer nomination confirmations.
14. gore's remarks at swearing-in of justice stephen g. breyer 08-12-9...
```

6. White House Email Addresses: president@whitehouse.gov and vice.president@whitehouse.gov.

7. Catalog of Government Publications: telnet pac.carl.org. At the *Enter Choice>* prompt, enter **PAC**.

   At the opening menu, choose *1.Library Catalogs (including Government Publications)*. At the next level choose *22. Government Publications*. At this level you will be given the following menu:

```
FEDERAL
     83.  U.S. Government Publications
     66.  U.S. Dept. of Energy
     52.  ERIC (Education Resources)
          (Access Restricted as of 11/1/92)
     88.  Federal Domestic Assistance Catalog

STATE
     84.  Colorado State Government Publications
```

   By typing **83** and pressing ENTER, the following screen will appear:

```
04/06/94

12:41 P.M.      SELECTED DATABASE:  Government Publication
U.S. Government Publications contains titles published by agencies
of the U.S. Government and cataloged by the U.S. government Printing
Office since 1976. Denver Public Library and the University of Colorado,
as regional depositories, receive all depository publications. Numerous
other libraries in Colorado and Wyoming receive selected publications.
See the list of depository libraries under 'library News' for U.S.
```

```
government publications. Consult with your librarian to access
publications before 1976.
                Enter   N   for  NAME search
```

As an example of a 'name' search, I entered the words, "water sup-ply systems" and pressed ENTER. This is what appeared on the screen:

```
WORKING...
WATER 13920 ITEMS         Government Publication
WATER + SUPPLY  1609 ITEMS
WATER + SUPPLY + SYSTEMS    63 ITEMS


WATER + SUPPLY + SYSTEMS    63 ITEMS  Government Publication
You may make your search more specific  (and reduce
the size of the list)  by adding another word
to your search. The result will be items in
your current list that also contain the new
word.

 to ADD a new word, enter it,
 <D>ISPLAY to see the current list, or
 <Q>UIT for a new search:
NEW WORD(S): d
```

By entering a **d** at the *NEW WORD(S):* prompt, the first page of a total of 63 items was displayed:

```
1                                           DOCS DPL CU US     1993
   Risk analysis of highly combustible gas storage  Y 3.N 88:25/5759
2 United states marine                      DOCS DPL CU US     1992
   Materiel fielding plan (mfp) for the family of w  D 214.29:11330.4
3 Gumerman robert c                         DOCS DPL CU US     1992
   Standardized costs for water supply distribution  EP 1.23/6:600/R-92/009
4 Monical jim e                             DOCS DPL CU US     1992
   A user's guide to the arkansas rural water-deliv  I 19.76:92-108
5 Mcvey eileen                              DOCS DPL CU US     1991
   Aquaculture in recirculating systems :  january  A 17.18/4:91-130
6                                           DOCS DPL CU US     1991
   Why do wellhead protection?  microform :  issues  EP 2.2:W 45
7                                           DOCS DPL CU US     1991
   Manual of individual and non-public water supply  EP 2.8:In 2/3
 <RETURN> To continue display
Enter <Line number(s)> To Display Full Records (Number +  B  for Brief)
<P>revious For Previous Page OR <Q>uit For New Search
4
```

I chose item number 4 and pressed ENTER which brought up the following bibliographic record:

```
---------------------------------------------------Government Publication-----
AUTHOR(s):      Monical, Jim E.
TITLE(s):       A user's guide to the Arkansas Rural Water-Delivery Network
                Geographic Information System (GIS) software  microform /
                by Jim E. Monical ; prepared in cooperation with the
                Arkansas Soil and Water Conservation Commission.
                Little Rock, Ark. :  U.S. Geological Survey ;  Denver,
                Colo. :  Books and Open-File Reports Section [distributor],
                1992.
```

```
                        iii, 22 p. :  ill. ;  28 cm.
                        U.S. Geological Survey open-file report ;  92-108
                        Distributed to depository libraries in microfiche.
                        Shipping list no.: 93-0914-M.
                        Microfiche. [Denver, Colo. :  U.S. Geological Survey,
                          1993]  1 microfiche : negative.
                        [vm]
        OTHER ENTRIES:  Municipal water supply  Arkansas  Computer programs.
                        Geographic information systems.
        more follows -- press <RETURN> (Q to quit)
        YOU HAVE 30 SECONDS TO RESPOND:  -- ENTER <T> FOR MORE TIME:
                        Geological Survey (U.S.)
                        Arkansas Soil and Water Conservation Commission.
        CALL #: I 19.76:92-108          LIBRARY:         DPL CU US


        ----4 of 63-------------------------------------Government Publication------
```

8. Government Documents at the Electronic Frontier Foundation: ftp ftp.eff.org /pub/academic/civics.

   This is a directory of documents relating to government in general located at the Electronic Frontier Foundation. This directory called *Civics* includes information on such diverse topics as Affirmative Action, Civil Rights Law, and the full-text of *Civil Disobedience* by Henry David Thoreau. For further details, download the README file.

9. Email Address for Congress: congress@hr.house.gov.

10. United Nations Information: telnet fatty.law.cornell.edu Login: **gopher**

11. White House Publications: ftp whitehouse.gov, or via email to publications@whitehouse.gov.

    If you want to use the mail server, begin by sending the command **help** which will retrieve a file that explains how to use the mail server for locating and downloading files. To fully explore the Gopher server, begin in the /pub directory and branch out, reading the README files for details on holdings. If you'd like to obtain an index of all the files residing at whitehouse.gov, send the command **send index** in the body of an email message to the mail server at publications@whitehouse.gov. (This is a big file, about 400Kb.)

12. Federal Agency Information: telnet fedworld.gov.

13. White House Almanac Information Server: Email queries to almanac@esusda.gov.

    Contains White House documents relating to press briefings, Executive Orders and other information. For instructions on how to use, send an email message with the command **send guide** in the body of the message. To request a specific document, send an email message with the command **send white-house <doc#>** in the body of the message, where **<doc#>** is the number of the document you wish to receive. To see a catalog of what's available, send the command **send catalog** in the body of an email message. To receive a daily summary of White House press releases, send the command **subscribe whsummary** to almanac@esusda.gov. For text of current legislation, testimonies from Congressional hearings, speeches, and other policy papers, send the command **send congress catalog** to the almanac server.

14. Budget Information: ftp sunsite.unc.edu /pub/academic/political-science. View the directory for a list of available files.

15. Social Security Administration Phone Book: ftp soaf1.ssa.gov /pub; sea.phone.book.Z

16. Arizona State University Gopher, Government Agency Information: gopher info.asu.edu /6. Other sources (explore the Internet!)/10. United States Government/Agencies Information.

17. U.S. Department of Labor: ftp://stats.bls.gov/pub/doc/overview.doc

18. U.S. Government Budget: gopher gopher.esa.doc.gov, or telnet ebb.stat-usa.

   Beginning in fiscal year 1995, the U.S. Government budget will be available on the Internet.

19. U.S. Census: gopher gopher.census.gov.

20. The Crown Jewels Campaign is an organized effort to make some of the U.S. federal government's most important information systems available to the public online or on CD-ROM. These include systems like JURIS (federal legal information), the SEC's EDGAR system, the House of Representatives' LEGIS system and the Trademark Automated Patent System (APS).

   The Crown Jewels Campaign memorandums are distributed through *tap-info*, a low-volume 'list' that can be subscribed to by sending a request to *tap-info-request@essential.org*. ('TAP' stands for the Taxpayer Assets Project, a Ralph Nader organization.) *tap-info* postings are archived and accessible via FTP at site *ftp.cpsr.org* in the */taxpayer_assets* directory and WAIS source *wais.cspr.org*.

21. *The National Information Infrastructure: Agenda for Action.* ftp ftp.ntia.doc.gov /pub; niiagenda.asc (ASCII text) OR niiagenda.exe (self extracting compressed file). Remember to issue the binary command before "getting" the compressed file.

22. ACLU Free Reading Room: gopher aclu.org /6. Society, Law, Politics/11. aclu/.

   Online publications and information resources relating to the American Civil Liberties Union. The root menu is presented below:

```
-->  1.  About the ACLU Free Reading Room.
     2.  The ACLU: The Voice of Liberty for 75 Years.
     3.  Civil Liberties: Our Membership Newsletter/
     4.  ACLU Newsroom (under construction -- please pardon our mess)/
     5.  The ACLU Speaks: Op-eds, Speeches, Letters to the Editor (coming s../
     6.  Publications and Reports/
     7.  Legislative Alerts (under construction)/
     8.  The ACLU in Court: Supreme Court and Other Filings (coming soon)/
     9.  Spotlight on Civil Liberties Issues (coming soon)/
```

```
10. Seeking Help from the ACLU/
11. Ordering ACLU Publications and Merchandise/
12. Join the ACLU/
```

## Ham Radio

1. Online Ham Radio Call Book: telnet callsign.cs.buffalo.edu 2000. Type **help** at the system prompt for information on searching database.

2. General Information: ftp world.std.com /pub/hamradio. View the directory for a list of available files.

3. Mail Server for the American Radio Relay League, Inc.: info@arrl.org.

   To receive an index of the files available from INFO, send the command **index** in the body of an email message. A sample of available files is shown below:

```
ARRL-JOIN         2k 930621 How become an ARRL member
ARRL-SERVICES     5k 930621 A condensed list of ARRL membership services
ARRL-TOUR        28k 930621 An electronic tour of ARRL Headquarters
BANDS-HF          7k 921203 Breakdown of users of HF spectrum
Q-SIGNALS         1k 921203 ARRL list of Amateur Radio Q-signals
EMI-GEN          37k 930120 How to solve an EMI/RFI problem - QST Lab Notes
ADDRESSES        16k 930318 Lots and lots of ham/electonic company addresses
KITS              6k 930430 List of companies that sell kits
BBS              12k 930601 List of ham-radio land-line bulletin boards
FAQ-1            25k 930707 Introduction to the FAQ and Amateur Radio
FAQ-2            45k 930707 Amateur Radio Orgs, Services and Info Sources
FAQ-3            32k 930707 Amateur Radio Advanced and Technical Questions
```

   Other valid commands that can be sent to this mail server are listed below. You can send as many commands as you like in a single email message as long as you enter each command on a separate line.

   **send <FILENAME>**—Retrieves the specified file.

   **quitB**—Terminates the transaction. If you have a signature or other text at the end of your message, you should use this command to notify the mail server that you have come to the end of your commands.

   **reply <address>**—Asks the mail server to sends its response to the specified address. This command should be placed at the beginning of your message if your 'From: address' in the header isn't a valid Internet address.

## Health Sciences

1. MedNews: Subscribe to MedNews by sending the message **sub mednews <your name>** to listserv@brownvm.brown.edu.

   This is a weekly digest of medical news. You can either receive mailings from the above named discussion lists, or read it on USENET news where it is distributed in the *bit.listserv.mednews* newsgroup.

2. Guide Dog Laws for all 50 states, Canadian Provinces and all US Territories: ftp handicap.shel.isc-br.com [129.189.4.189] /pub/dogs. View the directory for a list of available files.

3. SMDM-L by sending the message **subscribe smdm-l <your name>** to listserv@dartcms1.dartmouth.edu.

4. Cornucopia of Disability Information (CODI): gopher val-dor.cc.buffalo.edu.

   This Gopher site serves as a community resource for consumers and professionals. The root menu is shown below:

   ```
                    Internet Gopher Information Client v1.11
                       Cornucopia of Disability Information
   -->  1.   About the Cornucopia of Disability Information.
        2.   What's New in CODI.
        3.   State & Local Services/
        4.   College Services and Resources/
        5.   National Information Sources on Disabilities/
        6.   Digest of Data on Persons with Disabilities 1992/
        7.   Coming to Terms with Disabilities/
        8.   WNY TDD Directory/
        9.   Government Documents/
       10.   Computing/
       11.   Legal/
       12.   Publications/
       13.   Electronic Resources/
       14.   Other Directories/
       15.   Independent Living/
       16.   Bibliographic Information/
       17.   Heath Resource Center - Resource Directory/
       18.   NAtional Rehabilitation Information Center (NARIC)/
   ```

   Currently, the material is accessible via 19 main menu items. As with most information servers on the Internet, the organization of the menus is bound to change, along with the contents. Because of CODI's size and its frequency of change, #2. What's New in Codi, is included for the frequent browser. This menu item lists modifications, their dates and locations.

5. CancerNet: gopher helix.hig.gov /3.Health and Clinical Information/1.cancernet Information/3.PDQ Treatment Information for Patients.

6. Directory of Health Science Resources compiled by Lee Hancock: Send the email message **get medical rscrs f=mail** to listserv@vm.temple.edu.

7. List of Molecular Biology Databases: ftp ucselx.sdsu.edu /pub/doc/netinfo; molecular-biology.resources.

8. Medical Resource List: ftp ftp2.cc.ukans.edu /pub/hmatrix; medlst03.txt or medlst03.zip.

   Lee Hancock, Educational Technologist at University of Kansas Medical Center, created this list which includes LISTSERV and USENET discussion groups, Free-Nets, databases, archives, and etexts.

9. Archive of Information on Carpal Tunnel Syndrome: ftp soda.berkeley.edu /pub/typing-injury. View the directory to see a list of available files.

10. *Health Info-Com Network Newsletter*: gopher gopher.uic.edu /Library/Mednews/

    This newsletter is distributed biweekly. A recent issue included three articles relating to FDA News, six articles relating to Centers for Disease Control, and two feature articles: "Bone, Muscle, Motion" and "Probability EEG Tomography."

11. OncoLink Cancer Information: gopher cancer.med.upenn.edu 80.

    A sample of the root menu is shown below. (Note in the above Gopher address that you must specify port 80.)

```
               Internet Gopher Information Client 2.0 p19
                Root gopher server: cancer.med.upenn.edu
     1.  What's NEW on OncoLink/
     2.  Breast Cancer/
     3.  Ovarian Cancer/
     4.  Cancer News/
     5.  Pediatric Oncology/
     6.  Gynecologic Oncology/
     7.  Radiation Oncology/
     8.  Medical Oncology/
     9.  Surgical Oncology/
    10.  Medical Physics/
    11.  Psychosocial Support/
    12.  Other Oncology Resources/
    13.  Frequently Asked Questions (FAQ) about CANCER/
    14.  Send us your comments on OncoLink.
    15.  Meeting Announcement: Controversies in Pediatric Radiation Therapy...
    16.  Meeting Announcement: New Approaches to Cancer Chemotherapy.
    17.  Information on Testicular Cancer.
    18.  Chemotherapy/
```

12. PREVline: telnet ncadi.health.org

    PREVline is an Internet service providing access to the Center for Substance Abuse Prevention's National Clearinghouse for Alcohol and Drug Information. PREVline offers a public forum where questions and comments can be posted, access to information specialists, a keyword searchable online library of research material, and more.

## History

1. Civil War Timeline: ftp cse.unl.edu /pub/brad/txt; timeline.txt.

2. The University of Kansas HNSOURCE: telnet hnsource.cc.ukans.edu Login: **history**

   HNSOURCE is a Web server running Lynx (see chapter 9.2.1) maintained by Academic Computer Service and the Department of History for the University of Kansas. Affiliated with the History Network, it links together all of the major sources of historical materials in electronic format.

3. "Electronic Mail and Historians" from *Perspectives* (February 1991), Newsletter of the American Historical Association: ftp ra.msstate.edu /docs/General; Email.art.

4. Discussion groups:

> Discussion group on history in general. Send message **subscribe history \<your name\>** to listserv@finhutc.bitnet.

> Discussion group of the Canadian Historical Association Conference on Computing. Send message **subscribe l-cha \<your name\>** to l-cha@uqam.bitnet.

> 18th Century Interdisciplinary Discussion. Send message **subscribe c18-l \<your name\>** to listserv@psuvm.psu.edu.

> Discussions on The United Society of Believers. Send message **subscribe shaker \<your name\>** to listserv@ukc.uky.edu.

> Discussion on Early American history (before ca.1860) including Native Amercans, colonial and federal materials. Send message **subscribe eram-l \<your name\>** to listserv@kentvm.kent.edu.

5. International Electronic Mail Directory of Historians compiled by Michael J. McCarthy: ftp ra.msstate.edu /pub/docs/history/directories; HSTDIR.TXT

6. Almanac information on important birthdays, sports schedules and events in history: finger copi@oddjob.uchicago.edu.

A sample of the output is shown below.

```
            Day 65 and Week 10 of current year
        5,591,781 seconds elapsed in current year
            294 shopping days until Christmas
               Phase of moon: last quarter
         Age of moon 6 days (to next new moon)
                  The year of the Dog
******************** Special Events ********************
********** Birth: Aaron Burr (238 years ago) **********
***** Birth: Joseph von Fraunhofer (207 years ago) *****
** Birth: Elizabeth Barrett Browning (188 years ago) ***
****** Birth: Marie Alfred Cornu (153 years ago) ******
********* Birth: Alan Greenspan (68 years ago) *********
********* Birth: David Gilmour (50 years ago) **********
******* Death: Louisa May Alcott (106 years ago) *******
******* Death: John Philip Sousa (62 years ago) ********
******* Death: Elie Joseph Cartan (43 years ago) *******
* Event: Alamo fell after 13 day siege (158 years ago) *
****** Event: Dred Scott decision (137 years ago) ******
****** Event: All US banks closed (61 years ago) *******
********************************************************
```

Please email me event (mm/dd/YYYY) information to add to my list
Here is a list of upcoming games

```
(note: all times are EST)
NHL schedule for Sunday, 3/6...
       Anaheim      at San Jose
       Buffalo      at Detroit
       Calgary      at Washington
       Los Angeles  at Chicago
       Montreal     at Dallas
       Philadelphia at Tampa Bay
       Pittsburgh   at Winnipeg

NBA schedule for Sunday, 3/6...
   (NBC) Chicago       at Cleveland    (1:00 pm)
         Minnesota     at Denver       (9:00 pm)
         Philadelphia  at New Jersey   (6:00 pm)
         Utah          at Phoenix      (9:00 pm)
         Seattle       at Sacramento   (9:00 pm)
   (NBC) Orlando       at San Antonio  (3:30 pm)

If ya didn't pipe this to more then you are missing half the fun
(Try finger copi@oddjob.uchicago.edu | more (or less if you prefer))
```

7. Mississippi State History Archive: ftp ra.msstate.edu.

   Mississippi State University is the home of the National Archive's Center for Electronic Records. Here you can trace the history of the U.S. by exploring numerous text and image files. This archive is provided as a scholarly service of the college of Arts and Sciences and the Tramel Computing Center of Mississippi State University.

   To get to the American History section, change directories to /pub/docs/history/USA and then type **dir** and press ENTER. For information on the Vietnam War, change directories to /pub/docs/history/Vietnam and enter **dir**. For more information on the Revolutionary War, go to the /pub/docs/history/Revolution directory.

   In the USA directory you'll find documents from colonial days to papers relating to the Gulf War. In the 'Revolution' directory you'll find such things as *The Virginia Declaration of Rights* and the *Articles of Confederation*. Files can be retrieved via FTP from site ra.msstate.edu in subdirectory /docs/history.

8. Welsch, Erwin K. *Electronic Sources for West European History & Culture.* gopher dewey.lib.ncsu.edu /6. NCSU's Library Without Walls/3. Reference Desk/4. Guides (to subject literature, to Internet resources, etc.)/

   This resource identifies LISTSERVs and other electronic information sources related to West European history.

9. *Bryn Mawr Classical Review*: An ejournal that reviews current work in Greek and Roman studies. Send message **subscribe bmcr-l <your name>** to listserv@cc.brynmawr.edu.

10. *The Australian Electronic Journal of History*: Accessed through the Campus Wide Information System at James Cook University. gopher gopher.jcu.edu.au.

## Law

1. Cleveland State University Law Library: gopher gopher.law.csuhio.edu. To access via the Web: gopher://gopher.law.csuohio.edu:70/

2. Columbia Law Library Catalog: http://info.cern.ch:8001/pegun.law.columbia.edu:210/catalog.columnbia?

3. Columbia Law School Index to Hispanic Legislation: http://info.cern.ch:8001/pegun.law.columbia.edu:210/columbia.spanish.legal?

4. Cornell Law School: gopher://fatty.law.cornell.edu:70/

   Can also be accessed via gopher fatty.law.cornell.edu.

   This site is the source of a wealth of legal information ranging from copyright law to commercial law. On the Gopher server, librarians may find it worthwhile exploring the documents on ADA that are in the path */4. U.S. Law: Primary Documents.../5. Americans With Disabilities Act.* Here you'll find information on such things as how to make software more accessible to people and universal access in facility design. The root menu for this Gopher server is shown below.

```
                                                 Page: 1/1
                  Internet Gopher Information Client 2.0 p19
                  Root gopher server: fatty.law.cornell.edu
       1.  Cornell Law School Information/
       2.  Directory of Legal Academia/
       3.  Discussions and Listserv Archives/
 -->   4.  U.S. Law: Primary Documents and Commentary/
       5.  Foreign and International Law: Primary Documents and Commentary/
       6.  Other References Useful in Legal Education and Research/
       7.  Government (US) and Agency Information/
       8.  Information Services: Academic Institutions/
       9.  Library Resources (online catalogs)/
       10. Periodicals, News, and Journals/
       11. Other Gophers and Information Services/
       12. WAIS-based information/
       13. Internet (FTP sources, Archie, listserv directory)/
       14. Locators (where to find people and things)/
       15. Miscellaneous/
       16. Other Internet Law Sites/
       17. +---+ Please give us feedback! +---+.
```

5. International Environmental Law: http://vms.huji.ac.il/www_teva/law_international.html

6. Records of Clerkship Application Requirements for US Courts: http://info.cern.ch:8001/pegun.law.columbia.edu:210/us-judges?

7. US Patent Office: http://info.cern.ch:8001/cmns-moon.think.com:210/PTNT?

8. US Supreme Court Decisions (Project Hermes): ftp ftp.cwru.edu /hermes.

   This directory contains two subdirectories and several readme files. The *ascii* subdirectory contains plain ASCII text files.

9. University of Chicago Law School: gopher://lawnext.uchicago.edu:70/

10. US Copyright law: http://fatty.law.cornell.edu.:80/usr2/wwwtext/lii.table.html

11. Washington and Lee University Law Library: gopher liberty.uc.wlu.edu, or telnet liberty.uc.wlu.edu Login: **lawlib,** or gopher://liberty.uc.wlu.edu:70/11/W%26L%20Law %20Library%20FTP%20Files

This site provides access to law libraries and legal research. A convenient way to access this database is via Gopher. The sample session illustrated below demonstrates a keyword search in the W & L library catalog using the word "censorship."

```
$ gopher liberty.uc.wlu.edu

                Internet Gopher Information Client 2.0 p19
                    Root gopher server: liberty.uc.wlu.edu
        1.   W&L University Information/
        2.   Netlink Server/
  -->   3.   Libraries and Information Access/
        4.   Explore Internet Resources/
        5.   Finding Gopher Resources/
        6.   W&L Gopher - All Menu Entries  <?>
        7.   W&L Gopher - Local Entries  <?>


                    Libraries and Information Access
        1.   About W&L Libraries and what's in this part of the Burrow/
        2.   Reference Sources/
        3.   Electronic Journals/
        4.   Humanities/
        5.   History/
        6.   Social Sciences/
        7.   Sciences/
        8.   Law/
  -->   9.   Annie (W&L Library Catalog) <TEL>
        10.  Library Catalogs on the Internet (Yale)/
        11.  Library of Congress (Online Catalog and Gopher)/
        12.  Careers Information/
        13.  Commercial Services/
        14.  Forecasts, Reports, Advisories (travel, weather, US Government)/
        15.  Recreational goodies (recipes, lyrics, Monty Python, etc.)/
        16.  Subject Browsers/
        17.  Gophers of Scholarly Societies (via Waterloo)/
        18.  W&L Pathfinders and Guides/
                                                            Page: 1/1


   +--------------------Annie (W&L Library Catalog)--------------------+
   |                                                                   |
   |  Warning!!!!!, you are about to leave the Internet                |
   |  Gopher program and connect to another host. If                   |
   |  you get stuck press the control key and the                      |
   |  ^ key, and then type q.                                          |
   |                                                                   |
   |  Connecting to iii.library.wlu.edu, port 23 using telnet.         |
   |                                                                   |
   |  Use the account name "expect "*login*";send "library\r"" to log in  |
```

```
    |                                                                      |
    |                                      [Cancel: ^G] [OK: Enter]        |
    |                                                                      |
    +----------------------------------------------------------------------+


Trying... Connected to III.LIBRARY.WLU.EDU, a MIPS running UNIX.

login: lawlib




                             Welcome to ANNIE
        The Washington and Lee University Online Information Access System
                              **MAIN MENU**


                  C > The Washington and Lee Library CATALOG

                  L > LIBERTY
                  D > DISCONNECT
                              Choose one (C,L,D) c
                      Ask for assistance at the Reference Desk
                           Leyburn Library - 463-8644
                              Law Library - 463-8555




                  Washington and Lee University Library Catalog
                  W > WORDS in Subjects or Titles
                  H > Subject HEADING
                  A > AUTHOR
                  T > TITLE
                  L > LIBRARY of Congress Call Number
                  G > GOVERNMENT Documents (SuDocs Number)
                  R > RESERVE Lists
                  I > Library INFORMATION and User Suggestions
                  M > Return to MAIN menu
           The Washington and Lee Library catalog contains records of the
    books, periodicals, media programs, and other materials in campus libraries.
                      Choose one (W,H,A,T,L,G,R,I,M) w



               KEYWORD : censorship

        Type keywords you expect in titles, subjects, or contents notes.
              Lee Gettysburg ---> finds book Lee and Longstreet at Gettysburg.
              college ethics ---> finds book Education and Ethics.
        The connector OR may be used between words.
              federal law or state law
              dogs or cats
        You may truncate after 3 or more letters using *
              federal*  ---> retrieves federalism, federalist, etc.


    CENSORSHIP   is in 252  titles.
    There are 252 entries with CENSORSHIP.
```

```
You searched for the KEYWORD: censorship
252 entries found, entries 1-8 are:                           LOCATIONS
       1  Advertising and a democratic press          JOURNALISM
       2  Alexander Solsjenitsyn.                      LEYBURN
       3  An American paradox : censorship in a nation of LEYBURN
       4  The anatomy of censorship                    JOURNALISM
       5  The anatomy of censorship                    LAW
       6  Arresting images : impolitic art and uncivil ac LAW
       7  Arresting images : impolitic art and uncivil ac LEYBURN
       8  Art made tongue-tied by authority : Elizabethan LEYBURN
```

### A sample record for line number 3 is shown below:

```
AUTHOR       Garry, Patrick M.
 TITLE       An American paradox : censorship in a nation of free speech /
               Patrick Garry.
 PUBLISHER   Westport, Conn. : Praeger, c1993.
 DESCRIPT    xviii, 157 p. ; 24 cm.
 SUBJECT     Censorship --United States.
```

12. The Federal Register: gopher fatty.law.cornell.edu /7.Government (US) and Agency Information/6. Federal Register/1.United States Federal Register. The following online introduction explains this special service:

```
Welcome to Counterpoint Publishing's
DAILY FEDERAL REGISTER ON INTERNET
(Guest Account)
You are looking at the world's first and only complete Federal Register
updated daily via the global Internet.
Counterpoint's Daily Federal Register on Internet contains the identical text
found in the printed version of the Federal Register.  The text is searchable
using standard Internet tools such as Gopher, WAIS and telnet.
Tens of thousands of Internet users worldwide access the Counterpoint Federal
Register routinely to view the latest regulatory information and important
notices from all U.S. Government agencies.  Counterpoint provides free access
to the entire Table of Contents of the daily Federal Register and a portion
of the notices and articles as a public service.  Unlimited access is also
provided to certain agencies with a broad public appeal.  Please feel free to
let others know about how to access this account.
For commercial organizations, educational users and individuals, annual
licenses are available to provide unlimited access to the Federal Register,
including the capability to download articles to your computer or network.
Please contact Counterpoint Publishing for details.

                   Counterpoi   Publishing, Inc.
                   PO Box 928
                   84 Sherman Street
                   Cambridge, MA 02140
                   fedreg@counterpoint.com
                   Telephone: 800-998-4515  or 617-547-4515
                   Fax: 617-547-9064
Please also be sure to view our companion services: the complete updated U.S.
Code of Federal Regulations, the remarkably inexpensive Commerce Business
Daily and coming soon, state by state environmental regulations.  Technical
assistance provided by The Internet Company, a world leader in publishing
solutions on the global Internet.
```

After choosing the last menu item listed above (1. United States Federal Register), you can access data different ways. For example, /3.Federal Register Listed by Date of Issue/2. 040794/5. 040794 will bring you to the following menu:

```
                Internet Gopher Information Client 2.0 p19
                                  040794
    -->  1.   59 FR 16511:Milk in the New England and New York-New Jersey Market...
         2.   59 FR 16513:Small Business Size Standards; Inflation Adjusted Size...
         3.   59 FR 16537:Standards for Electronic Bulletin Boards Required Unde...
         4.   59 FR 16538:Utah Permanent Regulatory Program.
         5.   59 FR 16548:Haitian Transaction Regulations; Blocked Individuals o...
         6.   59 FR 16558:Simplified Alternative Procedure for Resolving Civil P...
         7.   59 FR 16560:Special Local Regulations: Key West Super Boat Race.
         8.   59 FR 16561:Special Local Regulations: Second Annual Run for the G...
         9.   59 FR 16562:Drawbridge Operation Regulations, Unnecessary Openings.
        10.   59 FR 16563:Temporary Amendment to Inland Waterways Navigation Reg...
        11.   59 FR 16566:North Dakota; Final Authorization of State Hazardous W...
        12.   59 FR 16568:Colorado; Final Authorization of State Hazardous Waste...
        13.   59 FR 16570:Groundfish of the Bering Sea and Aleutian Islands Area.
        14.   59 FR 16571:Lime Research, Promotion, and Consumer Information Ord...
        15.   59 FR 16574:Airworthiness Directives; de Havilland Model DHC-8-100...
        16.   59 FR 16576:Revisions to Rules Regulatory Money Market Funds-Exten...
        17.   59 FR 16577:Dietary Fiber and Cancer and Coronary Heart Disease; N...
        18.   59 FR 16578:Colorado Permanent Regulatory Program.
```

## Upon entering menu item number 1, the following article appears:

```
<ARTICLE>
Date="04/07/94"
Citation="59 FR 16511"
Group="agriculture"
Type="RULE"
Department="DEPARTMENT OF AGRICULTURE"
Agency="AGRICULTURAL MARKETING SERVICE, USDA"
Subject="Milk in the New England and New York-New Jersey Marketing Areas; Termin
ation of Certain Provisions of the Orders"
<HEADER>
DEPARTMENT OF AGRICULTURE
Agricultural Marketing Service
7 CFR Parts 1001 and 1002
[DA-94-09]
Milk in the New England and New York-New Jersey Marketing Areas;
Termination of Certain Provisions of the Orders
+-------------------------------------------------------------------------+

[PageDown: <SPACE>] [Help: ?] [Exit: u]
                                                                       46


AGENCY: Agricultural Marketing Service, USDA.
ACTION: Final rule.
</HEADER>
DEPARTMENT OF AGRICULTURE
Agricultural Marketing Service
7 CFR Parts 1001 and 1002
[DA-94-09]
Milk in the New England and New York-New Jersey Marketing Areas;
```

```
Termination of Certain Provisions of the Orders
AGENCY: Agricultural Marketing Service, USDA.
ACTION: Final rule.
+
                                                            100%

------------------------------------------------------------
SUMMARY: This rule terminates the seasonal production incentive
plans for paying producers under the New England and New York-
New Jersey Federal milk orders. This termination was requested
by cooperative associations that represent producers who supply
about one-half of the milk regulated under the orders. The seasonal
incentive plans have been suspended during each of the last
three years and are no longer effective in carrying out their
intended purpose.
EFFECTIVE DATE: April 7, 1994.
---------------------------------------------------------------------
Full access to this file is restricted to subscribers only.  To become a
subscriber to this service, please read the information provided at the
top level of the Counterpoint Publishing Internet Federal Register Gopher.
Please send all comments to 'fedreg@counterpoint.com'  -- Thanks.
---------------------------------------------------------------------
```

13. Jensen, Mary. *List of Law Realted Internet Resources*. gopher dewey.lib.ncsu.edu /6. NCSU's Library Without Walls/3. Reference Desk/4. Guides (to subject literature, to Internet resources, etc.)/25. List of law related Internet resources, Jensen.

    This resource lists law library catalogs on the Internet, FTP sites, USENET Newsgroups, and Electronic Conferences related to law, politics, government, and librarianship.

## Marketplace

1. Browse and Place Online Orders for Audio CD's, Videotapes, and Computer Software: telnet columbia.ilc.com [38.145.77.221] Login: **cas**

   For "Books Online" choose: /F. Access FREE Information Services/1) Infinity Link Corp/ 2) Books Online

2. The Electronic Newsstand: gopher gopher.internet.com /4. The Electronic Newsstand(tm)/6. Titles Listed Alphabetically.

   This service makes several print magazines available for review in electronic format on the Internet. Serving as a marketing outlet for magazine publishers, this free service describes the contents of current issues and offers full-length articles as samples. The Electronic Newsstand provides a table of contents and sample article for current issues of the following titles:

```
                 All Titles Listed Alphabetically
   -->   1. American Demographics/
         2. American Journal of International Law/
         3. American Quarterly/
         4..Arthritis Today/
         5. Best Friends/
```

```
 6. Bio/Technology/
 7. Blue & Gold Illustrated - Notre Dame Football/
 8. Body Politic/
 9. Cadalyst Magazine/
10. California Mining Journal/
11. Computerworld/
12. Cornell Magazine/
13. Current History/
14. Decanter/
15. Destination Discovery - The Discovery Channel Magazine/
16. Discover: The World of Science/
17. E, The Environmental Magazine/
18. Economist, The/
19. Educom Review/
20. Financial World/
21. Foreign Affairs/
22. Foreign Policy/
23. Free Inquiry
24. Games/
25. Growing Edge/
26. Health After Fifty -- John Hopkin's Medical Letter/
27. Human Ecology Forum/
28. Inc. Magazine/
29. Individual Investor/
30. International Legal Materials/
31. International Security/
32. Internet World/
33. Journal of Democracy/
34. Journal of Economics and Management Strategy/
35. Journal of NIH Research, The/
36. Kennedy Institute of Ethics Journal/
37. Maclean's/
38. Midrange Computing/
39. Museums New York/
40. National Review/
41. New Age Journal/
42. New Perspectives Quarterly/
43. New Republic, The/
44. New Yorker, The/
45. Out Magazine/
46. Outside Magazine/
47. PC Novice/
48. PC Today/
49. Policy Review/
50. Reason Magazine/
51. Reviews in American History/
52. Rozek's/
53. Saturday Night/
54. Scientist, The/
55. Skeptical Inquirer/
56. Sloan Management Review/
57. Source, The/
58. Stage Directions/
59. TCI: Theatre Craft International/
60. TDR: The Drama Review/
61. TLC Monthly - The Learning Channel Magazine/
```

```
62. Technology Review/
63. Times Higher Education Supplement, The/
64. Times Literary Supplement, The/
65. Today's Traveler Magazine/
66. Travel Holiday/
67. Washington Quarterly, The/
68. Wellness Letter -- University of California at Berkeley/
69. Western Journal of Medicine, The/
70. Whole Earth Review/
71. World Politics
72. Worth Magazin
73. Yellow Silk, Journal of Erotic Arts/
74. Yoga Journal/
```

3. MarketPlace.com: gopher marketplace.com.

This is an Information Mall operated by Cyberspace Development of Boulder, CO, that leases space to businesses that want a commercial presence on the Internet. Great idea for businesses that want to offer on-line shopping via Internet, but don't want to set up and operate a full-scale server. Contact Cyberspace Development at 303-938-8684; for an automated response, send email to info@marketplace.com; for a personal response, send email to office@marketplace.com. Here is a view of the Gopher server's root menu:

```
              Internet Gopher Information Client 2.0 p19
                   Root gopher server: marketplace.com
-->  1.  About MarketPlace.com - The Internet Information Mall.
     2.  Online Bookstore/
     3.  Interactive Publishing Alert/
     4.  INFOMARK - International Telecom Information/
     5.  Harmony Games/
     6.  How to open a storefront in Marketplace.com.
     7.  Commercial Internet Directory/
     8.  Cyberspace Development: Builders of Internet Storefronts.
     9.  Frequently Asked Questions about Internet Commerce.
```

Menu item 2. *Online Bookstore* is mentioned earlier in this section under the heading 'Bookstores'. Some of the titles currently available in ASCII by way of Gopher are listed below:

```
John Ashbery, _Flow Chart_, a poem ($5.00)
John Ashbery, Lyrics from _Selected Poems_ and _Hotel Lautreamont_ ($5.00)
Paulina Borsook, _Virtual Romance_, a novel ($5.00)
Robert Coover, selected short fiction ($5.00)
Robert Coover, _Pricksongs & Descants_, stories ($5.00)
Stephen King, "Umney's Last Case", a story ($5.00)
Frederik Leboyer, _Birth Without Violence_, nonfiction ($5.00)
Dianne Brinson and Mark Radcliffe, _Multimedia Law Handbook_,
    nonfiction ($30.00) with options to buy bound book
John Ashbery, _Flow Chart_, a poem ($5.00)
John Ashbery, Lyrics from _Selected Poems_ and _Hotel Lautreamont_ ($5.00)
Paulina Borsook, _Virtual Romance_, a novel ($5.00)
Robert Coover, selected short fiction ($5.00)
Robert Coover, _Pricksongs & Descants_, stories ($5.00)
```

```
Stephen King, "Umney's Last Case", a story ($5.00)
Frederik Leboyer, _Birth Without Violence_, nonfiction ($5.00)
Dianne Brinson and Mark Radcliffe, _Multimedia Law Handbook_,
    nonfiction ($30.00) with options to buy bound book
```

Other tiles are available in Postscript, Mosaic, and Voyager Expanded Book format.

4.  Infinity Link Corporation Consumer Access Services (ILC/CAS): telnet columbia.ilc.com Login:**cas**

    This service provides access to a wide variety of products including music CDs, Unix software, bookstores, movies on VHS video cassettes, and more. Mathematics

5.  Internet Business Pages: ftp ftp.msen.com /pub/vendor/msen; ipb.

    Directory of commercial vendors on the Internet.

## Movies

1.  Movie Database: For instructions on how to use, send email with message **help** to movie@ibmpcug.co.uk.of.

    A database of movies, actors, and directors.

2.  Movie Trivia: ftp grasp1.univ-lyon1.fr /pub/faq-by-news-group/rec/rec.arts.movies/movies; trivia-faq.

## Museums

1.  U.S. National Gallery of Art, Washington, D.C.: telnet ursus.maine.edu Login:**ursus**. At the Main Menu select **B** and then **4** to connect to the Gallery database.

    Search a database of over 1,600 works of art by artist, title, style, and medium.

2.  Jane Addams' Hull-House Museum, Chicago, Illinois: gopher nuinfo.nwu.edu /Local recreation, food and entertainment/Galleries and Museums/Hull-House.

3.  University of California at Berkeley Museum of Paleontology: gopher ucmpl.berkeley.edu.

4.  Bishop Museum, Honolulu: gopher bishop.bishop.hawaii.hawaii.

5.  Archive of Photographs and Art Collections at the Smithsonian Institution: ftp sunsite.unc.edu /pub/multimedia/pictures/smithsonian. View the directory for a listing of available files. This is a mirror site of ftp photo1.si.edu /pub/images.

## Newspapers

1.  *Middlesex News*, Farmingham, Massachusetts:
    gopher world.std.com /Periodicals and Journals.

2. Internet-based Newspaper Service: Contact usa@americast.com via email.

   The American Cybercasting Corporation offers an Internet-based newspaper service. Anyone with an Internet connection can have home delivery of the following newspapers: *Washington Post, Washington Times, Los Angeles Times*, and *USA Today*.

3. *The Tech*: telnet the-tech.mit.edu Login:**archive**.

   MIT's oldest and largest newspaper can be searched at this site. Searches are case sensitive.

## Religion

1. The Bible (King James Version): ftp mrcnext.cso.uiuc.edu /etext/etext92; bible10.txt.

2. The Electric Mystic's Guide: ftp panda1.uottawa.ca /pub/religion. View the directory to see the available files. This document is also available via email by sending the commands **GET MYSTICS V1-TXT F=MAIL** and **GET MYSTICS V2-TXT F=MAIL** on separate lines to listserv@acadvm1.uottawa.ca.

3. The Book of Mormon: ftp mrcnext.cso.uiuc.edu /etext/etext92; mormon13.txt.

4. The Koran (Quran): ftp quake.think.com /pub/etext/koran.

5. The Love Teachings of the Kama Sutra: ftp oes.orst.edu /pub/almanac/etext; kama-sutra.

## Science and Technology

1. Science and Technology Information (STIS):

   STIS provides access to National Science Foundation publications and awards abstracts. STIS documents are available through various Internet applications including:

   > EMAIL—Send email to stisserv@nsf.gov (Internet) or stisserv@NSF (BITNET) and request that a STIS document be mailed to your email address. You can request an index of all the documents on STIS and instructions for retrieving them by sending the following email message: get index. You can also get more details on the email service by connecting to site stis.nsf.gov via anonymous FTP and then downloading the file called "stisdirm" located in the root directory.

   > FTP—Use FTP to transfer any STIS document to your local computer. An index is available via FTP at site stis.nsf.gov (128.150.195.40). After you have logged on, you can retrieve a copy of this index by typing the command: **get index**. This file does not contain publications of NSF's Division of Science Resources

Studies (SRS). These files are indexed separately in a file called: srsindex.

TELNET—telnet stis.nsf.gov. STIS documents can also be accessed through an online system that features full-text search and retrieval system called TOPIC. Your PC or terminal must be able emulate a VT100 terminal. You will be prompted for a UNIX login name at which point you type: **public** (in lower case). The rest is self-explanatory. The online system provides a menu-driven interface with which documents can be located and read.

GOPHER—The STIS Gopher server is on host stis.nsf.gov and provides a hierarchical view of the documents. Keyword searching is available in the NSF Award Abstracts and NSF Publications indexes.

# Index

# About the Author

Allen C. Benson is the Director of the Saline County Library, Saline County, Arkansas, where he has been actively involved with integrating Internet services with traditional library practices for the past year.

Benson has taken the do-it-yourself approach to the Internet as he has with other projects ranging from capturing springs and building houses in the Ozark Mountains to publishing manuals on how to teach yourself the art of Swiss Basel drumming. Benson's interests include making information more accessible to more people, musical composition, and building restoration and renovation.

Benson earned a B.F.A. degree from the University of Minnesota in 1974 and an M.L.S. Degree from the University of Alabama in 1993. The University of Alabama awarded him the M.L.S. Faculty Scholar Award in 1992. He is affiliated with the American Library Association, The Internet Society, and the Beta Phi Mu International Library Science Honor Society.